Better Homes and Gardens®
❧ OLD-FASHIONED ❧
HOME BAKING

© Copyright 1990 by Meredith Corporation, Des Moines, Iowa.
All Rights Reserved. Printed in the United States of America.
First Edition. Printing Number and Year: 10 9   97 96 95 94
Library of Congress Catalog Card Number: 89-82439
ISBN: 0-696-01872-1
ISBN: 0-696-02497-7 (trade paperback)

BETTER HOMES AND GARDENS® BOOKS

Editor: Gerald M. Knox
Art Director: Ernest Shelton
Managing Editor: David A. Kirchner
Project Editors: James D. Blume, Marsha Jahns
Project Managers: Liz Anderson, Jennifer Speer Ramundt, Angela K. Renkoski

Food and Family Life Editor: Sharyl Heiken
Associate Department Editors: Sandra Granseth, Rosemary C. Hutchinson, Elizabeth Woolever
Senior Food Editors: Linda Henry, Mary Jo Plutt, Joyce Trollope
Associate Food Editors: Jennifer Darling, Debra-Ann Duggan, Heather M. Hephner, Mary Major, Shelli McConnell
Test Kitchen: Director, Sharon Stilwell; Photo Studio Director, Janet Herwig; Home Economists: Lynn Blanchard, Kay Cargill, Marilyn Cornelius, Maryellyn Krantz, Jennifer Nuese, Marge Steenson, Colleen Weeden

Associate Art Directors: Neoma Thomas, Linda Ford Vermie, Randall Yontz
Assistant Art Directors: Lynda Haupert, Harijs Priekulis, Tom Wegner
Graphic Designers: Mary Schlueter Bendgen, Michael Burns, Mick Schnepf
Art Production: Director, John Berg; Associate, Joe Heuer; Office Manager, Michaela Lester

President, Book Group: Jeramy Lanigan
Vice President, Retail Marketing: Jamie L. Martin
Vice President, Administrative Services: Rick Rundall

BETTER HOMES AND GARDENS® MAGAZINE
President, Magazine Group: James A. Autry
Editorial Director: Doris Eby
Food and Nutrition Editor: Nancy Byal

MEREDITH CORPORATION OFFICERS
Chairman of the Executive Committee: E. T. Meredith III
Chairman of the Board: Robert A. Burnett
President and Chief Executive Officer: Jack D. Rehm

OLD-FASHIONED HOME BAKING

Senior Editor: Mary Jo Plutt
Editors: Debra-Ann Duggan, Heather M. Hephner, Shelli McConnell
Project Manager: Jennifer Speer Ramundt
Graphic Designer: Michael Burns
Electronic Text Processor: Paula Forest
Contributing Editors: Sandra Mosley, Marcia Stanley
Food Stylists: Lynn Blanchard, Suzanne Finley, Carol Grones, Janet Herwig, Mabel Hoffman
Contributing Photographers: Dennis E. Becker, de Gennaro Associates, M. Jensen Photography

On the front cover: Pear-Almond Muffins, Apple Pie, Chocolate Chip Cookies, French Bread, Buttermilk Chocolate Cake with Butter Frosting, Whole Wheat Potato Bread, Gingerberry Lattice Pie, Streusel-Topped Ladder Loaf, Lemon Bars (see Index for recipe page numbers)
Cover Photo Location: 1900s Farmhouse, Living History Farms, Urbandale, Iowa
Photographer: M. Jensen Photography

Our seal assures you that every recipe in *Old-Fashioned Home Baking* has been tested in the Better Homes and Gardens® Test Kitchen. This means that each recipe is practical and reliable, and meets our high standards of taste appeal.

Remember asking your grandmother for a recipe? She'd say, "Just add a pinch of this and a dash of that. Then mix it until the dough looks right. . . ."

Our baking know-how probably will never match that of your grandmother's. So to help you, Better Homes and Gardens® Books has remade many old-time family recipes, giving you the exact measurements and easy-to-follow directions.

In re-creating these favorites for today's baker, we streamlined and simplified the baking techniques, yet kept the delicious tastes of yesteryear. And to ensure success, each section of this book begins with a host of hints to get you started and useful tips for solving common baking problems.

In addition to this collection of memorable homemade recipes, you'll find exciting decorating and gift-giving ideas throughout this book. These special features will show you easy ways to personalize your baked goods.

So whether you're a novice or a seasoned baker, now you can enjoy those old-fashioned breads, pies, cakes, and cookies you grew up with, right from your own kitchen.

HOMEMADE BREADS 6

Nothing quite compares to the aroma and flavor of freshly baked bread right from the oven.

OLD-TIME BAKED DESSERTS 92

A tummy-tempting array of after-dinner favorites.

HOME-STYLE COOKIES AND CRACKERS 126

Enjoy one of the simple pleasures in life—cookies or crackers and a tall glass of milk.

* Indicates extra-special decorating and gift-giving ideas.

Crunchy Parmesan Herb Breadsticks
(see recipe, page 57)

Cherry Twist
(see recipe, page 68)

Sage Wheat Bread
(see recipe, page 47)

Cherry Oat Bran Muffins
(see recipe, page 26)

Cheese Danish
(see recipe, page 89)

Independent Baking Co.

Davenport Iowa

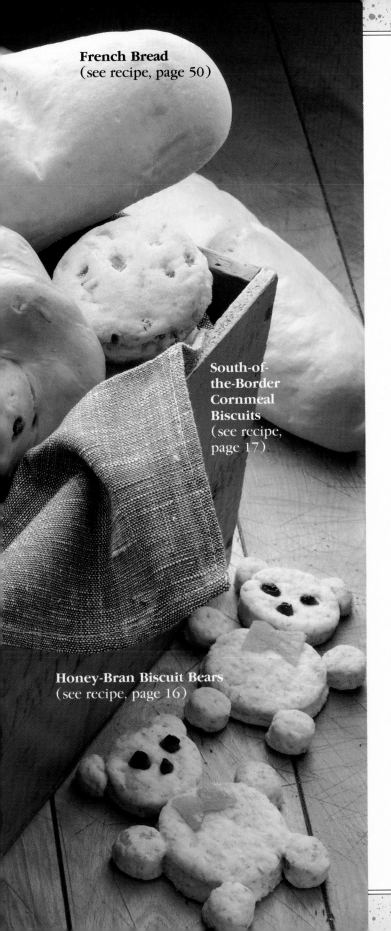

French Bread
(see recipe, page 50)

South-of-the-Border Cornmeal Biscuits
(see recipe, page 17)

Honey-Bran Biscuit Bears
(see recipe, page 16)

HOMEMADE BREADS

For centuries, bread has been a symbol of all that is good in life. It accompanies our simplest and most humble meals, and is present at our most festive celebrations.

In this chapter, we have collected a wide array of breads. Select a warm Danish pastry or a popover for breakfast, a buttery croissant or a fruit-filled coffee cake for a mid-morning break, or a fresh-from-the-oven yeast bread stacked high with thinly sliced cold cuts and cheeses for lunch. A soft pretzel makes a fun afternoon snack and warm rolls or biscuits add to any dinner.

Whichever you choose, you'll find the special flavor and aroma of freshly baked bread a joy to be around.

POPOVERS

With a few ingredients and a hot oven, you can create these crisp, hollow puffs in just a matter of minutes. Since popovers are easy to make and fun to serve, they'll be a hit for all occasions, from casual family meals to elegant entertaining.

☐ Pans used for baking popovers must be greased so that the popovers will be easy to remove. For regular-size popovers, use ½ teaspoon of shortening for *each* custard cup or cup of a popover pan or generously spray with nonstick spray coating. (For larger popovers, use *1 teaspoon* of shortening; for mini popovers, use *about ⅛ teaspoon.*)

☐ A blender or food processor makes quick work of mixing popover batter. To use this method, in a blender container or food processor bowl combine eggs, milk, cooking oil, flour, and salt. Cover; blend or process about 30 seconds or till smooth.

☐ To prevent popovers from overbrowning, place the oven shelf in the lower portion of the oven so the top of the custard cups or popover pan is in the center. A popover is done when it is very firm, and the crust is glossy and golden brown.

☐ After removing popovers from the oven, prick each one with a fork to let steam escape. This prevents popovers from becoming soggy. For crisper popovers, turn off the oven; return them to the oven for 5 to 10 minutes more or to desired crispness. Remove popovers from pans while warm.

☐ Popovers are best when served hot from the oven. But if you should have some left over, place them in a sealed freezer bag. Freeze for up to 3 months. Reheat frozen popovers on a shallow baking pan in a 400° oven for 10 to 15 minutes.

Yorkshire Pudding

This British popover is a variation of the American popover. It's usually served as a meat accompaniment.

> Beef pan drippings
> Cooking oil
> 4 eggs
> 2 cups milk
> 2 cups all-purpose flour
> ½ teaspoon salt
> ½ teaspoon dried basil, chervil, marjoram, rosemary, *or* thyme, crushed (optional)

After roasting a beef roast, remove meat from the pan. Reserve *2 tablespoons* of the beef pan drippings (if necessary, add enough cooking oil to drippings to equal 2 tablespoons). Spoon the reserved drippings into a 15½x10½x2-inch roasting pan. Brush drippings over bottom and sides of the pan. Set pan aside.

For batter, in a large mixing bowl use a wire whisk or rotary beater to beat eggs and milk together till combined. Add flour, salt, and, if desired, herb. Beat till mixture is smooth. Pour batter into the prepared roasting pan. Bake in a 450° oven for 20 to 25 minutes or till done. Immediately cut into squares to serve. Makes 8 to 10 servings.

Individual Yorkshire Puddings: Prepare Yorkshire Pudding as directed above, *except* reserve about ⅓ cup beef pan drippings (if necessary, add cooking oil). Spoon *1 teaspoon* of the drippings into *each* of sixteen 4-inch Yorkshire pudding pans or 4¼-inch pie pans.

Pour ¼ cup of the batter into *each* prepared Yorkshire pudding pan or pie pan. (If you don't have enough pans, set remaining batter aside. Then repeat preparing pans and baking the remaining batter. Stir batter before using.) Bake in the 450° oven about 15 minutes or till done. Remove Yorkshire puddings from pans and serve immediately. Makes 16 servings.

Popovers

If you like, serve these crispy, hollow puffs plain with butter or filled with a seafood or poultry salad, fruit, or pudding.

1 **tablespoon shortening *or* nonstick spray coating**
2 **eggs**
1 **cup milk**
1 **tablespoon cooking oil**
1 **cup all-purpose flour**
¼ **teaspoon salt**

Using *½ teaspoon* of shortening for *each* cup, grease the bottom and sides of six 6-ounce custard cups or the cups of a popover pan. *Or,* spray cups with the nonstick coating. Place the custard cups on a 15x10x1-inch baking pan. Set pan aside.

In a medium mixing bowl use a wire whisk or rotary beater to beat eggs, milk, and cooking oil together till combined. Add flour and salt. Beat till smooth.

Fill the prepared cups *half* full with batter. Bake in a 400° oven about 40 minutes or till done.

Immediately after removing popovers from the oven, use the tines of a fork to prick each popover to let the steam escape. Turn off the oven. For crisper popovers, return the popovers to the oven for 5 to 10 minutes or till desired crispness is reached. Remove popovers from cups and serve immediately. Makes 6.

Pick-a-Flour Popovers: Prepare Popovers as directed above, *except* reduce all-purpose flour to ⅔ *cup* and add ⅓ cup *whole wheat or rye flour* or ¼ cup *Masa Harina tortilla flour.*

Lemon-Poppy Seed Popovers: Prepare Popovers as directed above, *except* add 1 tablespoon *poppy seed* and 1½ teaspoons finely shredded *lemon or orange peel* with the flour and salt.

Spiced Popovers: Prepare Popovers as directed at left, *except* add 2 teaspoons *brown sugar,* ½ teaspoon ground *cinnamon,* ¼ teaspoon ground *ginger,* and ⅛ teaspoon ground *cloves* with the flour and salt.

Buttermilk Popovers: Prepare Popovers as directed at left, *except* substitute 1 cup *buttermilk* for the milk.

Garlic 'n' Chive Popovers: Prepare Popovers as directed at left, *except* add 1 tablespoon snipped *chives or parsley* and ⅛ teaspoon *garlic powder* with the flour and salt.

Select-a-Size Popovers

Here's how you can adjust our recipes to make the size popover you want. For all sizes, fill the prepared cups or pans *half* full with the batter and bake in a 400° oven.

For regular-size popovers, use 6-ounce custard cups, heavy cast-iron or heavy steel popover pans, or 2½-inch muffin pans. Prepare batter as directed in the recipe. Bake the popovers about 40 minutes or till done.

For larger popovers, use 4-inch Yorkshire pudding pans, 4½-inch quiche dishes, 4¼-inch pie pans, or 10-ounce custard cups. Prepare batter as directed in the recipe. Bake for 20 to 25 minutes or till done.

For mini popovers, use 1¾-inch muffin pans. Prepare batter as directed in the recipe. Bake about 25 minutes or till done.

Puffy Surprise Pancake

2 tablespoons margarine *or* butter
3 eggs
¼ cup milk
½ teaspoon finely shredded orange peel
¼ cup orange juice
2 tablespoons cooking oil
½ cup all-purpose flour
⅛ teaspoon ground ginger
4 cups sliced fresh fruit (such as strawberries, kiwi fruit, *or* peaches)
¼ cup packed brown sugar
1 8-ounce carton dairy sour cream *or* vanilla yogurt

Place margarine or butter in a 10-inch *ovenproof* skillet. Place skillet in a *cold* oven, then turn oven on to preheat to 400° (allow about 10 minutes).

Meanwhile, in a medium mixing bowl use a wire whisk or rotary beater to beat eggs, milk, orange peel, orange juice, and cooking oil together till combined. Add flour and ginger. Beat till mixture is smooth.

Remove skillet from oven. Immediately pour the batter into the skillet. Return skillet to the 400° oven and bake about 25 minutes or till done.

To serve, transfer the popover pancake to a serving plate. Spoon fruit into center of the popover. Sprinkle with brown sugar. Top with or pass the sour cream or yogurt. Makes 6 to 8 servings.

Individual Puffy Surprise Pancakes: Prepare Puffy Surprise Pancake as directed at left, *except* use six 4-inch Yorkshire pudding pans or 4¼-inch pie pans instead of the 10-inch ovenproof skillet. Place *1 teaspoon* of the margarine or butter into *each* pan, then preheat pans as directed. Fill the preheated pans *half* full with batter. Bake in the 400° oven for 15 to 20 minutes or till done. Serve as directed. Makes 6 servings.

Secrets to Successful Popovers

Popovers are a simple treat for brunch, lunch, or dinner. If your popovers have one of these problems, here's what to do next time.

If your popovers don't "pop":
■ Use large eggs when making popovers. The right size eggs will help set the popovers.
■ More is not always better. Do not add more cheese or meat than the recipe directs. Their heaviness will prevent popovers from "popping."
■ Be sure to stir the batter while filling the cups because popover batter is thin and settles out.
■ Under-greasing the cups keeps popovers from "popping." See page 8 for proper amounts to use.

■ Expect larger (wider) popovers to "pop" less than regular-size popovers (see tip, page 9). This is because the batter "grips" the sides of the cups during baking. In smaller cups, the batter can only rise upward. In a wider pan or cup, there is nothing to hold the center of the popover up.

If your popovers fall:
■ Do not underbake. Popovers should be baked for the time the recipe indicates or until very firm.
■ Do not peek at the popovers during baking. Opening the oven door lets in cool air, which can cause the popovers to fall.

Pepperoni Pizza Popovers

Serve these cheesy, herb-flavored popovers as a hearty snack or a light lunch.

  4 **teaspoons shortening *or* nonstick spray coating**
  2 **eggs**
  1 **cup milk**
  1 **tablespoon olive oil *or* cooking oil**
  1 **cup all-purpose flour**
  ½ **teaspoon dried basil, crushed**
  ¼ **teaspoon dried oregano, crushed**
  ⅛ **teaspoon garlic powder**
  2 **tablespoons finely snipped pepperoni**
  1 **cup shredded provolone cheese, mozzarella cheese, *or* pizza-flavored cheese (4 ounces)**

Using *½ teaspoon* of shortening for *each* pan or cup, grease the bottoms and sides of eight 4-inch Yorkshire pudding pans, 4¼-inch pie pans, 4½-inch quiche dishes, or 10-ounce custard cups. *Or,* spray pans or cups with the nonstick coating; set aside.

In a medium mixing bowl use a wire whisk or rotary beater to beat eggs, milk, and oil together till combined. Add flour, basil, oregano, and garlic powder. Beat till well combined. Stir in pepperoni.

Fill the prepared pans or cups *half* full with batter. Bake in a 400° oven about 20 minutes or till done.

Sprinkle cheese on top of popovers. Then return the popovers to the oven about 5 minutes or till cheese is melted. Remove popovers from pans or cups and serve immediately. Makes 8 servings.

Cheese Buttons

These bite-size popovers taste great when served with a salad or soup, or as an appetizer.

     Nonstick spray coating *or* 2 teaspoons shortening
  1 **egg**
  ½ **cup milk**
  ¼ **cup *finely* shredded Monterey Jack cheese with jalapeño peppers *or* cheddar cheese, *or* 2 tablespoons grated Parmesan cheese**
  ½ **cup all-purpose flour**

Spray eighteen 1¾-inch muffin cups with the nonstick coating or grease with shortening; set aside.

In a medium bowl use a wire whisk or rotary beater to beat egg, milk, and cheese together till well combined. Add flour. Beat till well combined.

Fill the prepared cups *half* full with the batter. Bake in a 400° oven about 25 minutes or till popovers are done. Makes 18 mini popovers.

Note: To freeze Cheese Buttons, arrange them in a single layer and place in the freezer till firm. Then, place them in a freezer bag, seal, and freeze for up to 3 months. To reheat, place popovers on a shallow baking pan and heat in a 400° oven for 5 to 6 minutes.

Why Do Popovers Pop?

Popovers pop because of the steam that forms inside them when they bake.

Before the invention of baking powder in the 1850s, popovers were one of the few breads cooks could make quickly. The name popover came about because the batter "popped over" the edge of the pan as it baked.

BISCUITS AND SCONES

Biscuits and scones are close cousins. Scones are usually a little richer than biscuits because of the addition of eggs and cream. But whether you serve a biscuit or a scone, the tender, flaky texture and sweet to savory flavors are sure to be palate pleasers anywhere, anytime.

☐ Avoid blending the fat with the flour beyond coarse crumbs. Overblending produces mealy biscuits and scones rather than flaky ones. If margarine or butter is called for in the recipe, make sure you use it chilled. This will make it easier to cut it into the flour mixture and get coarse crumbs.

☐ Try not to overknead the biscuit or scone dough. For most recipes, folding and pressing the dough *gently* for 10 to 12 strokes is enough to distribute the moisture for a flaky product.

☐ Try to cut out as many biscuits and scones as possible from a single rolling of dough. Too many rerollings of the dough causes biscuits and scones to be tough. Also, the extra flour needed for rerolling will cause biscuits and scones to be dry.

☐ If you have a preference for soft or crusty biscuits, bake them just the way you like them. For soft sides, place the biscuits close together on the baking sheet. If you like crusty sides, place the biscuits about 1 inch apart on the baking sheet. Then bake as the recipe directs.

☐ A biscuit or scone is done baking when both the bottom and top crusts are an even golden brown. To check the bottom crust, slightly lift the biscuit or scone up from the baking sheet.

Garden-Angel Biscuits

These light and airy biscuits are named "angel" because the yeast makes them extra light.

  1 package active dry yeast
  2 tablespoons warm water (105° to 115°)
2½ cups all-purpose flour
  1 tablespoon sugar
1½ teaspoons baking powder
  ½ teaspoon baking soda
  ¼ teaspoon salt
  ½ cup shortening *or* lard
  ¼ cup finely shredded carrot
  2 tablespoons snipped parsley
  2 tablespoons finely chopped green onion
  1 cup buttermilk *or* sour milk

In a small mixing bowl dissolve the yeast in warm water. Let stand for 5 minutes.

Meanwhile, in a large mixing bowl stir together flour, sugar, baking powder, baking soda, and salt. Using a pastry blender, cut in shortening or lard till mixture resembles coarse crumbs. Stir in carrot, parsley, and green onion. Make a well in center of dry mixture, then add softened yeast and buttermilk or sour milk all at once. Using a fork, stir *just till moistened.*

Turn the dough out onto a well-floured surface. Quickly knead the dough by gently folding and pressing the dough for 6 to 8 strokes or till the dough is *nearly* smooth. Pat or lightly roll dough to ½-inch thickness. Cut dough with a floured 2½-inch biscuit cutter, dipping the cutter into flour between cuts.

Place biscuits on an ungreased baking sheet. Bake in a 450° oven for 10 to 12 minutes or till biscuits are done. Remove biscuits from the baking sheet and serve hot. Makes 12 to 14.

Best-Ever Buttermilk Biscuits
(see recipe, page 15)

Buttery Breakfast Biscuits

2 **cups all-purpose flour**
1 **tablespoon baking powder**
1 **tablespoon sugar**
½ **teaspoon cream of tartar**
¼ **teaspoon salt**
½ **cup margarine** *or* **butter**
¾ **cup whipping cream, light cream,** *or* **milk**

In a bowl stir together flour, baking powder, sugar, cream of tartar, and salt. Using a pastry blender, cut in margarine till mixture resembles coarse crumbs. Make a well in center of dry mixture, then add cream all at once. Using a fork, stir *just till moistened.*

Turn the dough out onto a lightly floured surface. Quickly knead the dough by gently folding and pressing dough for 10 to 12 strokes or till the dough is *nearly* smooth. Pat or lightly roll dough to ½-inch thickness. Cut dough with a floured 2½-inch biscuit cutter, dipping the cutter into flour between cuts. Place biscuits on an ungreased baking sheet. Bake in a 450° oven for 10 to 12 minutes or till done. Remove biscuits from baking sheet; serve hot. Makes 10 to 12.

Almond Buttery-Biscuit Twists: For filling, in a small bowl beat 1 *egg white,* ½ cup *almond paste,* and ¼ cup packed *brown sugar* with an electric mixer till smooth; set aside.

Prepare dough for Buttery Breakfast Biscuits as directed above, *except* pat or roll dough into a 15x9-inch rectangle. Spread filling over dough. Fold dough lengthwise in half to make a 15x4½-inch rectangle. Cut rectangle into fifteen 1-inch-wide strips. Holding a strip at both ends, twist in opposite directions twice. Place twisted strips 1 inch apart on a greased baking sheet, pressing both ends down. Bake in a 450° oven for 10 to 12 minutes or till done. Remove twists from baking sheet. If desired, drizzle warm twists with *Powdered Sugar Icing* (see page 230). Makes 15.

Buttery Breakfast Turnovers: For filling, in a small mixing bowl beat one 3-ounce package *cream cheese,* softened, and 1 *egg yolk* with an electric mixer till combined. Stir in ⅓ cup *pineapple or peach preserves.* Set filling aside.

Prepare dough for Buttery Breakfast Biscuits as directed at left, *except* roll dough to ⅛-inch thickness. Cut dough with a 4-inch round biscuit cutter. Spoon *1 rounded teaspoon* of filling onto center of *each* circle of dough. Fold each in half, sealing edges with tines of a fork. Place turnovers 1 inch apart on an ungreased baking sheet. Bake in a 450° oven for 10 to 12 minutes or till done. Remove turnovers from baking sheet. Sift *powdered sugar* over tops. Serve warm. Makes 15.

Great Scott, It's Scones!

Immigrants from the British Isles have made scones popular in America, but the Scots take most of the credit for creating them.

Some scones are savory and biscuitlike, and others are sweet and cakelike. Traditionally, scones are cut into triangles and served as part of a tea menu in which they're lavishly spread with butter or jam. Some believe that when scones became Americanized, the biscuit was the result.

Best-Ever Buttermilk Biscuits

Buttermilk adds a subtle tangy flavor to quick breads and cakes, including these biscuits. (Pictured on page 13.)

2 cups all-purpose flour
1 tablespoon baking powder
2 teaspoons sugar
½ teaspoon cream of tartar
¼ teaspoon salt
¼ teaspoon baking soda
½ cup lard *or* shortening
⅔ cup buttermilk *or* sour milk

In a medium mixing bowl stir together flour, baking powder, sugar, cream of tartar, salt, and baking soda. Using a pastry blender, cut in lard or shortening till mixture resembles coarse crumbs. Make a well in center of dry mixture, then add buttermilk or sour milk all at once. Using a fork, stir *just till moistened.*

Turn the dough out onto a lightly floured surface. Quickly knead the dough by gently folding and pressing the dough for 10 to 12 strokes or till the dough is *nearly* smooth. Pat or lightly roll dough to ½-inch thickness. Cut dough with a floured 2½-inch biscuit cutter, dipping the cutter into flour between cuts.

Place biscuits on an ungreased baking sheet. Bake in a 450° oven for 10 to 12 minutes or till the biscuits are done. Remove biscuits from the baking sheet and serve hot. Makes 10 to 12.

Drop Best-Ever Buttermilk Biscuits: Prepare Best-Ever Buttermilk Biscuits as directed above, *except* increase buttermilk or sour milk to *1 cup. Do not knead, roll, or cut dough.* Drop dough from a tablespoon 1 inch apart on a greased baking sheet. Bake and serve as directed above. Makes 10 to 12.

▶ *For biscuits, make a well in the center of the dry mixture, then add liquid all at once. Using a fork, stir just till moistened. For rolled-out biscuits, the mixture will cling together in a ball, forming a soft dough. Too much mixing may result in biscuits that are tough and not as light as desired.*

Storing Biscuits And Scones

Tender flaky biscuits and scones are a wonderful addition to any breakfast, lunch, or dinner menu.

When there are too many biscuits or scones for one meal, wrap the leftovers in foil or place them in a plastic bag and seal it. Then store the biscuits or scones at room temperature for 2 or 3 days. To reheat, wrap the biscuits or scones in foil and heat in a 300° oven for 10 to 12 minutes.

To freeze biscuits or scones, wrap them in *heavy* foil. Label and freeze them for up to 3 months. To reheat, place the frozen wrapped biscuits or scones in a 300° oven and heat for 20 to 25 minutes.

Honey-Bran Biscuit Bears

Serve a cheery biscuit bear or angel for a special-occasion brunch, a leisurely family breakfast, or a children's party. (Bears are pictured on pages 6–7.)

⅔ cup buttermilk *or* sour milk
¼ cup wheat bran
1 tablespoon honey
1¾ cups all-purpose flour
1 tablespoon baking powder
1 tablespoon finely shredded orange peel
½ teaspoon cream of tartar
¼ teaspoon salt
½ cup margarine *or* butter
1 beaten egg
Dried fruit *or* nuts (optional)

In a small bowl stir together buttermilk or sour milk, wheat bran, and honey. Let stand for 5 minutes.

In a bowl stir together flour, baking powder, orange peel, cream of tartar, and salt. Using a pastry blender, cut in margarine till mixture resembles coarse crumbs. Make a well in center of dry mixture; add buttermilk mixture all at once. Using a fork, stir *just till moistened.* Turn dough out onto a lightly floured surface. Quickly knead dough by gently folding and pressing dough for 10 to 12 strokes or till dough is *nearly* smooth. (Dough will be soft.) Pat or lightly roll dough to ¼-inch thickness. Using floured biscuit cutters and dipping them into flour between cuts, cut *six* 2½-inch circles, *six* 2-inch circles, and *thirty* 1-inch circles. Combine egg and 1 tablespoon *water.*

To assemble *each* bear, place *one* 2½-inch circle (body) on an ungreased baking sheet. Brush the side of *one* 2-inch circle (head) with egg mixture; join to body. Brush sides of *four* 1-inch circles (arms and legs) with egg mixture; join to body. Cut *one* 1-inch circle in half (ears). Brush flat sides with egg mixture; join to head. Repeat making bears with remaining circles. If desired, decorate with fruit or nuts. Bake in a 450° oven for 8 to 10 minutes or till done. Makes 6.

Honey-Bran Biscuit Angels: Prepare and knead dough for Honey-Bran Biscuit Bears as directed at left. Pat or lightly roll dough into an 8x6-inch rectangle. Cut *one* 6x2-inch strip off one side of the rectangle. Set strip aside. Then cut *four* 3-inch squares from the remaining rectangle. Cut *each* square diagonally from the two bottom corners to about ¼ inch from the center of the top edge. Place the squares 3 inches apart on an ungreased baking sheet, separating the dough pieces to form wings and body. Curve the tips of the wings slightly.

Using a floured 1¼- or 1½-inch biscuit cutter, cut *four* circles from the remaining 6x2-inch strip of dough. Brush the sides of the circles with a mixture of egg and 1 tablespoon *water.* Join circles to bodies to form heads. Brush tops with egg mixture. If desired, decorate with dried fruits or nuts. Bake as directed. Makes 4.

Biscuit Preferences

You almost can tell what part of the country you're in just by sampling the local biscuits.

Most Northerners prefer a tender, flaky biscuit with large volume, and Southerners tend to like a crusty biscuit with a soft, tender crumbly inside that doesn't flake. Southerners also are more likely to add buttermilk or sour milk to their biscuits.

The variance in flours is one reason for the difference in the biscuits. All-purpose flour (made from a combination of soft and hard wheats) contributes to the flakiness of a northern-style biscuit. Whereas, soft-wheat flour is used to produce a southern-style biscuit.

South-of-the-Border Cornmeal Biscuits

Cornmeal is a staple in American cooking dating back to early colonial times. (Pictured on pages 6–7.)

1½ cups all-purpose flour
½ cup yellow cornmeal
2 teaspoons baking powder
¼ teaspoon baking soda
¼ teaspoon salt
½ cup margarine *or* butter
½ cup shredded cheddar cheese (2 ounces)
½ cup buttermilk *or* sour milk
1 4-ounce can diced green chili peppers

In a medium mixing bowl stir together flour, cornmeal, baking powder, baking soda, and salt. Using a pastry blender, cut in margarine or butter till mixture resembles coarse crumbs. Stir in cheese. Make a well in the center of the dry mixture; set aside.

In a bowl stir together buttermilk and *undrained* chili peppers. Add buttermilk mixture all at once to the dry mixture. Using a fork, stir *just till moistened.*

Turn the dough out onto a lightly floured surface. Quickly knead dough by gently folding and pressing dough for 10 to 12 strokes or till dough is *nearly* smooth. Pat or lightly roll dough to ½-inch thickness. Cut the dough with a floured 2½-inch biscuit cutter, dipping the cutter into flour between cuts.

Place biscuits on an ungreased baking sheet. Bake in a 450° oven for 12 to 15 minutes or till done. Remove biscuits. Serve hot. Makes 10 to 12.

Drop South-of-the-Border Cornmeal Biscuits: Prepare South-of-the-Border Cornmeal Biscuits as above, *except* increase the buttermilk or sour milk to *¾ cup. Do not knead, roll, or cut dough.* Drop dough from a well-rounded tablespoon 1 inch apart on an ungreased baking sheet. Bake and serve as directed. Makes 12 to 14.

Gruyère-Pecan Biscuits

Gruyère cheese has a slightly sweet, nutlike flavor.

2 cups all-purpose flour
1 tablespoon baking powder
½ teaspoon cream of tartar
½ cup margarine *or* butter
½ shredded Gruyère *or* Swiss cheese (2 ounces)
½ cup finely chopped pecans
⅔ cup milk

In a medium mixing bowl stir together flour, baking powder, and cream of tartar. Using a pastry blender, cut in margarine or butter till mixture resembles coarse crumbs. Stir in cheese and pecans. Make a well in the center of the dry mixture, then add milk all at once. Using a fork, stir *just till moistened.*

Turn the dough out onto a lightly floured surface. Quickly knead dough by gently folding and pressing dough for 10 to 12 strokes or till dough is *nearly* smooth. Pat or lightly roll dough to ½-inch thickness. Cut the dough with a floured 2½-inch biscuit cutter, dipping the cutter into flour between cuts.

Place biscuits on an ungreased baking sheet. Bake in a 450° oven for 10 to 12 minutes or till biscuits are done. Remove biscuits from the baking sheet and serve hot. Makes 10 to 12.

Oatmeal Soda Bread

Oatmeal Soda Bread

We stirred in oatmeal as a hearty addition to the traditional Irish soda bread.

- 1⅔ cups all-purpose flour
- ¾ cup quick-cooking rolled oats
- 1 teaspoon baking powder
- ½ teaspoon baking soda
- ¼ teaspoon salt
- 3 tablespoons margarine *or* butter
- 1 beaten egg
- ⅔ cup buttermilk *or* sour milk
- 1 beaten egg

Grease a baking sheet; set aside. In a large mixing bowl stir together flour, oats, baking powder, baking soda, and salt. Using a pastry blender, cut in margarine or butter till mixture resembles coarse crumbs. Make a well in center of the dry mixture. Stir together one beaten egg and buttermilk or sour milk, then add mixture all at once to the dry mixture. Using a fork, stir *just till moistened*. (Dough will be sticky.)

Turn the dough out onto a well-floured surface. Quickly knead dough by gently folding and pressing dough for 10 to 12 strokes or till dough is *nearly* smooth. On the prepared baking sheet, shape dough into a 6-inch-round loaf. On the top of the loaf, cut a 4-inch cross, ¼ inch deep. Brush with the one remaining beaten egg. Bake in a 375° oven about 35 minutes or till done. Remove from baking sheet and serve warm. Makes 1 loaf.

Raisin-Oatmeal Soda Bread: Prepare Oatmeal Soda Bread as directed above, *except* stir 2 tablespoons *brown sugar* and, if desired, 1 teaspoon ground *cinnamon* into the dry mixture. Stir ⅓ cup *raisins, dried currants,* or snipped *dried apricots* into the buttermilk mixture.

So-Easy Yogurt Shortcake

- 1½ cups self-rising flour*
- 3 tablespoons brown sugar
- ¼ cup margarine *or* butter
- 1 beaten egg
- 1 8-ounce carton vanilla *or* desired fruit-flavored yogurt (such as strawberry, peach, apricot, banana, *or* lemon)
- 2 tablespoons milk
- 4 cups sliced strawberries *or* nectarines; peeled and sliced peaches, bananas, *or* kiwi fruit; *or* whole raspberries *or* blueberries
- 1 cup whipping cream
- 1 tablespoon sugar

Grease an 8x1½-inch round baking pan. Set pan aside. In a medium mixing bowl stir together self-rising flour and brown sugar. Using a pastry blender, cut in margarine or butter till mixture resembles coarse crumbs. Make a well in the center of the dry mixture. In a small mixing bowl stir together egg, yogurt, and milk. Add yogurt mixture all at once to dry mixture. Using a fork, stir *just till moistened.*

Spread dough evenly in the prepared pan. Bake in a 450° oven for 18 to 20 minutes or till done. Cool in the pan on a wire rack for 10 minutes. Remove shortcake from pan. Cool completely on the wire rack.

In a small mixing bowl combine whipping cream and sugar. Beat with an electric mixer on medium speed till soft peaks form.

To serve shortcake, cut it into wedges. Place wedges on dessert plates and top each with fruit, then whippped cream. Makes 6 servings.

*If you don't have 1½ cups of self-rising flour for this recipe, then substitute 1½ cups *all-purpose flour* plus 1½ teaspoons *baking powder,* ¾ teaspoon *salt,* and ¼ teaspoon *baking soda.*

Country Scones

½ **cup dried currants**
2 **cups all-purpose flour**
3 **tablespoons brown sugar**
2 **teaspoons baking powder**
½ **teaspoon baking soda**
½ **teaspoon salt**
⅓ **cup margarine *or* butter**
1 **8-ounce carton dairy sour cream**
1 **beaten egg yolk**
1 **slightly beaten egg white**
1 **tablespoon brown sugar**
⅛ **teaspoon ground cinnamon**

In a small bowl pour enough *hot water* over currants to cover them. Let stand for 5 minutes, then drain well. In a large bowl stir together flour, 3 tablespoons brown sugar, baking powder, baking soda, and salt. Using a pastry blender, cut in margarine or butter till mixture resembles coarse crumbs. Add cur-

rants, then toss till mixed. Make a well in the center of the dry mixture. In a bowl combine sour cream and egg yolk. Add sour cream mixture all at once to dry mixture. Using a fork, stir *just till moistened.*

Turn the dough out onto a lightly floured surface. Quickly knead dough by gently folding and pressing dough for 10 to 12 strokes or till *nearly* smooth. Pat or lightly roll dough to ½-inch thickness. Cut dough with a floured 4-inch round biscuit cutter.

Place scones 1 inch apart on an ungreased baking sheet. Using a sharp knife, cut *each* scone into *four* wedges. *Do not separate wedges.* Brush tops of scones with a mixture of egg white and 1 tablespoon *water.* Combine the 1 tablespoon brown sugar and cinnamon, then sprinkle mixture over tops of scones. Bake in a 425° oven for 12 to 15 minutes or till done. Remove scones from baking sheet. Cool on a wire rack for 5 minutes. Break scone circles apart into wedges and serve warm. Makes 20 to 24.

Secrets to Successful Biscuits and Scones

You'll win compliments when you serve tender, flaky biscuits or scones warm from the oven. If you feel your biscuits or scones aren't perfect, next time try some of our suggestions.

If your biscuits or scones are heavy:
■ Be sure you're not cutting the fat into the dry mixture beyond the coarse crumb stage (see photo, page 235).
■ When adding liquid, stir *just till moistened* (see photo, page 15). Do not overmix dough.

If biscuits or scones have a dry, tough crumb:
■ Try handling the dough more gently. Use your fingers to *gently* knead the dough for the number of strokes indicated in the recipe.

If your biscuits or scones have yellow specks on the top crust:
■ Make sure you're stirring together the dry ingredients well enough to distribute the baking soda or baking powder.

If your biscuits or scones have a hard crust:
■ Check your oven temperature with an oven thermometer. If the temperature is too high or low, adjust it to the proper temperature.
■ Check the biscuits or scones for doneness at the minimum baking time. Biscuits or scones are done when both the top and bottom crusts are an even golden brown.

Sweetheart Chocolate Scones

For a different twist, omit the nuts and powdered sugar garnish, and frost the warm scones with sour cream or yogurt. Then arrange fresh strawberry slices on top.

1¾ cups all-purpose flour
⅓ cup packed brown sugar
3 tablespoons unsweetened cocoa powder
1 tablespoon baking powder
¼ teaspoon salt
⅓ cup margarine *or* butter
½ cup miniature semisweet chocolate pieces
2 beaten eggs
¼ cup milk
½ cup chopped nuts (optional)
Powdered sugar

In a large mixing bowl stir together flour, brown sugar, cocoa powder, baking powder, and salt. Using a pastry blender, cut in margarine or butter till the mixture resembles coarse crumbs. Add the chocolate pieces, then toss till mixed. Make a well in the center of the dry mixture.

In a small mixing bowl stir together beaten eggs and milk. Then add the milk mixture all at once to the dry mixture. Using a fork, stir *just till moistened.*

Turn the dough out onto a lightly floured surface. Quickly knead dough by gently folding and pressing the dough for 10 to 12 strokes or till *nearly* smooth. Pat or lightly roll dough to ½-inch thickness. Cut dough into heart shapes with a floured 2- to 3-inch cookie cutter, dipping cutter into flour between cuts.

Place scones 1 inch apart on an ungreased baking sheet. If desired, garnish by pressing chopped nuts around top edge of each scone.

Bake scones in a 375° oven for 12 to 15 minutes or till done. Cool scones on the baking sheet for 5 minutes, then transfer scones to a wire rack. Sift powdered sugar over the tops of the scones. Serve warm. Makes 20 (2-inch) or 12 (3-inch) scones.

Cranberry-Orange Scones

Cranberries once were known as "bounce berries" because they bounce when they are ripe.

1½ cups all-purpose flour
¼ cup sugar
2 teaspoons baking powder
1 teaspoon finely shredded orange peel
⅛ teaspoon salt
¼ cup margarine *or* butter
⅔ cup cranberries, coarsely chopped
⅓ cup chopped pecans *or* walnuts
1 beaten egg
⅓ cup orange yogurt
1 slightly beaten egg white
2 tablespoons chopped pecans *or* walnuts
Powdered sugar

Grease a baking sheet; set aside. In a large mixing bowl stir together flour, sugar, baking powder, orange peel, and salt. Using a pastry blender, cut in margarine or butter till mixture resembles coarse crumbs. Add cranberries and ⅓ cup nuts, then toss till mixed. Make a well in the center of the dry mixture. In a small mixing bowl stir together beaten egg and yogurt. Add yogurt mixture all at once to the dry mixture. Using a fork, stir *just till moistened.*

Turn the dough out onto a lightly floured surface. Quickly knead dough by gently folding and pressing dough for 6 to 8 strokes or till dough is *nearly* smooth. Divide the dough in half. On the prepared baking sheet, pat or lightly roll one portion of the dough into a 4-inch circle. Repeat with the remaining portion of dough. Using a sharp knife, cut *each* circle into *six* wedges. *Do not separate wedges.*

Brush tops of scones with beaten egg white, then sprinkle with 2 tablespoons nuts. Bake in a 400° oven for 15 to 18 minutes or till done. Remove scones from baking sheet. Cool on a wire rack for 5 minutes. Sift powdered sugar over tops. Break scone circles apart into wedges and serve warm. Makes 12.

MUFFINS AND QUICK BREADS

Taste the old-fashioned goodness of freshly baked breads in less than an hour when you bake a batch of muffins or a quick-bread loaf. Because you use baking powder and baking soda instead of yeast to make the dough rise, these breads are ready to serve in a jiffy.

☐ "Ledges on the edges" are those unwanted rims around the edges of your muffins or quick breads. To get nicely rounded products without ledges, grease the muffin cups or baking pans on the bottoms and only *half* way up the sides.

☐ After adding the liquid mixture to the flour mixture, stir the ingredients *just till* they are moistened. If you stir out all the lumps, your muffins and quick breads will have peaks, tunnels, and a tough texture.

☐ Once the batter is mixed, pop the muffins or quick bread into the preheated oven right away. Batters with baking powder and baking soda need to be baked immediately so that the leavening power is not lost.

☐ Muffins are done when their tops are golden, and quick breads are done when a wooden toothpick inserted near the center of each loaf comes out clean. (A slight crack across the top of a loaf is typical of quick breads.)

☐ To avoid soggy sides and bottoms, cool muffins and quick breads in their baking pans only as long as directed in the recipe.

Cheesy Bacon Vegetable Muffins

Serve these savory muffins for brunch, a soup lunch, or dinner.

- 1¾ cups all-purpose flour
- 2 tablespoons sugar
- 2 teaspoons baking powder
- ¼ teaspoon salt
- 1 beaten egg
- ¾ cup milk
- ⅓ cup cooking oil
- 6 slices bacon, crisp-cooked, drained, and crumbled (⅓ cup)
- ¼ cup finely chopped onion
- ¼ cup finely chopped green pepper
- 2 ounces Swiss *or* American cheese, cut into 12 (¾-inch) cubes

Grease twelve 2½-inch muffin cups or line them with paper bake cups. Set muffin cups aside.

In a medium mixing bowl stir together flour, sugar, baking powder, and salt. Make a well in the center of the dry mixture.

In another medium mixing bowl combine the egg, milk, and cooking oil. Add the egg mixture all at once to the dry mixture. Stir *just till moistened* (batter should be lumpy). Fold in the crumbled bacon, onion, and green pepper.

Spoon *half* of the batter into the prepared muffin cups. Place *one* cheese cube in the center of *each* muffin, then add the remaining batter to the muffin cups, filling each cup ⅔ full. Bake in a 400° oven about 20 minutes or till done. Remove muffins from muffin cups and cool slightly on a wire rack. Serve warm. Makes 12.

Cream Cheese Savory Muffins

In Britain, muffins, known as bannocks, once were baked on a hearth.

    2 cups all-purpose flour
    1 tablespoon sugar
 2½ teaspoons baking powder
    ¼ teaspoon salt
    1 3-ounce package cream cheese
    ¼ cup finely chopped onion
    ¼ cup snipped fresh parsley
    1 beaten egg
    ¾ cup milk
    ¼ cup margarine *or* butter, melted

Grease twelve 2½-inch muffin cups or line them with paper bake cups. Set muffin cups aside.

In a large bowl stir together flour, sugar, baking powder, and salt. Using a pastry blender, cut in cream cheese till mixture resembles coarse crumbs. Stir in onion and parsley. Stir together egg, milk, and melted margarine or butter. Add all at once to flour mixture. Stir *just till moistened* (batter should be lumpy).

Spoon batter into the prepared muffin cups, filling each ⅔ full. Bake in a 400° oven for 20 to 25 minutes or till done. Remove from muffin cups and cool slightly on a wire rack. Serve warm. Makes 12.

Thyme and Onion Muffins: Prepare Cream Cheese Savory Muffins as directed above, *except* stir ⅛ teaspoon dried *thyme,* crushed, into the flour mixture and omit the parsley.

Cheesy Broccoli Muffins: Prepare Cream Cheese Savory Muffins as directed above, *except* omit the onion and parsley. Fold ½ cup cooked, drained, and finely chopped *broccoli* and ½ cup shredded *cheddar cheese* (2 ounces) into batter.

Double Cheese Wheat Muffins

    1 cup all-purpose flour
    ½ cup whole wheat flour
    ½ cup shredded cheddar cheese
    ¼ cup grated Parmesan cheese
    2 teaspoons baking powder
    1 beaten egg
    ¾ cup milk
    ¼ cup honey
    ¼ cup cooking oil

Grease twelve 2½-inch muffins cups. Set muffin cups aside. In a large mixing bowl stir together all-purpose flour, whole wheat flour, cheddar cheese, Parmesan cheese, and baking powder. Make a well in the center of the dry mixture.

In another bowl stir together the beaten egg, milk, honey, and cooking oil. Add the egg mixture all at once to the dry mixture. Stir *just till moistened* (batter should be lumpy).

Spoon batter into the prepared muffin cups, filling each ⅔ full. Bake in a 400° oven for 18 to 20 minutes or till done. Remove muffins from muffin cups and cool slightly on a wire rack. Serve warm. Makes 12.

Muffin Gems

In the mid-1800s, a special baking pan for muffins was introduced. This early pan was an arrangement of iron or tin "gem" cups fastened together by a rack. To this day, muffins frequently are called gems in many parts of the country.

HISTORY OF BAKING

**Oatmeal-Blueberry
Teatime Muffins**

Oatmeal-Fig Teatime Muffins

If snipping the fruit for these muffins becomes a sticky mess, dip your scissors in warm water.

1⅓ **cups all-purpose flour**
 ¾ **cup rolled oats**
  2 **teaspoons baking powder**
 ½ **teaspoon baking soda**
 ¼ **teaspoon salt**
  1 **beaten egg**
 ¾ **cup milk**
 ½ **cup packed brown sugar**
 ¼ **cup cooking oil**
 ½ **teaspoon vanilla**
 ½ **cup snipped dried figs**
 ½ **cup chopped pecans**

Grease eighteen 1¾-inch or six 2½-inch muffin cups or line them with paper bake cups; set aside. In a bowl stir together flour, oats, baking powder, baking soda, and salt. Make a well in center of dry mixture.

In a bowl combine the egg, milk, brown sugar, oil, and vanilla. Add egg mixture all at once to the dry mixture. Stir *just till moistened* (batter should be lumpy). Fold figs and pecans into the batter.

Spoon *half* of the batter into the prepared muffin cups, filling each ¾ full. Bake in a 400° oven for 10 to 12 minutes for 1¾-inch muffins or 16 to 18 minutes for 2½-inch muffins or till done. Cool in muffin cups on a wire rack 5 minutes; remove muffins from cups. Repeat with remaining batter. Serve warm. Makes 36.

Oatmeal-Blueberry Teatime Muffins: Prepare Oatmeal-Fig Teatime Muffins as directed above, *except* substitute ¾ cup fresh *or* frozen *blueberries* for the dried figs and omit the pecans.

Oatmeal-Prune Teatime Muffins: Prepare Oatmeal-Fig Teatime Muffins as directed at left, *except* substitute 1 cup snipped dried pitted *prunes* for the dried figs and omit the pecans.

Maple Pecan Muffins

1½ **cups all-purpose flour**
 ½ **cup whole wheat flour**
1½ **teaspoons baking powder**
 ½ **teaspoon baking soda**
 ¼ **teaspoon salt**
  1 **beaten egg**
 ¾ **cup milk**
 ⅓ **cup cooking oil**
 ⅓ **cup maple syrup *or* maple-flavored syrup**
 ½ **cup chopped pecans**
 ½ **cup sifted powdered sugar**
  1 **tablespoon maple syrup *or* maple-flavored syrup**

Grease twelve 2½-inch muffin cups. Set muffin cups aside. In a bowl stir together all-purpose flour, whole wheat flour, baking powder, baking soda, and salt. Make a well in the center of the dry mixture.

In a medium mixing bowl combine egg, milk, cooking oil, and ⅓ cup syrup. Add egg mixture all at once to dry mixture. Stir *just till moistened* (batter should be lumpy). Fold in chopped pecans.

Spoon batter into the prepared muffin cups, filling each ⅔ full. Bake in a 400° oven about 20 minutes or till done. Transfer muffins from muffin cups to a wire rack. In a small bowl combine powdered sugar, the 1 tablespoon syrup, and 1 teaspoon *water;* drizzle over muffins. Cool slightly before serving. Makes 12.

Granola-Topped Blueberry Muffins

Crunchy granola tops these cakelike muffins that are dotted with blueberries.

  1 **cup frozen *or* fresh blueberries**
  ¼ **cup granola *or* 100% natural cereal**
  1 **tablespoon brown sugar**
  1 **tablespoon margarine *or* butter, softened**
  ¼ **teaspoon pumpkin pie spice**
1½ **cups all-purpose flour**
  2 **teaspoons baking powder**
  ½ **cup sugar**
  ⅓ **cup shortening**
  1 **egg**
     Several drops almond extract
  ⅓ **cup milk**
     Powdered Sugar Icing (see page 230)
     (optional)

If using frozen blueberries, *do not thaw*. Line twelve 2½-inch muffin cups with paper bake cups. Set muffin cups aside. In a small mixing bowl combine granola, brown sugar, margarine or butter, and pumpkin pie spice; set aside. In another bowl stir together flour, baking powder, and ⅛ teaspoon *salt*.

In a small mixing bowl beat sugar and shortening with an electric mixer on medium to high speed till light and fluffy. Add egg and almond extract. Beat till combined.

Alternately add the flour mixture and milk to shortening mixture, beating on low to medium speed after each addition just till smooth. Fold in blueberries. (Batter will be very thick.)

Spoon batter into the prepared muffin cups, filling each ⅔ full. Sprinkle granola mixture on top of each muffin. Bake in a 400° oven for 20 to 25 minutes or till a wooden toothpick inserted near center comes out clean. Let stand for 5 minutes in muffin cups on a wire rack. Remove muffins from muffin cups. If desired, lightly drizzle with Powdered Sugar Icing. Serve warm. Makes 12.

Cherry Oat Bran Muffins

Look for dried cherries at specialty food shops or order them through mail order catalogs. (Pictured on pages 6–7.)

1½ **cups all-purpose flour**
  1 **cup oat bran**
2½ **teaspoons baking powder**
  ¼ **teaspoon salt**
  1 **beaten egg**
  1 **cup milk**
  ½ **cup packed brown sugar**
  ¼ **cup margarine *or* butter, melted,**
     ***or* cooking oil**
  1 **teaspoon finely shredded lemon peel**
  ½ **cup snipped dried cherries *or* apricots**
  ¼ **cup chopped almonds *or* walnuts**
  2 **tablespoons margarine *or* butter, melted**

Grease twelve 2½-inch muffin cups or line them with paper bake cups. Set muffin cups aside.

In a medium mixing bowl stir together flour, oat bran, baking powder, and salt. Make a well in the center of the dry mixture.

In another medium mixing bowl stir together egg; milk; brown sugar; ¼ cup margarine, butter, or oil; and lemon peel. Add egg mixture all at once to the dry mixture. Stir *just till moistened* (batter should be lumpy). Fold in dried fruit and nuts.

Spoon batter into the prepared muffin cups, filling each ¾ full. Bake in a 400° oven for 20 to 25 minutes or till done. Remove muffins from muffin cups and cool slightly on a wire rack. Brush with 2 tablespoons melted margarine or butter. Serve warm. Makes 12.

Cranberry-Nut Upside Down Muffins

1½ **cups cranberries**
¾ **cup sugar**
¼ **teaspoon ground nutmeg**
1¾ **cups all-purpose flour**
⅓ **cup sugar**
⅓ **cup chopped nuts**
2 **teaspoons baking powder**
¼ **teaspoon salt**
1 **beaten egg**
¾ **cup milk**
¼ **cup cooking oil**
½ **teaspoon finely shredded lemon peel**

Grease twelve 2½-inch muffin cups or line them with paper bake cups. Set muffin cups aside.

In a small covered saucepan cook cranberries and the ¾ cup sugar over low heat just till mixture starts to form juice, stirring occasionally. Uncover and heat to boiling, stirring frequently. Boil gently, uncovered, about 5 minutes or till berries pop. Stir in nutmeg. Divide the cranberry mixture evenly among the prepared muffin cups. Set muffin cups aside.

In a medium mixing bowl stir together the flour, the ⅓ cup sugar, nuts, baking powder, and salt. Make a well in the center of the dry mixture.

In another medium mixing bowl combine egg, milk, cooking oil, and lemon peel. Add the egg mixture all at once to the dry mixture. Stir *just till moistened* (batter should be lumpy). Spoon batter on top of the cranberry mixture in the muffin cups, filling each ⅔ full. Bake in a 400° oven about 20 minutes or till done. Cool in muffin cups on a wire rack for 5 minutes. To remove muffins from muffin cups, invert them onto the wire rack. Makes 12.

▶ *To fill the muffin cups, first spoon in the cranberry mixture and set the muffin cups aside. Then mix the muffin batter just till moistened. (The batter still should be lumpy.) Using a rubber spatula, push batter off a spoon to fill each cup ⅔ full.*

▶ *Bake the muffins about 20 minutes or till golden. Cool the muffins in the muffin cups for 5 minutes. Then to remove the Cranberry-Nut Upside Down Muffins, just invert the muffin pan onto a wire rack.*

Flavored Butters and Spreads

Pair your favorite muffin or bread with one of these great-tasting, easy-to-make, flavored butters or spreads. Each recipe makes enough so you can enjoy some now and save some for later. Store leftovers, covered, for up to 2 weeks in the refrigerator or for up to 2 months in the freezer.

■**Peach-Nut Butter:** Place 1 cup *nuts* in a blender container or food processor bowl. Cover and blend or process till finely chopped. Transfer nuts to a small mixing bowl.

Place ½ cup *butter or margarine,* cut up and softened, and ½ cup *peach preserves* in the blender container or food processor bowl. Cover and blend till combined, stopping to scrape down the sides as necessary. Add preserves mixture to the nuts in the bowl. Mix well. Cover and chill for at least 1 hour before serving. Makes 1½ cups.

■**Apricot-Nut Butter:** Prepare Peach-Nut Butter as directed above, *except* substitute *apricot preserves* for the peach preserves. Makes 1½ cups.

■**Strawberry-Nut Butter:** Prepare Peach-Nut Butter as directed above, *except* use 1 cup blanched *almonds* as the desired nuts; cover and blend or process almonds till ground. Substitute *strawberry preserves* for the peach preserves. If desired, add 4 drops *red food coloring* to the preserves mixture while blending. Makes 1½ cups.

■**Orange Butter:** In a small mixing bowl beat ½ cup softened *butter or margarine,* 1 tablespoon *powdered sugar,* ½ teaspoon finely shredded *orange peel,* and 1 teaspoon *orange juice* with an electric mixer until smooth. Cover and chill. Let butter stand at room temperature about 30 minutes before serving. Makes ⅔ cup.

■**Full-of-Fruit Spread:** In a bowl stir together one 8-ounce carton soft-style *cream cheese with pineapple or strawberries,* ½ of a 6-ounce package (¾ cup) *mixed dried fruit bits,* ¼ cup finely choppped *pecans or almonds,* 1 to 2 tablespoons *milk.* Cover and chill till serving. Makes 1⅓ cups.

■**Praline Butter:** In a heavy 6-inch skillet evenly spread ¼ cup *sugar.* Heat over medium-high heat till sugar begins to melt, shaking skillet occasionally to heat sugar evenly. Carefully add ½ cup coarsely chopped *pecans* and 1 tablespoon *butter or margarine.* Reduce heat to low; cook till sugar melts and turns golden brown, stirring constantly. Remove skillet from the heat; spread candied nuts on a buttered baking sheet or piece of foil. Cool. Break into clusters. Place clusters in a plastic bag; use a rolling pin to crush the candied nuts.

In a mixing bowl stir together ½ cup softened *butter or margarine,* ½ teaspoon *vanilla,* and the crushed candied nuts. If not serving immediately, cover and chill. Let butter stand at room temperature about 1 hour before serving. Makes ¾ cup.

■**Chocolate-Nut Butter:** Melt ¼ cup *semisweet chocolate pieces* and 1 tablespoon *butter or margarine;* cool. Mix ½ cup softened *butter or margarine,* ½ cup chopped *pecans,* ½ teaspoon *vanilla,* and chocolate mixture. Chill. Let stand at room temperature 1 hour before serving. Makes ¾ cup.

■**Parmesan-Garlic Butter:** In a bowl beat ½ cup softened *butter or margarine,* ⅓ cup grated *Parmesan cheese,* and ¼ teaspoon *garlic powder* with an electric mixer till smooth. Stir in 2 tablespoons snipped *fresh parsley or* 2 teaspoons *dried parsley flakes.* Cover and chill. Bring to room temperature before serving. Makes ⅔ cup.

Pear-Almond Muffins With Lemon Butter

A basket of warm, fruit-filled muffins with a jar of lemony butter makes a perfect "welcome to our neighborhood" gift. (Pictured on the cover.)

1¾ cups all-purpose flour
⅓ cup sugar
2½ teaspoons baking powder
¼ teaspoon salt
1 beaten egg
¾ cup milk
⅓ cup cooking oil
1 cup finely chopped, peeled pear
½ cup chopped almonds, toasted
  Lemon Butter

Grease twelve 2½-inch muffin cups or line with paper bake cups. Set muffin cups aside. In a medium mixing bowl stir together flour, sugar, baking powder, and salt. Make a well in center of dry mixture.

In another medium bowl combine egg, milk, and oil. Add egg mixture all at once to the dry mixture. Stir *just till moistened* (batter should be lumpy). Carefully fold in pear and *¼ cup* of the almonds.

Spoon batter into the prepared muffin cups, filling each ⅔ full. Sprinkle remaining almonds on top. Bake in a 400° oven for 20 to 25 minutes or till done. Remove muffins from muffin cups and cool slightly on a wire rack. Serve warm with Lemon Butter. Makes 12.

> **Lemon Butter:** In a small mixing bowl combine ½ cup *butter or margarine,* 1 tablespoon *powdered sugar,* and 1 teaspoon *lemon juice.* Beat with an electric mixer on medium to high speed till light and fluffy. Stir in ½ teaspoon finely shredded *lemon peel.* Cover and let stand about 1 hour to develop flavors. Makes about ½ cup.

Pumpkin Praline Muffins

3 tablespoons brown sugar
1 tablespoon dairy sour cream
⅓ cup broken pecans
2 cups all-purpose flour
2 teaspoons baking powder
1 teaspoon ground cinnamon
½ teaspoon baking soda
¼ teaspoon ground nutmeg
⅛ teaspoon ground cloves
1 beaten egg
¾ cup buttermilk
¾ cup canned pumpkin
⅔ cup packed brown sugar
⅓ cup margarine *or* butter, melted

Grease twelve 2½-inch muffin cups or line them with paper bake cups. Set muffin cups aside. In a small bowl stir together 3 tablespoons brown sugar and sour cream. Stir in pecans. Set aside.

In a medium mixing bowl stir together flour, baking powder, cinnamon, baking soda, nutmeg, and cloves. Make a well in the center of the dry mixture.

In another medium mixing bowl stir together egg, buttermilk, pumpkin, ⅔ cup brown sugar, and melted margarine or butter. Add the pumpkin mixture all at once to the dry mixture. Stir *just till moistened* (batter should be lumpy).

Spoon batter into the prepared muffin cups, filling each ¾ full. Drop *1 teaspoon* of pecan mixture on top of *each* muffin. Bake in a 400° oven about 20 minutes or till done. Remove muffins from muffin cups and cool slightly on a wire rack. Serve warm. Makes 12.

Corn Bread

Freeze extra servings to have on hand for busy days when you don't have time to bake.

1 **cup all-purpose flour**
1 **cup yellow, white, *or* blue cornmeal**
2 **to 4 tablespoons sugar**
1 **tablespoon baking powder**
½ **teaspoon salt**
2 **beaten eggs**
1 **cup milk**
¼ **cup cooking oil *or* shortening, melted**

Grease a 9x9x2-inch baking pan; set aside. In a large mixing bowl stir together flour, cornmeal, sugar, baking powder, and salt. Make a well in the center of the dry mixture. In a medium mixing bowl combine eggs, milk, and cooking oil or melted shortening. Add egg mixture all at once to dry mixture. Stir *just till moistened* (batter should be lumpy).

Pour batter into the prepared baking pan. Bake in a 425° oven for 20 to 25 minutes or till a wooden toothpick inserted near the center comes out clean. Cut into squares. Makes 9 servings.

Corn Sticks *or* Corn Muffins: Prepare batter for Corn Bread as directed above. Spoon batter into greased corn stick pans or 2½-inch muffin cups, filling each pan or muffin cup ⅔ full. Bake in a 425° oven for 12 to 15 minutes or till golden brown. Makes 24 to 26 sticks or 12 muffins.

Crunchy Corn Bread: Prepare Corn Bread as directed above, *except* pour 1 cup *boiling water* over ¼ cup *cracked wheat or bulgur.* Let stand for 5 minutes; drain. Stir ½ cup *quick-cooking rolled oats* into flour mixture; add the cracked wheat or bulgur and egg mixture. Stir *just till moistened.* Fold in ½ cup chopped *pecans.* Makes 9 servings.

Corny Corn Bread: Prepare Corn Bread as directed at left, *except* fold one 12-ounce can *whole kernel corn with sweet peppers,* drained, into the batter. Makes 9 servings.

Green Chili Corn Bread: Prepare Corn Bread as at left, *except* fold 1 cup shredded *cheddar or Monterey Jack cheese* and one 4-ounce can diced *green chili peppers,* drained, into batter. Serves 9.

Corn Bread Loaves: Prepare batter for Corn Bread as at left; pour into two greased 9x5x3-inch loaf pans. Bake in a 425° oven for 20 to 25 minutes or till golden brown. Makes 2 loaves.

Cheese 'n' Turkey Corn Bread: Prepare Corn Bread as directed at left, *except* fold 1 cup (2 ounces) shredded *cheddar cheese* and ½ cup (2½ ounces) finely chopped, fully cooked *smoked turkey* into batter. Makes 9 servings.

Storing Muffins and Quick Breads

You can enjoy your muffins or quick-bread loaves later if you store them properly.

To store muffins and quick breads, place them in a plastic bag, seal, and store at room temperature for up to 3 days.

To freeze muffins and quick-bread loaves, wrap them tightly in *heavy* foil or place them in freezer bags, and freeze for up to 3 months. To reheat, wrap frozen muffins or loaves in *heavy* foil. Heat in a 300° oven for 12 to 15 minutes for 1¾-inch muffins and 15 to 18 minutes for 2½-inch muffins.

Cranberry-Apple Mini Loaves

½ cup whole cranberry sauce
½ cup chopped nuts
½ teaspoon finely shredded orange peel
1½ cups all-purpose flour
1 cup sugar
1 teaspoon ground cinnamon
½ teaspoon baking soda
¼ teaspoon salt
¼ teaspoon baking powder
¼ teaspoon ground allspice
1 beaten egg
½ cup finely shredded, peeled apple
¼ cup cooking oil
½ cup sifted powdered sugar
2 to 3 teaspoons orange juice

Grease four 4½x2½x1½-inch individual loaf pans. In a small mixing bowl stir together cranberry sauce, chopped nuts, and orange peel. Set pans and cranberry mixture aside.

In a medium mixing bowl stir together flour, sugar, cinnamon, baking soda, salt, baking powder, and allspice. Make a well in the center of the dry mixture.

In another medium mixing bowl combine the egg, shredded apple, and cooking oil till well mixed. Add apple mixture all at once to the dry mixture. Stir *just till moistened* (batter should be lumpy).

Pour *half* of the batter evenly into the prepared pans (use about ⅓ *cup* for *each* pan). Spoon about *2 tablespoons* of cranberry mixture on top of the batter in *each* pan. Top with remaining batter. Spoon the remaining cranberry mixture down the center of each loaf. Bake in a 350° oven for 35 to 40 minutes or till done. Cool on a wire rack for 10 minutes.

Remove quick breads from pans. In a small mixing bowl stir together powdered sugar and enough orange juice to make an icing of drizzling consistency. Drizzle over warm loaves. Makes 4 small loaves.

Spicy Pumpkin Loaf

A cinnamon- and nutmeg-flavored glaze adds zest to this pumpkin loaf.

2 cups all-purpose flour
1 cup sugar
2½ teaspoons baking powder
1 teaspoon ground cinnamon
½ teaspoon baking soda
½ teaspoon ground nutmeg
⅛ teaspoon ground cloves
1 cup canned pumpkin
½ cup cream sherry *or* milk
2 eggs
⅓ cup shortening
1 cup raisins
Spiced Glaze

Grease a 7-cup fluted tube mold or two 7½x3½x2-inch loaf pans. Set the mold or loaf pans aside.

In a medium mixing bowl stir together *1 cup* of the flour, sugar, baking powder, cinnamon, baking soda, nutmeg, cloves, and ¼ teaspoon *salt*. Add pumpkin, cream sherry or milk, eggs, and shortening. Beat with an electric mixer on low to medium speed about 30 seconds or till combined. Then beat on high speed for 2 minutes, scraping sides of bowl occasionally. Add remaining flour; beat till well mixed. Stir in raisins.

Pour batter into the prepared mold or pans. Bake in a 350° oven for 60 to 65 minutes for mold or 45 to 50 minutes for loaves or till done. Cool in mold or pans on a wire rack for 10 minutes. Remove bread; cool on rack. Wrap and store overnight. Before serving, drizzle with glaze. Makes 1 bread ring or 2 loaves.

Spiced Glaze: In a bowl stir together ½ cup sifted *powdered sugar*, ⅛ teaspoon ground *cinnamon*, ⅛ teaspoon ground *nutmeg*, and 2 to 3 teaspoons *cream sherry or water* to make an icing of drizzling consistency. Makes about ¼ cup.

Zucchini Bread

When the zucchini patch has you crying "uncle," here's how to use one or two.

 1½ **cups all-purpose flour**
  1 **cup sugar**
  1 **teaspoon ground cinnamon**
  ½ **teaspoon baking soda**
  ¼ **teaspoon salt**
  ¼ **teaspoon baking powder**
  ¼ **teaspoon ground nutmeg**
  1 **beaten egg**
  1 **cup finely shredded, unpeeled zucchini**
  ¼ **cup cooking oil**
  ¼ **teaspoon finely shredded lemon peel**
  ½ **cup chopped walnuts**

Grease an 8x4x2-inch loaf pan. Set loaf pan aside. In a medium mixing bowl stir together flour, sugar, cinnamon, baking soda, salt, baking powder, and nutmeg. Make a well in the center of the dry mixture.

In another medium mixing bowl combine the egg, shredded zucchini, cooking oil, and lemon peel. Add zucchini mixture all at once to the dry mixture. Stir *just till moistened* (batter should be lumpy). Fold in chopped walnuts.

Pour batter into the prepared pan. Bake in a 350° oven for 55 to 60 minutes or till done. Cool bread in pan on wire rack for 10 minutes. Then remove bread from the pan and completely cool on the wire rack. Wrap and store overnight before slicing. Makes 1 loaf.

Apple Bread: Prepare Zucchini Bread as directed at left, *except* substitute 1 cup finely shredded, peeled *apple* for the shredded zucchini.

Carrot and Pineapple Bread: Prepare Zucchini Bread as directed at left, *except* omit zucchini. Drain one 8¼-ounce can *crushed pineapple* (juice pack), reserving *2 tablespoons* juice. Stir drained pineapple, reserved pineapple juice, and ½ cup finely shredded *carrot* into egg mixture.

Secrets to Successful Muffins and Quick Breads

Although muffins and quick-bread loaves are different products, the techniques for making them are nearly the same. If you've been disappointed with your muffins or quick breads, here are some tips for improving your technique.

If your muffins or quick breads have peaks and tunnels:
■ Avoid mixing too much. When adding liquid to the dry ingredients, stir until the dry ingredients are *just moistened.* The batter should be lumpy.

If your muffins or quick breads are tough:
■ Be sure to thoroughly mix the egg and milk together before adding them to the dry ingredients.

If your muffins or quick breads crumble:
■ Mix the batter as the recipe directs, usually until the dry ingredients are *just moistened.* Muffins and quick breads don't need much mixing.
■ Be sure quick-bread loaves are completely cool before slicing. Storing some breads overnight makes slicing easier. Wrap the cooled bread tightly in foil and store at room temperature.

Festive Fruit Bread

No time to spare? Then decorate by sifting powdered sugar over the top of the bread instead of using the icing.

1½ cups all-purpose flour
¾ cup sugar
2 teaspoons baking powder
¼ teaspoon baking soda
¼ teaspoon salt
¾ cup mashed ripe banana (2 medium bananas)
⅓ cup margarine *or* butter, softened
2 tablespoons milk
2 eggs
⅓ cup red maraschino cherries, drained and coarsely chopped
⅓ cup green maraschino cherries, drained and coarsely chopped
⅓ cup chopped nuts
⅓ cup miniature semisweet chocolate pieces
Decorating Icing (optional)

Grease six 4-inch individual fluted tube pans, one 6-cup tube mold, or sixteen 2½-inch fluted muffin cups; set aside. In a large mixing bowl stir together *1 cup* of the flour, the sugar, baking powder, baking soda, and salt. Add mashed banana, margarine or butter, and milk. Beat with an electric mixer on low to medium speed about 30 seconds or till combined. Then beat on high speed for 2 minutes. Add eggs and remaining flour. Beat on low speed *just till combined*. Fold in red and green maraschino cherries, nuts, and chocolate pieces.

Pour batter into the prepared pans. (Use *¼ cup* batter for *each* fluted muffin cup. Refrigerate batter between batches.) Bake in a 350° oven for 25 to 30 minutes for the 4-inch fluted tube pans, for 50 to 55 minutes for the 6-cup tube mold, about 20 minutes for the fluted muffin cups, or till done. Cool in pans on a wire rack for 10 minutes. Remove bread from pans; cool on rack. If desired, use Decorating Icing to pipe berries and holly leaves on the breads. Makes 6 small bread rings, 1 large bread ring, or 16 muffins.

Decorating Icing: In a small bowl beat 1 cup sifted *powdered sugar,* 1 tablespoon *margarine or butter,* and ¼ teaspoon *vanilla* till combined. Beat in 2 to 3 teaspoons *milk* to make an icing of piping consistency. Divide in half. Tint one portion with *red food coloring;* tint one portion with *green food coloring.* Makes ½ cup.

Aloha Loaf

2 cups all-purpose flour
½ cup sugar
1½ teaspoons baking powder
½ teaspoon baking soda
1 beaten egg
½ cup milk
1 8¼-ounce can crushed pineapple
¼ cup margarine *or* butter, melted
¾ cup chopped Brazil nuts *or* macadamia nuts
1 3½-ounce can flaked coconut, toasted

Grease a 9x5x3-inch loaf pan or two 7½x3½x2-inch loaf pans; set aside. In a bowl stir together flour, sugar, baking powder, baking soda, and ¼ teaspoon *salt.* Make a well in center of dry mixture. In another bowl combine the egg, milk, *undrained* pineapple, and melted margarine. Add egg mixture all at once to the dry mixture. Stir *just till moistened* (batter should be lumpy). Fold in nuts and coconut.

Pour batter into the prepared loaf pan. Bake in a 350° oven for 55 to 60 minutes for the 9x5x3-inch pan or for 45 to 50 minutes for the 7½x3½x2-inch pans or till done. Cool bread in pan on a wire rack for 10 minutes. Remove bread from pan and completely cool on the wire rack. Wrap and store overnight before slicing. Makes 1 large loaf or 2 small loaves.

COFFEE CAKES

You don't need to get up with the rooster to enjoy freshly baked bread at your mid-morning brunch or coffee break. Choose one of the recipes in this section and it'll take just a few minutes to stir together the batter and pop the coffee cake into the oven.

☐ The coffee cakes in this section are related to biscuits and scones, muffins and quick-bread loaves, and creamed cakes. For more information on the baking techniques of each, refer to these other sections.

☐ If you are baking your coffee cake in a metal pan, be sure to use a shiny one. Shiny pans will reflect heat, which is necessary to produce coffee cakes with golden, delicate, and tender crusts.

☐ Most coffee cakes are best served warm, but are too hot to eat right from the oven. To reach the "just-right-for-eating" stage, allow your coffee cake to cool for 20 to 30 minutes before cutting and serving it.

☐ To save leftover coffee cake for an afternoon snack or tomorrow's breakfast, place it in a container, tightly cover, and store at room temperature. If the coffee cake contains cream cheese, store it in the refrigerator.

Pecan Ripple Ring

  1 **cup finely chopped pecans**
  ⅓ **cup packed brown sugar**
  1 **teaspoon ground cinnamon**
2½ **cups all-purpose flour**
  1 **cup sugar**
  1 **tablespoon baking powder**
  ½ **teaspoon salt**
  ½ **cup margarine** *or* **butter**
  3 **beaten eggs**
  1 **8-ounce carton dairy sour cream**
  ⅓ **cup milk**
  1 **teaspoon vanilla**
     Powdered Sugar Icing (see page 230)
  ¼ **teaspoon rum flavoring (optional)**

Generously grease a 10-inch fluted tube pan. Sprinkle *½ cup* of the pecans evenly over the bottom. For filling, in a bowl combine the remaining pecans, brown sugar, and cinnamon. Set pan and filling aside.

In a medium mixing bowl stir together flour, sugar, baking powder, and salt. Using a pastry blender, cut in margarine or butter till mixture resembles coarse crumbs. Make a well in the center of the dry mixture.

In another medium bowl stir together eggs, sour cream, milk, and vanilla. Add sour cream mixture all at once to dry mixture. Stir *just till moistened*. Remove *1 cup* of the batter and stir it into the filling.

Spread *half* of the plain batter into the prepared pan. Spoon the filling over batter. Then carefully spoon remaining plain batter over filling. Bake in a 325° oven for 45 to 50 minutes or till a wooden toothpick inserted near the center comes out clean. Cool in the pan on a wire rack for 10 minutes. Then invert onto a serving plate. Remove pan and cool for 15 minutes more. If desired, stir rum flavoring into the Powdered Sugar Icing. Drizzle icing over coffee cake. Serve warm. Makes 12 to 16 servings.

Apple-Wheat
Coffee Cake

*Apples, bran cereal, and whole wheat make this a
wholesome treat for breakfast or brunch.*

½ **cup finely snipped dried apples**
¼ **cup sugar**
¼ **cup whole wheat flour**
2 **tablespoons margarine *or* butter**
1 **cup whole bran cereal**
1 **cup all-purpose flour**
⅔ **cup sugar**
½ **cup whole wheat flour**
1 **teaspoon baking powder**
1 **teaspoon ground cinnamon**
½ **teaspoon baking soda**
¼ **teaspoon ground allspice**
1 **beaten egg**
½ **cup apple juice *or* apple cider**
⅓ **cup margarine *or* butter, melted**

Grease and flour a 9x1½-inch round baking pan;
set aside. Place dried apples in a small mixing bowl;
cover with *warm water.* Let apples stand for 10 minutes, then drain. For streusel mixture, in a small mixing bowl stir together ¼ cup sugar and ¼ cup whole
wheat flour. Using a pastry blender, cut in 2 tablespoons margarine or butter till the mixture resembles
coarse crumbs. Stir in about *half* of the drained dried
apples. Set the streusel mixture and the remaining
apples aside.

In a small mixing bowl stir together *½ cup* of the
whole bran cereal and ½ cup *boiling water.* Set bran
mixture aside.

In a large mixing bowl stir together all-purpose
flour, ⅔ cup sugar, ½ cup whole wheat flour, baking
powder, cinnamon, baking soda, and allspice. Make a
well in the center of the dry mixture.

Stir beaten egg, apple juice or cider, and melted
margarine or butter into the softened bran. Add egg-
bran mixture all at once to dry mixture. Stir *just till
moistened* (batter should be lumpy). Fold in apple
and remaining unsoaked bran cereal.

Spread batter into prepared pan. Sprinkle with
streusel mixture. Bake in a 375° oven for 30 to 35
minutes or till a wooden toothpick inserted near center comes out clean. Slightly cool in pan on a wire
rack. Cut into wedges and serve warm. Serves 10.

An Apple Tale

Early settlers took advantage of the versatili-
ty and long-storing capacity of apples by using
them in everything from breads and pies to
puddings and side dishes.

Apples were not growing in America when
the first colonists arrived. But by 1615, James-
town settlers could enjoy apples raised locally.

The first commercial apple operation in the
United States started in 1730 on New York's
Long Island. Washington's reputation as a
prime apple-growing state was launched in
1824 with the start-up of commercial apple
orchards. Today, the U.S. produces 25 percent
of the apples grown worldwide.

HISTORY OF BAKING

35

Strawberry Ripple Tea Cake

Strawberry Ripple Tea Cake

1   10-ounce package frozen, sweetened, sliced strawberries *or* red raspberries, thawed
1   tablespoon cornstarch
2¼ cups all-purpose flour
¾   cup sugar
¾   cup margarine *or* butter
½   teaspoon baking powder
½   teaspoon baking soda
⅛   teaspoon salt
1   beaten egg
¾   cup buttermilk *or* sour milk

Grease and flour a 10x2-inch round tart pan with a removable bottom or an 11x7x1½-inch baking pan; set aside. For filling, in a small saucepan stir together *undrained* strawberries or raspberries and the cornstarch till well combined. Cook and stir till thickened and bubbly. Remove from heat. Sieve the mixture, discarding the seeds. Set filling aside to cool slightly.

In a large mixing bowl stir together flour and sugar. Using a pastry blender, cut in margarine or butter till mixture resembles coarse crumbs. Set *½ cup* flour mixture aside for crumb topping. Into the remaining flour mixture stir baking powder, baking soda, and salt; mix well. Make a well in center of dry mixture.

In a small bowl combine egg and buttermilk or sour milk. Add the egg mixture all at once to the dry mixture. Stir *just till moistened.*

Spread *two-thirds* of the batter over the bottom and about 1 inch up the sides of the prepared pan. Carefully spread the filling on top of the batter in pan. Spoon remaining batter in small mounds on top of the entire surface. Sprinkle with the crumb topping.

Bake in a 350° oven for 30 to 35 minutes or till a wooden toothpick inserted near center comes out clean. Cool in pan on a rack for 15 minutes. Remove coffee cake from *tart* pan (leave in *baking* pan). Cut into wedges or squares. Serve warm. Serves 8.

Plum Kuchen

For many German and Austrian cooks, the weekly baking wasn't complete without at least one kuchen.

2   tablespoons all-purpose flour
1   tablespoon sugar
1   tablespoon margarine *or* butter
1½ cups all-purpose flour
¾   cup sugar
2   teaspoons baking powder
¼   teaspoon salt
1   beaten egg
½   cup milk
¼   cup cooking oil
4   medium plums, pitted and sliced; 2 pears, peeled, cored, and sliced; *or* one 16-ounce can unpeeled purple plum halves, drained and sliced

Grease and flour an 11-inch flan pan with a removable bottom. Set pan aside.

For topping, in a small mixing bowl stir together 2 tablespoons flour and 1 tablespoon sugar. Using a pastry blender, cut in margarine or butter till the mixture resembles coarse crumbs. Set topping aside.

In a medium mixing bowl stir together the 1½ cups flour, ¾ cup sugar, baking powder, and salt. Make a well in the center of the dry mixture. In a small bowl stir together egg, milk, and cooking oil. Add the egg mixture all at once to the dry mixture. Stir *just till moistened* (batter should be lumpy).

Spread batter into the prepared pan. Arrange fruit slices on top. Sprinkle with topping. Bake in a 375° oven for 30 to 35 minutes or till a wooden toothpick inserted near the center comes out clean. Cool kuchen in pan on a wire rack for 15 minutes. Remove the sides of the pan and serve the kuchen warm. Makes 10 to 12 servings.

Peanut Butter 'n' Chocolate Bubble Ring

If you like chocolate and peanut butter, you'll love the combo in this coffee cake.

> 2 **cups all-purpose flour**
> ½ **cup packed brown sugar**
> 1 **tablespoon baking powder**
> ¼ **teaspoon salt**
> ¼ **cup margarine *or* butter**
> 2 **beaten eggs**
> ¼ **cup creamy peanut butter**
> ¼ **cup milk**
> ½ **teaspoon vanilla**
> 20 **milk chocolate kisses**
> ¼ **cup margarine *or* butter, melted**
> 1 **cup honey roasted peanuts *or* cocktail peanuts, ground**
> ½ **of a recipe Semisweet Chocolate Glaze (see page 221) (optional)**

Grease a 5-cup ring mold. Set ring mold aside. For dough, in a bowl stir together flour, brown sugar, baking powder, and salt. Using a pastry blender, cut in ¼ cup margarine or butter till mixture resembles coarse crumbs. Make a well in center of dry mixture.

In another bowl stir together eggs, peanut butter, milk, and vanilla with a wire whisk till well combined. Add the peanut butter mixture all at once to the dry mixture. Using a fork, stir *just till moistened.*

Turn dough out onto a lightly floured surface. Quickly knead dough by gently folding and pressing for 10 to 12 strokes or till dough is *nearly* smooth.

Divide dough into 20 portions. Using lightly floured hands, shape each portion of dough into a ball around a chocolate kiss.

Dip each ball in melted margarine or butter, then roll in ground peanuts. Arrange the coated balls of dough in 2 layers in the prepared pan, using 10 balls for each layer. Position the balls of dough in the second layer between the balls of dough in the first layer. Drizzle with any remaining melted margarine.

Bake in a 375° oven about 25 minutes or till golden. Cool in the pan for 1 minute. Invert onto a serving plate; remove ring mold. If desired, drizzle with Chocolate Glaze. Serve warm. Makes 10 servings.

▲ *To shape dough for the Peanut Butter 'n' Chocolate Bubble Ring, pat dough out flat and cut it into 20 equal portions. Shape each portion of dough into a ball. Then holding a ball of dough in the palm of one hand, use the other hand to place a chocolate kiss, point side up, into the center of the dough. Shape the dough back into a ball around the chocolate kiss.*

Mocha Chip Coffee Cake

Serve this sweet, chocolate-studded treat with coffee for a mid-morning or afternoon pick-me-up.

- ¼ cup sugar
- 1 tablespoon margarine *or* butter, softened
- 1 tablespoon all-purpose flour
- ⅛ teaspoon ground cinnamon
- ¾ cup miniature semisweet chocolate pieces
- ½ cup milk
- 1 teaspoon instant coffee crystals
- 1¼ cups all-purpose flour
- ¾ cup sugar
- 3 tablespoons unsweetened cocoa powder
- 2 teaspoons baking powder
- ½ teaspoon salt
- ½ teaspoon ground cinnamon
- 1 beaten egg
- ¼ cup cooking oil

Grease a 9x9x2-inch baking pan. Set pan aside. For topping, in a small mixing bowl stir together the ¼ cup sugar, margarine or butter, 1 tablespoon flour, and ⅛ teaspoon cinnamon till crumbly. Stir in *¼ cup* of the chocolate pieces. Set topping aside.

In a small mixing bowl stir together milk and coffee crystals; set aside. In a medium bowl stir together 1¼ cups flour, ¾ cup sugar, cocoa powder, baking powder, salt, and ½ teaspoon cinnamon. Stir in the remaining chocolate pieces. Make a well in the center of the dry mixture.

Stir egg and cooking oil into the coffee mixture. Then add the egg mixture all at once to the dry mixture. Stir *just till moistened* (batter should be lumpy). Spread batter into the prepared baking pan. Sprinkle topping on top of the batter.

Bake in a 375° oven for 20 to 25 minutes or till a wooden toothpick inserted near center comes out clean. Cool in pan on a wire rack about 15 minutes. Cut into squares and serve warm. Makes 16 servings.

Tropical Sourdough Coffee Cake

- ½ cup Sourdough Starter (see page 52)
- 1 8¼-ounce can crushed pineapple
- 1 tablespoon cornstarch
- 1 tablespoon lemon juice
- 1½ cups all-purpose flour
- ½ cup sugar
- ½ teaspoon baking powder
- ½ teaspoon baking soda
- ¼ teaspoon salt
- ½ cup margarine *or* butter
- 1 beaten egg
- ¼ cup milk
- 1 teaspoon vanilla
- ¼ cup sugar
- ¼ cup all-purpose flour
- 2 tablespoons margarine *or* butter
- ¼ cup coconut
- ¼ cup chopped almonds *or* macadamia nuts

Bring Sourdough Starter to room temperature. Grease a 9x9x2-inch baking pan; set aside. For pineapple filling, in a medium saucepan combine *undrained* pineapple, cornstarch, and lemon juice. Cook and stir till thickened and bubbly. Cool.

In a large mixing bowl stir together the 1½ cups flour, the ½ cup sugar, baking powder, baking soda, and salt. Using a pastry blender, cut in the ½ cup margarine or butter till mixture resembles fine crumbs. In a small mixing bowl stir together egg, milk, vanilla, and Sourdough Starter. Add to the flour mixture and stir *just till moistened.*

Spread *two-thirds* of the batter in the prepared pan. Spread pineapple filling on top. Drop remaining batter in small mounds on the filling. In a medium bowl combine the ¼ cup sugar and the ¼ cup flour. Cut in 2 tablespoons margarine or butter till mixture resembles coarse crumbs. Stir in the coconut and nuts; sprinkle over the batter. Bake in a 350° oven for 35 to 40 minutes or till golden. Cool in pan on a wire rack. Cut into squares. Serve warm or cooled. Serves 9.

Cream Cheese and Raspberry Coffee Cake

The swirls of red preserves in this rich cream cheese coffee cake make it as eye-catching as it is yummy.

 1 **8-ounce package cream cheese, softened**
 ½ **cup margarine *or* butter**
1¾ **cups all-purpose flour**
 1 **cup sugar**
 2 **eggs**
 ¼ **cup milk**
 1 **teaspoon baking powder**
 ½ **teaspoon baking soda**
 ½ **teaspoon vanilla**
 ½ **cup seedless red raspberry preserves *or* strawberry preserves**
   Powdered sugar

Grease a 13x9x2-inch baking pan; set aside. In a large mixing bowl beat cream cheese and margarine or butter with an electric mixer on medium to high speed about 30 seconds or till combined.

Add about *half* of the flour to the cream cheese mixture. Then add the sugar, eggs, milk, baking powder, baking soda, and vanilla. Beat on low speed till thoroughly combined, scraping the sides of the bowl. Beat on medium speed for 2 minutes. Then beat in remaining flour on low speed *just till combined.*

Spread batter evenly in the prepared pan. Dollop preserves in small spoonfuls on top of the batter. Using a small narrow spatula or knife, gently swirl preserves into the batter to create a marbled effect.

Bake in a 350° oven for 30 to 35 minutes or till a wooden toothpick inserted near the center comes out clean. Cool in the pan on a wire rack for 15 minutes. Sift powdered sugar over the top. Cut into squares and serve warm or cooled. Makes 12 servings.

Cream Cheese and Raspberry Ring: Prepare Cream Cheese and Raspberry Coffee Cake as directed at left, *except* spread *half* of the batter in a greased and floured 6-cup fluted tube pan. Dollop with *half* of the preserves. Repeat with remaining batter and preserves. Swirl as directed. Bake in a 350° oven about 50 minutes or till a wooden toothpick inserted near the center comes out clean. Cool in the pan on a wire rack for 10 minutes. Loosen and invert the coffee cake onto the wire rack; cool completely. Sift powdered sugar over the top. Serve warm or cooled. Makes 12 servings.

◄*Using a small narrow metal spatula or a knife, gently swirl or zigzag the preserves into the cream cheese batter to create a marbled effect. Do not swirl or zigzag too vigorously or the marbled effect will be lost.*

Banana Berry Crunch

Coffee cakes were created during the early 1900s when cooks started embellishing plain butter cakes with spices, nuts, and fruits.

  1 **10-ounce package frozen, sweetened, sliced strawberries *or* raspberries, thawed**
  4 **teaspoons cornstarch**
1½ **cups all-purpose flour**
  2 **teaspoons baking powder**
  ¼ **teaspoon baking soda**
  ¼ **teaspoon salt**
  ½ **cup margarine *or* butter**
  ⅔ **cup sugar**
  2 **eggs**
  2 **ripe medium bananas, mashed (1 cup)**
  ¼ **cup milk**
  1 **teaspoon vanilla**
  ⅓ **cup chopped peanuts**
  ¼ **cup sugar**
  1 **tablespoon all-purpose flour**
  1 **tablespoon margarine *or* butter, softened**

Grease and lightly flour a 9x9x2-inch baking pan; set aside. In a saucepan combine *undrained* berries and cornstarch. Cook and stir till thickened and bubbly. If desired, sieve berry mixture; set aside.

In a small bowl stir together 1½ cups flour, baking powder, soda, and salt; set aside. In a medium bowl beat ½ cup margarine with an electric mixer on medium speed about 30 seconds or till softened. Add ⅔ cup sugar; beat till combined. Add eggs, one at a time, beating on medium speed till combined. Combine banana, milk, and vanilla. Alternately add flour mixture and banana mixture to beaten mixture, beating on low speed after each addition *just till combined.*

Pour batter into the prepared pan. Spoon the berry mixture on top. Combine peanuts, ¼ cup sugar, 1 tablespoon flour, and 1 tablespoon margarine. Sprinkle over berry mixture. Bake in a 375° oven for 30 to 35 minutes or till a wooden toothpick inserted near center comes out clean. Serve warm. Makes 9 servings.

Pineapple Apricot Coffee Cake

Here's a new twist to the traditional pineapple upside down cake—the fruit is swirled throughout.

  ⅓ **cup chopped walnuts**
  2 **tablespoons brown sugar**
  1 **tablespoon margarine *or* butter, softened**
1¼ **cups all-purpose flour**
  2 **teaspoons baking powder**
  ¼ **teaspoon salt**
  ½ **cup margarine *or* butter**
  ½ **cup sugar**
  1 **egg**
  1 **teaspoon vanilla**
  ½ **cup milk**
  ½ **of an 8-ounce can crushed pineapple, drained**
  2 **tablespoons apricot preserves**

Grease and lightly flour an 8x8x2-inch baking pan. Set pan aside. In a small mixing bowl combine the walnuts, brown sugar, and 1 tablespoon margarine or butter. Set nut mixture aside. In another small mixing bowl stir together the flour, baking powder, and salt. Set the flour mixture aside.

In a medium mixing bowl beat ½ cup margarine or butter with an electric mixer on medium to high speed about 30 seconds or till softened. Add sugar and beat till combined. Add egg and vanilla; beat till well combined (batter may appear curdled). Alternately add flour mixture and milk to beaten mixture, beating on low to medium speed after each addition *just till combined.*

Spread the batter into the prepared pan. In a small bowl stir together pineapple and apricot preserves, then dollop pineapple mixture in small spoonfuls on top of batter. Using a narrow spatula, gently swirl pineapple mixture into the batter. Sprinkle with the nut mixture. Bake in a 350° oven for 30 to 35 minutes or till a wooden toothpick inserted near the center comes out clean. Makes 9 servings.

YEAST BREADS

Nothing quite compares to the aroma and eye appeal of freshly baked yeast breads. Whether you choose a loaf or a special shape, homemade yeast bread is fun to make and a great way to treat your family to a bit of wholesome goodness.

□ Working with yeast can be tricky. If it gets too hot or too cold, the bread won't rise. Use a thermometer to make sure you heat the liquid mixture to just the right temperature, and choose a warm but not hot area for rising.

□ Kneading the dough (see photo, page 43) can be a sticky mess when you use too little flour or a tough task if you use too much flour. Our bread recipes give a range for the amount of flour, so start by using the minimum amount as a guideline. If the dough seems sticky, add more flour a little at a time, but do not go over the maximum amount given.

□ Choose a draft-free area with the optimum temperature of 80° to 85° for raising your dough. Our Test Kitchen found that the oven or the microwave oven are good places for raising dough. To use your oven, place the bowl of dough in an unheated oven, then set a large pan of hot water under the bowl on the oven's lower rack. To use your microwave, see the tip on page 64.

□ You easily can check your bread for doneness by tapping the top of the loaf with your finger. When you get a hollow sound, the bread is done. Rolls and coffee cakes don't need to be tapped. When their tops are golden brown, remove them from the oven.

Oatmeal Molasses Bread

2¾ to 3¼ cups all-purpose flour
2 packages active dry yeast
1 12-ounce can dark beer *or* beer
½ cup molasses
3 tablespoons margarine *or* butter
2 teaspoons salt
2 cups whole wheat flour
½ cup quick-cooking rolled oats
½ cup yellow cornmeal
Yellow cornmeal
1 slightly beaten egg white
Quick-cooking rolled oats

In a large bowl combine *2 cups* of all-purpose flour and yeast; set aside. In a saucepan heat and stir beer, molasses, margarine, and salt *just till warm* (120° to 130°) and margarine almost melts. Add to flour mixture. Beat with an electric mixer on low to medium speed for 30 seconds, scraping bowl. Beat on high speed for 3 minutes. Stir in whole wheat flour, the ½ cup oats, and the ½ cup cornmeal. Then stir in as much of the remaining all-purpose flour as you can.

On a lightly floured surface, knead in enough of the remaining flour to make a moderately stiff dough that is smooth and elastic (6 to 8 minutes total). Shape into a ball. Place in a greased bowl; turn once. Cover; let rise in a warm place till double (about 1½ hours).

Punch dough down. Turn out onto a lightly floured surface. Divide in half. Cover; let rest 10 minutes. Grease a large baking sheet. Sprinkle with additional cornmeal. Shape *each* half into a ball. Place on prepared baking sheet. Flatten to 6 inches in diameter. Cover; let rise till *nearly* double (about 1 hour).

Brush loaves with a mixture of egg white and 1 tablespoon *water*. Sprinkle tops with additional oats. Bake in a 375° oven for 35 to 40 minutes or till done (if necessary, cover with foil the last 15 minutes of baking to prevent overbrowning). Remove from baking sheet. Cool on a wire rack. Makes 2 loaves.

Whole Wheat Bread

3 to 3½ cups all-purpose flour
1 package active dry yeast
1¾ cups water
⅓ cup packed brown sugar
3 tablespoons shortening, margarine, *or* butter
1 teaspoon salt
2 cups whole wheat flour

In a large mixing bowl combine *2 cups* of all-purpose flour and yeast; set aside. In a medium saucepan heat and stir water, brown sugar, shortening, and salt *just till warm* (120° to 130°) and shortening almost melts. Add to flour mixture. Beat with an electric mixer on low to medium speed for 30 seconds, scraping bowl. Beat on high speed for 3 minutes. Using a wooden spoon, stir in whole wheat flour and as much of the remaining all-purpose flour as you can.

Turn dough out onto a lightly floured surface. Knead in enough of the remaining all-purpose flour to make a moderately stiff dough that is smooth and elastic (6 to 8 minutes total). Shape into a ball. Place in a greased bowl; turn once. Cover and let rise in a warm place till double (1 to 1½ hours).

Punch dough down. Turn out onto a floured surface. Divide in half. Cover; let rest 10 minutes. Lightly grease two 8x4x2-inch loaf pans. Shape *each* half into a loaf (see tip, page 52). Place in prepared pans. Cover; let rise till *nearly* double (45 to 60 minutes).

Bake in a 375° oven for 40 to 45 minutes or till bread tests done (if necessary, cover with foil the last 15 minutes of baking to prevent overbrowning). Remove from pans. Cool on a wire rack. Makes 2 loaves.

Bran Bread: Prepare Whole Wheat Bread as directed above, *except* reduce whole wheat flour to *1½ cups* and stir in ½ cup *unprocessed wheat bran (miller's bran)*.

▶ *To knead the dough, place it on a lightly floured surface. Knead by folding the dough and pushing it down with the heels of your hands, curving your fingers over the dough. Turn, fold, and push down again.*

▶ *To check the dough to see if it has doubled and is ready for shaping, press two fingers ½ inch into the dough. Remove your fingers; if the indentations remain, the dough has doubled in size and is ready to be punched down.*

▶ *To punch the dough down, push your fist into the center of the dough, pressing beyond the surface. Pull the edges of the dough to the center. Turn the dough over and place it on a lightly floured surface.*

Old-Fashioned Potato Bread

Old-Fashioned Potato Bread

Freshly cooked potato is the secret to the moist goodness of this bread. (Whole wheat version is pictured on cover.)

1½ cups water
1 medium potato, peeled and cubed
1 cup buttermilk *or* sour milk
3 tablespoons sugar
2 tablespoons margarine *or* butter
2 teaspoons salt
6 to 6½ cups all-purpose flour
2 packages active dry yeast
All-purpose flour

In a saucepan combine the water and potato. Bring to boiling. Cook, covered, about 12 minutes or till very tender. *Do not drain*. Mash potato in the water. Measure the potato-water mixture. If necessary, add additional *water* to make *1¾ cups* total. Return mixture to saucepan. Add buttermilk, sugar, margarine or butter, and salt. Heat or cool as necessary to 120° to 130°. In a large bowl combine *2 cups* of the all-purpose flour and yeast. Add the potato mixture. Beat with an electric mixer on low to medium speed for 30 seconds, scraping bowl. Beat on high speed for 3 minutes. Using a spoon, stir in as much of the remaining 6 to 6½ cups of all-purpose flour as you can.

On a lightly floured surface, knead in enough of the remaining 6 to 6½ cups of all-purpose flour to make a moderately stiff dough that is smooth and elastic (6 to 8 minutes total). Shape into a ball. Place in a greased bowl; turn once to grease surface. Cover and let rise in a warm place till double (45 to 60 minutes).

Punch dough down. Turn out onto a lightly floured surface. Divide in half. Cover and let rest for 10 minutes. Lightly grease two 8x4x2-inch loaf pans. Shape *each* half of dough into a loaf (see tip, page 52). Lightly dip tops of loaves in the additional all-purpose flour. Place in prepared loaf pans, flour side up. Cover and let rise till *nearly* double (about 30 minutes).

Bake in a 375° oven for 35 to 40 minutes or till done (if necessary, cover with foil the last 15 minutes of baking to prevent overbrowning). Remove bread from pans and cool on a wire rack. Makes 2 loaves.

Whole Wheat Potato Bread: Prepare Old-Fashioned Potato Bread as directed at left, *except* reduce all-purpose flour to *4 to 4½ cups* and add 2 cups *whole wheat flour*. Stir in the whole wheat flour along with as much of the remaining all-purpose flour as you can.

Potato Buns: Prepare Old-Fashioned Potato Bread *or* Whole Wheat Potato Bread as directed, *except* divide *each* half of dough into 12 pieces. Shape into balls. Lightly dip tops of balls in the additional all-purpose flour. Place evenly on 2 greased baking sheets so rolls don't touch. Cover; let rise till *nearly* double (about 30 minutes). Bake in a 375° oven for 20 to 25 minutes or till golden brown. Makes 24 buns.

Saving Time with Quick-Rising Yeast

Using quick-rising yeast can be a great shortcut for bread bakers. It can cut the dough's rising time by a third. The yeast bread and roll recipes in this chapter were tested using active dry yeast. However, you can prepare these recipes (except for the Sourdough Starter on page 52 and any yeast doughs requiring a refrigerated rise) using the quick-rising active dry yeast. Follow the same directions, but check rising earlier.

Barley Wheat Bread

½ cup quick-cooking barley
3½ to 4 cups all-purpose flour
2 packages active dry yeast
1 cup water
1 cup cream-style cottage cheese
⅓ cup packed brown sugar
3 tablespoons margarine *or* butter
1½ teaspoons salt
2 cups whole wheat flour
   Margarine *or* butter, melted

Cook barley according to package directions, then drain well. In a large mixing bowl combine *2 cups* of all-purpose flour and yeast. In a medium saucepan heat and stir water, cottage cheese, brown sugar, 3 tablespoons margarine, and salt *just till warm* (120° to 130°) and margarine almost melts. Add to flour mixture. Beat with an electric mixer on low to medium speed for 30 seconds, scraping bowl. Beat on high speed for 3 minutes. Using a wooden spoon, stir in barley, whole wheat flour, and as much of the remaining all-purpose flour as you can.

Turn dough out onto lightly floured surface. Knead in enough of the remaining all-purpose flour to make a moderately stiff dough that is smooth and elastic (6 to 8 minutes total). Shape into a ball. Place in a greased bowl, turning once to grease surface. Cover; let rise in a warm place till double (about 1¼ hours).

Punch dough down. Turn out onto a lightly floured surface. Divide in half. Cover and let rest 10 minutes. Meanwhile, lightly grease two 9x5x3-inch loaf pans. Shape *each* half of dough into a loaf (see tip, page 52). Place in prepared loaf pans. Cover and let rise till *nearly* double (45 to 60 minutes).

Bake in a 375° oven about 35 minutes or till done (if necessary, cover loosely with foil the last 15 minutes of baking to prevent overbrowning). Remove bread from pans and cool on a wire rack. Brush tops with melted margarine or butter. Makes 2 loaves.

Pepper-Cheese Bread

If you use aged provolone cheese, be sure to crumble rather than shred it.

2¾ to 3¼ cups all-purpose flour
1 package active dry yeast
1½ to 2 teaspoons cracked black pepper
½ teaspoon salt
1 cup warm water (120° to 130°)
2 tablespoons olive oil *or* cooking oil
1 cup shredded provolone cheese (4 ounces)
½ cup grated Parmesan *or* Romano cheese
1 slightly beaten egg white

In a medium mixing bowl stir together *1 cup* of the flour, yeast, pepper, and salt. Add warm water and oil. Beat with an electric mixer on low to medium speed for 30 seconds, scraping the sides of bowl. Beat on high speed for 3 minutes. Using a wooden spoon, stir in as much of the remaining flour as you can.

On a lightly floured surface, knead in enough of the remaining flour to make a stiff dough that is smooth and elastic (8 to 10 minutes total). Shape into a ball. Place in a greased bowl; turn once. Cover and let rise in a warm place till double (1 to 1¼ hours).

Punch dough down. Turn out onto a lightly floured surface. Cover and let rest 10 minutes. Meanwhile, lightly grease a large baking sheet. Roll the dough into a 12x10-inch rectangle. Sprinkle provolone and Parmesan or Romano cheese on top of dough. Roll up, jelly-roll style, starting from a long side. Moisten edge with water and seal. Taper ends. Place, seam side down, on prepared baking sheet. Brush with a mixture of egg white and 1 tablespoon *water.* Cover and let rise till *nearly* double (about 45 minutes).

With a very sharp knife, make 3 or 4 diagonal cuts about ¼ inch deep across top of the loaf. Bake in a 375° oven for 15 minutes. Brush again with egg white mixture. Bake for 20 to 25 minutes more or till done. Remove from baking sheet and cool on a wire rack. Makes 1 loaf.

Sage Wheat Bread

Sage, the seasoning used in stuffing, makes this a wonderful bread to jazz up a turkey sandwich. (Pictured on pages 6–7.)

2¼ to 2¾ cups all-purpose flour
  2 packages active dry yeast
  1 tablespoon snipped fresh sage *or* 1 teaspoon dried sage, crushed
1¾ cups milk
  ¼ cup packed brown sugar
  3 tablespoons margarine *or* butter
  2 teaspoons salt
  2 cups whole wheat flour
  ½ cup yellow cornmeal
    Yellow cornmeal
  1 slightly beaten egg
  2 sage sprigs (optional)

In a large mixing bowl combine *2 cups* of the all-purpose flour, yeast, and fresh or dried sage; set aside. In a medium saucepan heat and stir milk, brown sugar, margarine or butter, and salt *just till warm* (120° to 130°) and margarine almost melts. Add to flour mixture. Beat with an electric mixer on low to medium speed for 30 seconds, scraping bowl. Beat on high speed for 3 minutes. Using a spoon, stir in the whole wheat flour, ½ cup cornmeal, and as much of the remaining all-purpose flour as you can.

On a floured surface, knead in enough remaining all-purpose flour to make a moderately stiff dough that is smooth and elastic (6 to 8 minutes). Shape into a ball. Place in a greased bowl; turn once. Cover; let rise in a warm place till double (1 to 1¼ hours).

Punch dough down. Turn out onto a lightly floured surface. Divide in half. Cover and let rest 10 minutes. Lightly grease a large baking sheet and lightly sprinkle it with additional cornmeal. Shape *each* half of dough into a ball. Place on prepared baking sheet. Flatten to about 5 inches in diameter.

Brush loaves with a mixture of egg and 1 tablespoon *water*. If desired, place sage sprigs on top of loaves *or* use a very sharp knife to slash a leaf design. Cover; let rise till *nearly* double (30 to 45 minutes).

Brush again with egg mixture. Bake in a 375° oven for 30 to 35 minutes or till done (if necessary, cover with foil the last 15 minutes of baking to prevent overbrowning). Cool on a wire rack. Makes 2 loaves.

Yogurt Dill Bread

This no-knead yeast bread is a batter instead of a dough.

2¼ cups all-purpose flour
  1 package active dry yeast
  1 teaspoon dried dillweed
  1 8-ounce carton plain yogurt
  ¼ cup sugar
  ¼ cup water
  ¼ cup margarine *or* butter
  ½ teaspoon salt
  1 egg

Grease an 8-inch fluted tube pan. Set pan aside. In a large mixing bowl stir together *1 cup* of the flour, yeast, and dillweed; set aside. In a medium saucepan heat and stir the yogurt, sugar, water, margarine or butter, and salt *just till warm* (120° to 130°) and margarine almost melts. Add to flour mixture. Add egg. Beat with an electric mixer on low to medium speed for 30 seconds, scraping the sides of bowl. Then beat on high speed for 3 minutes. Using a spoon, stir in remaining flour (batter will be sticky).

Spoon batter into the prepared pan. Cover and let rise in a warm place till *nearly* double (about 30 minutes). Bake in a 375° oven for 35 to 40 minutes or till bread tests done (if necessary, cover with foil the last 15 minutes to prevent overbrowning). Remove bread from pan. Cool on a wire rack. Makes 1 loaf.

SPECIAL LOAF-SHAPING IDEAS

With a few easy twists and turns, you can transform a basic bread into something extraordinary. Try these shaping ideas with our Whole Wheat Bread, Old-Fashioned Potato Bread, Cheese 'n' Onion Bread, and Sourdough Bread. (See recipes, pages 43, 45, 51, and 52.)

CHRISTMAS TREES: For *each* loaf, divide dough into 17 pieces. Shape *each* piece into a 1½-inch ball, pulling dough under to make a smooth top. On a greased baking sheet form a tree shape with balls, starting with a row of 5 balls, then 4, 3, 2, and 1. Combine the last *two* balls into one larger ball. Flatten slightly and place at the base of the tree. Let rise and bake as directed. If desired, decorate with Powdered Sugar Icing (see recipe, page 230) and candied fruit.

COILS: For *each* loaf, roll the dough into an evenly thick 36-inch rope. Starting in the center of a greased 9x1½-inch round baking pan, loosely coil the rope to form a snail shape; tuck end under. Let rise and bake as directed.

TWISTS AND BRAIDS: For *each* twisted loaf, divide dough into two portions. Roll *each* portion into an evenly thick 14-inch rope. Loosely twist the two ropes together; press ends together to seal. Place on a greased baking sheet. Let rise and bake as directed.

For *each* braided loaf, divide dough into three portions. Roll *each* portion into an evenly thick 16-inch rope. Line up the three ropes, 1 inch apart, on a greased baking sheet. Starting in the middle, *loosely* braid by bringing left rope underneath the center rope. Then bring the right rope under the new center rope. Repeat to end. On the other end, braid to center by bringing the outside ropes alternately *over* center rope. Press ends together to seal. Let rise and bake as directed.

WREATHS: For *each* wreath, shape dough into a twist or braid as directed at left, *except* make the ropes 30 inches long. Make a wreath by forming the twist or braid into a circle. Press the ends together to seal. Let rise and bake as directed.

French Bread

A crisp, crunchy crust and slightly chewy center make this bread as traditional as the breads served in France. (Pictured on pages 6–7 and on the cover.)

5½ to 6 cups all-purpose flour
2 packages active dry yeast
1½ teaspoons salt
2 cups warm water (120° to 130°)
    Cornmeal
1 slightly beaten egg white
1 tablespoon water

In a large mixing bowl combine *2 cups* of the flour, the yeast, and salt. Add the 2 cups warm water. Beat with an electric mixer on low to medium speed for 30 seconds, scraping sides of bowl. Beat on high speed for 3 minutes. Using a wooden spoon, stir in as much of the remaining flour as you can.

On a lightly floured surface, knead in enough remaining flour to make a stiff dough that is smooth and elastic (8 to 10 minutes total). Shape into a ball. Place in a greased bowl; turn once. Cover and let rise in a warm place till double (about 1 hour).

Punch dough down. Turn out onto a lightly floured surface. Divide dough in half. Cover; let rest for 10 minutes. Lightly grease a large baking sheet. Sprinkle with cornmeal. Roll *each* half of dough into a 15x10-inch rectangle. Roll up, starting from a long side. Moisten edge with water and seal. Taper ends. Place, seam side down, on the prepared baking sheet. Brush with a mixture of egg white and 1 tablespoon water. Cover; let rise till *nearly* double (35 to 45 minutes).

With a very sharp knife, make 3 or 4 diagonal cuts about ¼ inch deep across top of each loaf. Bake in a 375° oven for 20 minutes. Brush again with egg white mixture. Then bake for 15 to 20 minutes more or till bread tests done (if necessary, cover loosely with foil the last 15 minutes of baking to prevent overbrowning). Remove from baking sheet and cool on a wire rack. Makes 2 loaves.

Secrets to Successful Breads

With a little know-how, you can master the art of bread baking in no time. If your bread has one of the following problems, next time try an appropriate recommendation.

If your bread is heavy and compact:
■ Be sure the liquid added to the yeast is at the temperature recommended in the recipe. Check the accuracy of the thermometer you used to test the temperature of the liquid.
■ Don't exceed the maximum amount of flour given in the recipe. Add just enough flour to make the dough the proper stiffness.
■ Use an oven thermometer to check the temperature of your oven. Baking at too low a temperature can result in heavy bread.

If the top crust separates from the bottom of the loaf:
■ Shape into a loaf by gently pulling dough into a loaf shape and tucking edges beneath.
■ Loosely cover the loaf with a dish towel or waxed paper during rising.
■ Let the loaf rise *just till nearly* double, then pop it in the oven.

If the crust is thick:
■ Use an oven thermometer to check the temperature of your oven. Baking at too low a temperature can result in a thick crust.

If the texture is crumbly:
■ Be sure not to add too much flour. Use the amount of flour called for in the recipe.
■ Let dough rise *just till* double for the first rise, and till *nearly* double for the second rise.

Rye Bread

For a delicious molasses flavor, reduce the water to 1½ cups and substitute ½ cup molasses for the brown sugar.

- 3½ to 4 cups all-purpose flour
- 2 packages active dry yeast
- 2 cups warm water (120° to 130°)
- ¼ cup packed brown sugar
- 2 tablespoons cooking oil
- 1 teaspoon salt
- 2 cups rye flour
- 1 tablespoon caraway seed
- Cornmeal

In a large mixing bowl combine *2¾ cups* of the all-purpose flour and the yeast. Add water, brown sugar, oil, and salt. Beat with an electric mixer on low to medium speed for 30 seconds, scraping the sides of bowl. Beat on high speed for 3 minutes. Using a wooden spoon, stir in rye flour, caraway seed, and as much of the remaining all-purpose flour as you can.

On a lightly floured surface, knead in enough of the remaining all-purpose flour to make a moderately stiff dough that is smooth and elastic (6 to 8 minutes total). Shape into a ball. Place in a greased bowl, turning once to grease the surface. Cover and let rise in a warm place till double (about 1 hour).

Punch dough down. Turn out onto a lightly floured surface. Divide in half. Cover and let rest for 10 minutes. Meanwhile, lightly grease a large baking sheet. Sprinkle with cornmeal. Shape *each* half of dough into a ball. Place on the prepared baking sheet. Flatten to 6 inches in diameter. Cover and let rise in a warm place till *nearly* double (30 to 45 minutes).

Bake in a 375° oven for 35 to 40 minutes or till bread tests done (if necessary, cover loosely with foil the last 15 minutes of baking to prevent overbrowning). Remove from baking sheet and cool on a wire rack. Makes 2 loaves.

Cheese 'n' Onion Bread

- 1 cup finely chopped onion
- 2 cloves garlic, minced
- ½ cup water
- ¾ cup milk
- 1 tablespoon sugar
- ½ teaspoon salt
- 4 to 4½ cups all-purpose flour
- 1 package active dry yeast
- 1 egg
- 2 cups shredded American cheese (8 ounces)

In a small saucepan combine onion and garlic, then add water. Bring to boiling; reduce heat. Cover and simmer about 10 minutes or till onion is tender. Stir milk, sugar, and salt into the onion mixture. Heat or cool as necessary to 120° to 130°. In a large mixing bowl combine *1 cup* of the flour and yeast. Add the onion mixture and egg. Beat with an electric mixer on low to medium speed for 30 seconds, scraping sides of bowl. Then beat on high speed for 3 minutes. Using a spoon, stir in cheese and as much of the remaining flour as you can.

On a lightly floured surface, knead in enough of the remaining flour to make a moderately stiff dough that is smooth and elastic (6 to 8 minutes total). Shape into a ball. Place in a greased bowl; turn once to grease surface. Cover and let rise in a warm place till double (about 1½ hours).

Punch dough down. Turn out onto a lightly floured surface. Divide in half. Cover and let rest for 10 minutes. Meanwhile, lightly grease two 8x4x2-inch loaf pans. Shape *each* half of dough into a loaf (see tip, page 52). Place in prepared loaf pans. Cover and let rise till *nearly* double (35 to 45 minutes).

Bake in a 375° oven for 35 to 40 minutes or till bread tests done (if necessary, cover loosely with foil the last 15 minutes of baking to prevent overbrowning). Remove bread from pans and cool on a wire rack. Makes 2 loaves.

Sourdough Starter

Don't use quick-rising yeast when making this starter.

1 package active dry yeast
2½ cups warm water (105° to 115°)
2 cups all-purpose flour
1 tablespoon sugar *or* honey

In a large mixing bowl dissolve yeast in ½ *cup* of the warm water. Stir in the remaining water, flour, and sugar or honey. Stir till smooth. Cover the bowl with 100% cotton cheesecloth. Let stand at room temperature (75° to 85°) for 5 to 10 days or till the mixture has a sour fermented aroma, stirring 2 or 3 times *each* day. (Fermentation time depends upon the room temperature: a warmer room hastens fermentation.)

When fermented, transfer Sourdough Starter to a 1-quart jar. Cover with the cheesecloth and refrigerate. *Do not cover jar with a tight-fitting lid.* If starter isn't used within 10 days, stir in 1 teaspoon *sugar or honey.* Repeat every 10 days till used.

To use starter, bring desired amount to room temperature. For every 1 cup used, stir ¾ cup *all-purpose flour,* ¾ cup *water,* and 1 teaspoon *sugar or honey* into the remaining amount. Cover and let stand at room temperature at least 1 day or till bubbly. Then refrigerate for later use. Makes about 2 cups.

Shaping a Loaf

You can achieve a prizewinning shaped loaf by either patting or rolling the dough into shape. To shape dough by patting, gently pull dough into a loaf shape and tuck edges beneath. To shape dough by rolling, on a lightly floured surface, roll dough into a 12x8-inch rectangle. Tightly roll up, starting from a short side. Seal with your fingertips as you roll.

Sourdough Bread

A tangy flavor and chewy texture are the hallmarks of Sourdough Bread.

1 cup Sourdough Starter (see recipe at left)
5½ to 6 cups all-purpose flour
1 package active dry yeast
1½ cups water
3 tablespoons sugar
3 tablespoons margarine *or* butter
1 teaspoon salt
Cornmeal

Bring Sourdough Starter to room temperature. In a large mixing bowl combine *2½ cups* of the flour and yeast; set aside. In a saucepan heat and stir water, sugar, margarine or butter, and salt *just till warm* (120° to 130°) and margarine almost melts. Add to flour mixture. Add Sourdough Starter. Beat with an electric mixer on low to medium speed for 30 seconds, scraping bowl. Beat on high speed for 3 minutes. Stir in as much of the remaining flour as you can.

On a lightly floured surface, knead in enough of the remaining flour to make a moderately stiff dough that is smooth and elastic (6 to 8 minutes total). Shape into a ball. Place dough in a lightly greased bowl, turning once to grease the surface. Cover and let rise in a warm place till double (45 to 60 minutes).

Punch dough down. Turn out onto a lightly floured surface. Divide in half. Cover and let rest for 10 minutes. Meanwhile, lightly grease a large baking sheet. Sprinkle with cornmeal. Shape *each* half of dough into a ball. Place on prepared baking sheet. Flatten slightly to 6 inches in diameter. With a sharp knife, make crisscross slashes about ¼ inch deep across the tops of the loaves. Cover and let rise in a warm place till *nearly* double (about 30 minutes).

Bake in a 375° oven for 30 to 35 minutes or till bread tests done (if necessary, cover loosely with foil the last 15 minutes of baking to prevent overbrowning). Cool on a wire rack. Makes 2 loaves.

German
Sourdough Bread

Serving suggestion: Place a custard cup filled with flavored butter in the center of this bread (see recipes, page 28).

1½ **cups Sourdough Starter (see recipe, page 52)**
  2 **to 2½ cups all-purpose flour**
  1 **package active dry yeast**
  1 **cup buttermilk *or* sour milk**
  3 **tablespoons margarine *or* butter**
  1 **tablespoon brown sugar *or* sugar**
 ½ **teaspoon salt**
  1 **cup whole wheat flour**
 ¾ **cup rye flour**
  1 **slightly beaten egg white (optional)**
  1 **tablespoon water (optional)**

Bring Sourdough Starter to room temperature. In a large mixing bowl combine *1¼ cups* of the all-purpose flour and the yeast; set aside. In a saucepan heat and stir buttermilk or sour milk, margarine, brown sugar or sugar, and salt *just till warm* (120° to 130°) and margarine almost melts. Add to flour mixture. Add Sourdough Starter. Beat with an electric mixer on low to medium speed for 30 seconds, scraping sides of bowl. Beat on high speed for 3 minutes. Using a spoon, stir in the whole wheat flour, rye flour, and as much of the remaining all-purpose flour as you can.

On a lightly floured surface, knead in enough of the remaining all-purpose flour to make a moderately stiff dough that is smooth and elastic (6 to 8 minutes total). Shape into a ball. Place dough in a greased bowl, turning once to grease the surface. Cover and let rise in a warm place till double (45 to 60 minutes).

Punch dough down. Turn out onto a floured surface. Cover and let rest for 10 minutes. Grease a large baking sheet and the outside of a 6-ounce custard cup. Place the custard cup, upside down, in the center of the baking sheet. Shape dough into a 10½-inch round loaf. Flatten loaf to about 1½ inches thick. Use your fingers to pierce a hole in the center.

Place the dough on prepared baking sheet. Stretch the hole to fit around the custard cup. With a sharp knife, gently cut a ½-inch-deep ring on top of the loaf, halfway between the custard cup and outside edge. Then make 8 cuts perpendicular to the ring, from the ring to the outside edge, cutting all the way through. Tuck corners of each piece under to form scallops around the loaf. Cover and let rise in a warm place till *nearly* double (about 30 minutes).

If desired, brush a mixture of the egg white and water over the bread. Bake in a 375° oven for 40 to 45 minutes or till bread tests done (if necessary, cover loosely with foil the last 15 minutes of baking to prevent overbrowning). Remove from baking sheet and cool on a wire rack. Remove the custard cup when bread is cool. Makes 1 loaf.

◀*Shape the bread by making eight cuts perpendicular to the ring and the outside edge. Then form scallops around the edge of the loaf by gently tucking under each corner.*

Wheat 'n' Walnut Butterhorns
(see recipe, page 56)

Country Herb Rolls
(see recipe, page 57)

Egg Dinner Rolls

Egg Dinner Rolls

Shape these egg-rich rolls into pretty rosettes.

3½ to 4 cups all-purpose flour
  1 package active dry yeast
  1 cup milk
  ¼ cup sugar
  ¼ cup margarine *or* butter
  ½ teaspoon salt
  3 egg yolks
  1 slightly beaten egg yolk
  1 tablespoon water

In a large mixing bowl combine *1½ cups* of the flour and the yeast; set aside. In a medium saucepan heat and stir the milk, sugar, margarine or butter, and salt *just till warm* (120° to 130°) and margarine almost melts. Add to the flour mixture. Then add the 3 egg yolks. Beat with an electric mixer on low to medium speed for 30 seconds, scraping the sides of the bowl. Beat on high speed for 3 minutes. Stir in as much of the remaining flour as you can.

On a lightly floured surface, knead in enough of the remaining flour to make a moderately stiff dough that is smooth and elastic (6 to 8 minutes total). Shape into a ball. Place in a greased bowl; turn once. Cover; let rise in a warm place till double (about 1 hour).

Punch dough down. Turn out onto a lightly floured surface. Divide in half. Then divide *each* half into *12* pieces. Cover and let rest for 10 minutes. Meanwhile, grease baking sheets. To shape rolls, roll each piece into a 12-inch rope. Tie in a loose knot. Tuck top end under the roll. Then bring bottom end up and tuck it into center of roll (see photo for shaping rosettes, page 59). Place 3 inches apart on prepared baking sheets. Cover and let rise in a warm place till *nearly* double (about 30 minutes).

Brush rolls with a mixture of one egg yolk and water. Bake in a 375° oven for 10 to 12 minutes or till golden. Remove rolls from baking sheets and cool on a wire rack. Makes 24.

Achieving the Proper Stiffness of Dough

Terms such as soft dough, moderately soft dough, moderately stiff dough, and stiff dough often seem confusing to the novice bread baker. The following hints will help you to achieve the proper stiffness of dough. All you have to do is use the proper technique for kneading (see photo, page 43), knead the dough for the suggested length of time, and identify the stiffness specified in the recipe.

To double-check and make sure you've kneaded the dough long enough, set a timer for the time period suggested in the recipe. You can take a break during the kneading time; just be sure the total kneading time is as long as the recipe suggests.

Here is how to identify the stiffness of dough specified in our recipes:
■ *Soft dough* is very sticky and used for breads that don't require kneading, such as batter breads.
■ *Moderately soft dough* is slightly sticky and may be kneaded on a floured surface. It is used for most sweet breads.
■ *Moderately stiff dough* is not sticky but yields slightly to the touch. It kneads easily when on a floured surface, and is used for most unsweet breads.
■ *Stiff dough* is firm to the touch and kneads easily when on a lightly floured surface. It will, however, have some resilience and will hold its shape after it is kneaded. Chewy-textured breads, such as French breads, are made from this type of dough.

Wheat 'n' Walnut Butterhorns

These cinnamon-flavored dinner rolls are a delicious complement to a spinach salad. (Pictured on page 54.)

> 3 to 3½ **cups all-purpose flour**
> 2 **packages active dry yeast**
> ½ **teaspoon ground cinnamon**
> 1 **cup milk**
> ½ **cup margarine *or* butter**
> ½ **cup packed brown sugar**
> 2 **eggs**
> 1½ **cups whole wheat flour**
> ¼ **cup margarine *or* butter, melted**
> ½ **cup finely chopped walnuts, toasted**

In a large mixing bowl combine *2 cups* of the all-purpose flour, yeast, and cinnamon. In a saucepan heat and stir milk, ½ cup margarine, and brown sugar *just till warm* (120° to 130°) and margarine almost melts. Add to flour mixture. Add eggs. Beat with an electric mixer on low to medium speed for 30 seconds, scraping bowl. Beat on high speed for 3 minutes. Stir in whole wheat flour and as much of the remaining all-purpose flour as you can. On a lightly floured surface, knead in enough remaining all-purpose flour to make a moderately soft dough that is smooth and elastic (3 to 5 minutes total). Shape into a ball. Place in a greased bowl; turn once. Cover and let rise in a warm place till double (1 to 1½ hours).

Punch dough down. Turn out onto a lightly floured surface. Divide in half. Cover and let rest 10 minutes. Grease baking sheets. Roll *each* half of dough into a 12-inch circle. Brush *each* circle with *half* of the ¼ cup melted margarine and sprinkle with *half* of the walnuts. Cut *each* circle into *12* wedges. To shape, begin at wide end of each wedge and roll toward point. Place, point side down, 3 inches apart on prepared baking sheets. Cover and let rise in a warm place till *nearly* double (about 30 minutes).

Bake in a 375° oven for 12 to 15 minutes or till lightly browned. Cool on a wire rack. Makes 24.

Buttermilk Rolls

> 4 to 4½ **cups all-purpose flour**
> 1 **package active dry yeast**
> 1¼ **cups buttermilk *or* sour milk**
> ⅓ **cup sugar**
> ⅓ **cup margarine, butter, *or* shortening**
> ¾ **teaspoon salt**
> 1 **egg**
> 2 **tablespoons margarine *or* butter, melted**

In a large mixing bowl stir together *2 cups* of the flour and the yeast; set aside. In a medium saucepan heat and stir buttermilk or sour milk; sugar; the ⅓ cup margarine, butter, or shortening; and salt *just till warm* (120° to 130°) and margarine almost melts. Add to flour mixture. Add egg. Beat with an electric mixer on low to medium speed for 30 seconds, scraping sides of bowl. Beat on high speed for 3 minutes. Using a wooden spoon, stir in as much of the remaining flour as you can.

On a lightly floured surface, knead in enough of the remaining flour to make a moderately stiff dough that is smooth and elastic (6 to 8 minutes total). Shape into a ball. Place in a lightly greased bowl, turning once to grease surface. Cover and let rise in a warm place till double (about 1 hour).

Punch dough down. Turn out onto a lightly floured surface. Divide dough in half. Then divide *each* half into *36* pieces. Cover and let rest for 10 minutes. Meanwhile, grease 24 muffin cups. Shape each piece into a ball, pulling edges under to make a smooth top. Place *three* balls in *each* muffin cup. Cover and let rise till *nearly* double in size (about 45 minutes). (*Or,* cover with oiled waxed paper, then cover with plastic wrap and refrigerate for up to 24 hours. Let stand at room temperature 20 minutes before baking.)

Brush rolls with the 2 tablespoons melted margarine. Bake in a 375° oven for 15 to 18 minutes or till golden. Remove rolls from muffin cups and cool on a wire rack. Makes 24.

Country Herb Rolls

For a tasty change, add 2 tablespoons poppy seed to the flour-yeast mixture. (Basic rolls are pictured on page 54.)

3¼ to 3¾ cups all-purpose flour
½ cup yellow cornmeal
1 package active dry yeast
½ teaspoon dried basil, crushed
½ teaspoon dried oregano, crushed
¾ cup milk
⅓ cup margarine *or* butter
¼ cup sugar
½ teaspoon salt
2 eggs
3 tablespoons margarine *or* butter, melted

In a large mixing bowl combine *1 cup* of the flour, cornmeal, yeast, basil, and oregano; set aside. In a saucepan heat and stir milk, ⅓ cup margarine, sugar, and salt *just till warm* (120° to 130°) and margarine almost melts. Add to flour mixture. Then add eggs. Beat with an electric mixer on low to medium speed for 30 seconds, scraping bowl. Beat on high speed for 3 minutes. Stir in as much of the remaining flour as you can. On a floured surface, knead in enough remaining flour to make a moderately stiff dough that is smooth and elastic (6 to 8 minutes total). Shape into a ball. Place in greased bowl; turn once. Cover and let rise in a warm place till double (about 1 hour).

Punch dough down. Turn out onto a floured surface. Cover; let rest for 10 minutes. Roll dough to ¼-inch thickness. Cut with a floured 2½-inch round biscuit cutter. Brush with some of the 3 tablespoons melted margarine. To shape, use a wooden spoon handle to make a slight off-center crease in each round. Fold large half over small half, slightly overlapping. Press folded edge firmly. Place 3 inches apart on greased baking sheets. Cover; let rise till *nearly* double (about 20 minutes).

Brush top of rolls with remaining melted margarine. Bake in a 375° oven about 12 minutes or till golden. Cool on a wire rack. Makes about 24.

Crunchy Parmesan Herb Breadsticks

Eat 'em plain or dip 'em in your favorite mustard, pizza sauce, or sour cream dip. (Pictured on pages 6–7.)

2 to 2½ cups all-purpose flour
⅓ cup grated Parmesan cheese
1 package active dry yeast
1 teaspoon Italian seasoning, crushed
¾ cup warm water (120° to 130°)
1 tablespoon cooking oil
1 slightly beaten egg white
1 tablespoon water
   Grated Parmesan cheese

In a medium mixing bowl stir together ¾ *cup* of the flour, the ⅓ cup Parmesan cheese, yeast, and Italian seasoning. Add the ¾ cup warm water and oil to the flour mixture. Beat with an electric mixer on low to medium speed for 30 seconds, scraping sides of bowl. Beat on high speed 3 minutes. Using a spoon, stir in as much of the remaining flour as you can.

On a lightly floured surface, knead in enough of the remaining flour to make a stiff dough that is smooth and elastic (8 to 10 minutes total). Shape into a ball. Place dough in a lightly greased bowl, turning once to grease the surface. Cover and let rise in a warm place till double (45 to 60 minutes).

Punch dough down. Turn out onto a lightly floured surface. Divide into quarters. Then divide *each* quarter into *six* pieces. Cover and let rest for 10 minutes. Grease baking sheets. To shape breadsticks, roll each piece into an 8-inch-long rope. Place 2 inches apart on prepared baking sheets. Cover and let rise in a warm place till *nearly* double (about 30 minutes).

Brush breadsticks with a mixture of egg white and 1 tablespoon water. Then sprinkle with additional Parmesan cheese. Bake in a 375° oven for 10 minutes. Reduce oven temperature to 300°. Bake for 20 to 25 minutes more or till golden brown and crisp. Remove breadsticks from baking sheets and cool on a wire rack. Makes 24.

SPECIAL ROLL-SHAPING IDEAS

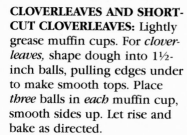

A few quick snips and folds can turn traditional dinner rolls into impressively shaped buns every time. Try these shaping ideas with our Egg Dinner Rolls, Buttermilk Rolls, Country Herb Rolls, and the dough from the Wheat 'n' Walnut Butterhorns. (See recipes, pages 55–57.)

CLOVERLEAVES AND SHORT-CUT CLOVERLEAVES: Lightly grease muffin cups. For *cloverleaves,* shape dough into 1½-inch balls, pulling edges under to make smooth tops. Place *three* balls in *each* muffin cup, smooth sides up. Let rise and bake as directed.

For *shortcut cloverleaves,* shape dough into 2-inch balls, pulling edges under to make smooth tops. Place *one* ball in *each* muffin cup, smooth side up. With floured kitchen scissors, snip top in half, making a cut about 1 inch deep. Make a second snip to form an X. Let rise and bake as directed.

PARKER HOUSE ROLLS: Lightly grease baking sheets. On a lightly floured surface, roll dough to ¼-inch thickness. Cut with a 2½-inch round biscuit cutter, dipping the cutter into flour between cuts. Brush with melted *margarine or butter.* To shape, use a wooden spoon handle to make a slight off-center crease in each round. Fold large half over small half, overlapping slightly. Press folded edge firmly. Place 3 inches apart on the baking sheets. Let rise; bake as directed.

BUTTERHORNS: Lightly grease baking sheets. Divide the dough in half. On a lightly floured surface, roll each *half* of dough into a 12-inch circle. Brush with melted *margarine* or *butter*. Cut *each* circle into 12 wedges. To shape, begin at wide end of the wedge and roll toward the point. Place rolls point side down, 3 inches apart on prepared baking sheets. Let rise and bake as directed.

FLOWER-SHAPED ROLLS: Lightly grease baking sheets. Shape dough into 2-inch balls, pulling edges under to make smooth tops. Place 3 inches apart on baking sheets. Cover; let rise till *nearly* double (about 30 minutes). Using kitchen scissors, make five snips from edge *almost* to center, cutting completely through dough. Bake as directed.

BOWKNOTS AND ROSETTES: Lightly grease baking sheets. Shape dough into 2-inch balls. For *bowknots,* on a lightly floured surface, roll *each* piece into a 10-inch rope. Tie the rope in a loose knot, leaving two long ends. Place 3 inches apart on baking sheets. Let rise and bake as directed.

For *rosettes,* on a lightly floured surface, roll *each* piece into a 12-inch rope. Tie the rope in a loose knot, leaving two long ends. Tuck the top end under the roll. Bring the bottom end up and tuck it into the center of roll. Place 3 inches apart on baking sheet. Let rise and bake as directed.

Bagels

Three steps—broiling, boiling, and baking—make these bagels crusty on the outside and chewy on the inside.

>   4   to 4½ cups all-purpose flour
>   1   package active dry yeast
>   1½ cups warm water (120° to 130°)
>   2   tablespoons sugar
>   1½ teaspoons salt
>   1   tablespoon sugar
>   1   beaten egg

In a large mixing bowl combine *2 cups* of the flour and the yeast. Add the warm water, 2 tablespoons sugar, and salt. Beat with an electric mixer on low to medium speed for 30 seconds, scraping the sides of the bowl. Beat on high speed for 3 minutes. Stir in as much of the remaining flour as you can.

On a lightly floured surface, knead in enough of the remaining flour to make a moderately stiff dough that is smooth and elastic (6 to 8 minutes total). Cover; let rest for 10 minutes. Grease 2 baking sheets. Working quickly, divide dough into 12 portions. Shape each portion into a smooth ball. Cover and let rest for 5 minutes. With a floured finger, punch a hole in the center of each ball. Make about a 2-inch hole, keeping a uniform shape. Place 2 inches apart on the prepared baking sheets. Reshape so the holes are 2 inches in diameter. Cover and let rise for 20 minutes (start timing after the first bagel is shaped).

Broil raised bagels about 5 inches from the heat for 3 to 4 minutes or till bagels look set, turning once (tops should not brown). Meanwhile, in a 12-inch skillet or 4½-quart Dutch oven bring 6 cups *water* and 1 tablespoon sugar to boiling. Reduce heat; simmer bagels, 4 or 5 at a time, for 7 minutes, turning once. Drain on paper towels. Let stand on towels only a few seconds. (If left too long, they stick.) Place drained bagels 2 inches apart on well-greased baking sheets. Brush with egg. Bake in a 375° oven for 20 to 25 minutes or till tops are golden. Makes 12.

Egg Bagels: Prepare Bagels at left, *except* reduce warm water to *1¼ cups*. Add 2 egg *yolks* to the flour mixture along with the warm water.

Onion Bagels: Prepare Bagels at left, *except* omit brushing with egg. Cook ½ cup finely chopped *onion* in 3 tablespoons *margarine or butter* till tender but not brown. Brush over tops of bagels after the first 15 minutes of baking.

Parmesan Bagels: Prepare Bagels at left, *except* stir ¼ cup grated *Parmesan cheese* into the flour-yeast mixture.

Poppy Seed *or* Sesame Bagels: Prepare Bagels at left, *except* before baking, sprinkle with 2 teaspoons *poppy seed* or toasted *sesame seed*.

Light Rye Bagels: Prepare Bagels at left, *except* substitute 1¼ cups *rye flour* for 1¼ cups of the stirred-in all-purpose flour. Stir in 1 teaspoon *caraway seed* with the rye flour.

Whole Wheat Bagels: Prepare Bagels at left, *except* substitute 1½ cups *whole wheat flour* for 1½ cups of the stirred-in all-purpose flour.

◀ *To shape into bagels, use a floured finger to punch a hole in the center of each ball. Using four fingers, gently pull the dough to make about a 2-inch hole. While pulling, try to keep each bagel uniform in shape.*

Soft Pretzels

Oh, so yummy, served plain or with the cheese sauce.

     4 to 4½ cups all-purpose flour
     1 package active dry yeast
    1½ cups milk
     ¼ cup sugar
     2 tablespoons cooking oil
     1 teaspoon salt
     2 tablespoons salt
     3 quarts boiling water
     1 slightly beaten egg white
     1 tablespoon water
        Sesame seed, poppy seed, *or* coarse salt
        Cheddar Sauce (optional)

In a large mixing bowl combine *1½ cups* of the flour and the yeast. In a medium saucepan heat and stir milk, sugar, oil, and 1 teaspoon salt *just till warm* (120° to 130°). Add to the flour mixture. Beat with an electric mixer on low to medium speed for 30 seconds, scraping the sides of the bowl. Then beat on high speed for 3 minutes. Using a wooden spoon, stir in as much of the remaining flour as you can.

Turn dough out onto a lightly floured surface. Knead in enough of the remaining flour to make a moderately stiff dough that is smooth and elastic (6 to 8 minutes total). Shape into a ball. Place in a greased bowl, turning once to grease the surface. Cover and let rise in a warm place till double (about 1¼ hours).

Punch dough down. Turn out onto a lightly floured surface. Cover and let rest for 10 minutes. Meanwhile, grease 2 baking sheets. Roll dough into a 12x10-inch rectangle. Cut into twenty 12x½-inch strips. Gently pull each strip into a rope about 16 inches long. Shape into pretzels (see photo for shaping pretzels at right). Place pretzels ½ inch apart on the prepared baking sheets. Bake in a 475° oven for 4 minutes. Remove from oven. Reduce oven temperature to 350°.

Meanwhile, dissolve the 2 tablespoons salt in the boiling water. Reduce heat. Lower pretzels, 4 or 5 at a time, into simmering water. Simmer for 2 minutes, turning once. Remove with a slotted spoon and drain on paper towels. Let stand on towels only a few seconds. (If left too long, they stick.) Then place ½ inch apart on well-greased baking sheets.

Brush pretzels with a mixture of egg white and 1 tablespoon water. Lightly sprinkle with sesame seed, poppy seed, or coarse salt. Bake in the 350° oven for 20 to 25 minutes or till golden brown. Remove from baking sheet and cool on a wire rack. If desired, serve with Cheddar Sauce. Makes 20.

Cheddar Sauce: In a small saucepan melt 1 tablespoon *margarine or butter*. Stir in 4 teaspoons *all-purpose flour* and dash ground *red pepper*. Add ½ cup *milk* all at once. Cook and stir over medium heat till thickened and bubbly. Cook and stir 1 minute more. Stir in ½ cup shredded *cheddar cheese* till melted. Makes ⅔ cup.

Whole Wheat Soft Pretzels: Prepare Soft Pretzels as directed at left, *except* substitute 1½ cups *whole wheat flour* for *1½ cups* of the stirred-in all-purpose flour.

◀ *Shape each pretzel by crossing one end over the other to form a circle, overlapping about 4 inches from each end. Take one end of dough in each hand and twist once at the point where dough overlaps. Lift each end across to the edge of the circle opposite it. Tuck ends under; moisten and press to seal.*

Vaňočka Braid

The name Vaňočka (VAN och ka) comes from the Czech word for Christmas.

5½ **to 6 cups all-purpose flour**
1 **package active dry yeast**
1¼ **cups milk**
⅔ **cup sugar**
¼ **cup margarine** *or* **butter**
½ **teaspoon salt**
2 **eggs**
1 **egg white**
¼ **teaspoon ground mace**
1½ **cups light raisins**
1 **teaspoon finely shredded lemon peel**
1 **beaten egg yolk**
¼ **cup sliced almonds**

In a large bowl combine *2½ cups* of the flour and the yeast; set aside. In a saucepan heat and stir the milk, sugar, margarine, and salt *just till warm* (120° to 130°) and margarine almost melts. Add to flour mixture. Then add the whole eggs, the egg white, and mace. Beat with an electric mixer on low to medium speed for 30 seconds, scraping bowl. Beat on high speed for 3 minutes. Using a spoon, stir in raisins, lemon peel, and as much remaining flour as you can.

On a floured surface, knead in enough of the remaining flour to make a moderately stiff dough that is smooth and elastic (6 to 8 minutes total). Shape into a ball. Place in a greased bowl; turn once. Cover and let rise in a warm place till double (1 to 1½ hours).

Punch dough down. Turn the dough out onto a lightly floured surface. Divide in half. Cover and let rest 10 minutes. Meanwhile, grease 2 large baking sheets. Set half of the dough aside.

To shape, divide the remaining half of dough in half. Cut *one* of the portions into thirds. Roll *each* third into an evenly thick 18-inch rope. To braid, line up the 3 ropes, 1 inch apart, on a prepared baking sheet. Starting in the middle, loosely bring left rope

underneath center rope; lay it down. Then bring the right rope under the new center rope; lay it down. Repeat to end. Then on the other end, braid by bringing the outside ropes alternately *over* center rope to the center. Press ends together to seal and tuck under. Stretch braid to a length of 11 inches. Divide the other portion of dough into quarters. Roll *three* of the four pieces into evenly thick 14-inch ropes. Braid loosely; press ends together to seal and tuck under. Stretch braid to a length of 9 inches. Brush top of first braid with enough water to moisten; place second braid on top of first braid. Cut remaining quarter of dough into thirds. Roll *each* third into an evenly thick 12-inch rope. Braid loosely; press the ends together to seal and tuck under. Stretch braid to a length of 7 inches. Brush top of second braid with enough water to moisten; place third braid on top of second braid.

Repeat shaping directions with the other half of the dough. Cover braids and let them rise till *nearly* double (30 to 45 minutes).

Brush braids with a mixture of beaten egg yolk and 2 teaspoons *water*. Sprinkle with sliced almonds. Bake in a 350° oven for 15 minutes. Cover loosely with foil. Then bake 20 to 25 minutes more or till the bread tests done. Cool on wire rack. Serve warm or cool. Makes 2 loaves.

Iced Vaňočka Braid: Prepare Vaňočka Braid as directed above, *except* omit the egg yolk-water mixture and the sliced almonds. After bread is baked and cooled, prepare 2 recipes *Powdered Sugar Icing* (see recipe, page 230), *except* substitute ¼ teaspoon *almond extract* for the ½ teaspoon vanilla. Frost *each* loaf. Decorate with chopped *almonds* and halved red and green *candied cherries.*

Vaňočka Braid

Whole Wheat Raisin Bread

2¾ to 3¼ cups all-purpose flour
  1 package active dry yeast
1⅓ cups milk
  ⅓ cup packed brown sugar
  3 tablespoons margarine *or* butter
  ½ teaspoon salt
  2 eggs
  2 cups whole wheat flour
  2 cups raisins
  1 recipe Powdered Sugar Icing (optional)
    (see page 230)

In a large mixing bowl combine *2 cups* of the all-purpose flour and the yeast; set aside. In a saucepan heat and stir the milk, brown sugar, margarine, and salt *just till warm* (120° to 130°) and margarine almost melts. Add to the flour mixture. Then add eggs. Beat with an electric mixer on low to medium speed for 30 seconds, scraping bowl. Beat on high speed for 3 minutes. Stir in the whole wheat flour, raisins, and as much remaining all-purpose flour as you can.

On a lightly floured surface, knead in enough of the remaining all-purpose flour to make a moderately stiff dough that is smooth and elastic (6 to 8 minutes total). Shape into a ball. Place in a lightly greased bowl, turning once to grease the surface. Cover and let rise in a warm place till double (1 to 1½ hours).

Punch dough down. Turn out onto a lightly floured surface. Divide in half. Cover and let rest for 10 minutes. Meanwhile, grease two 8x4x2-inch loaf pans. Shape *each* half of dough into a loaf (see tip, page 52). Place in prepared pans. Cover and let rise in a warm place till *nearly* double (45 to 60 minutes).

Bake in a 375° oven for 30 to 35 minutes or till the bread tests done (if necessary, cover loosely with foil the last 15 minutes of baking to prevent overbrowning). Remove bread from pans and cool on a wire rack. If desired, drizzle warm loaves with Powdered Sugar Icing. Makes 2 loaves.

Proofing Yeast Dough In Your Microwave

With a little help from your microwave oven, you may be able to significantly shorten the time it takes to proof (raise) yeast breads.

Before you begin, check your owner's manual to see if proofing is recommended. *Or,* use the following test to check your oven:

Place 2 tablespoons cold stick margarine (do not use corn oil margarine) in a custard cup in the center of your oven. Micro-cook, uncovered, on 10% power (low) for 4 minutes. If the margarine doesn't completely melt, your microwave can proof yeast dough. But if the margarine does completely melt, your microwave puts out too much power at this low setting and will kill the yeast before the bread has a chance to rise. If so, you should raise your yeast breads conventionally.

If your oven passed the test, here's how to proceed. While kneading your dough, place 3 cups water in a microwave-safe 4-cup measure. Cook on 100% power (high) for 6½ to 8½ minutes or till boiling. Move measure to back of oven. Place kneaded dough in a microwave-safe greased bowl, turning once. Cover with waxed paper and place in microwave oven with hot water. Heat dough and water on 10% power (low) 13 to 15 minutes or till dough has *nearly* doubled. Punch dough down; shape into loaves. (For any shape other than loaves, you'll have to do the second proofing step conventionally.)

Place the shaped loaves in microwave-safe 8x4x2- or 9x5x3-inch loaf dishes. Return to microwave oven with the hot water. Cover with waxed paper. Heat on low for 6 to 8 minutes or till *nearly* doubled.

Walnut Potica

2 to 2½ cups all-purpose flour
1 package active dry yeast
⅓ cup milk
¼ cup margarine *or* butter
2 tablespoons sugar
½ teaspoon salt
2 eggs
3 cups ground walnuts
¾ cup sugar
¼ cup margarine *or* butter, softened
¼ cup honey
1 slightly beaten egg
3 tablespoons milk
½ teaspoon vanilla

In a medium bowl combine *1 cup* of the flour and the yeast; set aside. In a saucepan heat ⅓ cup milk, ¼ cup margarine, 2 tablespoons sugar, and salt *just till warm* (120° to 130°) and margarine almost melts. Add to flour mixture. Then add 2 eggs. Beat with an electric mixer on low to medium speed for 30 seconds, scraping bowl. Beat on high speed 3 minutes. Stir in as much of the remaining flour as you can.

On a lightly floured surface, knead in enough of the remaining flour to make a moderately soft dough that is smooth and elastic (3 to 5 minutes total). Shape into a ball. Place in a greased bowl, turning dough once to grease surface. Cover and let rise in a warm place till double (1 to 1¼ hours). Meanwhile, for filling, in a medium mixing bowl stir together walnuts, ¾ cup sugar, ¼ cup margarine, honey, one slightly beaten egg, 3 tablespoons milk, and vanilla. Set aside.

Punch dough down. Cover and let rest 10 minutes. Meanwhile, lightly grease two 7½x3½x2- or 8x4x2-inch loaf pans. Cover a large surface (at least 3x3 feet) with a floured cloth. On the cloth, roll dough into a 15-inch square. Cover and let rest 10 minutes. Then roll dough into a 30x20-inch rectangle.

To assemble, cut dough lengthwise in half, forming two 30x10-inch sheets. Spread the filling evenly over the surface of the dough, keeping to within 1 inch of the edges. Using the cloth as a guide, roll up jelly-roll style, starting from the short sides. Pinch seams and ends to seal. Place loaves, seam sides down, in the prepared loaf pans. Cover and let rise till *nearly* double (45 to 60 minutes).

Bake in a 325° oven for 45 to 50 minutes or till done (if necessary, cover with foil the last 15 minutes of baking to prevent overbrowning). Remove from pans and cool on a wire rack. Makes 2 loaves.

◀ *Carefully spread the nut filling evenly over the surface of each portion of dough. Keep the filling to within 1 inch of the edges to allow enough room for the seams and ends to be sealed.*

◀ *To roll up both loaves at once, use the cloth underneath the dough as a guide. Slowly and evenly lift the cloth to roll up the dough, jelly-roll style, beginning from the short sides.*

Date and Nut Bread

Date and Nut Bread

3¼ to 3¾ cups all-purpose flour
  1 package active dry yeast
  ¾ cup milk
  ¼ cup sugar
  ¼ cup margarine *or* butter
  ½ teaspoon salt
  2 eggs
  1 egg yolk
  1 teaspoon finely shredded lemon peel
  3 tablespoons currant jelly
  ⅔ cup ground walnuts
  ½ cup pitted whole dates, snipped
  3 tablespoons sugar
  1 egg white
  ¼ teaspoon lemon juice
  1 egg

In a large mixing bowl stir together *1½ cups* of the flour and the yeast; set aside. In a medium saucepan heat and stir the milk, the ¼ cup sugar, margarine, and salt *just till warm* (120° to 130°) and margarine almost melts. Add to flour mixture. Then add the 2 whole eggs and the egg yolk. Beat with an electric mixer on low to medium speed for 30 seconds, scraping the sides of the bowl. Beat on high speed for 3 minutes. Using a wooden spoon, stir in lemon peel and as much of the remaining flour as you can.

Turn the dough out onto a lightly floured surface. Knead in enough remaining flour to make a moderately soft dough that is smooth and elastic (3 to 5 minutes total). Shape into a ball. Place in a greased bowl, turning once to grease the surface. Cover and let rise in a warm place till double (1 to 1½ hours).

For filling, in a small saucepan heat currant jelly *just till melted*. Remove the saucepan from heat and stir in the walnuts, dates, 3 tablespoons sugar, egg white, and lemon juice. Set aside. In a bowl beat together one whole egg and 1 tablespoon *water*.

Punch dough down. On a floured surface, divide dough in half. Cover; let rest 10 minutes. Grease a baking sheet. Roll *each* half to 12x10 inches. Cut each into three 10x4-inch strips. Spread *3 tablespoons* filling down center of *each* strip. Brush egg mixture on edges. Fold long sides of dough over filling; seal.

To shape, line up 3 filled ropes, seam sides down, 1 inch apart on half of prepared baking sheet. Starting in middle, loosely braid by bringing left rope *underneath* center rope; lay it down. Bring right rope under new center rope; lay it down. Repeat to end. On the other end, braid by bringing outside ropes alternately *over* center rope to center. Press ends together to seal; tuck under. Repeat braiding with remaining 3 ropes. Brush loaves with some egg mixture. Cover; let rise in a warm place till *nearly* double (45 to 60 minutes). Brush loaves again with egg mixture. Bake in a 350° oven about 30 minutes or till done (if necessary, cover with foil the last 15 minutes of baking to prevent overbrowning). Cool on a rack. Makes 2 loaves.

High-Altitude Bread Baking

At high altitudes, bread dough may rise faster than the time given in the recipe. In fact, the higher the altitude at which you live, the faster your dough probably will rise. Because overrising causes bread to be coarse in texture, watch it closely; let it rise till just *nearly* double. If you'd like the yeast flavor to develop more, punch the dough down once and let rise a second time.

Also, flours are drier at high altitudes so they absorb more liquid. When you knead in flour, be sure to knead in only enough to reach the desired stiffness (see tip, page 52).

Sally Lunn

3 cups all-purpose flour
1 package active dry yeast
1 cup milk
3 tablespoons sugar
3 tablespoons margarine *or* butter
½ teaspoon salt
2 eggs

In a large mixing bowl stir together *1½ cups* of the flour and the yeast; set aside. In a medium saucepan heat and stir the milk, sugar, margarine, and salt *just till warm* (120° to 130°) and margarine almost melts. Add to the flour mixture. Then add eggs. Beat with an electric mixer on low to medium speed for 30 seconds, scraping sides of bowl. Beat on high speed for 3 minutes. Using a spoon, stir in enough of the remaining flour to make a stiff batter. Cover batter and let rise in a warm place till double (about 1 hour).

Stir down batter. Turn batter into a well-greased Turk's head mold or 7-cup tube mold. Cover and let rise in a warm place till *nearly* double (about 45 minutes). Bake in a 375° oven about 40 minutes or till bread sounds hollow when tapped. Remove bread from pan. Serve warm or cool. Makes 1 loaf.

The Story of Sally Lunn

Traditionally served in colonial America as a tea bread, this bread is said to have been named for an eighteenth-century English-woman, Sally Lunn. She baked and sold the coffee cake-type bread in her tea shop, which was located in Bath, England. Typically baked in a Turk's head mold (a round, fluted tube pan), this batter bread is wonderful served warm from the oven or cooled and toasted.

Cherry Twist

Great to give as a homemade gift. (Pictured on pages 6–7.)

3½ to 4 cups all-purpose flour
2 packages active dry yeast
1 cup milk
¼ cup sugar
¼ cup margarine *or* butter
1 teaspoon salt
1 egg
1 cup dried cherries, chopped, *or* dried mixed fruit bits
1 beaten egg yolk

In a large bowl combine *1½ cups* of the flour and the yeast; set aside. In a saucepan heat and stir milk, sugar, margarine, and salt *just till warm* (120° to 130°) and margarine almost melts. Add to flour mixture. Then add egg. Beat with an electric mixer on low to medium speed for 30 seconds, scraping bowl. Beat on high speed for 3 minutes. Stir in cherries and as much of the remaining flour as you can.

On a floured surface, knead in enough of the remaining flour to make a moderately stiff dough that is smooth and elastic (6 to 8 minutes total). Shape into a ball. Place in a greased bowl; turn once. Cover and let rise in a warm place till double (about 1 hour).

Punch dough down. Turn the dough out onto a lightly floured surface. Divide dough into quarters. Cover and let rest 10 minutes. Meanwhile, grease 2 baking sheets. Roll *each* quarter of dough into a 26-inch rope. Place 2 ropes, side by side, on each prepared baking sheet (ropes will extend beyond ends of the baking sheet). Twist the 2 ropes together. Shape into a figure 8, tucking ends under in the center. Cover and let rise till *nearly* double (about 40 minutes).

Brush loaves with mixture of egg yolk and 1 tablespoon *water*. Bake in a 350° oven for 25 to 30 minutes or till bread tests done (if necessary, cover with foil the last 15 minutes of baking). Remove from baking sheets and cool on a wire rack. Makes 2 loaves.

Fruit-Filled Ladder Loaf

Surprise! The filling tastes like peach pie, but it's baked in a bread. (Streusel-topped version is pictured on the cover.)

 1 **package active dry yeast**
 ¼ **cup warm water (105° to 115°)**
 ½ **cup margarine *or* butter**
 ⅓ **cup sugar**
 ¾ **teaspoon salt**
 4 **cups all-purpose flour**
 ½ **cup milk**
 4 **eggs**
 ⅓ **cup packed brown sugar**
 2 **tablespoons all-purpose flour**
 1¼ **teaspoons ground cinnamon**
 ½ **teaspoon ground nutmeg**
 ⅛ **teaspoon ground allspice**
 4 **cups thinly sliced, peeled peaches, *or* thinly sliced, peeled apples**
 ¼ **cup margarine *or* butter, softened**
 1 **recipe Powdered Sugar Icing (see recipe, page 230)**

In a small bowl dissolve the yeast in the warm water. In a large bowl beat the ½ cup margarine or butter, the sugar, and salt with an electric mixer on medium to high speed till combined. Add *1 cup* of the flour, the milk, eggs, and dissolved yeast. Beat till well combined. Stir in the remaining flour. Stir till dough is smooth. Place dough in a large greased bowl. Cover and refrigerate for 6 to 24 hours.

For filling, in a medium mixing bowl stir together the brown sugar, the 2 tablespoons flour, cinnamon, nutmeg, and allspice. Add the peaches or apples. Toss to coat the fruit. Set aside.

Grease 2 baking sheets. Stir dough down. Turn the dough out onto a lightly floured surface. Divide dough in half. Roll each half of the dough into a 12x9-inch rectangle. Carefully transfer each rectangle

to a prepared baking sheet. Spread with the ¼ cup margarine or butter. Spread the filling in a 3-inch-wide strip down the center of each rectangle to within 1 inch of the ends.

On the long sides, make 3-inch cuts from the edges toward center at 1-inch intervals. Starting at one end, alternately fold opposite strips of dough, at an angle, across the filling. Slightly press the ends in the center together to seal. Cover and let rise in a warm place till *nearly* double (45 to 60 minutes).

Bake in a 350° oven for 25 to 30 minutes or till done. Remove from oven. Drizzle with Powdered Sugar Icing. Serve warm. Makes 2 loaves.

Streusel-Topped Ladder Loaf: Prepare Fruit-Filled Ladder Loaf as directed at left, *except* after the strips of dough are folded over the filling and before rising in a warm place, brush the loaves with *milk*. In a small mixing bowl stir together 3 tablespoons *all-purpose flour* and 3 tablespoons *sugar*. Cut in 2 tablespoons *margarine or butter* till mixture resembles coarse crumbs. Sprinkle over loaves. Cover, let rise, and bake as directed. Omit the Powdered Sugar Icing.

◀ *To form a ladder loaf, make 3-inch cuts from the side edges toward the center, keeping the cuts 1 inch apart. Then, starting at one end of the rectangle, alternately fold opposite strips of dough, at an angle, across fruit filling. To seal, slightly press strips together in the center.*

Chocolate-Almond Crescent

2¼ to 2¾ cups all-purpose flour
⅓ cup unsweetened cocoa powder
1 package active dry yeast
¾ cup milk
¼ cup sugar
¼ cup margarine *or* butter
½ teaspoon salt
1 egg
½ cup almond paste
¼ cup margarine *or* butter, softened
2 tablespoons sugar
1 egg
¼ cup finely chopped almonds
1 beaten egg white
Sliced almonds
Powdered sugar

In a medium mixing bowl stir together *1 cup* of the flour, the cocoa powder, and yeast; set aside. In a medium saucepan heat and stir the milk, the ¼ cup sugar, the ¼ cup margarine, and salt *just till warm* (120° to 130°) and margarine almost melts. Add to flour mixture. Then add one whole egg. Beat with an electric mixer on low to medium speed for 30 seconds, scraping the sides of the bowl constantly. Then beat on high speed for 3 minutes. Using a spoon, stir in as much of the remaining flour as you can.

Turn the dough out onto a lightly floured surface. Knead in enough of the remaining flour to make a moderately soft dough that is smooth and elastic (3 to 5 minutes total). Shape into a ball. Place the dough in a lightly greased bowl, turning once to grease the surface. Cover and let rise in a warm place till double (about 1½ hours).

Meanwhile, for filling, in another medium mixing bowl combine almond paste, the ¼ cup softened margarine, the 2 tablespoons sugar, and one whole egg. Beat with the electric mixer on medium to high speed till smooth. Stir in chopped almonds. Set aside.

Punch dough down. Turn dough out onto a lightly floured surface. Cover and let rest for 10 minutes. Grease a large baking sheet. Roll dough into a 24x10-inch rectangle. Spread filling to within ½ inch of the edges. Roll up, jelly-roll style, starting from one of the long sides. Pinch seam to seal. Place dough, seam side down, on the prepared baking sheet. Shape dough into a crescent shape. Seal ends. Cover; let rise till *nearly* double (30 to 40 minutes).

Brush loaf with mixture of egg white and 1 tablespoon *water*. Decorate the top of loaf with sliced almonds. Bake in a 350° oven for 10 minutes. Cover bread loosely with foil. Then bake for 15 to 20 minutes more or till bread tests done. Remove from baking sheet and cool on a wire rack. Lightly sift powdered sugar over the top of loaf. Makes 1 loaf.

Storing Yeast Breads

It's a fact, you just can't keep that tantalizing aroma of fresh baked bread lingering through the kitchen very long. But you can keep breads fresh by storing them properly.

To store yeast breads, completely cool them. Then wrap them in foil or plastic wrap, or place them in plastic bags. Store them in a cool, dry place for 2 to 3 days. (Do not refrigerate baked yeast breads, since refrigerator storage causes bread to stale.)

To freeze yeast breads, place completely cooled, unfrosted breads in a freezer bag or container, or tightly wrap in *heavy* foil. Freeze for up to 3 months. Thaw the wrapped breads at room temperature for 1 hour. (*Or,* wrap in foil and heat in a 300° oven about 20 minutes.) Frost sweet breads after thawing.

Almond Sourdough Rolls

1 cup Sourdough Starter (see recipe, page 52)
1 cup sliced almonds, toasted
1 package active dry yeast
¼ cup warm water (105° to 115°)
4 to 4½ cups all-purpose flour
½ cup buttermilk *or* sour milk
⅓ cup sugar
¼ cup margarine *or* butter, melted
1 egg
1 teaspoon salt
½ teaspoon baking soda
3 tablespoons margarine *or* butter, melted
½ cup sugar
1 teaspoon ground cinnamon
   Almond Icing

Bring Sourdough Starter to room temperature. Set ¼ *cup* of the almonds aside for garnishing. Finely chop remaining almonds; set aside. Dissolve yeast in warm water. In a large mixing bowl combine *1½ cups* of the flour, the buttermilk, the ⅓ cup sugar, the ¼ cup margarine or butter, egg, salt, Sourdough Starter, and dissolved yeast. Beat with an electric mixer on low to medium speed for 30 seconds, scraping the sides of the bowl constantly. Then beat on high speed for 3 minutes. Using a wooden spoon, stir in the soda and as much of the remaining flour as you can.

Turn the dough out onto a lightly floured surface. Knead in enough of the remaining flour to make a moderately soft dough that is smooth and elastic (3 to 5 minutes total). Shape into a ball. Place in a greased bowl, turning once to grease surface. Cover and let rise in a warm place till double (about 1½ hours).

Punch dough down. Turn dough out onto a lightly floured surface. Divide dough in half. Cover; let rest for 10 minutes. Meanwhile, grease two 9x1½-inch round or 9x9x2-inch baking pans. Roll *each* half of the dough into a 12x8-inch rectangle. Brush with the 3 tablespoons melted margarine. In a small mixing bowl combine the ½ cup sugar and cinnamon. Sprin-kle sugar-cinnamon mixture on top of dough. Then sprinkle finely chopped almonds over the dough.

Roll up each rectangle, jelly-roll style, starting from one of the long sides. Pinch seams to seal. Cut *each* roll into twelve 1-inch pieces (see photo for cutting the roll, page 73). Place pieces, cut side down, in the prepared baking pans. Cover and let rise in a warm place till *nearly* double (about 30 minutes).

Bake in a 375° oven for 20 to 25 minutes or till rolls test done. Invert onto a wire rack; cool. Drizzle with Almond Icing. Sprinkle with the ¼ cup sliced almonds. Makes 24.

Almond Icing: In a mixing bowl stir together 1 cup sifted *powdered sugar,* ¼ teaspoon *almond extract,* and 1 to 2 tablespoons *milk* to make an icing of drizzling consistency. Makes ⅓ cup.

The Sourdough Legend

HISTORY OF BAKING

Sourdough dates back to the pioneers and cowboys of the Old West, when cooks saved a piece of dough from one batch of bread to leaven the next. Many believed the "starter" got the ability to leaven and create a tangy flavor in bread from a mysterious force.

Since sourdough was the critical ingredient needed for making bread, frontier families considered it their most important possession after the Bible. In fact, most old strains were heavily guarded and shared only among family and friends. Not only was sourdough used in bread, flapjacks, and biscuits, but it also was used to fill cracks in log cabins, to treat wounds, and, some said, even to resole shoes.

Basic Sweet Dough

4 to 4⅓ cups all-purpose flour
1 package active dry yeast
1 cup milk
⅓ cup sugar
⅓ cup margarine *or* butter
½ teaspoon salt
2 eggs

In a large mixing bowl combine *1½ cups* of the flour and the yeast; set aside. In a saucepan heat and stir milk, sugar, margarine, and salt *just till warm* (120° to 130°) and margarine almost melts. Add to flour mixture. Then add eggs. Beat with an electric mixer on low to medium speed for 30 seconds, scraping sides of bowl. Beat on high speed for 3 minutes. Stir in as much of the remaining flour as you can.

On a floured surface, knead in enough of the remaining flour to make a moderately soft dough that is smooth and elastic (3 to 5 minutes total). Shape into a ball. Place in a greased bowl; turn once. Cover and let rise in a warm place till double (about 1 hour).

Punch dough down. Turn out onto a lightly floured surface. Divide in half. Cover and let rest for 10 minutes. Shape and bake dough as directed in the recipe.

Cinnamon Rolls

Enjoy fresh-baked cinnamon rolls for breakfast. Just mix and shape them the night before, then bake them in the morning. (Pictured on page 74.)

1 recipe Basic Sweet Dough (see above)
3 tablespoons margarine *or* butter, melted
½ cup sugar
2 teaspoons ground cinnamon
¾ cup raisins (optional)
1 recipe Powdered Sugar Icing (see page 230)

Prepare Basic Sweet Dough as directed. Grease two 9x1½-inch round baking pans. On a lightly floured surface, roll *each* half of the dough into a 12x8-inch rectangle. Brush with margarine or butter. In a small mixing bowl stir together sugar and cinnamon. Sprinkle the sugar-cinnamon mixture on top of the dough. If desired, sprinkle with raisins.

Roll up each rectangle, jelly-roll style, starting from one of the long sides. Pinch seams to seal. Cut *each* roll into 10 to 12 pieces. Place pieces, cut side down, in prepared baking pans. Cover and let rise till *nearly* double (about 30 minutes). *Or,* cover with oiled waxed paper, then with plastic wrap, and refrigerate for 2 to 24 hours.

If chilled, let stand, covered, for 20 minutes at room temperature. Puncture any surface bubbles with a greased wooden toothpick. Bake in a 375° oven for 20 to 25 minutes or till rolls test done. Cool slightly. Remove rolls from pans. Drizzle with Powdered Sugar Icing. Serve warm or cool. Makes 20 to 24.

Cinnamon 'n' Apple Rolls: Prepare Cinnamon Rolls as directed at left, *except* sprinkle *½ cup* raisins and 2 cups finely chopped *apple* on top of the dough after sprinkling with sugar-cinnamon mixture. Add dash ground *cinnamon* and dash ground *nutmeg* to the Powdered Sugar Icing.

Cinnamon 'n' Chocolate Rolls: Prepare Cinnamon Rolls as directed at left, *except* stir 3 tablespoons *unsweetened cocoa powder* into the sugar-cinnamon mixture. Omit the raisins and sprinkle ¾ cup miniature *semisweet chocolate pieces* on top of dough. Add 2 tablespoons miniature *semisweet chocolate pieces,* melted, to the Powdered Sugar Icing along with the milk.

Caramel Pecan Rolls

The miniature rolls are just the right size for a special coffee, tea, or brunch.

> 1 **recipe Basic Sweet Dough (see page 72)**
> 1/3 **cup margarine *or* butter**
> 2/3 **cup packed brown sugar**
> 2 **tablespoons light corn syrup**
> 24 **pecan halves *or* 2/3 cup chopped pecans**
> 3 **tablespoons margarine *or* butter, melted**
> 1/2 **cup sugar**
> 1 **teaspoon ground cinnamon**

Prepare Basic Sweet Dough as directed. While the dough is resting, in a small saucepan melt the 1/3 cup margarine or butter. Stir in the brown sugar and corn syrup. Cook and stir *just till blended*. Divide syrup mixture evenly among 24 well-greased muffin cups or two 9x1½-inch round baking pans. Place 1 pecan half in the bottom of each muffin cup. *Or,* sprinkle pecan halves or chopped pecans evenly in the bottom of each round baking pan. Set pans aside.

On a lightly floured surface, roll *each* half of the dough into a 12x8-inch rectangle. Brush dough with the 3 tablespoons melted margarine. In a small mixing bowl stir together sugar and cinnamon. Sprinkle the sugar-cinnamon mixture on top of the dough. Roll up each rectangle, jelly-roll style, starting from one of the long sides. Pinch seams to seal. Cut *each* roll into 10 to 12 pieces. Place pieces, cut side down, in the prepared muffin cups or round baking pans. Cover; let rise till *nearly* double (about 30 minutes). *Or,* cover with oiled waxed paper, then with plastic wrap. Chill in the refrigerator 2 to 24 hours.

If chilled, let stand, covered, 20 minutes at room temperature. Puncture any surface bubbles with a greased wooden toothpick. Bake in a 375° oven for 20 to 25 minutes or till done. Invert rolls onto wire racks or serving platter. Serve warm. Makes 20 to 24.

Miniature Caramel Pecan Rolls: Prepare Caramel Pecan Rolls as directed at left, *except* place the syrup mixture in a 15½x10½x2-inch baking pan. *Or,* divide the syrup mixture between two 9x9x2-inch baking pans or one 13x9x2-inch baking pan and one 8x8x2-inch baking pan. Sprinkle *chopped pecans* over the syrup. Set aside.

Divide *each* half of the dough in half. Roll *each* portion of the dough into a 12x6-inch rectangle. Using 1/4 *cup* melted margarine or butter instead of 3 tablespoons, brush on top of the dough and sprinkle with the sugar-cinnamon mixture. Roll up each rectangle, jelly-roll style, starting from one of the long sides. Pinch seams to seal. Slice the dough into twelve 1-inch pieces. Place pieces, cut side down, in prepared pan. Let rise and bake as directed. Makes 48.

◀ *To easily cut the dough, place a piece of heavy-duty thread under the roll where you want to make the cut. Then pull the ends up and around the sides. Crisscross the thread at the top of the roll and pull quickly as though tying a knot.*

Cinnamon Rolls
(see recipe, page 72)

St. Lucia Buns

5¼ to 5¾ cups all-purpose flour
  2 packages active dry yeast
1½ cups milk
  ½ cup sugar
  ½ cup margarine *or* butter
  1 teaspoon salt
  ⅛ teaspoon ground saffron *or* ¾ teaspoon
      ground cardamom
  2 eggs
  ½ cup blanched almonds, ground
  1 tablespoon finely shredded lemon peel
      Raisins
  1 slightly beaten egg white
      Sugar

In a large mixing bowl stir together *2 cups* of the flour and the yeast; set aside. In a medium saucepan heat and stir the milk, ½ cup sugar, margarine or butter, salt, and saffron or cardamom *just till warm* (120° to 130°) and margarine almost melts. Add to the flour mixture. Then add the 2 whole eggs. Beat with electric mixer on low to medium speed for 30 seconds, scraping bowl. Then beat on high speed for 3 minutes. Stir in the ground almonds, lemon peel, and as much of the remaining flour as you can.

Turn dough out onto a lightly floured surface. Knead in enough of the remaining flour to make a moderately soft dough that is smooth and elastic (3 to 5 minutes total). Shape into a ball. Place dough in a lightly greased bowl, turning once to grease the surface. Cover and let rise in a warm place till double (1 to 1¼ hours).

Punch dough down. Turn dough out onto a lightly floured surface. Divide dough into quarters. Cover and let rest for 10 minutes.

Grease baking sheets. To shape buns, divide *each* quarter of dough into 12 equal pieces. Roll *each* piece of dough into a 10-inch-long rope. Place 3 inches apart on prepared baking sheets. Form each rope into an S-shape, coiling ends in a snail fashion. (If desired, make double buns by pressing the centers of 2 of the S-shaped pieces together to form a cross.) Press *one* raisin into center of *each* coil. Cover and let rise in a warm place till *nearly* double (30 to 40 minutes).

Stir together the slightly beaten egg white and 1 tablespoon *water*. Lightly brush mixture over buns. Sprinkle with additional sugar. Bake in a 375° oven about 10 minutes or till golden brown. Remove from baking sheets. Serve warm or cool. Makes 48 single buns or 24 double buns.

A Swedish Holiday Tradition

St. Lucia buns take their name from the holiday for which they're traditionally baked. Lucia's Day, celebrated December 13, is the beginning of the Christmas season in Sweden. The holiday is named for a young Sicilian woman, Lucia, who was a devout Christian.

When Sweden suffered from famine one frigid winter, Lucia, wearing a white robe and a crown of candles, appeared with food. She became known as the Queen of Light.

Today she is honored during the dark northern winter by young girls all over Sweden. On Lucia's Day, in households with girls, the eldest daughter dons a white robe and a crown of candles, and awakens her parents with the St. Lucia buns and coffee.

Kolaches

For another version, substitute purchased poppy seed cake and pastry filling for the fruit fillings.

3¾ **to 4¼ cups all-purpose flour**
1 **package active dry yeast**
1 **cup milk**
¾ **cup margarine *or* butter**
½ **cup sugar**
½ **teaspoon salt**
4 **egg yolks**
1 **teaspoon finely shredded lemon peel**
  Apricot *or* Prune Filling
2 **tablespoons margarine *or* butter, melted, *or* milk**
  Powdered sugar

In a large mixing bowl stir together *2 cups* of the flour and the yeast. In a medium saucepan heat and stir the 1 cup milk, the ¾ cup margarine or butter, sugar, and salt *just till warm* (120° to 130°) and margarine almost melts. Add to the flour mixture. Then add the egg yolks. Beat with an electric mixer on low to medium speed for 30 seconds, scraping the sides of the bowl constantly. Then beat on high speed for 3 minutes. Using a wooden spoon, stir in the lemon peel and as much of the remaining flour as you can.

Turn dough out onto a lightly floured surface. Knead in enough of the remaining flour to make a moderately soft dough that is smooth and elastic (3 to 5 minutes total). Place dough in a greased bowl, turning once to grease the surface. Cover and let rise in a warm place till double (1 to 1½ hours). Meanwhile, prepare desired filling. Set aside to cool.

Punch down dough. Turn the dough out onto a lightly floured surface. Divide in half. Cover and let rest for 10 minutes. Grease baking sheets. Shape *each* half of dough into 12 balls, pulling the edges under to make a smooth top. Place the balls 3 inches apart on the prepared baking sheets. Flatten each ball to 2½ inches in diameter. Cover; let rise till *nearly* double (about 35 minutes).

Using your thumb or two fingers, make an indentation in the center of each dough circle. Spoon about *2 teaspoons* filling into *each* indentation. Lightly brush the 2 tablespoons melted margarine or milk around the edges of rolls. Bake in a 375° oven for 10 to 12 minutes or till rolls are golden brown. Remove rolls from baking sheets and cool on a wire rack. Lightly sift powdered sugar over the tops. Makes 24.

Apricot Filling: In a small saucepan combine 1 cup snipped dried *apricots* and enough *water* to come 1 inch above the apricots. Bring to boiling. Reduce heat. Cover and simmer for 10 to 15 minutes or till apricots are very soft. Drain, reserving *2 tablespoons* cooking liquid. In a blender container or food processor bowl place apricots, reserved liquid, ¼ cup *sugar,* 1 teaspoon *lemon juice,* ¼ teaspoon ground *cinnamon,* and ⅛ teaspoon ground *nutmeg.* Cover and blend or process till smooth, stopping to scrape down the sides as necessary. Makes 1 cup.

Prune Filling: In a medium saucepan combine 1½ cups *water* and 1 cup diced dried *prunes.* Bring to boiling. Reduce heat. Cover and simmer for 25 minutes. Drain prunes. In a small bowl stir together prunes, 2 tablespoons *sugar,* ½ teaspoon *lemon juice,* ¼ teaspoon ground *cinnamon,* and dash ground *cloves.* Makes 1¼ cups.

Kolache Shapes

Kolaches, an Eastern European favorite, traditionally were shaped into circles. To the people of this region, the circle was a symbol of good luck, prosperity, and eternity. Today you'll find kolaches that are made into not only circles, but squares and diamonds, too.

Ensaimada Rolls

1 package active dry yeast
¼ cup warm water (105° to 115°)
½ cup margarine *or* butter
⅓ cup sugar
4 cups all-purpose flour
½ cup milk
4 eggs
½ cup margarine *or* butter, melted
1 cup finely shredded Edam cheese (4 ounces)
  Sugar

Dissolve yeast in the warm water. In a large bowl beat the ½ cup margarine or butter with an electric mixer on medium to high speed about 30 seconds or till softened. Add the ⅓ cup sugar and ½ teaspoon *salt*. Beat well. Stir in *1 cup* of the flour, the milk, and eggs. Add softened yeast. Beat till thoroughly combined, scraping bowl. Using a spoon, stir in the remaining flour till dough is smooth. Turn into a large greased bowl. Cover; refrigerate for 12 to 48 hours.

Stir dough down. Turn out onto a floured surface. Divide in half. Cover and let rest 10 minutes. Grease baking sheets. Roll *each* half of dough into an 18x15-inch rectangle. Brush some of the ½ cup melted margarine on top. Sprinkle cheese on top of each rectangle. With a sharp knife, cut each rectangle lengthwise into three 18x5-inch strips. Roll up each strip, jelly-roll style, from a long side. Seal. Cut each rolled strip crosswise into 3 pieces. Roll each piece of dough into a rope about 10 inches long. To shape rolls, make a loop in the center of each rope, leaving about 3 inches free at each end. Bring ends together in front of the loop. Pinch the ends together. Pull the loop over the top of sealed ends. Place 3 inches apart on the prepared baking sheets. Cover; let rise in a warm place till *nearly* double (40 to 45 minutes).

Bake in a 375° oven for 12 to 15 minutes or till golden. Transfer rolls to a wire rack and brush with the remaining melted margarine. Sprinkle rolls with additional sugar. Serve warm. Makes 18.

▶ Roll up each strip, jelly-roll style, starting from one of the long sides. Pinch edge to seal. Cut each rolled strip crosswise into three pieces, each 6 inches long. Then, on a lightly floured surface, roll each piece of dough into a thin rope about 10 inches long.

▶ To shape the rolls, make a loop in the center of each rope, leaving about 3 inches free at each end. Bring the ends together in front of the loop. Then pinch the ends together to seal.

▶ To finish shaping, gently pull the loop over the top of the sealed ends.

CROISSANTS AND DANISH PASTRIES

The smell of success can't be more satisfying than when you bake croissants or Danish pastries in your own oven. A batch of the light, flaky, melt-in-your-mouth pastries is likely to get compliments from anyone lucky enough to get a sample.

□ Although margarine is an easy substitute for butter in most baked goods, we recommend using only butter in croissants and Danish pastries. Butter produces the lightest and most airy pastry.

□ Cut 40 minutes off most chilling steps by using the freezer. In our recipes that call for 1 hour of chilling in the refrigerator, you instead may chill the dough for 20 minutes in the freezer. Don't skip these important chilling stages. Chilling relaxes the dough, which reduces shrinking during rolling and baking, and keeps the butter firm, which makes rolling easier.

□ Take the time to evenly roll and fold the dough to the size the recipe indicates. The rolling and folding steps ensure even and proper rising and a nice appearance.

□ For golden pastries, brush the tops with the egg-water mixture, being careful not to drip the mixture down the sides of the pastries. Then to even out the color, brush both the tops and sides of the pastries the last 2 to 3 minutes of baking.

□ To freeze dough for later use, store it tightly wrapped in foil or freezer bags for up to 1 month. (Do not shape before freezing.) Thaw dough in the refrigerator overnight or for up to 24 hours. Shape and bake dough as directed in recipes.

Classic Croissants

Croissants made the traditional way taste just like the ones the French make. (Pictured on page 84.)

  1½ **cups butter**
  ⅓   **cup all-purpose flour**
  3¾ **to 4¼ cups all-purpose flour**
  1   **package active dry yeast**
  1¼ **cups milk**
  ¼   **cup sugar**
  2   **eggs**

In a large mixing bowl beat butter with an electric mixer about 30 seconds or till softened. Add ⅓ cup flour; mix well. Roll butter mixture between 2 large sheets of waxed paper into a 12x6-inch rectangle. Chill 1 hour in refrigerator or 20 minutes in freezer.

For dough, in the same large mixing bowl stir together *2 cups* of the remaining flour and the yeast; set aside. In a medium saucepan heat and stir milk, sugar, and ¼ teaspoon *salt* just till warm (120° to 130°). Add to the flour mixture. Add *one* of the eggs. Beat with an electric mixer on low to medium speed for 30 seconds, scraping sides of bowl constantly. Beat on high speed for 3 minutes. Using a wooden spoon, stir in as much of the remaining flour as you can.

Turn the dough out onto a lightly floured surface. Knead in enough of the remaining flour to make a moderately soft dough that is smooth and elastic (3 to 5 minutes total). Cover and let rest for 10 minutes.

On a floured surface, roll the dough into a 14-inch square. Remove the top sheet of waxed paper from the chilled butter mixture. Invert butter mixture onto half of the dough to within 1 inch of the edges. Remove remaining waxed paper from butter mixture. Fold over the other half of dough and press edges together to seal. Roll dough into a 21x12-inch rectangle.

Fold dough crosswise into thirds to form a 12x7-inch rectangle. Loosely wrap in plastic wrap; chill for 1 hour in the refrigerator or 20 minutes in the freezer.

On a lightly floured surface, roll chilled dough into a 21x12-inch rectangle. Fold, chill, and roll twice more. Fold the dough into thirds to form a 12x7-inch rectangle. Loosely wrap the dough and chill it in the refrigerator for several hours or overnight.

To shape, cut the dough crosswise into fourths. Wrap and return *three* portions to the refrigerator till ready to use. On a floured surface, roll the fourth portion of dough into a 16x8-inch rectangle. Cut the rectangle crosswise in half to form *two* squares. Then cut *each* square diagonally in half to form *two* triangles. (You will have *four* triangles total from *each* rectangle.) Loosely roll up each triangle, starting from an 8-inch side and rolling to the opposite point.

Repeat shaping with the remaining 3 portions of the dough. Place croissants 4 inches apart on ungreased baking sheets, points down. Curve ends to form crescent shapes. Cover and let rise in a warm place till *nearly* double (about 1 hour).

Brush croissants with a mixture of remaining egg and 1 tablespoon *water*. Bake in a 375° oven for about 15 minutes or till golden. Remove croissants from baking sheets; cool on a wire rack. Makes 16.

Rolling Pins

Choosing the proper rolling pin is much like choosing the right golf club. Getting one to fit your hands is most important. An all-purpose wooden rolling pin suits most needs, from rolling out pie pastry to rolling out cookies. Beyond choosing a basic rolling pin, you might want to consider other types, such as marble or hollow rolling pins, or tapered French rolling pins, for specialty baking needs.

▶ *Remove top sheet of waxed paper from the butter mixture. Invert the butter mixture onto half of the 14-inch square of dough to within 1 inch of the edges. Remove remaining sheet of waxed paper. Fold over other half of dough; press edges to seal. Roll into a 21x12-inch rectangle.*

▶ *Fold dough crosswise into thirds, forming a 12x7-inch rectangle. Chill for 1 hour. Then roll into a 21x12-inch rectangle. Fold, chill, and roll two more times. Fold dough into thirds to form a 12x7-inch rectangle. Chill several hours or overnight. Cut dough crosswise into fourths.*

▶ *Roll one portion into a 16x8-inch rectangle. Cut rectangle crosswise to form two squares. Then cut each square into two triangles. Loosely roll up each triangle, starting from an 8-inch side and rolling to the point. Then place croissants on baking sheets with their point sides down; curve ends.*

Quick-Method Croissants

Save yourself some steps without sacrificing quality with our easy-mix method.

> 1½ cups *cold* butter
>   3 cups all-purpose flour
> 1½ cups all-purpose flour
>   1 package active dry yeast
> 1¼ cups milk
>   ¼ cup sugar
>   ¼ teaspoon salt
>   1 egg
>   ¼ to ½ cup all-purpose flour
>   1 egg
>   1 tablespoon water *or* milk

Cut butter into ½-inch *slices.* In a medium mixing bowl stir butter slices into the 3 cups flour till slices are coated and separated. Chill butter mixture while preparing the dough.

For dough, in a large mixing bowl stir together the 1½ cups flour and the yeast; set aside. In a medium saucepan heat and stir the milk, sugar, and salt *just till warm* (120° to 130°). Add the milk mixture to the flour mixture. Then add one egg. Beat with an electric mixer on low to medium speed for 30 seconds, scraping the sides of the bowl constantly. Beat on high speed for 3 minutes. Using a wooden spoon, stir in the chilled flour-butter mixture till the flour is well moistened (butter will remain in large pieces).

Sprinkle a board or pastry cloth with ¼ *cup* of the remaining flour. Turn the dough out onto the floured surface. With floured hands, gently knead the dough for 8 strokes. With a well-floured rolling pin, roll the dough into a 21x12-inch rectangle (if necessary, sprinkle surface of the dough with enough remaining flour to prevent sticking). Fold dough crosswise into thirds to form a 12x7-inch rectangle. Loosely wrap in plastic wrap and chill for 1 to 1½ hours in the refrigerator or for 20 to 30 minutes in the freezer or till dough is firm but not excessively stiff.

On a well-floured surface, roll dough into a 21x12-inch rectangle. Fold dough crosswise into thirds again and give dough a quarter-turn. Roll, fold, and turn twice more, flouring the surface as needed (it is *not* necessary to chill dough between each rolling). Place dough in a plastic bag. Seal bag, leaving room for the dough to expand. Chill dough for 4 to 24 hours.

To shape, cut dough crosswise into fourths. Wrap and return *three* portions to the refrigerator till ready to use. On a lightly floured surface, roll the fourth portion of dough into a 16x8-inch rectangle. Cut the rectangle crosswise in half to form *two* squares. Then cut *each* square diagonally in half to form *two* triangles. (You will have *four* triangles total from *each* rectangle.) Loosely roll up each triangle, starting from an 8-inch side and rolling toward the opposite point.

Repeat shaping with the remaining 3 portions of dough. Place croissants 4 inches apart on ungreased baking sheets, points down. Curve the ends to form crescent shapes. Cover and let rise in a warm place till *nearly* double (about 1 hour).

In a small mixing bowl use a fork to beat one egg with 1 tablespoon water or milk. Lightly brush the egg mixture over croissants. Bake in a 375° oven about 15 minutes or till golden. Remove croissants and cool on a wire rack. Makes 16.

Wheat Croissants: Prepare Quick-Method Croissants as directed at left, *except* use 2 cups *all-purpose flour* and 1 cup *whole wheat flour* for the 3 *cups* all-purpose flour.

Orange-Chocolate-Filled Croissants

▶ *For light and flaky croissants, it's important to cut butter into ½-inch slices rather than chunks or cubes. In a bowl stir butter slices into 3 cups of flour till coated and separated. Chill while preparing the dough so the butter stays firm. Prepare dough, then stir the chilled butter mixture into the dough.*

▶ *Turn dough out onto a floured surface. With floured hands, gently knead dough for eight strokes. With a well-floured rolling pin, evenly roll dough into a 21x12-inch rectangle. Fold dough crosswise into thirds to form a 12x7-inch rectangle, then chill.*

The French love this chocolate-filled snack, and you will too when you taste this version.

1 recipe Classic Croissants, Quick-Method Croissants, Wheat Croissants, *or* Orange-Pecan Croissants (see pages 78–80 and 85)
⅔ cup sugar
⅓ cup orange juice
2 tablespoons cornstarch
2 squares (2 ounces) unsweetened chocolate, coarsely chopped
1 slightly beaten egg

Prepare the dough for croissants as directed. For filling, in a small saucepan combine sugar, orange juice, cornstarch, and chocolate. Cook and stir till chocolate melts and mixture bubbles. Cook and stir 2 minutes more. Cool (filling will thicken).

To shape, cut dough crosswise into fourths. Wrap and return *three* portions of dough to the refrigerator till ready to use. On a lightly floured surface, roll the fourth portion of dough into a 16x8-inch rectangle. Then cut the rectangle into four 8x4-inch rectangles. Spoon *2 teaspoons* filling onto the center of *each* 8x4-inch rectangle. Brush edges with a mixture of egg and 1 tablespoon *water*. Fold short sides of rectangles over filling to overlap in the center, forming 4x3½-inch bundles. Pinch edges together to seal.

Repeat shaping with remaining portions. Place 4 inches apart, seam sides down, on ungreased baking sheets. Cover; let rise in a warm place till *nearly* double (about 1 hour). Brush again with egg mixture. Bake in a 375° oven about 15 minutes or till golden. Remove croissants and cool on a wire rack. Makes 16.

Honey-Nutmeg Croissants

1½ **cups** *cold* **butter**
  3 **cups all-purpose flour**
  ¼ **teaspoon ground nutmeg**
1½ **cups all-purpose flour**
  1 **package active dry yeast**
1¼ **cups milk**
  ¼ **cup honey**
  ¼ **teaspoon salt**
  2 **eggs**
  ¼ **to ½ cup all-purpose flour**

Cut butter into ½-inch *slices*. In a bowl stir together the 3 cups flour and nutmeg. Stir the butter slices into the flour-nutmeg mixture till slices are coated and separated. Chill while preparing the dough.

For dough, in another bowl stir together the 1½ cups flour and yeast; set aside. In a saucepan heat and stir the milk, honey, and salt *just till warm* (120° to 130°). Add to the flour mixture. Then add *one* egg. Beat with an electric mixer on low to medium speed for 30 seconds, scraping the sides of the bowl constantly. Beat on high speed for 3 minutes. Using a wooden spoon, stir in the chilled flour-butter mixture till the flour is well moistened (butter will remain in large pieces).

Sprinkle a board or pastry cloth with ¼ *cup* of the remaining flour. Turn the dough out onto the floured surface. With floured hands, gently knead the dough for 8 strokes. With a well-floured rolling pin, roll the dough into a 21x12-inch rectangle (if necessary, sprinkle surface of dough with enough of the remaining flour to prevent sticking). Fold dough crosswise into thirds to form a 12x7-inch rectangle. Loosely wrap in plastic wrap and chill for 1 to 1½ hours in the refrigerator or for 20 to 30 minutes in the freezer or till dough is firm but not excessively stiff.

On a well-floured surface, roll dough into a 21x12-inch rectangle. Fold dough crosswise into thirds again and give dough a quarter-turn. Roll, fold, and turn twice more, flouring surface as needed (it is *not* necessary to chill dough between each rolling). Place dough in a plastic bag. Seal bag, leaving room for dough to expand. Chill dough for 4 to 24 hours.

To shape, cut dough crosswise into fourths. Wrap and return *three* portions to the refrigerator till ready to use. On a lightly floured surface, roll the fourth portion of dough into a 16x8-inch rectangle. Cut rectangle crosswise in half to form *two* squares. Then cut *each* square diagonally in half to form *two* triangles. (You will have *four* triangles total from *each* rectangle.) Loosely roll up each triangle, starting from an 8-inch side and rolling toward the opposite point.

Repeat shaping with the remaining 3 portions of dough. Place croissants 4 inches apart on ungreased baking sheets, points down. Curve the ends to form crescent shapes. Cover and let rise in a warm place till *nearly* double (about 1 hour). Lightly brush with a mixture of remaining egg and 1 tablespoon *water*. Bake in a 375° oven about 15 minutes or till golden. Cool on a wire rack. Makes 16.

Time for Tea

What better way to enjoy a delicate croissant or warm bread than with a cup of tea? In fact, get out your best china, sit down, and enjoy teatime as the English do. It is a welcome respite from the hustle and bustle of daily life.

Teatime, a great English tradition, became popular there in the mid-1800s when tea arrived from China along with the elegant tea services known as *china*. The custom of teatime, usually observed from 4 to 5 p.m., became synonymous with gentility when Queen Victoria and her court adopted the tradition.

Chocolate-Coconut-Filled Croissants

**1 recipe Classic Croissants, Quick-Method
        Croissants, Wheat Croissants, or Orange-
        Pecan Croissants (see pages 78–80 and 85)**
1 cup miniature semisweet chocolate pieces
½ cup shredded coconut
1 slightly beaten egg

Prepare the dough for croissants as directed. To shape, cut dough crosswise into fourths. Wrap and return *three* portions to the refrigerator till ready to use. On a lightly floured surface, roll the fourth portion of dough into a 16x8-inch rectangle. Then cut the rect-angle into four 8x4-inch rectangles. Spoon about *1 tablespoon* chocolate pieces onto the center of *each* 8x4-inch rectangle. Then sprinkle each with about *1 rounded teaspoon* coconut. Brush edges with a mixture of egg and 1 tablespoon *water*. Fold short sides of rectangles over filling to overlap in center, forming 4x3½-inch bundles. Pinch edges together to seal.

Repeat shaping with the remaining portions of dough. Place bundles 4 inches apart, seam sides down, on ungreased baking sheets. Cover and let rise in a warm place till *nearly* double (about 1 hour).

Brush again with the egg mixture. Bake in a 375° oven about 15 minutes or till golden. Remove from baking sheets; cool on a wire rack. Makes 16.

Secrets to Successful Croissants and Danish Pastries

Making wonderful croissants and Danish pastries is easier than you think. If your pastries aren't tender, flaky, and airy, here's what you can do next time:

■ Be sure to chill the dough for the length of time the recipe indicates. The dough should feel firm and cold to the touch when thoroughly chilled.

■ If it's above 75° and you don't have air conditioning, plan to bake on a cooler day. The dough needs to stay cold while you're working with it so the butter stays firm and sealed into the dough. If the butter softens, the pastries will become compact and the butter may leak out during baking.

■ Sticks of butter used in Quick-Method Croissants and Quick-Method Danish Pastry must be cut into ½-inch *slices* as the recipes indicate. The size and shape of the butter pieces affect the flakiness of the pastry. (If the butter is cut into cubes, the butter pieces are too small and eventually mix into the dough instead of staying in chunks.) When the butter slices melt during baking, steam is created. As the steam tries to escape and the yeast begins to work, the dough puffs, producing light, buttery layers.

■ Gently knead the Quick-Method Croissants and Quick-Method Danish Pastry doughs as the recipes indicate to keep the butter in chunks. Overkneading mixes the butter into the yeast dough, which keeps the dough from forming puffy pastry layers.

■ Always be sure to preheat the oven. Croissants and Danish need a constant oven temperature for proper rising.

Classic Croissants
(see recipe, page 78-79)

Orange-Pecan Croissants

1½ **cups *cold* butter**
3 **cups all-purpose flour**
1½ **teaspoons finely shredded orange peel**
1½ **cups all-purpose flour**
1 **package active dry yeast**
1¼ **cups milk**
¼ **cup sugar**
2 **eggs**
¼ **to ½ cup all-purpose flour**
⅔ **cup finely chopped pecans, toasted**

Cut butter into ½-inch *slices*. Mix 3 cups flour and orange peel. Stir in butter slices till coated and separated. Chill. For dough, stir together the 1½ cups flour and yeast. Heat and stir milk, sugar, and ¼ teaspoon *salt* just till warm (120° to 130°). Add to the flour mixture. Add *one* egg. Beat with an electric mixer on low to medium speed for 30 seconds, scraping bowl. Beat on high speed for 3 minutes. Using a wooden spoon, stir in butter mixture till flour is well moistened (butter will remain in large pieces.)

Sprinkle a board with ¼ *cup* of the remaining flour. Turn dough out onto floured surface. With floured hands, gently knead for 8 strokes. Using a well-floured rolling pin, roll into a 21x12-inch rectangle. Fold crosswise into thirds to form a 12x7-inch rectangle. Loosely wrap in plastic wrap and refrigerate for 1 to 1½ hours or till firm but not excessively stiff.

On a well-floured surface, roll dough into a 21x12-inch rectangle. Fold crosswise into thirds again and give a quarter-turn. Roll, fold, and turn twice more, flouring the surface as needed. Place the dough in a plastic bag. Seal the bag, leaving room for the dough to expand. Chill for 4 to 24 hours.

To shape, cut dough crosswise into fourths. Wrap and return *three* portions to the refrigerator. On a lightly floured surface, roll the fourth portion into a 16x8-inch rectangle. Cut crosswise in half to form *two* squares. Then cut *each* square diagonally in half to form *two* triangles. Sprinkle *2 teaspoons* pecans on *each* triangle. Loosely roll up each triangle, starting from an 8-inch side and rolling toward the opposite point. Repeat shaping with the remaining dough. Place croissants 4 inches apart on ungreased baking sheets, points down. Curve ends. Cover and let rise in a warm place till *nearly* double (about 1 hour).

Lightly brush croissants with a mixture of the remaining egg and 1 tablespoon *water*. Bake in a 375° oven about 15 minutes or till golden. Remove and cool on a wire rack. Makes 16.

Storing Croissants and Danish Pastries

Retain the quality of freshly made pastries by taking the time to store them properly.

To store baked croissants and Danish pastries, wrap them in foil or place them in plastic bags. Then refrigerate for up to 3 days. (Room temperature storage is not recommended because of the high butter content and spoilage of fillings.) To serve refrigerated croissants or Danish, allow them to stand at room temperature for 20 to 30 minutes.

To freeze baked croissants and Danish pastries, tightly wrap them in *heavy* foil. Freeze them for up to 2 months. To serve, heat wrapped frozen croissants or Danish in a 400° oven for 5 to 8 minutes.

Classic Danish Pastry

Danish pastry originated when the Danes added sweet fillings to Austrian pastry. The result—flaky pastry with a luscious surprise—earned praise even from the Austrians.

1½ cups butter
⅓ cup all-purpose flour
3¾ to 4¼ cups all-purpose flour
1 package active dry yeast
1¼ cups light cream *or* milk
¼ cup sugar
¼ teaspoon salt
1 egg

In a large bowl beat butter with an electric mixer on medium to high speed about 30 seconds or till softened. Add the ⅓ cup flour and mix well. Roll the butter mixture between 2 large sheets of waxed paper into a 12x6-inch rectangle. Chill for 1 hour.

For dough, in the large bowl combine *1¼ cups* of remaining flour and yeast. Heat and stir cream, sugar, and salt *just till warm* (120° to 130°). Add to flour mixture. Add egg. Beat with an electric mixer on low to medium speed for 30 seconds, scraping bowl. Then beat on high speed for 3 minutes. Using a wooden spoon, stir in as much remaining flour as you can.

Turn the dough out onto a lightly floured surface. Knead in enough of the remaining flour to make a moderately soft dough that is smooth and elastic (3 to 5 minutes total). Cover and let rest for 10 minutes.

On a lightly floured surface, roll the dough into a 14-inch square. Remove top sheet of waxed paper from the butter mixture. Carefully invert butter mixture onto half of the dough to within 1 inch of edges. Remove waxed paper. Fold over the other half of dough and seal edges. Roll into a 21x12-inch rectangle. Fold crosswise into thirds forming a 12x7-inch rectangle. Chill for 1 hour. Repeat rolling into a 21x12-inch rectangle, folding, and chilling three more times. Fill, shape, and bake as directed in the recipes.

Quick-Method Danish Pastry

Use this dough or Classic Danish Pastry as the base for the seven pastry recipes on the following pages.

1½ cups *cold* butter
3 cups all-purpose flour
1½ cups all-purpose flour
1 package active dry yeast
1¼ cups light cream *or* milk
¼ cup sugar
¼ teaspoon salt
1 egg
¼ to ½ cup all-purpose flour

Cut butter into ½-inch *slices.* In a bowl stir butter slices into 3 cups flour till coated and separated; chill.

For dough, in a large bowl combine 1½ cups flour and yeast. Heat and stir the cream, sugar, and salt *just till warm* (120° to 130°). Add to flour mixture. Add the egg. Beat with an electric mixer on low to medium speed for 30 seconds, scraping bowl. Beat on high speed for 3 minutes. Using a wooden spoon, stir in the chilled flour-butter mixture till the flour is well moistened (butter will remain in large pieces).

Sprinkle a pastry cloth or surface with ¼ *cup* of remaining flour. Turn dough out onto the floured surface. With floured hands, gently knead dough for 8 strokes. With a well-floured rolling pin, roll into a 21x12-inch rectangle. Fold crosswise into thirds to form a 12x7-inch rectangle. Loosely wrap; chill 1 to 1½ hours in refrigerator or for 20 to 30 minutes in freezer or till dough is firm but not excessively stiff.

On a well-floured surface, roll dough into a 21x12-inch rectangle. Fold dough crosswise into thirds; give a quarter-turn. Then roll, fold, and turn twice more, flouring the surface as needed (it is *not* necessary to chill dough between rollings). Place in plastic bag. Seal bag, leaving room for expansion. Chill 4 to 24 hours. Fill, shape, and bake as directed in recipes.

Bear Claws

Scandinavians call them "cockscombs." Others know them as "scrubbing brushes." By whatever name you call them, these golden, tender pastries are a cherished treat.

1   **recipe Classic Danish Pastry *or* Quick-Method Danish Pastry (see page 86)**
1   **slightly beaten egg white**
¾   **cup sifted powdered sugar**
½   **cup almond paste**
1   **egg**
1   **tablespoon water**
     Pearl sugar, crushed sugar cubes, *or* sugar
     Sliced almonds

Prepare Danish pastry dough as directed. For filling, in a medium mixing bowl beat together the egg white, powdered sugar, and almond paste with an electric mixer on low to medium speed until smooth.

To shape, cut the chilled dough crosswise in half. On a lightly floured surface, roll *each* half of dough into a 12-inch square. Cut each square into three 4-inch-wide strips (6 strips total).

Spread about *2 tablespoons* filling down the center of *each* strip. Fold the strips lengthwise in half to cover filling. Pinch the edges to seal. Cut each strip into three 4-inch-long pieces. Make 4 or 5 evenly spaced cuts in each piece, snipping from the sealed edge almost to the folded edge. Place 1½ inches apart on ungreased baking sheets, curving slightly to separate slits. Cover; let rise in a warm place till *nearly* double (45 to 60 minutes).

In a small mixing bowl use a fork to beat the whole egg and water. Lightly brush egg mixture over dough. Sprinkle with sugar and almonds. Bake in a 375° oven about 15 minutes or till golden. Remove pastries and cool slightly on a wire rack. Serve warm. Makes 18.

◀ *To shape Bear Claws, cut each filled strip into pieces 4 inches long. Make four or five cuts in each piece, snipping from the sealed edge almost to the folded edge at about 1-inch intervals, as shown. Transfer pastries to an ungreased baking sheet. Then curve the pastries slightly to form crescents.*

Danish Pinwheels

1   **recipe Classic Danish Pastry *or* Quick-Method Danish Pastry (see page 86)**
1   **10-ounce jar desired flavor of preserves *or* spreadable fruit**
1   **egg**
1   **tablespoon water *or* milk**

Prepare Danish pastry dough as directed. To shape, on a lightly floured surface, roll the chilled dough into a 21x12-inch rectangle. Cut the dough into twenty-eight 3-inch squares. Cut 1-inch slits from the corners toward the center of *each* square. Place squares 4 inches apart on ungreased baking sheets. Spoon *1 rounded teaspoon* preserves onto the center of *each* square. Fold points to center over preserves, alternating points to form a pinwheel. Moisten points in the center and pinch together. Cover; let rise in a warm place till *nearly* double (45 to 60 minutes).

In a small mixing bowl use a fork to beat the egg and water or milk. Lightly brush mixture over pinwheels. Bake in a 375° oven for 12 to 15 minutes or till golden. Remove pastries from baking sheets and cool slightly on a wire rack. Serve warm. Makes 28.

Danish Braids

1 recipe Classic Danish Pastry *or* Quick-Method Danish Pastry (see page 86)
1¼ cups sugar
4 slightly beaten eggs
2 teaspoons finely shredded orange peel
1 teaspoon vanilla
3 cups hazelnuts *or* walnuts, very finely chopped
  Orange Glaze (optional)

Prepare Danish pastry dough as directed. For filling, in a large mixing bowl stir together sugar, 3 eggs, orange peel, and vanilla. Fold in nuts. Set aside.

To shape, cut the chilled dough crosswise in half. On a lightly floured surface, roll *each* half into an 18x12-inch rectangle. Cut each lengthwise into three 18x4-inch strips. Spoon about ⅔ *cup* filling down the center third of *each* strip. Fold strips lengthwise in half to cover filling. Moisten and seal edges and ends, forming 6 ropes. On 2 ungreased baking sheets, make 2 braids using 3 ropes for each braid (see directions for braided loaves, page 49). Cover and let rise in a warm place till *nearly* double (45 to 60 minutes).

Lightly brush the braids with a mixture of the remaining egg and 1 tablespoon *water*. Bake in a 375° oven for 25 minutes. Cover loosely with foil. Bake about 10 minutes more or till golden. Remove braids from baking sheets and cool on a wire rack. If desired, drizzle with Orange Glaze. Makes 2 loaves.

Orange Glaze: In a small bowl stir together 1 cup sifted *powdered sugar,* 1 tablespoon *orange juice or orange liqueur,* and 1 to 2 teaspoons *orange juice or water* to make a glaze of drizzling consistency. Makes about ⅓ cup.

Fruit-Filled Danish Turnovers

1 recipe Classic Danish Pastry *or* Quick-Method Danish Pastry (see page 86)
½ cup dried cherries, snipped dried prunes, *or* snipped dried apricots
½ cup chopped walnuts
¼ cup packed brown sugar
1 tablespoon all-purpose flour
  Dash ground cinnamon
1 recipe Powdered Sugar Icing (see page 230)

Prepare Danish pastry dough as directed. For filling, in a small saucepan combine dried fruit and enough *water* to cover (about 1 cup) the fruit. Bring to boiling. Remove from heat. Let stand, covered, for 5 minutes. Drain. Stir in walnuts, brown sugar, flour, and cinnamon. Set filling aside.

To shape, cut the chilled dough crosswise in half. On a lightly floured surface, roll *each* half of dough into a 12-inch square. Cut each square of dough into nine 4-inch squares (18 squares total). Spoon about *1 tablespoon* of filling onto the center of *each* square. Brush edges with *water*. Fold squares diagonally in half, forming triangles. Press the edges to seal. Place the triangles 4 inches apart on ungreased baking sheets. Cover and let rise in a warm place till *nearly* double (45 to 60 minutes).

Bake in a 375° oven for 18 to 20 minutes or till golden. Remove turnovers from baking sheets and cool slightly on a wire rack. Drizzle Powdered Sugar Icing over warm turnovers. Serve warm or cool. Makes 18.

Pecan Snails

If you like the taste of cinnamon rolls, you'll love these easy-to-form snail-shaped pastries.

1 recipe Classic Danish Pastry *or* Quick-Method Danish Pastry (see page 86)
1 cup pecans, finely chopped
⅔ cup packed brown sugar
½ teaspoon ground cinnamon
⅓ cup margarine *or* butter, softened
1 egg
½ teaspoon instant coffee crystals
1 cup sifted powdered sugar

Prepare Danish pastry dough as directed. Grease 24 muffin cups. For topping, in a small mixing bowl stir together the pecans, brown sugar, and cinnamon. Set muffin cups and topping aside.

To shape, cut the chilled dough crosswise in half. On lightly floured surface, roll *each* half of dough into a 12-inch square. Spread the dough with the softened margarine or butter. Sprinkle with the topping. Roll up each square, jelly-roll style, starting from one of the sides. Pinch seams to seal. Cut each roll into 12 pieces. Place pieces, cut sides down, in the prepared muffin cups. Cover and let rise in a warm place till *nearly* double (45 to 60 minutes).

In a small mixing bowl use a fork to beat the egg and 1 tablespoon *water*. Lightly brush over the tops. Bake in a 375° oven about 20 minutes or till golden. Invert pastries onto wire racks. Cool slightly.

Meanwhile, in a small mixing bowl stir together 1 tablespoon *hot water* and coffee crystals till coffee is dissolved. Stir into powdered sugar. If necessary, stir in additional *water* to make frosting of drizzling consistency. Drizzle over pastries. Serve warm. Makes 24.

Cheese Danish

The buttery flavor and rich aroma of these luscious cheese-filled pastries makes them a hands-down coffee break favorite. (Pictured on pages 6–7.)

1 recipe Classic Danish Pastry *or* Quick-Method Danish Pastry (see page 86)
1 8-ounce package cream cheese, softened
¼ cup sugar
1 egg yolk
2 teaspoons finely shredded lemon peel
½ teaspoon vanilla
1 egg
1 tablespoon water
Powdered sugar (optional)

Prepare Danish pastry dough as directed. For filling, in a small mixing bowl stir together cream cheese, sugar, egg yolk, lemon peel, and vanilla. Set aside.

To shape pastries, on a lightly floured surface, roll the chilled dough into a 20x12-inch rectangle. Cut rectangle into twenty 12x1-inch strips. With one end of a strip in each hand, twist ends in opposite directions 3 or 4 times. Place the twisted strip on an ungreased baking sheet, forming a wide U-shape. Repeat with remaining strips, placing them 4 inches apart on baking sheets. Then coil one end of each U-shaped strip into the center to form a snail shape. Tuck the end underneath. Coil the opposite end of the U-shaped strip into the center so the 2 coils nearly touch. Tuck the second end under in the same manner as the first.

Spoon *1 heaping teaspoon* of filling onto the center of *each* coil. Cover and let rise in a warm place till *nearly* double (30 to 45 minutes).

In a small mixing bowl use a fork to beat the whole egg and water. Lightly brush egg mixture over dough portions of pastries. Bake in a 375° oven for 18 to 20 minutes or till golden. Remove pastries and cool slightly on a wire rack. If desired, sift powdered sugar over tops of pastries. Serve warm. Makes 20.

Date-Filled Danish

1 recipe Classic Danish Pastry *or* Quick-Method Danish Pastry (see page 86)
½ cup finely snipped pitted whole dates
½ cup water
3 tablespoons corn syrup
2 tablespoons sugar
2 tablespoons all-purpose flour
½ teaspoon finely shredded lemon peel
1 teaspoon lemon juice
1 recipe Powdered Sugar Icing (see page 230)

Prepare Danish pastry dough as directed. For filling, in a small saucepan combine the dates and water. Bring to boiling. Reduce heat. Cover and simmer for 20 minutes. Remove from heat. Stir in corn syrup. Stir together sugar and flour. Then stir sugar mixture into the date mixture. Cook and stir about 1 minute more or till thickened and bubbly. Remove from heat. Stir in lemon peel and lemon juice. Set filling aside to cool slightly before using.

To shape, on a lightly floured surface, roll chilled pastry dough into a 20x12-inch rectangle. Cut dough crosswise into twenty 12x1-inch strips. Take a strip, one end in each hand, and twist ends in opposite directions 3 or 4 times. Place the twisted strip on an ungreased baking sheet, forming it into a snail shape. Tuck the ends underneath. Repeat with remaining strips, placing them 4 inches apart on baking sheets.

Using your thumb or 2 fingers, make a 2-inch indentation in the center of each pastry. Spoon *1 rounded tablespoon* of the filling into *each* indentation. Cover and let rise in a warm place till *nearly* double (45 to 60 minutes).

Bake in a 375° oven for 18 to 20 minutes or till golden. Remove pastries and cool slightly on a wire rack. Drizzle with Powdered Sugar Icing. Serve warm. Makes 20.

Nutrition Analysis

Recipes	Servings	Calories	Protein (g)	Carbohydrates (g)	Total Fat (g)	Saturated Fat (g)	Cholesterol (mg)	Sodium (mg)
Almond Buttery-Biscuit Twists, 14	15	209	3	21	13	4	16	182
Almond Sourdough Rolls, 71	24	198	4	33	6	1	9	155
Aloha Loaf, 33	16	197	4	25	10	4	14	129
Apple Bread, 32	16	155	2	23	6	1	13	69
Apple-Wheat Coffee Cake, 35	10	281	5	49	9	2	21	234
Apricot-Nut Butter, 28	24	85	0	6	7	3	10	33
Bagels, 60	12	172	5	35	1	0	18	273
Banana Berry Crunch, 41	9	369	6	54	16	3	48	323
Barley Wheat Bread, 46	32	115	4	21	2	1	1	145
Bear Claws, 87	18	336	6	33	21	11	71	177
Best-Ever Buttermilk Biscuits, 15	10	195	3	21	11	4	10	189
Bran Bread, 43	32	82	2	16	1	0	0	68
Buttermilk Popovers, 9	6	156	6	18	7	2	73	153
Buttermilk Rolls, 56	24	126	3	19	4	1	9	124
Buttery Breakfast Biscuits, 14	10	241	3	21	16	6	24	265
Buttery Breakfast Turnovers, 14	15	206	3	19	13	5	37	194
Caramel Pecan Rolls, 73	20	267	4	38	11	2	22	162
Carrot and Pineapple Bread, 32	16	160	2	25	6	1	13	70
Cheddar Sauce, 61	20	21	1	1	2	1	4	27
Cheese Buttons, 11	18	27	2	3	1	0	14	15
Cheese Danish, 89	20	305	5	26	21	12	87	190
Cheese 'n' Onion Bread, 51	32	93	4	13	3	2	14	140
Cheese 'n' Turkey Corn Bread, 30	9	263	10	27	13	4	67	379
Cheesy Bacon Vegetable Muffins, 22	12	180	5	17	10	3	26	169
Cheesy Broccoli Muffins, 23	12	174	5	19	9	4	32	214
Cherry Oat Bran Muffins, 26	12	212	5	32	8	2	20	194
Cherry Twist, 68	32	90	2	16	2	0	14	93
Chocolate-Almond Crescent, 70	24	142	4	16	7	1	18	102
Chocolate-Coconut-Filled Croissants, 83	16	365	6	36	23	14	75	199
Chocolate-Praline Butter, 28	16	95	0	2	10	5	18	55
Cinnamon 'n' Apple Rolls, 72	20	217	4	38	6	1	23	123
Cinnamon 'n' Chocolate Rolls, 72	20	240	4	38	9	3	23	124
Cinnamon Rolls, 72	20	200	4	33	6	1	23	123
Classic Croissants, 78	16	301	5	29	19	11	75	197
Corn Bread, 30	9	202	5	27	8	1	50	243
Corn Bread Loaves, 30	8	228	6	31	9	2	56	274

Per Serving

◀ *To shape the Date-Filled Danish pastries, on a baking sheet, form each twisted strip into a snail shape. Tuck the ends underneath. Press your thumb in the center of each pastry to make a 2-inch-wide indentation. Spoon a rounded tablespoon of the date filling into each indentation.*

Per Serving

Recipes	Servings	Calories	Protein (g)	Carbohydrates (g)	Total Fat (g)	Saturated Fat (g)	Cholesterol (mg)	Sodium (mg)
Corn Muffins, 30	12	152	4	20	6	1	37	182
Corn Sticks, 30	24	76	2	10	3	1	19	91
Corny Corn Bread, 30	9	232	6	34	8	1	50	364
Country Herb Rolls, 57	24	126	3	18	5	1	18	100
Country Scones, 20	20	121	2	16	6	2	16	149
Cranberry-Apple Mini Loaves, 31	16	179	2	29	6	1	13	71
Cranberry-Nut Upside Down Muffins, 27	12	179	3	35	3	1	19	107
Cranberry-Orange Scones, 21	12	155	3	19	8	1	18	128
Cream Cheese and Raspberry Coffee Cake, 40	12	320	5	42	15	6	57	219
Cream Cheese Savory Muffins, 23	12	155	4	18	7	3	27	184
Crunchy Corn Bread, 30	9	280	7	35	13	2	50	243
Crunchy Parmesan Herb Breadsticks, 57	24	54	2	8	1	0	2	39
Danish Braids, 88	24	351	6	32	23	9	80	138
Danish Pinwheels, 87	28	208	3	23	12	7	46	112
Date and Nut Bread, 67	32	111	3	17	4	1	27	62
Date-Filled Danish, 90	20	297	4	35	16	10	54	155
Double Cheese Wheat Muffins, 23	12	158	5	18	8	2	25	123
Drop Best-Ever Buttermilk Biscuits, 15	10	198	3	21	11	4	11	197
Drop Country Scones, 20	24	100	2	13	5	2	13	123
Drop South-of-the-Border Cornmeal Biscuits, 18	12	174	4	18	10	3	6	246
Egg Bagels, 60	12	181	6	35	2	0	53	274
Egg Dinner Rolls, 55	24	107	3	17	3	1	36	74
Ensaimada, 77	18	255	6	27	13	4	54	257
Festive Fruit Bread, 33	16	174	3	25	8	2	27	136
French Bread, 50	30	86	3	18	0	0	0	109
Fruit-Filled Danish Turnovers, 88	18	345	5	38	20	11	60	172
Fruit-Filled Ladder Loaf, 69	24	196	4	30	7	2	36	149
Full-of-Fruit Spread, 28	21	41	1	4	3	1	0	34
Garden-Angel Biscuits, 12	12	186	4	23	9	2	1	138
Garlic 'n' Chive Popovers, 9	6	160	6	18	7	2	75	131
German Sourdough Bread, 53	16	176	5	33	3	1	1	109
Granola-Topped Blueberry Muffins, 26	12	179	3	25	8	2	18	97
Green Chili Corn Bread, 30	9	256	8	28	12	4	63	323
Gruyère-Pecan Biscuits, 17	10	245	5	21	16	3	8	232
Honey-Bran Biscuit Angels, 16	4	464	9	51	25	5	55	704
Honey-Bran Biscuit Bears, 16	6	310	6	34	17	3	37	470
Honey-Nutmeg Croissants, 82	16	324	6	34	19	11	75	197
Iced Vaňočka Braid, 62	32	170	4	34	2	1	14	63
Individual Puffy Surprise Pancake, 10	6	305	6	27	20	7	124	107
Individual Yorkshire Puddings, 8	16	129	4	14	6	3	61	98
Kolaches, 76	24	184	3	25	8	2	36	130
Lemon-Poppy Seed Popovers, 9	6	168	6	18	8	2	75	131
Light Rye Bagels, 60	12	166	5	34	1	0	18	273
Maple Pecan Muffins, 25	12	216	4	28	10	1	19	130
Miniature Caramel Pecan Rolls, 73	48	113	2	16	5	1	9	70
Mocha Chip Coffee Cake, 39	16	174	2	26	8	3	14	121
Oatmeal-Blueberry Teatime Muffins, 25	36	55	1	8	2	0	6	48
Oatmeal-Fig Teatime Muffins, 25	36	69	1	9	3	0	6	48
Oatmeal Molasses Bread, 42	24	140	4	26	2	0	0	199
Oatmeal-Prune Teatime Muffins, 25	36	62	1	10	2	0	6	48
Oatmeal Nut Bread, 19	16	95	3	13	3	1	27	121
Old-Fashioned Potato Bread, 45	32	105	3	21	1	0	0	151
Onion Bagels, 60	12	193	5	36	3	1	0	301
Orange Butter, 28	12	70	0	1	8	5	21	65

Per Serving

Recipes	Servings	Calories	Protein (g)	Carbohydrates (g)	Total Fat (g)	Saturated Fat (g)	Cholesterol (mg)	Sodium (mg)
Orange-Chocolate-Filled Croissants, 81	16	357	6	39	21	12	75	197
Orange-Pecan Croissants, 85	16	353	6	34	22	12	75	164
Parmesan Bagels, 60	12	179	6	35	1	1	19	304
Parmesan-Garlic Butter, 28	12	78	1	0	8	5	22	106
Peach-Nut Butter, 28	24	85	0	6	7	3	10	33
Peanut Butter 'n' Chocolate Bubble Ring, 38	10	407	11	39	24	4	43	365
Pear-Almond Muffins with Lemon Butter, 29	12	221	4	24	13	2	19	152
Pecan Ripple Ring, 34	12	413	6	54	20	5	62	284
Pecan Snails, 89	24	305	4	30	19	9	54	162
Pepper-Cheese Bread, 46	12	181	8	23	7	3	27	240
Pepperoni Pizza Popovers, 11	8	182	8	14	10	4	67	183
Pick-a-Flour Popovers, 9	6	157	6	17	7	2	75	131
Pineapple Apricot Coffee Cake, 41	9	283	4	34	15	3	25	274
Plum Kuchen, 37	10	224	3	36	8	1	22	138
Popovers, 9	6	160	6	18	7	2	75	131
Poppy Seed Bagels, 60	12	174	5	35	1	0	18	273
Potato Buns, 45	24	140	4	27	1	0	0	201
Praline Butter, 28	12	125	0	5	12	6	23	73
Puffy Surprise Pancake, 10	6	305	6	27	20	7	124	107
Pumpkin Praline Muffins, 29	12	223	4	34	8	2	19	172
Quick-Method Croissants, 80	16	320	6	33	19	11	75	197
Raisin-Oatmeal Soda Bread, 19	16	110	3	17	3	1	27	122
Rye Bread, 51	24	121	3	24	2	0	0	91
Sage Wheat Bread, 47	24	146	5	27	2	1	11	30
Sally Lunn, 68	12	175	5	28	4	1	37	144
Sesame Bagels, 60	12	174	5	35	1	0	18	273
So-Easy Yogurt Shortcake, 19	6	428	7	47	24	11	92	479
Soft Pretzels, 61	20	129	4	23	2	1	2	146
Sourdough Bread, 52	24	146	4	28	2	0	0	107
South-of-the-Border Cornmeal Biscuits, 18	10	206	5	21	11	3	6	289
Spiced Popovers, 9	6	167	6	20	7	2	75	132
Spicy Pumpkin Loaf, 31	16	208	3	37	5	1	27	115
St. Lucia Buns, 75	48	95	2	15	3	1	10	75
Strawberry-Nut Butter, 28	24	84	1	6	7	3	10	34
Strawberry Ripple Tea Cake, 37	8	410	6	57	18	4	28	338
Streusel-Topped Ladder Loaf, 69	24	198	4	28	8	2	36	160
Sweetheart Chocolate Scones (large), 21	12	191	4	25	9	3	36	193
Sweetheart Chocolate Scones (small), 21	20	115	2	15	5	2	22	116
Thyme and Onion Muffins, 23	12	155	4	18	7	3	27	184
Tropical Sourdough Coffee Cake, 39	9	522	6	91	17	4	24	285
Vaňočka Braid, 62	32	144	4	27	3	1	21	62
Walnut Potica, 65	30	176	3	17	11	1	22	81
Wheat Croissants, 80	16	316	6	32	19	11	75	197
Wheat 'n' Walnut Butterhorns, 56	24	179	4	23	8	2	19	80
Whole Wheat Bagels, 60	12	165	5	34	1	0	18	273
Whole Wheat Bread, 43	32	87	2	17	1	0	0	68
Whole Wheat Potato Bread, 45	32	102	3	20	1	0	0	151
Whole Wheat Raisin Bread, 64	32	120	3	24	2	0	14	58
Whole Wheat Soft Pretzels, 61	20	125	4	22	3	1	2	146
Yogurt Dill Bread, 47	10	187	5	28	6	1	23	184
Yorkshire Pudding, 8	8	210	8	27	7	3	115	196
Zucchini Bread, 32	16	151	2	23	6	1	13	69

We've analyzed the nutritional content of each recipe using the first choice if ingredient substitutions are given, and using the first serving size if a serving range is given. We've omitted optional ingredients from the analysis.

Chocolate Meringue Surprises
(see recipe, page 96)

Cream Cheese Fruited Flan
(see recipe, page 116)

Cheesecake and Brandied Berry Sauce
(see recipe, page 122)

Lemon Meringue Torte
(see recipe, page 95)

Cranberry-Apple Crisp
(see recipe, page 111)

OLD-TIME BAKED DESSERTS

From the simple to the elegant, dessert is the grand finale for any meal. Whether it's an everyday family meal or an important company affair, dessert is the course that leaves the lasting impression. Make it a memory to treasure with a wonderful old-fashioned baked creation. This selection covers the whole spectrum, from homey fruit crisps and cobblers to company-special meringues, cheesecakes, and custards.

HARD MERINGUES

Light and puffy as clouds, meringues make heavenly desserts. Hard meringues are used like pastry as shells or for crisp cookies. Not only are they delicious, but for a bonus, plain meringues have no fat or cholesterol.

☐ The key to making meringues is how you handle the egg whites. Eggs are easier to separate when they are cold. Be very careful not to get even a speck of yolk in the egg whites. Place the egg whites in a glass or metal mixing bowl. Do not use a plastic bowl. The fat from the egg yolk or any grease on the utensils will prevent you from getting good volume when beating the egg whites.

☐ You'll get more volume as you beat the egg whites if they are at room temperature. Allow about 1 hour for the egg whites to come to room temperature.

☐ Pipe or shape the beaten egg whites immediately after beating so none of the volume is lost.

☐ If only one cookie sheet of meringue cookies will fit on your oven rack, place the meringue mixture in the refrigerator until you are ready to drop and bake another cookie sheet full (chill for up to 1 hour).

Meringue Shell

Create a spectacular dessert by filling these shells with fresh fruit, scoops of ice cream or sherbet, or a favorite pudding.

    3 egg whites
    1 teaspoon vanilla
    ¼ teaspoon cream of tartar
    1 cup sugar

Line a baking sheet with parchment paper, plain brown paper, or foil. Draw one 9-inch circle or eight 3-inch circles on the paper. Set baking sheet aside. In a large bowl beat egg whites, vanilla, cream of tartar, and dash *salt* with an electric mixer on medium speed till soft peaks form (tips curl). Gradually add sugar, *1 tablespoon* at a time, beating on high speed about 7 minutes or till very stiff peaks form (tips stand straight) and sugar is *almost* dissolved.

Using a spoon or a spatula, spread meringue mixture over the circle or circles on the prepared baking sheet, building the sides up to form a shell or shells (sides on large circle should be 1¾ inches high). *Or,* spoon meringue mixture into a decorating bag fitted with a medium plain-round or star tip (about ¼-inch opening). Pipe shells on the prepared baking sheet.

Bake in a 300° oven for 45 minutes for a large shell or 35 minutes for small shells. Turn off oven. Let dry in oven with door closed for 1 hour (do not open oven). Peel shells from paper or foil. To serve, add desired filling. Makes 1 large or 8 individual shells.

Nut Meringue Shell: Prepare Meringue Shell as above, *except* fold in ½ cup finely chopped toasted *almonds, hazelnuts, walnuts, or pecans* after beating to very stiff peaks. Do not pipe shell.

Chocolate Meringue Shell: Prepare Meringue Shell as directed above, *except* fold in 1 square (1 ounce) grated *semisweet chocolate* after beating egg white mixture to very stiff peaks.

Lemon Meringue Torte

The luscious filling softens the meringue layers, giving them a marshmallowlike texture. (Pictured on pages 92–93.)

- 4 **egg whites**
- 1 **teaspoon vanilla**
- ¼ **teaspoon cream of tartar**
- ¾ **cup sugar**
- 2 **tablespoons sliced almonds**
  Lemon Filling
  Raspberry Sauce

Line a baking sheet with parchment paper, plain brown paper, or foil. Draw three 7-inch circles on the paper. Set baking sheet aside.

In a large mixing bowl beat egg whites, vanilla, and cream of tartar with an electric mixer on medium speed till soft peaks form (tips curl). Gradually add sugar, *1 tablespoon* at a time, beating on high speed about 9 minutes or till very stiff peaks form (tips stand straight) and sugar is *almost* dissolved.

Spoon about *one-third* of the meringue into a decorating bag fitted with a large star tip (about ½-inch opening). Pipe a lattice design on the prepared baking sheet over *one* of the circles, then pipe a border around the lattice. Sprinkle lattice with almonds.

Spread the remaining meringue mixture over the remaining circles. Bake in a 300° oven for 20 minutes. Turn off oven. Let meringues dry in the oven with door closed for 1 hour (do not open oven).

To assemble torte, peel meringue circles from paper. Place one solid meringue circle on a serving plate; spread *half* of the Lemon Filling on the meringue. Repeat layering with remaining solid meringue circle and filling. Top with meringue lattice. Loosely cover with plastic wrap. Chill 4 to 18 hours.

To serve, drizzle torte with some of the Raspberry Sauce. If desired, garnish with red raspberries and mint sprigs. Pass remaining sauce. Serves 8 to 10.

Lemon Filling: In a medium saucepan stir together ⅔ cup *sugar* and 1 envelope *unflavored gelatin.* Add 4 beaten *egg yolks,* ⅔ cup *water,* ½ teaspoon finely shredded *lemon peel,* ⅓ cup *lemon juice,* and 2 tablespoons *margarine or butter.* Cook and stir over medium heat till thickened and bubbly. Cook and stir for 2 minutes more. Remove from heat. Cool to room temperature, stirring occasionally. In a small mixing bowl beat ¾ cup *whipping cream* till soft peaks form. Fold whipped cream into lemon mixture. Chill till *partially* set. Makes about 2½ cups.

Raspberry Sauce: In a medium saucepan combine one 10-ounce package frozen *raspberries,* thawed; 3 tablespoons *sugar;* and 2 teaspoons *cornstarch.* Cook and stir till thickened and bubbly. Cook and stir for 2 minutes more. Press the mixture through a fine sieve. Discard seeds. Cover and chill sauce. Makes ¾ cups.

◄ *To see if the sugar is almost or completely dissolved, rub a little of the meringue between your fingers. A hard meringue is ready when it feels almost smooth, yet still slightly grainy. A soft meringue for a cream pie topping is ready when it feels completely smooth.*

Chocolate Meringue Surprises

Each crisp meringue hides a bite of smooth chocolate candy. (Pictured on pages 92–93.)

  2 **egg whites**
  ½ **teaspoon vanilla**
  ¼ **teaspoon cream of tartar**
  ½ **cup sugar**
  1 **tablespoon unsweetened cocoa powder**
 36 **milk chocolate kisses *or* bite-size peanut butter cups**
  3 **tablespoons ground unsalted cocktail peanuts (optional)**

Line 2 cookie sheets with parchment paper, plain brown paper, or foil. Set cookie sheets aside.

In a medium mixing bowl beat egg whites, vanilla, and cream of tartar with an electric mixer on medium speed till soft peaks form (tips curl). Gradually add sugar, *1 tablespoon* at a time, beating on high speed about 7 minutes or till very stiff peaks form (tips stand straight) and sugar is *almost* dissolved. Then beat in cocoa powder *just till combined.*

Spoon meringue mixture into a decorating bag fitted with a medium star tip (about ¼-inch opening). On the prepared cookie sheets, pipe some of the meringue into 36 rounds, each about 1¼ inches in diameter and 2 inches apart. Lightly press a chocolate kiss or peanut butter cup into each meringue round. Then pipe the remaining meringue around each candy in concentric circles, starting at the base and working toward the top, completely covering the candy. If desired, sprinkle with ground peanuts.

Bake cookies in a 325° oven for 25 minutes. Cool on cookie sheets for 1 to 2 minutes. Carefully peel cookies from paper. Completely cool meringues on a wire rack. Makes about 36.

Chocolate Amaretti Balls

  2 **egg whites**
  1 **tablespoon amaretto *or* ¼ teaspoon almond extract**
  ½ **teaspoon vanilla**
  ¼ **teaspoon cream of tartar**
  ½ **cup sugar**
  2 **tablespoons unsweetened cocoa powder**
  1½ **cups ground almonds**
  ½ **cup semisweet chocolate pieces *or* 3 ounces vanilla-flavored confectioners' coating, chopped (optional)**
  1 **tablespoon shortening (optional)**

Line 2 cookie sheets with parchment paper, plain brown paper, or foil. Set aside. In a medium mixing bowl beat egg whites, amaretto or almond extract, vanilla, and cream of tartar with an electric mixer on medium speed till soft peaks form (tips curl). Gradually add sugar, *1 tablespoon* at a time, beating on high speed about 7 minutes or till very stiff peaks form (tips stand straight) and sugar is *almost* dissolved. Then beat in cocoa powder *just till combined.* Fold in almonds.

Spoon meringue mixture into a decorating bag fitted with a large plain-round tip (about ½-inch opening). Pipe 1-inch mounds 1½ inches apart on the prepared cookie sheets. *Or,* drop from a rounded teaspoon 1½ inches apart on the cookie sheets. Bake in a 300° oven for 15 to 18 minutes or till set. Turn off oven. Let cookies dry in oven with door closed for 30 minutes (do not open oven). Peel cookies from the paper. Then completely cool cookies on a wire rack.

If desired, in a small heavy saucepan heat chocolate pieces or confectioners' coating and shortening over low heat just till melted, stirring occasionally. Dip the bottoms of *half* of the cookies in the melted chocolate. Then place each on top of a plain cookie. Let the cookies stand on the wire rack till set. Makes about 90 single or 45 double cookies.

After-Dinner Mint Meringues

For another look, drizzle the sticks or stars with the melted chocolate instead of dipping them in it.

- **2 egg whites**
- **¼ to ½ teaspoon peppermint *or* mint extract**
- **¼ teaspoon cream of tartar**
- **⅔ cup sugar**
  Several drops red *or* green food coloring
- **3 tablespoons grated semisweet chocolate**
- **3 squares (3 ounces) semisweet chocolate, chopped (optional)**
- **1 tablespoon shortening (optional)**

Line 2 cookie sheets with parchment paper, plain brown paper, or foil. Set cookie sheets aside. In a medium mixing bowl beat egg whites, peppermint or mint extract, and cream of tartar with an electric mixer on medium speed till soft peaks form (tips curl). Gradually add sugar, *1 tablespoon* at a time, beating on high speed about 7 minutes or till very stiff peaks form (tips stand straight) and sugar is *almost* dissolved. Beat in food coloring *just till* mixture is tinted. Fold in the 3 tablespoons grated chocolate.

Spoon meringue mixture into a decorating bag fitted with large plain-round tip (about ½-inch opening). Pipe 2-inch-long sticks 1 inch apart on the prepared cookie sheets. *Or,* use a medium star tip (about ¼-inch opening) and pipe stars ½ to ¾ inch in diameter 1 inch apart on the prepared sheets.

Bake meringues in a 300° oven for 10 to 12 minutes or till slightly dry and crisp but not brown. Turn off oven. Then let dry in the oven with door closed for 30 minutes (do not open oven). Peel sticks or stars from paper. Completely cool on a wire rack.

If desired, in a small saucepan heat 3 squares chopped chocolate and shortening over low heat just till melted, stirring occasionally. Dip half of *each* stick or the bottom of *each* star into the melted chocolate, allowing excess chocolate to drip off. Place on waxed paper; let stand till chocolate is set. Makes about 60.

Coconut Macaroons

- **2 egg whites**
- **½ teaspoon vanilla**
- **⅔ cup sugar**
- **1 3½-ounce can flaked coconut (1⅓ cups)**

Grease a cookie sheet. Set cookie sheet aside. In a medium mixing bowl beat egg whites and vanilla with an electric mixer on medium speed till soft peaks form (tips curl). Gradually add sugar, 1 *tablespoon* at a time, beating on high speed about 7 minutes or till very stiff peaks form (tips stand straight) and sugar is *almost* dissolved. Fold in coconut.

Drop coconut mixture from a rounded teaspoon 2 inches apart on the prepared cookie sheet. Bake in a 325° oven for 15 to 20 minutes or till edges are lightly browned. Remove cookies from cookie sheet and cool on a wire rack. Makes about 30.

Storing Hard Meringues

To keep hard meringues crisp, place the cooled meringues in an airtight container and seal. Store at room temperature for 2 to 3 days.

To freeze hard meringues, seal the meringues in an airtight container. Use them within 2 weeks. To thaw, uncover and let stand at room temperature about 30 minutes.

Coffee Meringue Doves

½ **teaspoon instant coffee crystals**
2 **egg whites**
¼ **teaspoon cream of tartar**
½ **cup sugar**
 Miniature semisweet chocolate pieces

Line 2 cookie sheets with parchment paper, plain brown paper, or foil. Set cookie sheets aside. Dissolve coffee crystals in ½ teaspoon *hot water.* In a medium mixing bowl beat dissolved coffee, egg whites, and cream of tartar with an electric mixer on medium speed till soft peaks form (tips curl). Gradually add sugar, *1 tablespoon* at a time, beating on high speed about 7 minutes or till very stiff peaks form (tips stand straight) and sugar is *almost* dissolved.

Spoon meringue mixture into a decorating bag fitted with a large plain-round tip (about ½-inch opening). Pipe doves 2 inches apart on the prepared cookie sheets as directed below. Place 2 chocolate pieces on each head for an eye and a beak. Bake in a 300° oven about 15 minutes or till slightly dry. Turn off oven. Then let meringues dry in the oven with the door closed for 30 minutes (do not open oven).

Peel meringues from paper. Completely cool the meringues on a wire rack. Makes about 24.

▶ *For a dove, pipe a 1-inch-long question mark for the head. For the body, continue piping without lifting the tip, moving the tip 2½ inches to the right. Move tip to the left, almost to the end of the question mark, then to the right again to form the wing tip, releasing pressure as you pull the tip up.*

Secrets to Successful Hard Meringues

Hard meringues are simple to make. However, if your meringues have one of the following problems, here's how to correct it next time.

If meringues are soft, sticky, or gummy:
■ Don't make meringues on a rainy or humid day because baked meringues will not dry properly.
■ Measure the sugar carefully (review Measuring Tips on page 297). Too much sugar can cause gumminess.
■ Check your oven temperature with an oven thermometer. Baking at too high a temperature can cause gumminess.
■ Carefully follow the recipe times for baking and drying. Underbaking and insufficient drying will cause gummy meringues.

If the volume is low and your meringues look curdled:
■ Start adding the sugar to the egg white mixture *as soon as* soft peaks form. At this stage, the tips will bend over in soft curls (see photo, page 195). Underbeating or overbeating the egg white mixture before adding the sugar can result in meringues with low volume.

Orange Meringue Fingers

For a fun look, dip the cookies diagonally into the chocolate.

    2 egg whites
    ¼ teaspoon cream of tartar
    ¼ teaspoon vanilla
    ⅔ cup sugar
    1 tablespoon finely shredded orange peel *or*
          tangerine peel
    ½ cup semisweet chocolate pieces *or* 3 ounces
          orange-colored vanilla-flavored
          confectioners' coating, chopped
    1 tablespoon shortening

Line 2 cookie sheets with parchment paper, plain brown paper, or foil. Set cookie sheets aside.

In a medium mixing bowl beat egg whites, cream of tartar, and vanilla with an electric mixer on medium speed till soft peaks form (tips curl). Gradually add sugar, *1 tablespoon* at a time, beating on high speed about 7 minutes or till very stiff peaks form (tips stand straight) and sugar is *almost* dissolved. Fold in orange or tangerine peel.

Spoon meringue mixture into a decorating bag fitted with a large plain-round tip (about ⅜-inch opening). Pipe 2½-inch-long strips about 2 inches apart on the prepared cookie sheets. Bake in a 300° oven for 13 to 15 minutes or till slightly dry and crisp but not brown. Turn off oven. Then let meringues dry in the oven with the door closed for 30 minutes (do not open oven). Carefully peel meringues from paper. Completely cool meringues on a wire rack.

In a small heavy saucepan place chocolate pieces or confectioners' coating. If using chocolate, add shortening; if using confectioners' coating, *omit* shortening. Cook over low heat just till melted, stirring often.

Dip one end of *each* meringue finger into the melted chocolate or confectioners' coating, allowing the excess to drip off. Place on waxed paper and let stand till chocolate or coating is set. Makes about 48.

Peaches 'n' Cream Meringue Pie

Top with fresh peach slices, whipped cream, and mint sprigs for an elegant yet easy garnish.

    2½ cups chopped, peeled peaches *or* frozen
           unsweetened peach slices, thawed and
           chopped
     1 recipe Nut Meringue Shell (see page 94)
    ⅓ cup sugar
     1 envelope unflavored gelatin
    ½ cup milk
    ½ of an 8-ounce package cream cheese, cubed

Thaw peaches, if frozen. *Do not drain.* Prepare Nut Meringue Shell as directed, *except* spread meringue mixture over a *7-inch* circle on the prepared baking sheet. Bake and cool as directed; set aside.

For filling, in a medium saucepan stir together sugar and gelatin. Add milk. Heat and stir over low heat till gelatin is dissolved. In a blender container or food processor bowl place *half* of the chopped peaches and their juices, *half* of the gelatin mixture, and *half* of the cream cheese. Cover and blend or process till smooth. Transfer mixture to a medium bowl. Repeat with remaining chopped peaches, gelatin mixture, and cream cheese. Cover and chill peach mixture about 30 minutes or till the mixture mounds.

Spoon peach mixture into the meringue shell. Cover and chill about 2 hours or till set. Makes 8 servings.

Let Them Eat Meringue

Legend has it that Marie Antoinette loved meringues so much that she made them herself for the French court. Whether she actually made a meringue herself or not, there's no doubt that this heavenly concoction always has been fit for kings and queens.

COBLERS

First cousin to a deep-dish pie, cobblers have the same bubbly fruit filling but sport a rich biscuit topping. The cobbled or bumpy appearance of the topping gives this favorite fruit dessert its name.

☐ Always use the size dish called for in the recipe. The filling will bubble rather high during baking and the dish needs to allow for this. For extra insurance, place a baking sheet or pizza pan under the baking dish to catch any spills.

☐ So that the bottom of the biscuit topping will cook, the filling must be *hot* when the biscuit mixture is dropped on it. Keep the filling over low heat while mixing the topping, then quickly pour the filling into the baking dish and drop on the biscuit topping.

☐ To check the doneness of cobblers, after the minimum baking time is up, insert a wooden toothpick into the center of one or two of the biscuit mounds. (Don't get the toothpick into the gooey filling.) If the toothpick comes out clean, the cobbler is done.

☐ Serve cobbler warm with a scoop of ice cream or pass a pitcher of light cream so each person can top his or her own dessert.

Cherry Cobbler

½   cup all-purpose flour
1   tablespoon sugar
¾   teaspoon baking powder
3   tablespoons margarine *or* butter
¾   cup sugar
1   tablespoon cornstarch
4   cups fresh *or* frozen unsweetened pitted tart
      red cherries
1   egg
1   tablespoon milk

For biscuit topping, in a medium mixing bowl stir together flour, the 1 tablespoon sugar, baking powder, and ⅛ teaspoon *salt.* Using a pastry blender, cut in *2 tablespoons* of the margarine or butter till the mixture resembles coarse crumbs. Make a well in the center, then set the dry mixture aside.

For filling, in a medium saucepan combine ¾ cup sugar and cornstarch. Add cherries and ⅓ cup *water.* Cook and stir till slightly thickened and bubbly. Stir in remaining margarine. Reduce heat and keep hot.

In a small bowl use a fork to beat together egg and milk. Add egg mixture all at once to dry topping mixture. Using the fork, stir *just till moistened.* Transfer *hot* filling to an ungreased 8x1½-inch round baking dish. *Immediately* spoon topping into 4 mounds on top of filling. Bake in a 400° oven for 20 to 25 minutes or till cobbler tests done. Serve warm. Serves 4.

Blueberry Cobbler: Prepare biscuit topping for Cherry Cobbler as directed above. For blueberry filling, in a medium saucepan stir together ½ cup packed *brown sugar* and 4 teaspoons *cornstarch.* Stir in 4 cups fresh or frozen *blueberries,* 1 cup *water,* and 1 tablespoon *lemon juice.* Cook and stir till thickened and bubbly. Reduce heat and keep hot. Continue as directed above.

Cherry Cobbler

Dried Fruit Cobbler

Tangy, mixed fruit filling tastes like a Swedish fruit soup.

- ½ cup whole wheat flour
- ⅓ cup all-purpose flour
- 2 tablespoons sugar
- 1½ teaspoons baking powder
- ⅛ teaspoon salt
- 3 tablespoons margarine *or* butter
- 1 8-ounce package mixed dried fruit
- 2½ cups apple juice
- ⅛ teaspoon ground nutmeg
- 4 teaspoons cornstarch
- 2 tablespoons water
- 2 tablespoons sugar
- 1 teaspoon vanilla
- ⅓ cup milk
- ¼ cup chopped walnuts

For biscuit topping, in a medium mixing bowl stir together whole wheat flour, all-purpose flour, 2 table-spoons sugar, baking powder, and salt. Using a pastry blender, cut in margarine or butter till the mixture resembles coarse crumbs. Make a well in the center, then set the dry mixture aside.

For filling, using kitchen scissors, snip the dried fruit into bite-size pieces. In a medium saucepan combine dried fruit, apple juice, and nutmeg. Bring to boiling. Cover and reduce heat. Simmer about 10 minutes or till nearly tender. Stir together cornstarch and water. Add to fruit mixture. Cook and stir till thickened and bubbly. Stir in the 2 tablespoons sugar and the vanilla. Reduce heat and keep filling hot.

Add milk all at once to the dry topping mixture. Using a fork, stir *just till moistened.* Transfer *hot* filling to an ungreased 1½-quart casserole. *Immediately* spoon biscuit topping into 6 mounds on top of the filling. Sprinkle walnuts on top of mounds. Bake in a 400° oven for 20 to 25 minutes or till cobbler tests done. Serve warm. Makes 6 servings.

Pear-Orange Cobbler

- 1 cup all-purpose flour
- 2 tablespoons sugar
- 1½ teaspoons baking powder
- 1 teaspoon finely shredded orange peel
- ¼ teaspoon ground nutmeg
- ¼ cup margarine *or* butter
- 1 16-ounce can pear slices
- ⅓ cup orange juice
- ⅓ cup packed brown sugar
- 2 tablespoons all-purpose flour
- ⅛ teaspoon ground ginger
- 1 11-ounce can mandarin orange sections, drained
- 1 egg
- ¼ cup milk
- ¼ cup coconut

For biscuit topping, in a medium mixing bowl stir together the 1 cup all-purpose flour, sugar, baking powder, orange peel, and nutmeg. Using a pastry blender, cut in margarine or butter till the mixture resembles coarse crumbs. Make a well in the center, then set the dry mixture aside.

For filling, drain pears, reserving liquid. Add enough of the reserved pear liquid to orange juice to measure *1½ cups.* Discard the remaining pear liquid. In a medium saucepan combine brown sugar, the 2 tablespoons all-purpose flour, and ginger. Add the orange juice mixture. Cook and stir over medium heat till thickened and bubbly. Stir in pears and orange sections. Reduce heat and keep filling hot.

In a small bowl use a fork to beat together egg and milk. Add egg mixture all at once to the dry topping mixture. Using the fork, stir *just till moistened.* Transfer *hot* filling to an ungreased 10x6x2-inch baking dish. *Immediately* spoon biscuit topping into 6 mounds on top of the hot filling. Sprinkle coconut on top of mounds. Bake in a 400° oven for 20 to 25 minutes or till cobbler tests done. Serve warm. Serves 6.

Whole Wheat Apple-Nut Cobbler

⅓ cup all-purpose flour
¼ cup whole wheat flour
2 tablespoons brown sugar
1 teaspoon baking powder
3 tablespoons margarine *or* butter
2 tablespoons finely chopped walnuts
¾ cup sugar
1 tablespoon all-purpose flour
½ teaspoon ground cinnamon
¼ teaspoon ground nutmeg
5 medium apples, peeled, cored, and sliced (5 cups)
½ cup chopped walnuts
1 tablespoon lemon juice
1 egg
2 tablespoons milk

For biscuit topping, in a medium mixing bowl stir together the ⅓ cup all-purpose flour, the whole wheat flour, brown sugar, and baking powder. Using a pastry blender, cut in margarine or butter till mixture resembles coarse crumbs. Stir in 2 tablespoons walnuts. Make a well in the center. Set dry mixture aside.

For filling, combine the sugar, the 1 tablespoon flour, cinnamon, and nutmeg, then set aside. In a large saucepan combine apples and ⅓ cup *water,* then bring to boiling. Cover and reduce heat. Simmer about 5 minutes or till apples are nearly tender, stirring often. Add cinnamon mixture. Cook and stir till thickened and bubbly. Stir in the ½ cup walnuts and lemon juice. Reduce heat and keep filling hot.

In a small bowl use a fork to beat together egg and milk. Add egg mixture all at once to dry topping mixture. Using the fork, stir *just till moistened.* Transfer *hot* filling to an ungreased 8x8x2-inch baking dish. *Immediately* spoon topping into 6 mounds on top of filling. Bake in a 400° oven for 20 to 25 minutes or till cobbler tests done. Serve warm. Makes 6 servings.

Rhubarb Swirl Cobbler

Some like it sweet, some like it tart. Add sugar to the filling according to your liking.

1 cup all-purpose flour
2 teaspoons baking powder
1 teaspoon sugar
¼ cup margarine *or* butter
¾ to 1 cup sugar
2 tablespoons cornstarch
4 cups fresh *or* frozen unsweetened sliced rhubarb
⅓ cup milk
2 tablespoons strawberry preserves
1 tablespoon sugar
¼ teaspoon ground cinnamon

For biscuit topping, in a medium mixing bowl stir together flour, baking powder, the 1 teaspoon sugar, and ¼ teaspoon *salt.* Using a pastry blender, cut in margarine till the mixture resembles coarse crumbs. Make a well in the center. Set the dry mixture aside.

For filling, in a medium saucepan stir together the ¾ to 1 cup sugar and the cornstarch. Add 1 cup *water.* Cook and stir over medium heat till thickened and bubbly. Add fresh or frozen rhubarb. Cook and stir till boiling. Reduce heat and keep filling hot.

Add milk all at once to the dry topping mixture. Using a fork, stir *just till moistened.* Turn dough out onto a lightly floured surface. Knead dough by gently folding and pressing dough for 10 to 12 strokes or till nearly smooth. Roll dough into a 12x8-inch rectangle, then spread with preserves to within ½ inch of the edges. Roll up, jelly-roll style, starting from one of the short sides. Moisten and seal edges. Cut into 8 slices.

Transfer *hot* filling to an ungreased 2-quart casserole. *Immediately* place biscuit slices, cut sides down, on top of the filling. Stir together the 1 tablespoon sugar and the cinnamon, then sprinkle it on top of biscuit slices. Bake in a 400° oven for 20 to 25 minutes or till biscuits are golden. Serve warm. Serves 8.

BREAD PUDDINGS

The proof of the pudding is in the eating. Try one of these bread puddings and you'll discover why this combination of bread and pudding baked together has been a favorite for generations.

☐ Various breads absorb pudding differently, so it doesn't work to substitute one type of bread for another. For instance, don't use sliced white bread in a recipe that calls for French bread.

☐ Take your choice—either tear or cut the bread into ½-inch pieces or cubes.

☐ You can oven-dry or air-dry the bread cubes. To oven-dry, spread the cubes in a single layer in a baking pan and bake in a 300° oven about 15 minutes or till the cubes are dry, stirring several times. To air-dry, spread the cubes in a single layer in a shallow baking pan and cover with a towel. Let them stand at room temperature for 8 to 12 hours or till the cubes are dry.

☐ To test if bread pudding is done, insert a knife near the center. If the bread pudding doesn't cling to the knife, then it is done.

Caramel-Apple Bread Pudding

Remember how great caramel apples rolled in nuts tasted when you were a kid? Here are the same flavors, but now they're easier to eat.

   4 **eggs**
2¼ **cups milk**
   ½ **cup sugar**
   ½ **teaspoon ground cinnamon**
   ½ **teaspoon vanilla**
   ⅛ **teaspoon ground nutmeg**
   2 **cups dry whole wheat bread cubes**
      (about 3 slices)
   1 **6-ounce package dried apples, snipped**
      Caramel-Nut Sauce

In a large mixing bowl use a rotary beater to beat together eggs, milk, sugar, cinnamon, vanilla, and nutmeg. Set the egg mixture aside.

In an ungreased 8x1½-inch round baking dish toss together dry bread cubes and dried apples. Pour the egg mixture evenly over the bread-apple mixture.

Bake in a 350° oven for 40 to 45 minutes or till the bread pudding tests done. Serve warm with Caramel-Nut Sauce. Makes 6 to 8 servings.

Caramel-Nut Sauce: In a small saucepan melt ¼ cup *margarine or butter*. Stir in ½ cup packed *brown sugar* and 1 tablespoon *light corn syrup*. Cook and stir over medium heat until the mixture comes to a full boil. Stir in ¼ cup *whipping cream*. Return to a full boil. Remove from the heat. Stir in ¼ cup chopped *pecans*. Serve warm. Makes about 1 cup.

Coconut Bread Pudding With Meringue Topper

½ cup light raisins
¼ cup cream sherry
4 cups dry French bread cubes
2½ cups milk
4 egg whites
4 egg yolks
¾ cup sugar
3 tablespoons margarine *or* butter, melted
1 teaspoon vanilla
½ cup coconut
¼ teaspoon cream of tartar
1 cup sifted powdered sugar

In a small bowl combine raisins and sherry. Let stand for 15 minutes. In a large mixing bowl combine bread and milk. Let stand for 10 to 15 minutes or till bread is softened, stirring once or twice. Place egg whites in a large mixing bowl and set aside to bring to room temperature.

In a medium mixing bowl use a rotary beater or fork to beat together egg yolks, sugar, melted margarine or butter, and vanilla. Add the egg yolk mixture, coconut, and raisin mixture to the bread mixture. Gently stir till combined.

Transfer bread-raisin mixture to an ungreased 8x8x2-inch baking pan. Bake in a 350° oven about 45 minutes or till the bread pudding tests done.

Meanwhile, for meringue, add cream of tartar to the egg whites. Beat with an electric mixer on medium speed till soft peaks form (tips curl). Gradually add powdered sugar, *1 tablespoon* at a time, beating on high speed till stiff, glossy peaks form (tips stand straight) and sugar is *completely* dissolved.

Spread meringue over *hot* bread pudding, making swirls and carefully sealing meringue to edges of the pan. Return pan to oven and bake for 10 to 15 minutes or till meringue is golden. Serve warm. Serves 8.

Chocolate Bread Pudding

A hint of cinnamon accents the chocolate flavor.

3 cups dry French bread cubes
2 cups milk
¾ cup sugar
¼ cup unsweetened cocoa powder
½ teaspoon ground cinnamon
2 eggs
1 tablespoon margarine *or* butter, melted
2 teaspoons vanilla
½ cup semisweet chocolate pieces
Unsweetened whipped cream *or* ice cream

In a large mixing bowl combine bread cubes and milk. Let stand for 10 to 15 minutes or till bread is softened, stirring once or twice.

In a small mixing bowl stir together sugar, cocoa powder, and cinnamon. In a medium mixing bowl use a rotary beater to beat together eggs, melted margarine or butter, and vanilla. Add sugar mixture, then beat till combined. Stir in chocolate pieces. Add egg mixture to bread mixture. Gently stir till combined.

Transfer bread-egg mixture to an ungreased 10x6x2-inch baking dish. Bake in a 350° oven for 40 to 45 minutes or till the bread pudding tests done. Serve bread pudding warm with whipped cream or ice cream. Makes 6 to 8 servings.

From Rags to Riches

The origins of bread pudding date back to the 1800s in England. Then it was eaten by the poor to make use of stale bread. Today, we dry the bread on purpose and think of bread pudding as a rich treat.

BAKED FRUITS

Dessert and good nutrition go hand in hand when you choose a baked fruit dessert. The naturally sweet fruit will satisfy that sweet tooth, plus supply fresh flavor, vitamins, and fiber.

☐ For baked fruit, choose apples and pears that will hold their shape when baked. The preferred apples for baking are Red Rome (Rome Beauty), Winesap, Granny Smith, McIntosh, Jonathan, and Golden Delicious. Although most pears work well for baking, some of the preferred varieties are Anjou, Bartlett, and Bosc.

☐ Coring whole fruit is easy if you invest in a long, cylindrical apple corer. With just a twist or two of the corer you can easily remove the core and seeds from apples and pears.

☐ To keep the peel from splitting during baking, use either the peeling edge of an apple corer or a vegetable peeler to remove a strip of the peel around the top of the fruit.

☐ Experiment with different fillings for baked apples and pears. For starters, try granola, chocolate chips, coconut, nuts, or a cinnamon-sugar mixture. Follow the baking times given in the following recipes.

☐ To see if the fruit is done, poke it with a fork. If the fork goes in and comes out easily, the fruit is done. If your apples or pears are larger or smaller than those specified in the recipe, they may take more or less time to bake.

Baked Apples

Apples stuffed with crunchy nuts and sweet raisins or dates make a homey treat.

4 medium baking apples (about 1¼ pounds)
⅓ cup raisins *or* snipped pitted whole dates
¼ cup chopped walnuts
⅓ cup packed brown sugar
⅓ cup water
1 tablespoon margarine *or* butter
½ teaspoon ground cinnamon
½ teaspoon ground nutmeg
Light cream *or* vanilla ice cream

Core apples. Peel off a strip around the top of each apple. Place apples in an ungreased 10x6x2-inch baking dish or a 2-quart casserole. In a small mixing bowl combine the raisins or dates and walnuts. Spoon raisin or date mixture into the centers of the apples.

In a small saucepan stir together brown sugar, water, margarine or butter, cinnamon, and nutmeg. Bring mixture to boiling. Pour the hot sugar mixture over the apples in the baking dish.

Bake in a 350° oven for 40 to 45 minutes or till apples test done, basting occasionally with the sugar mixture. Transfer apples to individual dessert bowls. Spoon the sugar mixture over apples. Serve warm with light cream or ice cream. Makes 4 servings.

Hawaiian-Style Baked Pears

6 medium pears
¼ cup pineapple preserves
2 tablespoons coconut
2 tablespoons chopped slivered almonds
½ cup packed brown sugar
½ cup orange juice
1 tablespoon margarine *or* butter
¼ teaspoon ground allspice
  Light cream

Core pears. Peel off a strip around the top of each pear. *Or,* peel entire pear. Place pears in an ungreased 10x6x2-inch baking dish. In a small mixing bowl stir together preserves, coconut, and almonds. Spoon the preserve mixture into the centers of the pears.

In a small saucepan stir together brown sugar, orange juice, margarine or butter, and allspice. Bring to boiling. Pour hot sugar mixture over pears. Bake in a 350° oven about 45 minutes or till pears test done, basting occasionally with sugar mixture. Transfer pears to individual dessert bowls. Spoon sugar mixture over pears. Serve warm with cream. Serves 6.

Baked Fruit Ambrosia

Toss this easy dessert together in about 10 minutes.

1 cup sliced peeled peaches *or* frozen
    unsweetened peach slices
1 8¾-ounce can unpeeled apricot halves,
    drained
1 cup seedless red grapes
1 cup cubed fresh pineapple *or* one 8¼-ounce
    can pineapple chunks, drained
¼ cup orange juice
2 tablespoons brown sugar
¼ teaspoon finely shredded lemon peel
1 tablespoon apricot brandy (optional)
¼ cup coconut

Thaw peaches, if frozen. *Do not drain.* In an ungreased 1½-quart casserole combine the peaches and their juices, apricots, grapes, and pineapple.

In a small mixing bowl stir together orange juice, brown sugar, and lemon peel. If desired, stir in apricot brandy. Pour juice mixture evenly over fruit. Sprinkle with coconut. Bake in a 425° oven about 15 minutes or till coconut is lightly browned. Serve warm. Makes 4 servings.

Storing Cobblers, Bread Puddings, Baked Fruits, Betties, and Crisps

On the outside chance that you'll have any of these wonderful desserts left over, you'll want to save them to enjoy later. Transfer the leftovers to a smaller casserole or ovenproof dish, cover, and chill. Be sure to quickly refrigerate desserts containing eggs or milk. Plan to serve the leftover dessert within 2 days. If you would like to reheat a cobbler, baked fruit, betty, or crisp, cover it with the casserole lid or foil and bake in a 350° oven till warm in the center.

BETTIES AND CRISPS

Hungry for something homey, warm, and crunchy? This is the place to look. Betties and crisps feature luscious, spicy, fruit fillings and crunchy toppings of bread cubes or an oat crumb mixture.

☐ Betties are made with soft bread cubes rather than dry cubes like bread puddings. Cubing bread for a betty is easier if the bread is frozen. Whether the bread is frozen or not, use a serrated knife and a gentle sawing motion when cutting the bread into the ½-inch cubes.

☐ If you have a special passion for crisps, try mixing a double batch of the topping the next time you make a crisp. Put the extra topping in a freezer bag, and seal, label, and freeze it for up to one month. Then, the next time you want to make a crisp, all you'll have to do is make the filling.

☐ Betties and crisps, like other baked fruit desserts, taste their best when eaten warm, not hot. To serve the dessert at that perfect temperature, let it cool about 30 minutes. If desired, top the warm dessert with vanilla ice cream, whipped cream, or light cream.

Rhubarb-Peach Betty

Complement the fresh-tasting fruit dessert with a dollop of whipped cream.

> 3 cups fresh *or* frozen unsweetened sliced rhubarb
> 2 cups sliced peeled peaches *or* frozen unsweetened peach slices
> 1 cup sugar
> 1 tablespoon all-purpose flour
> ¼ teaspoon salt
> 4 cups soft bread cubes (about 5 slices)
> ⅓ cup margarine *or* butter, melted
> ½ teaspoon finely shredded orange peel

Thaw rhubarb and peaches, if frozen. *Do not drain.* For filling, in a large mixing bowl stir together sugar, flour, and salt. Add rhubarb and peaches and their juices, then gently toss till coated. Add *2 cups* of the bread cubes. Drizzle with *2 tablespoons* of the melted margarine or butter, then toss till mixed. Transfer fruit filling to an ungreased 8x8x2-inch baking dish.

For topping, in a medium mixing bowl combine the remaining bread cubes and orange peel. Drizzle with the remaining melted margarine or butter, then toss till mixed. Sprinkle the bread topping on top of the fruit filling. Bake in a 375° oven for 25 to 35 minutes or till fruit is tender and topping is golden. Serve warm. Makes 6 servings.

Rhubarb-Peach Betty

Raspberry-Pear Betty

3 cups fresh red raspberries *or* one 12-ounce
  package frozen red raspberries
½ cup sugar
1 tablespoon all-purpose flour
¼ teaspoon salt
2 medium pears *or* apples, peeled, cored, and
  thinly sliced (2 cups)
4 cups soft bread cubes (about 5 slices)
2 tablespoons margarine *or* butter, melted

Thaw raspberries, if frozen. *Do not drain.* For filling, in a large mixing bowl stir together sugar, flour,
and salt. Add raspberries and their juices and sliced
pears or apples. Gently toss till coated. Add *2 cups* of
the bread cubes, then toss till mixed. Transfer fruit
filling to an ungreased 8x8x2-inch baking dish.

For topping, place remaining bread cubes in a medium mixing bowl. Drizzle with melted margarine or
butter, then toss till mixed. Sprinkle bread topping on
top of the fruit filling. Bake in a 375° oven for 25 to
35 minutes or till pears or apples are tender and topping is golden. Serve warm. Makes 6 servings.

Cones of Sugar

Sugar is such a basic ingredient in our
kitchens, it's hard to imagine baking without
it. However, early Americans considered sugar
a luxury to be used sparingly.
  In those days, sugar was imported from the
West Indies and sold in cones wrapped in
blue paper. (Enterprising homemakers saved
the blue paper to make blue dye.) The cones
were so hard that special tools were needed to
break them up. Indeed, a mortar and a pestle
were used to pulverize the sugar before it
could be used in baking.

Cherry-Orange Betty

Coconut and pecans dress up the topping.

5 cups fresh *or* frozen unsweetened pitted tart
  red cherries
2 medium oranges
1 cup sugar
2 tablespoons all-purpose flour
4 cups soft bread cubes (about 5 slices)
¼ cup margarine *or* butter, melted
¼ cup coconut
¼ cup chopped pecans

Thaw cherries, if frozen. *Do not drain.* Finely shred
½ teaspoon orange peel from the oranges, then set
shredded peel aside. Peel and section* oranges, then
set orange sections aside.

For filling, in a large mixing bowl stir together orange peel, sugar, flour, and ¼ teaspoon *salt.* Add
cherries and their juices and orange sections. Gently
toss till coated. Add *2 cups* of the bread cubes. Drizzle
with *2 tablespoons* of the melted margarine or butter,
then toss till mixed. Transfer the fruit filling to an ungreased 8x8x2-inch baking dish.

For topping, in a medium mixing bowl combine
the remaining bread cubes, coconut, and pecans.
Drizzle with the remaining melted margarine, then
toss till mixed. Sprinkle bread topping on top of the
fruit filling. Bake in a 375° oven for 25 to 35 minutes
or till topping is golden. Serve warm. Serves 6.

*To section an orange, first cut off the peel and all of
the white membrane. Over a bowl, use a thin sharp
knife to cut toward the center of the orange between
one section and the membrane. Then turn the knife
and slide it along the other side of the section next to
the membrane, pushing out the orange section. Repeat with the remaining sections. Remove any seeds.

Rhubarb Crisp

- **4 cups fresh *or* frozen unsweetened sliced rhubarb**
- **¼ cup rolled oats**
- **¼ cup packed brown sugar**
- **2 tablespoons all-purpose flour**
- **2 tablespoons margarine *or* butter**
- **½ cup sugar**
- **2 tablespoons all-purpose flour**
- **½ teaspoon ground cinnamon**
- **¼ cup orange juice *or* apple juice**

Thaw rhubarb, if frozen. *Do not drain.* For topping, in a small mixing bowl stir together the oats, brown sugar, and the 2 tablespoons flour. Using a pastry blender, cut in margarine or butter till the mixture resembles coarse crumbs. Set topping aside.

For filling, in a large mixing bowl stir together sugar, the 2 tablespoons flour, and cinnamon. Add rhubarb and its juices and orange or apple juice. Gently toss till coated. Transfer filling to an ungreased 8x1½-inch round baking dish.

Sprinkle topping on the filling. Bake in a 375° oven for 30 to 40 minutes or till the rhubarb is tender and topping is golden. Serve warm. Makes 4 servings.

Cranberry-Apple Crisp

Cranberry sauce gives a new twist to a favorite dessert. (Pictured on pages 92–93.)

- **½ cup rolled oats**
- **⅓ cup packed brown sugar**
- **¼ cup all-purpose flour**
- **½ teaspoon ground cinnamon**
- **¼ cup margarine *or* butter**
- **½ cup chopped walnuts**
- **3 medium apples, peeled, cored, and sliced (3 cups)**
- **1 16-ounce can whole cranberry sauce**
  Whipped cream, vanilla ice cream, *or* light cream (optional)
  Apple slices, halved (optional)

For topping, in a medium mixing bowl stir together rolled oats, brown sugar, flour, and cinnamon. Using a pastry blender, cut in margarine or butter till mixture resembles coarse crumbs. Stir in the chopped walnuts. Set topping aside.

For filling, in a large mixing bowl stir together 3 cups apple slices and cranberry sauce. Transfer filling to an ungreased 8x8x2-inch baking dish.

Sprinkle the topping on the filling. Bake in a 375° oven for 30 to 40 minutes or till apples are tender and topping is golden. Serve warm. If desired, top with whipped cream, ice cream, or light cream, and garnish with halved apple slices. Makes 6 servings.

Cherry-Apple Crisp

Crunchy granola makes an easy, no-mix topping.

> 3 cups fresh *or* frozen unsweetened pitted tart red cherries
> ⅓ cup sugar
> 2 tablespoons all-purpose flour
> ½ teaspoon ground cinnamon
> 3 medium apples, peeled, cored, and thinly sliced (3 cups)
> 1½ cups granola

Thaw cherries, if frozen. *Do not drain.* For filling, in a large mixing bowl stir together sugar, flour, and cinnamon. Add cherries and their juices and apples. Gently toss till coated. Transfer filling to an ungreased 8x1½-inch round baking dish.

Sprinkle granola on the filling. Bake in a 375° oven about 30 minutes or till the apples are tender. Serve warm. Makes 6 servings.

Mini Crisps

If you're cooking for only two or three, you may prefer to divide the crisp recipes in this book in half. If so, use an 8x4x2-inch loaf dish. Bake the crisp about 5 minutes less than the time given in the recipe or until the fruit is tender and the topping is golden.

Apple-Raisin Crisp

> ½ cup raisins
> ½ cup rolled oats
> ½ cup packed brown sugar
> ¼ cup all-purpose flour
> ½ teaspoon ground cinnamon
> ¼ cup margarine *or* butter
> ½ cup chopped pecans
> 6 medium apples, peeled, cored, and sliced (6 cups)
> 2 tablespoons sugar

In a small mixing bowl pour enough *boiling water* over the raisins to cover them. Let stand for 5 minutes, then drain raisins.

For topping, in a medium mixing bowl stir together rolled oats, brown sugar, flour, and cinnamon. Using a pastry blender, cut in margarine or butter till mixture resembles coarse crumbs. Stir in chopped pecans. Set topping aside.

For filling, in large mixing bowl combine drained raisins, sliced apples, and sugar, then gently toss till combined. Transfer the filling to an ungreased 9x9x2-inch baking pan.

Sprinkle the topping on the filling. Bake in a 375° oven for 30 to 35 minutes or till the apples are tender and topping is golden. Serve warm. Makes 6 servings.

Peach-Pineapple Crisp

Macaroon-almond topping transforms a traditional peach crisp into an elegant dessert.

- 3 cups sliced peeled peaches *or* frozen unsweetened peach slices
- 1½ cups crumbled soft macaroon cookies (6 *or* 7 cookies)
- ¼ cup chopped almonds, toasted
- 3 tablespoons margarine *or* butter, melted
- 1 15¼-ounce can pineapple chunks, drained, *or* one 16-ounce can pear slices, drained
- 2 tablespoons sugar
- 2 tablespoons amaretto

Thaw peaches, if frozen. *Do not drain.* For topping, in a medium bowl stir together the crumbled macaroons, chopped almonds, and melted margarine or butter. Set topping aside.

For filling, in a large mixing bowl stir together the peaches and their juices, drained pineapple chunks or pear slices, sugar, and amaretto. Transfer filling to an ungreased 1½-quart casserole.

Sprinkle the topping on the filling. Bake in a 350° oven for 30 to 35 minutes or till the topping is golden. Serve warm. Makes 6 servings.

Blueberry Crisp

- 4 cups fresh *or* frozen blueberries
- 1½ cups granola
- ⅓ cup coconut
- 2 tablespoons margarine *or* butter, melted
- ¼ cup sugar
- 1 tablespoon lemon juice
- ¼ teaspoon ground cinnamon

Thaw blueberries, if frozen. *Do not drain.* For topping, in a medium mixing bowl stir together granola, coconut, and margarine or butter. Set topping aside.

For filling, in a large mixing bowl stir together blueberries and their juices, sugar, lemon juice, and cinnamon. Transfer the filling to an ungreased 10x6x2-inch baking dish.

Sprinkle the topping on the filling. Bake in a 375° oven for 30 to 40 minutes or till the topping is crisp. Serve warm. Makes 6 servings.

Whipped Cream On Call

You don't need to get out the beaters each time you want whipped cream for a warm fruit dessert. Instead, when you have whipped cream left over, freeze it for another time.

Spoon the extra whipped cream into mounds on a baking sheet lined with waxed paper. Freeze till firm, then transfer the mounds to a container; seal, label, and freeze. Use the cream within 1 month.

When you want to use the frozen whipped cream, remove the number of mounds you need and let them stand at room temperature for 5 minutes.

CUSTARDS

Smooth and creamy, warm or chilled, custard goes from simple to exotic fare. Whether you're in the mood for a dish of plain custard or a caramel-coated flan, you'll find one in this section that's sure to please.

☐ The secret to a smooth custard is how you beat the eggs. Beat the eggs *just till* the egg yolks and whites are blended. Don't beat until foamy or your custard will have bubbles on the surface.

☐ If you're tempted to skip the hot water bath when baking the custard, don't. The hot water helps to even out the heat so the custard cooks slowly without overcooking the edges.

☐ When testing to see if the custard is done, insert a clean knife ½ inch into the custard about 1 inch from the center. If the knife comes out clean, the custard is done. If any of the custard clings to the knife, bake the custard a few more minutes and test it again.

☐ Once the custard tests done, remove it from the water immediately. If it stays in the hot water, the custard will continue to cook. Be careful not to drip the hot water on yourself as you lift the mold from the water.

☐ To unmold a custard, run a knife around the edges. Then slip the tip of the knife down the side of the mold to let in air. Invert a plate over the custard, and turn the mold and plate over together. Lift off the mold.

☐ As soon as the custard is cooled, cover it and place it in the refrigerator till serving time. Baked custard should be served within 2 or 3 days. Freezing custards is not recommended.

Coconut Cream Flan

¾ cup flaked coconut
2 tablespoons sliced almonds
½ cup sugar
4 eggs
1¾ cups light cream *or* milk
⅓ cup cream of coconut
⅓ cup sugar
¼ teaspoon almond extract
Edible violas and pansies (see tip, page 123)

Spread coconut in a thin layer in a large baking pan. Spread almonds in small baking pan. Bake both in a 350° oven 5 to 10 minutes or till golden, stirring once or twice; set aside.

To caramelize sugar, in a heavy 8-inch skillet cook the ½ cup sugar over medium-high heat (*do not stir*) till sugar begins to melt, shaking the skillet occasionally. Reduce heat to low and cook about 5 minutes more or till sugar is golden brown, stirring frequently. Remove the skillet from the heat and immediately pour caramelized sugar into an 8x1½-inch round baking pan. Holding baking pan with potholders, quickly rotate pan to coat bottom and sides evenly.

In a large mixing bowl use a rotary beater or wire whisk to lightly beat eggs *just till mixed*. Stir in light cream or milk, cream of coconut, ⅓ cup sugar, and almond extract. Fold in *½ cup* of the toasted coconut.

Place caramel-coated pan in a 13x9x2-inch baking dish or pan; set on the oven rack. Pour egg mixture into caramel-coated pan. Pour *boiling or hottest tap water* into the 13x9x2-inch dish or pan to a depth of 1 inch. Bake in a 325° oven for 50 to 55 minutes or till flan tests done. Remove pan with flan from water. Cool on a wire rack. Cover and chill at least 4 hours.

To serve, unmold flan onto a serving plate with sides. Spoon any sugar that remains in pan on top of flan. Sprinkle with remaining coconut and almonds. Garnish with violas and pansies. Serves 6 to 8.

Coconut Cream Flan

Cream Cheese Fruited Flan

Caramelized sugar coats each bite of smooth, rich custard. (Pictured on pages 92–93.)

⅓ cup sugar
1 14-ounce can (1¼ cups) *sweetened condensed* milk
1 8-ounce package cream cheese, softened
6 slightly beaten eggs
1¾ cups water
1 teaspoon vanilla
 Sliced strawberries, sliced bananas, and sliced, halved, peeled kiwi fruit

To caramelize sugar, in a heavy 8-inch skillet cook sugar over medium-high heat (*do not stir*) till sugar begins to melt, shaking the skillet occasionally. Reduce heat to low and cook about 5 minutes more or till sugar is golden brown, stirring frequently.

Remove skillet from heat and immediately pour caramelized sugar into an ungreased 6½-cup metal ring mold (9 inches in diameter). Holding mold with potholders, quickly rotate mold to coat bottom and sides.

In a large mixing bowl beat condensed milk and cream cheese with an electric mixer on low to medium speed till smooth. Stir in eggs, water, and vanilla.

Place ring mold in a 15½x10½x2-inch baking pan, then set pan on the oven rack. Pour egg mixture into the mold. Pour *boiling or hottest tap water* into the pan around the mold to a depth of 1 inch. Bake in a 325° oven for 55 to 60 minutes or till the flan tests done. Remove the ring mold from water in the pan. Cool the flan in the ring mold on a wire rack. Then cover and chill for at least 4 hours.

To serve, unmold flan onto a serving plate with sides. Spoon any caramelized sugar that remains in mold on top of flan. Pile sliced fruit in the center and around the edges of the flan. Makes 12 servings.

Baked Custards

Just four basic ingredients make a wonderful dessert.

3 eggs
1½ cups milk
⅓ cup sugar
1 teaspoon vanilla
 Ground nutmeg *or* cinnamon (optional)

In a 4-cup measuring cup or medium mixing bowl use a rotary beater or wire whisk to lightly beat eggs *just till mixed*. Stir in milk, sugar, and vanilla.

Place 4 ungreased 6-ounce custard cups or one 3½-cup soufflé dish in an 8x8x2-inch baking dish; set on the oven rack. Pour egg mixture evenly into cups or soufflé dish. If desired, sprinkle with nutmeg or cinnamon. Pour *boiling or hottest tap water* into the baking dish around cups or soufflé dish to a depth of 1 inch. Bake in a 325° oven for 30 to 45 minutes for cups (50 to 60 minutes for soufflé dish) or till custards test done. Remove cups or soufflé dish from water. Cool on a wire rack. Serve warm or chilled. If desired, unmold custards from cups. Makes 4 servings.

Caramel Flans: Prepare Baked Custards as above, *except* use custard cups. In a heavy 8-inch skillet cook ⅓ cup *sugar* over medium-high heat (*do not stir*) till sugar begins to melt, shaking skillet often. Reduce heat to low and cook about 5 minutes or till golden brown, stirring frequently. Remove from heat. Immediately divide caramelized sugar among cups; tilt cups to coat bottoms. Let stand 10 minutes. Add egg mixture. Bake; cool as directed above. Unmold to serve.

Baked Rice Pudding: Prepare Baked Custards as directed above, *except* stir 1 cup *cooked rice* and ½ cup *raisins* into egg mixture. Pour into an ungreased 1½-quart casserole. Bake in a 325° oven 45 to 55 minutes or till it tests done, stirring after 30 minutes. Continue as above. Serves 6.

Custards with Apricot Flummery

Flummery, an old-fashioned name for a thickened fruit, describes the warm apricot sauce that's often served over chilled custards.

- 4 **eggs**
- 2 **cups milk**
- ½ **cup sugar**
- 1 **teaspoon rose water** *or* **2 teaspoons vanilla**
  Apricot Flummery

In a medium mixing bowl use a rotary beater or wire whisk to lightly beat eggs *just till mixed.* Stir in milk, sugar, and rose water or vanilla.

Place 6 ungreased 6-ounce custard cups in a 13x9x2-inch baking pan, then set pan on the oven rack. Pour egg mixture evenly into the cups. Pour *boiling or hottest tap water* into the pan around the cups to a depth of 1 inch.

Bake in a 325° oven for 30 to 40 minutes or till the custards test done. Remove custard cups from the water in the pan. Cool custard in cups on a wire rack. Cover and chill for at least 1 hour.

To serve, unmold custards into individual dessert bowls. Spoon warm Apricot Flummery on top of the chilled custards. Makes 6 servings.

Apricot Flummery: In a medium saucepan stir together ⅓ cup *sugar* and 1 tablespoon *corn-starch.* Stir in one 5⅓-ounce can *apricot nectar* (⅔ cup). Cook and stir over medium heat till thickened and bubbly. Stir in one 16-ounce can unpeeled *apricot halves,* drained and chopped, *or* 1 pound *apricots* (10 to 12), peeled, pitted, and chopped (2 cups). Cook and stir for 2 minutes. Serve warm. Cover and chill any remaining sauce. Makes about 1¾ cups.

Orange Custards

- 4 **eggs**
- 2 **cups milk**
- ½ **cup sugar**
- 2 **tablespoons orange liqueur** *or* ½ **teaspoon**
  orange extract
- ½ **cup whipping cream**
- 2 **teaspoons sugar**

In a medium mixing bowl use a rotary beater or wire whisk to beat eggs *just till mixed.* Stir in milk, the ½ cup sugar, *1 tablespoon* of the orange liqueur or *¼ teaspoon* orange extract, and ⅛ teaspoon *salt.*

Place 6 ungreased 6-ounce custard cups in a 13x9x2-inch baking pan, then set pan on the oven rack. Pour egg mixture evenly into the custard cups. Pour *boiling or hottest tap water* into the pan around the cups to a depth of 1 inch.

Bake in a 325° oven for 30 to 45 minutes or till custards test done. Remove custard cups from water in the pan. Cool custard in cups on a wire rack. Cover and chill for at least 1 hour.

In a small mixing bowl beat whipping cream, the remaining liqueur or orange extract, and 2 teaspoons sugar till soft peaks form. Spoon on custards. Serves 6.

Coffee with Dessert

When you serve coffee with dessert, it's probably because of the Boston Tea Party. You may be surprised to learn that this event launched coffee as America's favorite beverage. Because of the shortage of tea and as a political protest, Americans began drinking coffee rather than traditional English tea.

HISTORY OF BAKING

CHEESECAKES

Which cheesecake is the ultimate cheesecake? Is it a creamy, heavy cheesecake, or one made of ricotta cheese, or a double chocolate one? You'll want to sample each recipe in this section before making up your mind.

☐ *Gently* beat the cheesecake batter. Overbeating incorporates too much air and causes the cheesecake to puff up, then fall and crack.

☐ If you use a portable electric mixer to mix the cheesecake filling and notice that the mixer strains or gets hot, finish the mixing by hand.

☐ A springform pan may leak, so place it on a shallow baking pan, such as a pizza pan with edges, to prevent a spill in the oven.

☐ Gently shake the cheesecake to see if it is done. The center should appear *nearly* set. A 1-inch area in the center will jiggle slightly when the cheesecake is done (this area will firm after cooling). A knife test does not work when checking the doneness of cheesecakes because the knife makes a crack. Also, if there is sour cream in the batter, the knife will not come out clean even when the cheesecake is done.

☐ Don't bother to remove the cheesecake from the bottom of the springform pan. Just set it on a serving plate and garnish around the edge with edible flowers, fresh fruit, or whipped cream.

Double Chocolate-Almond Cheesecake

For an extra boost of flavor, toast the almonds before grinding them.

  2 **teaspoons margarine *or* butter**
  ¾ **cup ground almonds**
 16 **ounces white baking bar with cocoa butter, chopped**
  4 **8-ounce packages cream cheese, softened**
  ½ **cup margarine *or* butter, softened**
  3 **tablespoons milk**
  1 **tablespoon vanilla**
     Dash salt
  4 **eggs**
  1 **egg yolk**
  4 **1½-ounce bars milk chocolate with almonds, chopped**
     Chocolate curls (optional)

Use the 2 teaspoons margarine or butter to grease bottom and sides of a 10-inch springform pan. Press ground almonds onto the bottom of the springform pan. Set pan aside.

For filling, in a heavy medium saucepan heat and stir the white baking bar over low heat *just till melted*. In a large mixing bowl beat melted baking bar, cream cheese, the ½ cup margarine or butter, milk, vanilla, and salt with an electric mixer on medium to high speed till combined. Add whole eggs and egg yolk all at once. Beat on low speed *just till combined*. Stir in chopped milk chocolate.

Pour filling into the prepared springform pan. Bake cheesecake on a shallow baking pan in a 375° oven for 45 to 50 minutes or till cheesecake tests done.

Cool cheesecake in springform pan on a wire rack for 10 minutes. Using a small metal spatula, loosen cheesecake from sides of the springform pan. Cool for 30 minutes more. Remove sides of the springform pan. Cool completely, then chill at least 4 hours. If desired, garnish with chocolate curls. Makes 16 servings.

Cheesecake Supreme

1¾ cups finely crushed graham crackers
¼ cup finely chopped walnuts
½ teaspoon ground cinnamon
½ cup margarine *or* butter, melted
3 8-ounce packages cream cheese, softened
1 cup sugar
2 tablespoons all-purpose flour
1 teaspoon vanilla
½ teaspoon finely shredded lemon peel
   (optional)
2 eggs
1 egg yolk
¼ cup milk
1 recipe Fruit Sauce (see recipe at right)
   (optional)

For crust, in a medium mixing bowl combine crushed crackers, nuts, and cinnamon. Stir in melted margarine or butter. If desired, reserve ¼ *cup* of the crumb mixture for topping. Press remaining crumb mixture onto the bottom and about 2 inches up the sides of an 8- or 9-inch springform pan. Set pan aside.

For filling, in a large bowl beat cream cheese, sugar, flour, vanilla, and, if desired, lemon peel with an electric mixer on medium to high speed till combined. Add whole eggs and yolk all at once. Beat on low speed *just till combined.* Stir in milk.

Pour filling into the crust-lined springform pan. If desired, sprinkle with reserved crumbs. Bake cheesecake on a shallow baking pan in a 375° oven for 45 to 50 minutes for the 8-inch pan (35 to 40 minutes for the 9-inch pan) or till cheesecake tests done.

Cool cheesecake in springform pan on a wire rack for 15 minutes. Using a small metal spatula, loosen crust from sides of pan. Cool for 30 minutes more. Remove sides of the springform pan. Cool cheesecake completely, then chill for at least 4 hours. If desired, serve with Fruit Sauce. Makes 12 to 16 servings.

Sour Cream Cheesecake: Prepare Cheesecake Supreme as directed at left, *except* reduce cream cheese to *2 packages* and omit the milk. Add three 8-ounce cartons dairy *sour cream* with the eggs. Bake about 55 minutes for the 8-inch pan (about 50 minutes for the 9-inch pan).

Liqueur Cheesecake: Prepare Cheesecake Supreme as directed at left, *except* substitute ¼ cup *white crème de menthe, crème de cacao, amaretto, or coffee liqueur* for the milk.

Chocolate Swirl Cheesecake: Prepare Cheesecake Supreme at left, *except* omit lemon peel. Stir 2 squares (2 ounces) *semisweet chocolate,* melted and cooled, into *half* of the filling. Gently pour *half* of plain filling into the crust-lined pan; pour in *half* of the chocolate filling. Repeat layers. Use a narrow spatula to gently swirl batters.

Fruit Sauce

½ teaspoon finely shredded orange peel
¼ cup orange juice
1 tablespoon cornstarch
¼ teaspoon ground cinnamon
1 8- to 8¾-ounce can fruit (unpeeled apricot halves, pitted light sweet cherries, peach slices, crushed pineapple, *or* fruit cocktail) *or* one 10-ounce package frozen red raspberries *or* strawberries, thawed

In a small saucepan stir together orange peel, orange juice, cornstarch, and cinnamon. Stir in *undrained* fruit (cut up any large pieces). Cook and stir till thickened and bubbly. Cook and stir for 2 minutes more. Serve warm or cool. Makes 1⅓ cups.

Hazelnut Chocolate Cheesecake

For a plain chocolate cheesecake, omit the liqueur and increase the milk to ¼ cup.

2   teaspoons margarine *or* butter
1   cup finely ground hazelnuts (filberts)
3   8-ounce packages cream cheese, softened
1   cup sugar
4   squares (4 ounces) semisweet chocolate,
      melted and cooled
2   tablespoons all-purpose flour
⅛   teaspoon salt
4   eggs
2   tablespoons milk
2   tablespoons hazelnut *or* coffee liqueur
1   teaspoon vanilla
      Chocolate leaves (see page 301) (optional)
      Chocolate-dipped hazelnuts (see page 301)
      (optional)

Use margarine or butter to grease the bottom and 1¾ inches up the sides of a 9-inch springform pan. Press ground hazelnuts (filberts) onto the bottom and 1¾ inches up the sides of the greased springform pan. Set springform pan aside.

For filling, in a large mixing bowl beat cream cheese, sugar, melted chocolate, flour, and salt with an electric mixer on medium to high speed till combined. Add eggs all at once. Beat on low speed *just till combined.* Stir in milk, hazelnut or coffee liqueur, and vanilla.

Pour filling into the crust-lined springform pan. Bake on a shallow baking pan in a 325° oven for 45 to 50 minutes or till cheesecake tests done.

Cool cheesecake in the springform pan on a wire rack for 10 minutes. Using a small metal spatula, loosen crust from sides of pan. Cool for 30 minutes more. Remove sides of the springform pan. Cool cheesecake completely, then chill for at least 2 hours. If desired, garnish with chocolate leaves and chocolate-dipped hazelnuts. Makes 12 to 16 servings.

Secrets to Successful Cheesecakes

A perfect cheesecake is not only delicious but also creamy and attractive. If your cheesecake has one of the following problems, here's what to do next time.

If the texture of your cheesecake is dry and the center has fallen:
■ Test the cheesecake for doneness at the minimum baking time to avoid overbaking.

If your cheesecake has large cracks:
■ Be sure to beat the filling *gently* after adding the eggs, and stir in the remaining ingredients by hand. Vigorous beating will incorporate too much air, which causes the cheesecake to puff up, then fall and crack.
■ Check the doneness by gently shaking the pan rather than inserting a knife. If a knife is inserted, the hole may grow into a large crack.
■ Set a minute timer for the exact cooling time given in the recipe. When it rings, follow the recipe directions for loosening the crust of the cheesecake from the sides of the pan. If you don't loosen the crust from the pan when the recipe specifies, the cheesecake may begin to pull away from the sides and crack.

Hazelnut Chocolate Cheesecake

Cheesecake and Brandied Berry Sauce

The ruby red cranberry sauce adds a festive touch for a holiday dessert. (Pictured on pages 92–93.)

 ¾ **cup all-purpose flour**
 3 **tablespoons sugar**
1½ **teaspoons finely shredded orange peel**
 6 **tablespoons margarine *or* butter**
 1 **beaten egg yolk**
 1 **teaspoon margarine *or* butter**
 3 **8-ounce packages cream cheese, softened**
 1 **cup sugar**
 2 **tablespoons all-purpose flour**
 1 **teaspoon vanilla**
 2 **eggs**
 1 **egg yolk**
 ¼ **cup milk**
  Brandied Berry Sauce
  Edible geranium blossoms (see tip, page 123)

For crust, in a medium mixing bowl stir together the ¾ cup flour, the 3 tablespoons sugar, and *1 teaspoon* of the orange peel. Using a pastry blender, cut in the 6 tablespoons margarine or butter till mixture resembles coarse crumbs. Stir in the one beaten egg yolk. Remove sides from an 8-inch springform pan. Press about *one-third* of the dough onto the bottom of the pan. Cover the remaining dough and set aside.

Bake bottom crust in a 375° oven about 7 minutes or till golden. Cool crust on springform pan bottom on a wire rack. Use the 1 teaspoon margarine or butter to grease 1½ inches up sides of springform pan. Attach sides to bottom of springform pan. Press remaining dough 1½ inches up sides of pan; set aside.

For filling, in a large mixing bowl beat cream cheese, the 1 cup sugar, 2 tablespoons flour, vanilla, and remaining orange peel with an electric mixer on medium to high speed till combined. Add whole eggs and one egg yolk all at once. Beat on low speed *just till combined.* Stir in milk. Pour filling into crust-lined springform pan. Bake on a shallow pan in a 375° oven for 45 to 50 minutes or till done.

Cool cheesecake in springform pan on a wire rack for 15 minutes. Using a small metal spatula, loosen crust from sides of pan. Cool for 30 minutes more. Remove sides of the springform pan. Cool completely, then chill at least 4 hours. To serve, spoon a little Brandied Berry Sauce on the cheesecake. Garnish with flowers. Pass remaining sauce. Serves 12.

Brandied Berry Sauce: In a small saucepan combine 1½ cups *cranberries,* 1 cup *sugar,* ½ cup *orange juice,* and dash ground *cloves.* Bring mixture to boiling, then reduce heat to medium. Simmer, uncovered, till cranberries pop. Stir together 1 tablespoon *cornstarch* and 1 tablespoon *cold water;* stir into cranberry mixture. Cook and stir till thickened and bubbly, then cook and stir for 2 minutes more. Stir in 2 tablespoons *blackberry brandy or brandy.* Cool to room temperature. Makes about 1¾ cups.

Storing Cheesecake

Have you ever hesitated to make a cheesecake because you might not be able to serve all 12 pieces at once? Go ahead and make that cheesecake, enjoy some today, and stash the extra for another day.

To refrigerate cheesecake, cover it and keep it refrigerated for up to 3 days.

To freeze cheesecake, seal a whole cheesecake or pieces in *heavy* foil or an airtight container. Plan on using a whole cheesecake within 1 month and individual pieces within 2 weeks. To serve, loosen the covering and thaw a whole cheesecake in the refrigerator for 24 hours or thaw individual pieces at room temperature for 2 hours.

Peaches 'n' Cream Cheesecake

Equally delicious with either peaches or apricots.

1½ **cups finely crushed graham crackers**
¼ **cup ground walnuts** *or* **pecans**
⅓ **cup margarine** *or* **butter, melted**
1 **10-ounce jar peach** *or* **apricot preserves**
¼ **cup peach nectar** *or* **apricot nectar**
3 **8-ounce packages cream cheese, softened**
¾ **cup sugar**
2 **tablespoons all-purpose flour**
3 **eggs**
½ **cup whipping cream**
1 **tablespoon powdered sugar (optional)**
2 **teaspoons lemon juice (optional)**
1 **medium peach, peeled, pitted, and sliced (optional)**

For crust, in a medium bowl stir together crushed crackers and nuts. Stir in melted margarine or butter. Press crumb mixture onto the bottom and about 2 inches up the sides of an 8- or 9-inch springform pan. Set springform pan aside.

In a small saucepan combine peach or apricot preserves and peach or apricot nectar. Cook and stir over low heat about 5 minutes or till preserves are melted. Set preserve mixture aside.

For filling, in a large mixing bowl beat cream cheese, sugar, and flour with an electric mixer on medium to high speed till combined. Add eggs all at once. Beat on low speed *just till combined.* Stir in preserve mixture. Pour filling into the crust-lined springform pan. Bake on a shallow baking pan in a 375° oven for 40 to 45 minutes or till done.

Cool cheesecake in springform pan on a wire rack for 15 minutes. Using a small metal spatula, loosen crust from sides of pan. Cool for 30 minutes more. Remove sides of springform pan. Cool cheesecake completely, then chill for at least 4 hours.

To serve, in a small mixing bowl beat whipping cream till soft peaks form. Spoon whipped cream in mounds on top of cheesecake. If desired, in a small mixing bowl stir together powdered sugar and lemon juice. Add peach slices and toss till coated. Arrange peach slices on whipped cream. Serves 12 to 16.

Garnishing with Edible Flowers

Gaily colored blossoms make an exquisite, yet easy, garnish. Be sure to use only edible flowers around food whether you plan to eat them or not. To be edible, the flower must be a nontoxic variety and free of any chemicals.

Some favorite edible flowers are the rose, viola, pansy, calendula (pot marigold), daylily, nasturtium, violet, chamomile, bachelor's button, carnation, geranium blossom (not leaf), and magnolia. If in doubt whether a variety of a flower's blossom, stem, or leaf is edible, check with your local poison control center or state extension service.

To find flowers for decorating food, you need to look no further than your own garden, if you and your neighbors do not use chemicals. Pick the flowers just before using, rinse, and gently pat dry.

Flowers from a florist usually are treated with chemicals and should not be used. A local source may be an herb garden, restaurant supplier, or produce supplier who specializes in edible flowers. You also can get flowers from mail-order flower and herb farms.

123

Coconut-Ricotta Cheesecake

½ cup all-purpose flour
3 tablespoons sugar
¼ cup margarine *or* butter
1 beaten egg yolk
1 cup flaked coconut
1 15-ounce carton ricotta cheese
1 8-ounce package cream cheese, softened
¼ teaspoon vanilla
1 cup sugar
2 tablespoons all-purpose flour
3 eggs
¼ cup milk
1 8-ounce carton dairy sour cream
¼ cup flaked coconut, toasted

For crust, in a bowl combine the ½ cup flour and *2 tablespoons* of the sugar. Using a pastry blender, cut in margarine or butter till crumbly. Stir in 1 egg yolk and 1 cup coconut. Press dough onto bottom and 1¾ inches up sides of an 8-inch springform pan. Bake in a 375° oven 15 minutes or till golden. Cool on a rack.

For filling, in a large mixing bowl beat ricotta cheese, cream cheese, and vanilla with an electric mixer on medium to high speed till combined. Add the 1 cup sugar, 2 tablespoons flour, and ⅛ teaspoon *salt.* Beat till combined. Add 3 whole eggs all at once. Beat on low speed *just till combined.* Stir in milk.

Pour filling into the crust-lined springform pan. Bake cheesecake on a shallow baking pan in a 375° oven about 45 minutes or till cheesecake tests done.

Meanwhile, in a small bowl stir together sour cream and remaining 1 tablespoon sugar. Remove spring-form pan from oven. Immediately spread sour cream mixture on top of cheesecake. Cool cheesecake in the springform pan on a wire rack for 15 minutes. Using a small metal spatula, loosen crust from sides of pan. Cool for 30 minutes more. Remove sides of pan. Cool cheesecake completely. Chill for at least 4 hours. Sprinkle with toasted coconut. Makes 12 servings.

Pumpkin Cheesecake Squares

With this spicy combination you'll satisfy the traditionalist who wants only pumpkin pie for the holiday dinner as well as those who want something new.

1 cup finely crushed graham crackers
2 tablespoons sugar
2 tablespoons margarine *or* butter, melted
1 8-ounce package cream cheese, softened
1 3-ounce package cream cheese, softened
½ cup sugar
1 cup canned pumpkin
1½ teaspoons pumpkin pie spice
½ teaspoon vanilla
⅛ teaspoon salt
3 eggs
¾ cup light cream *or* milk
1 8-ounce carton dairy sour cream
1 tablespoon sugar

For crust, in a small mixing bowl stir together crushed crackers and the 2 tablespoons sugar. Stir in melted margarine or butter. Press crumb mixture evenly onto the bottom of an 8x8x2-inch baking dish. Set baking dish aside.

For filling, in a large mixing bowl beat cream cheese and the ½ cup sugar with an electric mixer on medium to high speed till well combined. Add the pumpkin, pumpkin pie spice, vanilla, and salt. Beat till combined. Add eggs all at once. Beat on low speed *just till combined.* Stir in cream or milk.

Pour filling into the crust-lined dish. Bake in a 375° oven for 40 to 45 minutes or till cheesecake tests done. Cool on a wire rack for 10 minutes.

Meanwhile, in a small bowl stir together sour cream and the 1 tablespoon sugar. Spread over the cheese-cake. Using a small metal spatula, loosen sides of cheesecake. Cool cheesecake completely, then chill for at least 4 hours. Makes 9 servings.

Nutrition Analysis

Per Serving

Recipes	Servings	Calories	Protein (g)	Carbohydrates (g)	Total Fat (g)	Saturated Fat (g)	Cholesterol (mg)	Sodium (mg)
After-Dinner Mint Meringues, 97	60	11	0	2	0	0	0	3
Apple-Raisin Crisp, 112	6	365	3	58	15	2	0	100
Baked Apples, 106	4	299	3	51	12	3	11	57
Baked Custards, 116	4	165	8	21	6	2	168	93
Baked Fruit Ambrosia, 107	4	161	1	38	2	1	0	8
Baked Rice Pudding, 116	6	184	6	32	4	2	112	64
Blueberry Cobbler, 100	4	337	4	65	8	2	54	227
Blueberry Crisp, 113	6	266	4	43	10	5	0	110
Caramel-Apple Bread Pudding, 104	6	477	10	68	21	6	164	306
Caramel Flans, 116	4	229	8	38	6	2	168	94
Cheesecake and Brandied Berry Sauce, 122	12	469	7	49	28	14	133	254
Cheesecake Supreme, 119	12	446	8	34	32	15	116	379
Cherry-Apple Crisp, 112	6	247	4	49	5	3	0	59
Cherry Cobbler, 100	4	391	5	72	11	2	54	241
Cherry-Orange Betty, 110	6	401	4	69	14	3	0	310
Chocolate Amaretti Balls, 96	90	13	0	2	1	0	0	2
Chocolate Bread Pudding, 105	6	426	9	49	23	13	123	206
Chocolate Meringue Shell, 94	8	120	1	27	1	1	0	42
Chocolate Meringue Surprises, 96	36	38	1	6	2	0	0	8
Chocolate Swirl Cheesecake, 119	12	470	8	36	34	16	116	379
Coconut Bread Pudding with Meringue Topper, 105	8	340	8	53	11	4	113	214
Coconut Cream Flan, 114	6	347	7	36	20	13	168	74
Coconut Macaroons, 97	30	33	0	6	1	1	0	4
Coconut-Ricotta Cheesecake, 124	12	351	9	32	22	12	111	198
Coffee Meringue Doves, 98	24	20	0	4	0	0	0	6
Cranberry-Apple Crisp, 111	6	369	3	60	15	2	0	118
Cream Cheese Fruited Flan, 116	12	252	7	29	12	7	138	130
Custards with Apricot Flummery, 117	6	271	7	51	5	2	149	87
Double Chocolate-Almond Cheesecake, 118	16	423	9	14	38	18	130	284
Dried Fruit Cobbler, 102	6	304	4	55	10	2	1	201
Fruit Sauce, 119	12	22	0	6	0	0	0	1
Hawaiian-Style Baked Pears, 107	6	292	2	57	8	3	11	46
Hazelnut Chocolate Cheesecake, 120	12	418	8	28	32	16	133	222
Lemon Meringue Torte, 95	8	271	4	51	6	1	106	71
Liqueur Cheesecake, 119	12	464	7	36	32	15	115	376
Meringue Shell, 94	8	102	1	25	0	0	0	42
Nut Meringue Shell, 94	8	150	3	27	4	0	0	43
Orange Custards, 117	6	249	7	25	12	7	176	135
Orange Meringue Fingers, 99	48	23	0	4	1	0	0	3
Peaches 'n' Cream Cheesecake, 123	12	494	8	45	33	17	129	341
Peaches 'n' Cream Meringue Pie, 99	8	265	6	42	10	4	17	94
Peach-Pineapple Crisp, 113	6	414	3	56	20	1	0	140
Pear-Orange Cobbler, 102	6	336	4	59	10	3	36	190
Pumpkin Cheesecake Squares, 124	9	375	7	31	25	14	127	288
Raspberry-Pear Betty, 110	6	228	3	44	5	1	0	254
Rhubarb Crisp, 111	4	280	3	55	6	1	0	79
Rhubarb-Peach Betty, 108	6	323	3	55	11	2	0	330
Rhubarb Swirl Cobbler, 103	8	228	3	42	6	1	1	215
Sour Cream Cheesecake, 119	12	499	8	35	37	18	120	351
Whole Wheat Apple-Nut Cobbler, 103	6	363	5	56	15	2	36	133

We've analyzed the nutritional content of each recipe using the first choice if ingredient substitutions are given, and using the first serving size if a serving range is given. We've omitted optional ingredients from the analysis.

Gingersnaps
(see recipe, page 145)

Chocolate Revel Bars
(see recipe, page 131)

Apricot-Hazelnut Spirals
(see recipe, page 155)

Spiced Apple Drops (see recipe, page 136)

Holiday Cottage Cookies (see recipe, page 139)

HOME-STYLE COOKIES AND CRACKERS

Prepare a tantalizing collection of homemade cookies and crackers from the kitchen-tested recipes found in this chapter. From sweet to savory, you'll find a broad range of recipes sure to satisfy your cravings or suit any occasion. Included are cakelike Buttermilk Brownies, irresistible Snickerdoodles, crispy Buttery Rich Crackers, and much more. These recipes are all-time favorites that we are sure you will enjoy.

BAR COOKIES

Treat friends and family to the simple pleasures of homemade bar cookies. They're some of the easiest cookies to make—just stir and bake! In this section, you'll discover a variety of mouth-watering bar cookie recipes. Choose from elegant Viennese Raspberry Squares, crowd-pleasing Chocolate Revel Bars, scrumptious Peanut Butter and Chocolate Chip Bars, and many more.

☐ Using a baking pan that is too large or too small may alter the baking time and texture of your bar cookies. So, remember to bake bars only in the size pan indicated.

☐ To cut even squares or rectangles, use a ruler to measure and toothpicks to mark the lines.

☐ Dress up your bar cookies with a simple garnish. Try sprinkling unfrosted bars with powdered sugar or a spice used in the recipe. Or, top frosted bars with chocolate curls, nuts, miniature chocolate chips, dried fruit, or candied fruit.

☐ Serving bar cookies is easiest if you first remove a corner piece. Then remove the rest.

☐ Here's a trick for making batches of bars for future use. Line your baking pan with foil (see tip, page 130). Then, follow the recipe for baking and cooling. Lift the bars out of pan on the foil. Place the uncut and unfrosted bars in freezer bags or airtight containers, then seal, label, and freeze. Thaw the bars at room temperature about 15 minutes. Once thawed, bars can be frosted and cut.

Chocolate-Nut Cheesecake Bars

These fast-baking bars, featuring an easy nut crust, are a quick new twist to a traditional dessert favorite—cheesecake.

¾ **cup ground walnuts *or* pecans**
2 **8-ounce packages cream cheese, softened**
⅔ **cup sugar**
1 **tablespoon all-purpose flour**
2 **eggs**
1 **tablespoon milk**
½ **teaspoon vanilla**
2 **1.6-ounce bars milk chocolate, chopped (about ¾ cup)**
Walnut *or* pecan halves (optional)
Chocolate curls (optional)

Generously grease the bottom and sides of an 8x8x2-inch baking dish. Press ground nuts onto the bottom of the dish. Set the baking dish aside.

For filling, in a large mixing bowl beat cream cheese with an electric mixer on low to medium speed till creamy. Add sugar and flour. Beat till thoroughly combined, scraping sides of bowl occasionally. Add the eggs. Beat just till combined. (*Do not overbeat.*) Stir in milk and vanilla, then stir in chopped chocolate.

Carefully spread filling on top of nuts in the prepared baking dish. Bake in a 375° oven about 35 minutes or till center is nearly set. Cool bars in baking dish on a wire rack for 10 minutes. Using a narrow metal spatula, loosen sides of the bars from the dish. Cool about 2 hours more. Cover and chill thoroughly.

To serve, cut into bars. If desired, garnish each bar with a walnut half and a chocolate curl. Store in refrigerator. Makes 24.

Cocoa-Berry Bars

⅓ cup margarine *or* butter
¾ cup sugar
¼ cup unsweetened cocoa powder
1 egg
½ teaspoon vanilla
¼ cup milk
¾ cup all-purpose flour
¼ teaspoon baking powder
¼ teaspoon baking soda
⅓ cup red raspberry *or* apricot preserves
Cocoa Glaze
Fresh raspberries (optional)

Grease a 9x9x2-inch baking pan. Set pan aside. In a medium saucepan melt margarine or butter. Remove from heat. Stir in sugar and cocoa powder. Add egg and vanilla to saucepan. Using a wooden spoon, lightly beat just till combined. Stir in milk. Add flour, baking powder, and baking soda. Beat till combined.

Spread batter into the prepared baking pan. Bake in a 350° oven for 20 to 25 minutes or till a wooden toothpick inserted near the center comes out clean. Cool in pan on a wire rack for 10 minutes.

Meanwhile, if necessary, snip any large pieces of fruit in preserves. Then spread preserves over *warm* bars. Cool bars completely. Drizzle with Cocoa Glaze.

To serve, cut into bars. If desired, garnish each bar with a fresh raspberry. Makes 24.

Cocoa Glaze: In a small saucepan cook and stir 1 tablespoon *unsweetened cocoa powder,* 1 tablespoon *margarine or butter,* and 1 tablespoon *milk* till margarine is melted. Remove from heat. Stir in ¾ cup sifted *powdered sugar* and ¼ teaspoon *vanilla.* Stir till smooth. Makes ⅓ cup.

Pumpkin Bars

It's magic. Substitute one 16-ounce can of applesauce for the pumpkin and presto! You have applesauce bars.

2 cups all-purpose flour
1½ cups sugar
2 teaspoons baking powder
2 teaspoons ground cinnamon
1 teaspoon baking soda
¼ teaspoon salt
¼ teaspoon ground cloves
1 16-ounce can pumpkin
1 cup cooking oil
4 beaten eggs
1 cup chopped walnuts (optional)
½ of a recipe Cream Cheese Frosting
    (see page 226) *or* powdered sugar

In a large mixing bowl stir together flour, sugar, baking powder, cinnamon, baking soda, salt, and cloves. Stir in pumpkin, cooking oil, and eggs till thoroughly combined. If desired, stir in walnuts.

Spread batter into an ungreased 15x10x1-inch baking pan. Bake in a 350° oven for 25 to 30 minutes or till a wooden toothpick inserted near the center comes out clean. Cool in pan on a wire rack. Frost with Cream Cheese Frosting or sift powdered sugar over top. Cut into bars. Store, covered, in the refrigerator. Makes 48.

Frontier Baking

The frontier cook had lard, suet, or sometimes only bear fat to use as fat in cooking and baking. With these choices, it's no wonder lots of spices and sweeteners often were added to mask the strong fat flavor.

HISTORY OF BAKING

Apple Squares

½ **cup sugar**
2 **tablespoons all-purpose flour**
½ **teaspoon ground cinnamon**
¼ **teaspoon ground nutmeg**
2½ **cups sliced, peeled cooking apple**
1¼ **cups all-purpose flour**
1 **tablespoon sugar**
½ **teaspoon finely shredded lemon peel**
⅛ **teaspoon salt**
⅓ **cup margarine *or* butter**
1 **beaten egg**
1 **tablespoon milk**
1½ **teaspoons milk**
½ **of a recipe Powdered Sugar Icing**
  (see page 230)

In a large bowl combine the ½ cup sugar, 2 tablespoons flour, cinnamon, and nutmeg. Add apple slices, then toss till coated. Set mixture aside.

In a medium mixing bowl stir together the 1¼ cups flour, the 1 tablespoon sugar, lemon peel, and salt. Using a pastry blender, cut in the margarine till pieces are the size of small peas.

In a small bowl combine egg and the 1 tablespoon milk. Add to flour mixture. Using a fork, stir just till moistened. (If necessary, stir in additional milk, 1 teaspoon at a time, till all is moistened.) Divide dough in half. Form *each* half into a ball. On a lightly floured surface, roll *half* of the dough into a 10-inch square. Carefully place in an ungreased 8x8x2-inch baking pan, allowing dough to extend up the sides.

Evenly arrange apple mixture on dough in pan. Roll out remaining dough into an 8-inch square. Cut several slits to vent steam. Place on top of apple mixture. Press edges together to seal. Brush with 1½ teaspoons milk. Bake in a 375° oven for 35 to 40 minutes or till golden. Cool in pan on wire rack. Drizzle with Powdered Sugar Icing. Cut into squares. Makes 16.

Fudge Brownies

A chocolaty delight even without the frosting.

½ **cup margarine *or* butter**
2 **squares (2 ounces) unsweetened chocolate**
1 **cup sugar**
2 **eggs**
1 **teaspoon vanilla**
¾ **cup all-purpose flour**
½ **cup chopped nuts**
½ **of a recipe No-Cook Fudge Frosting *or* ½ of a**
  recipe Chocolate Glaze (see page 227)
  Chopped nuts (optional)

Grease an 8x8x2-inch baking pan; set aside. In a saucepan melt margarine and chocolate over low heat, stirring constantly. Remove from heat. Stir in sugar, eggs, and vanilla. Using a spoon, lightly beat just till combined. Stir in flour and ½ cup nuts.

Spread batter into the prepared baking pan. Bake in a 350° oven for 30 minutes. Cool in pan on a wire rack. Frost or glaze top. If desired, sprinkle with additional chopped nuts. Cut into bars. Makes 24.

Cookie Step-Saver

Lining your baking pan makes it easy to remove and cut bars, and simplifies cleanup.

Just line the pan with foil, extending foil over the edges of the pan. If the recipe directs, grease the foil instead of the pan. Then spread bar cookie dough in the pan. Bake and cool the bars in the pan. Lift the bars out of the pan and pull the edges of the foil down to the counter. With a long knife cut straight down into bars. For clean, straight edges, wipe the knife between cuts.

Chocolate Revel Bars

Vary these chewy, fudgy bars by adding 1 cup whole wheat flour in place of 1 cup all-purpose flour. (Basic bars are pictured on pages 126–127.)

    1   cup margarine *or* butter
 2½   cups all-purpose flour
    2   cups packed brown sugar
    2   eggs
    2   teaspoons vanilla
    1   teaspoon baking soda
    3   cups quick-cooking rolled oats
 1½   cups semisweet chocolate pieces
    1   14-ounce can (1¼ cups) *sweetened
         condensed* milk
    2   tablespoons margarine *or* butter
   ½   cup chopped walnuts *or* pecans
    2   teaspoons vanilla

In a very large mixing bowl beat 1 cup margarine or butter with an electric mixer on medium to high speed about 30 seconds or till softened. Add about *half* of the flour. Then add brown sugar, eggs, 2 teaspoons vanilla, and baking soda. Beat till thoroughly combined, scraping sides of bowl occasionally. Then beat or stir in the remaining flour. Stir in the oats. Set oat mixture aside.

For filling, in a medium saucepan heat chocolate pieces, sweetened condensed milk, and the 2 tablespoons margarine or butter over low heat till chocolate is just melted, stirring occasionally. Remove from heat. Stir in walnuts and 2 teaspoons vanilla.

For crust, press *two-thirds* (about 3⅓ cups) of the oat mixture into an ungreased 15x10x1-inch baking pan. Then spread the chocolate mixture on top of crust. Drop the remaining oat mixture from a rounded teaspoon on top of chocolate layer.

Bake in a 350° oven about 25 minutes or till top is light golden (chocolate layer will look slightly moist). Cool in pan on a wire rack. Cut into bars. Store in the refrigerator. Makes 64.

Peanut Butter and Chocolate Chip Bars

For a chewy oat version of these fabulous bar cookies, just reduce the flour to 1 cup, and stir in ¾ cup quick-cooking rolled oats with the peanuts.

   ¾   cup peanut butter
   ¼   cup cooking oil
 1½   cups all-purpose flour
    1   cup packed brown sugar
    2   eggs
   ¾   cup milk
   ½   teaspoon baking powder
   ¼   teaspoon baking soda
   ½   cup miniature semisweet chocolate pieces
   ⅓   cup chopped peanuts
        Peanut Butter Frosting

Grease a 13x9x2-inch baking pan. Set pan aside. In a large mixing bowl beat peanut butter and oil with an electric mixer on low to medium speed about 30 seconds or till combined.

Add about *half* of the flour to the peanut butter mixture. Then add brown sugar, eggs, about *half* of the milk, baking powder, and baking soda. Beat till thoroughly combined, scraping sides of bowl occasionally. Then stir in the remaining flour and milk. Stir in chocolate pieces and chopped peanuts.

Spread batter into the prepared baking pan. Bake in a 350° oven for 25 to 30 minutes or till a wooden toothpick inserted near center comes out clean. Cool in pan on a wire rack. Frost with Peanut Butter Frosting. Cut into bars. Makes 36.

Peanut Butter Frosting: In a large bowl beat 3½ cups sifted *powdered sugar,* ¼ cup *peanut butter,* and ¼ to ⅓ cup *milk* to make the frosting of spreading consistency. Makes about 1½ cups.

Buttermilk Brownies

Moist and chocolaty cakelike brownies.

2 cups all-purpose flour
2 cups sugar
1 teaspoon baking soda
¼ teaspoon salt
1 cup margarine *or* butter
1 cup water
⅓ cup unsweetened cocoa powder
2 eggs
½ cup buttermilk *or* sour milk
1½ teaspoons vanilla
¼ cup margarine *or* butter
3 tablespoons unsweetened cocoa powder
3 tablespoons buttermilk *or* sour milk
2¼ cups sifted powdered sugar
½ teaspoon vanilla
¾ cup coarsely chopped pecans (optional)

Grease a 15x10x1-inch baking pan. Set pan aside. In a large mixing bowl stir together flour, sugar, baking soda, and salt. Set flour mixture aside.

In a saucepan combine 1 cup margarine or butter, water, and ⅓ cup cocoa powder. Bring just to boiling, stirring constantly. Remove from heat. Add chocolate mixture to flour mixture. Beat with an electric mixer on medium to high speed till thoroughly combined. Add eggs, ½ cup buttermilk, and 1½ teaspoons vanilla. Beat for 1 minute (batter will be thin).

Pour batter into the prepared baking pan. Bake in a 350° oven about 25 minutes or till a wooden toothpick inserted near the center comes out clean. Cool slightly in pan on wire rack.

Meanwhile, for frosting, in a saucepan combine the ¼ cup margarine, 3 tablespoons cocoa powder, and 3 tablespoons buttermilk. Bring to boiling, then remove from heat. Stir in powdered sugar and ½ teaspoon vanilla till smooth. If desired, stir in pecans. Pour warm frosting over *warm* bars, spreading evenly. Cool completely. Cut into bars. Makes 36.

Fruit Crumb Bars

2 cups fresh *or* frozen blueberries *or* chopped,
  peeled apple
2 tablespoons sugar
2 tablespoons water
1 tablespoon lemon juice
½ teaspoon ground cinnamon
1 cup all-purpose flour
1 cup quick-cooking rolled oats
⅔ cup packed brown sugar
¼ teaspoon ground cinnamon
⅛ teaspoon baking soda
½ cup margarine *or* butter, melted

For filling, in a medium saucepan combine blueberries or apple, sugar, water, lemon juice, and ½ teaspoon cinnamon. Bring to boiling. Reduce heat. Simmer, uncovered, about 8 minutes or till slightly thickened, stirring frequently. Remove from heat.

In a mixing bowl stir together flour, oats, brown sugar, ¼ teaspoon cinnamon, and baking soda. Stir in melted margarine or butter till thoroughly combined. Set aside *1 cup* of the oat mixture for topping. Press remaining oat mixture into an ungreased 9x9x2-inch baking pan. Bake in a 350° oven for 12 minutes.

Carefully spread filling on top of baked crust. Sprinkle with reserved oat mixture. Lightly press oat mixture into filling. Bake in the 350° oven for 20 to 25 minutes more or till topping is set. Cool in pan on a wire rack. Cut into bars. Makes 24.

Cranberry-Date Crumb Bars: Prepare Fruit Crumb Bars as above, *except* omit the filling. For cranberry-date filling, in a medium saucepan combine 1½ cups *cranberries,* 1 cup chopped pitted *dates,* and 2 tablespoons *water.* Cook, covered, over low heat about 12 minutes or till cranberries pop, stirring frequently. Then stir in 1 teaspoon *vanilla.* Cool slightly before using.

Lemon Bars

A tasty crumb crust topped with fresh lemon custard. (Pictured on the cover.)

⅓ cup margarine *or* butter
1 cup sugar
1 cup all-purpose flour
2 eggs
2 tablespoons all-purpose flour
2 teaspoons finely shredded lemon peel
   (set aside)
3 tablespoons lemon juice
¼ teaspoon baking powder
   Powdered sugar

For crust, in a medium mixing bowl beat margarine or butter with an electric mixer on medium to high speed about 30 seconds or till softened. Add *¼ cup* of the sugar. Beat till thoroughly combined. Then beat in 1 cup flour till mixture resembles fine crumbs. Press mixture into an ungreased 8x8x2-inch baking pan. Bake in a 350° oven for 15 minutes.

Meanwhile, for lemon mixture, in the same mixing bowl beat eggs with an electric mixer on medium speed just till foamy. Add the remaining sugar, 2 tablespoons flour, lemon juice, baking powder, and ⅛ teaspoon *salt*. Beat on medium speed about 3 minutes or till slightly thickened. Stir in lemon peel. Pour lemon mixture over baked crust. Bake in the 350° oven for 20 to 25 minutes or till lightly golden around edges and center is set. Cool in pan on a rack. Sift powdered sugar over top. Cut into bars. Store, covered, in refrigerator. Makes 16.

Coconut-Lemon Bars: Prepare Lemon Bars as above, *except* for coconut-lemon mixture, increase baking powder to *½ teaspoon* and stir in 1 cup *coconut*. Pour mixture over top of baked crust. Bake in the 350° oven for 20 to 25 minutes or till center is set. Cool as above. Sift powdered sugar over top. Cut into bars.

Carrot-Walnut Bars

1½ cups all-purpose flour
1 cup packed brown sugar
1 teaspoon baking powder
1 teaspoon ground cinnamon
½ teaspoon baking soda
2 beaten eggs
⅔ cup cooking oil
1 teaspoon vanilla
1½ cups finely shredded carrot
¾ cup chopped walnuts
½ cup coconut
½ of a recipe Cream Cheese Frosting
   (see page 226)

Grease a 13x9x2-inch baking pan. Set pan aside. In a large mixing bowl stir together flour, brown sugar, baking powder, cinnamon, and baking soda. Stir in eggs, oil, and vanilla till thoroughly combined. Then stir in carrot, walnuts, and coconut.

Spread batter into the prepared baking pan. Bake in a 350° oven for 20 to 25 minutes or till a wooden toothpick inserted near the center comes out clean. Cool in pan on a rack. Frost with Cream Cheese Frosting. Cut into bars. Store in refrigerator. Makes 24.

Festive Bar Shapes

Here are some ideas for varying the shape of of your bar cookies.
For triangles, cut cookie bars into 2- to 2½-inch squares. Then, diagonally cut each of the squares in half.
For diamonds, first make straight parallel cuts 1 to 1½ inches apart down the length of the pan. Then, make diagonal cuts across the straight cuts 1 to 1½ inches apart, forming a diamond pattern.

Orange-Date Bars

¼ **cup margarine *or* butter**
1 **cup all-purpose flour**
½ **cup packed brown sugar**
1 **teaspoon finely shredded**
 orange peel (set aside)
½ **cup orange juice**
1 **egg**
½ **teaspoon baking powder**
¼ **teaspoon baking soda**
½ **cup chopped walnuts**
½ **cup chopped pitted dates**
 Powdered sugar

In a medium mixing bowl beat margarine or butter with an electric mixer on medium to high speed about 30 seconds or till softened.

Add about *half* of the flour to the margarine. Then add the brown sugar, *half* of the orange juice, egg, baking powder, and baking soda. Beat till thoroughly combined, scraping sides of bowl. Then beat or stir in the remaining flour and orange juice. Stir in orange peel, walnuts, and dates.

Spread batter into an ungreased 11x7x1½-inch baking pan. Bake in a 350° oven about 25 minutes or till a wooden toothpick inserted near the center comes out clean. Cool in the pan on a wire rack. Sift powdered sugar over the top. Cut into bars. Makes 24.

Spicy Prune Bars: Prepare Orange-Date Bars as directed above, *except* add ½ teaspoon ground *cinnamon* and dash ground *cloves* with the first half of flour. Also, substitute ½ cup snipped, dried, pitted *prunes* for the dates.

Cranberry-Pecan Bars: Prepare Orange-Date Bars as directed above, *except* substitute ½ cup chopped *pecans* for the walnuts and ½ cup chopped *cranberries* for the dates.

Viennese Raspberry Squares

This is a cookie rendition of the classic Austrian dessert, Linzer torte, popular for its almond crust and raspberry preserves filling.

2 **egg whites**
⅓ **cup margarine *or* butter**
1 **cup all-purpose flour**
⅓ **cup sugar**
2 **egg yolks**
¼ **teaspoon cream of tartar**
⅔ **cup sifted powdered sugar**
1 **cup finely chopped almonds *or* walnuts,**
 toasted
⅓ **cup red raspberry, peach, *or* apricot**
 preserves

In a medium mixing bowl bring egg whites to room temperature. Set aside.

For crust, in another medium mixing bowl beat margarine or butter with an electric mixer on medium to high speed about 30 seconds or till softened. Add about *half* of the flour. Then add the sugar and egg yolks. Beat on medium to high speed till thoroughly combined, scraping sides of bowl occasionally. Stir in the remaining flour. Press crust mixture into an ungreased 9x9x2-inch baking pan. Bake in a 350° oven for 15 minutes.

Meanwhile, thoroughly wash and dry the beaters. For meringue topping, add cream of tartar to the egg whites. Beat on medium speed till soft peaks form (tips curl). Gradually add the powdered sugar, beating till stiff peaks form (tips stand straight). Gently fold in the chopped nuts. Set meringue topping aside.

Spread preserves over top of the *hot* baked crust. Then carefully spread meringue topping over the preserves layer. Bake in the 350° oven about 20 minutes more or till top is golden. Cool in pan on a wire rack. Cut into squares. Store in refrigerator. Makes 36.

Viennese Raspberry Squares

DROP COOKIES

Warm the hearts in your household with these sweet satisfiers. Store-bought cookies simply don't compare with fresh-from-the-oven drop cookies. Choose from White Chocolate-Hazelnut Cookies, Apricot Tea Cookies, or any of the other terrific cookies featured on the following pages. Few things will bring a smile as fast as a plate full of homemade cookies.

☐ When recipes call for greased cookie sheets, use a light coating of shortening. When recipes specify ungreased cookie sheets, use regular or non-stick sheets, but do not grease them.

☐ If your electric mixer begins to strain and feel very warm when mixing cookie dough, stir in the last portion of flour by hand.

☐ To get the correct number of cookies from each recipe, drop cookie dough using spoons from your everyday flatware set, not measuring spoons.

☐ For even baking, be sure to bake on only one oven rack at a time. You might get uneven browning if you use more than one rack.

☐ To keep your drop cookies from spreading too much, allow cookie sheets to cool between batches before reusing them.

☐ Drop cookies are properly baked when the dough looks set, when a slight imprint remains after lightly touching one with a fingertip, or when edges and bottoms are lightly browned.

Spiced Apple Drops

Choose firm, tart baking apples for this flavorful cookie. (Pictured on pages 126–127.)

- ½ cup margarine *or* butter
- 2 cups all-purpose flour
- ⅔ cup sugar
- ⅔ cup packed brown sugar
- 1 egg
- ¼ cup apple juice *or* apple cider
- 1 teaspoon ground cinnamon
- ½ teaspoon baking soda
- ½ teaspoon ground nutmeg
- ⅛ teaspoon ground cloves
- 1 cup finely chopped apple
- 1 cup chopped walnuts
  Apple Frosting

Lightly grease a cookie sheet. (Repeat greasing cookie sheet for each batch.) Set aside. In a large mixing bowl beat margarine with electric mixer on medium to high speed about 30 seconds or till softened.

Add about *half* of the flour to margarine. Add sugar, brown sugar, egg, *half* of the juice, cinnamon, baking soda, nutmeg, and cloves. Beat till thoroughly combined, scraping sides of bowl occasionally. Then beat or stir in remaining flour and remaining apple juice or cider. Stir in chopped apple and walnuts.

Drop dough from a rounded teaspoon 2 inches apart on prepared cookie sheet. Bake in a 375° oven for 10 to 12 minutes or till edges are lightly browned. Cool on cookie sheet for 1 minute. Remove cookies and cool on a rack. Frost with Apple Frosting. Store iced cookies in refrigerator. Makes about 40.

Apple Frosting: In a medium mixing bowl beat 4 cups sifted *powdered sugar,* ¼ cup softened *margarine or butter,* 1 teaspoon *vanilla,* and 3 to 4 tablespoons *apple juice* to make a frosting of spreading consistency. Makes about 1¼ cups.

Florentines

Savor each irresistible cookie with its crisp, candylike texture and thin layer of chocolate.

- ⅓ cup margarine *or* butter
- ⅓ cup milk
- ¼ cup sugar
- 1 cup chopped almonds, toasted
- ¾ cup diced mixed candied fruits and peels, finely chopped
- 1 teaspoon finely shredded orange peel
- ¼ cup all-purpose flour
- ¾ cup semisweet chocolate pieces
- 2 tablespoons margarine *or* butter

Grease and flour a cookie sheet. (Repeat greasing and flouring cookie sheet for each batch.) Set aside.

In a heavy medium saucepan combine the ⅓ cup margarine or butter, milk, and sugar. Bring to a full rolling boil, stirring occasionally. Remove from heat. Stir in the almonds, candied fruits and peels, and orange peel. Then stir in the flour.

Drop batter from a *level tablespoon* at least 3 inches apart on prepared cookie sheet. Then, using the back of a spoon, spread the batter into 3-inch circles.

Bake in a 350° oven for 8 to 10 minutes or till the edges are lightly browned. Cool on the cookie sheet for 1 minute. Remove the cookies from the cookie sheet and cool on waxed paper.

In a small heavy saucepan heat chocolate pieces and 2 tablespoons margarine or butter over low heat just till melted, stirring occasionally. Spread a *scant teaspoon* of chocolate mixture evenly over the bottom of *each* cookie. When chocolate is *almost* set, use the tines of a fork to draw wavy lines through chocolate. Store, covered, in the refrigerator. Makes about 24.

Apricot Tea Cookies

- ¾ cup snipped dried apricots
- ⅓ cup apricot nectar *or* orange juice
- ¾ cup margarine *or* butter
- 1¼ cups all-purpose flour
- ¾ cup packed brown sugar
- 1 egg
- 1 teaspoon finely shredded orange peel
- ½ teaspoon baking powder
- ½ teaspoon ground cardamom
- ¼ teaspoon ground cinnamon
  Apricot Frosting

In a small bowl stir together dried apricots and apricot nectar or orange juice. Let stand for 15 minutes. Then drain, reserving liquid for frosting.

In a large mixing bowl beat margarine or butter with an electric mixer on medium to high speed about 30 seconds or till softened.

Add about *half* of the flour to the margarine. Then add the brown sugar, egg, orange peel, baking powder, cardamom, and ground cinnamon. Beat till thoroughly combined, scraping sides of the bowl occasionally. Then beat or stir in remaining flour. Stir in drained apricots.

Drop dough from a rounded teaspoon 2 inches apart on an ungreased cookie sheet. Bake in a 350° oven for 10 to 12 minutes or till edges are golden. Cool on cookie sheet for 1 minute. Then remove cookies from cookie sheet and cool on a wire rack. Frost cookies with Apricot Frosting. Makes about 30.

Apricot Frosting: In a medium mixing bowl beat 1½ cups sifted *powdered sugar,* 2 tablespoons *margarine or butter,* and 1 to 2 tablespoons of the *reserved liquid* to make a frosting of spreading consistency. Makes about ⅔ cup.

Chocolate Chip Cookies

Traditional favorites any time. (Pictured on the cover.)

- ½ **cup shortening**
- ½ **cup margarine *or* butter**
- 2½ **cups all-purpose flour**
- 1 **cup packed brown sugar**
- ½ **cup sugar**
- 2 **eggs**
- 1 **teaspoon vanilla**
- ½ **teaspoon baking soda**
- 1 **12-ounce package (2 cups) semisweet chocolate pieces *or* 2 cups candy-coated milk chocolate pieces**
- 1 **cup chopped walnuts, pecans, *or* hazelnuts (filberts) (optional)**

In a large mixing bowl beat shortening and margarine or butter with an electric mixer on medium to high speed about 30 seconds or till softened.

Add about *half* of the flour to the shortening mixture. Then add brown sugar, sugar, eggs, vanilla, and baking soda. Beat till thoroughly combined, scraping sides of bowl occasionally. Beat or stir in remaining flour. Stir in chocolate pieces. If desired, stir in nuts.

Drop dough from a rounded teaspoon 2 inches apart on an ungreased cookie sheet. Bake in a 375° oven for 8 to 10 minutes or till edges are lightly browned. Remove the cookies from the cookie sheet and cool on a wire rack. Makes about 60.

Cookie History

Did you know that the word *cookie* comes from the Dutch word for cake, *koekje*? The first cookies were actually tiny cakes baked as a test to make sure that the oven temperature was right for baking a large cake.

Peanut Butter Cup-Chocolate Cookies

Sink your teeth into the chunks of gooey, chocolate-covered peanut butter cups found throughout these heavenly cookies.

- ½ **cup shortening**
- ½ **cup margarine *or* butter**
- 2¼ **cups all-purpose flour**
- ¾ **cup sugar**
- ¾ **cup packed brown sugar**
- 2 **squares (2 ounces) unsweetened chocolate, melted and cooled**
- 2 **eggs**
- 1 **teaspoon baking soda**
- 1 **teaspoon vanilla**
- 2 **cups coarsely chopped chocolate-covered peanut butter cups**

In a large mixing bowl beat the shortening and margarine or butter with an electric mixer on medium to high speed about 30 seconds or till softened.

Add about *half* of the flour to the shortening mixture. Add sugar, brown sugar, unsweetened chocolate, eggs, baking soda, and vanilla. Beat till thoroughly combined, scraping the sides of the bowl occasionally. Beat or stir in the remaining flour. Stir in chopped peanut butter cups.

Drop dough from a rounded tablespoon 2½ inches apart on an ungreased cookie sheet. Bake in a 375° oven for 10 to 12 minutes or till tops look dry. Cool on cookie sheet for 1 minute. Then remove the cookies from the cookie sheet and cool on a wire rack. Makes about 30.

Peanutty Chocolate Cookies: Prepare Peanut Butter Cup Chocolate Cookies as above, *except* substitute 2 cups coarsely chopped *chocolate-covered peanuts* for chopped peanut butter cups.

Holiday Cottage Cookies

Cottage cheese is the secret ingredient in these moist, cakelike cookies. (Pictured on pages 126–127.)

½ **cup margarine *or* butter**
1½ **cups all-purpose flour**
⅔ **cup sugar**
½ **cup cream-style cottage cheese**
1 **egg**
2 **tablespoons milk**
½ **teaspoon baking powder**
½ **teaspoon vanilla**
¼ **teaspoon baking soda**
½ **cup diced mixed candied fruits and peels**
½ **cup chopped candied pineapple**
½ **cup chopped pecans *or* walnuts**
   Pecan *or* walnut halves (optional)
   Mixed candied fruits and peels (optional)

In a large mixing bowl beat margarine or butter with an electric mixer on medium to high speed about 30 seconds or till softened.

Add about *half* of the flour to the margarine. Add sugar, cottage cheese, egg, milk, baking powder, vanilla, and baking soda. Beat till combined, scraping the sides of the bowl occasionally. Beat or stir in the remaining flour. Stir in the ½ cup fruits and peels, pineapple, and ½ cup chopped nuts.

Drop the dough from a rounded teaspoon 2 inches apart on an ungreased cookie sheet. If desired, press a nut half and additional fruits and peels into the top of each cookie dough mound.

Bake in a 375° oven for 9 to 11 minutes or till the tops spring back when lightly touched. Cool on cookie sheet for 1 minute. Remove cookies from cookie sheet and cool on a wire rack. Makes about 48.

Secrets to Successful Drop Cookies

You can win approving "oohs!" and "ahhs!" for your drop cookies. If you don't get rave reviews look below for possible solutions.

If your cookies are doughy:
■ Try baking your next batch 1 to 2 minutes longer to avoid underbaking the cookies.
■ Use an oven thermometer to check your oven temperature. If necessary, adjust the setting.
■ Make sure you're not overloading the oven. For best results, bake on one oven rack at a time.

If your cookies spread too much:
■ When greasing cookie sheets, use a *light coating* of shortening.
■ Refrigerate your cookie dough until it feels cool to the touch.

■ Dropping cookie dough on warm cookie sheets causes excess spreading. Let cookie sheets cool before reusing.

If your cookies are dry and hard:
■ Overbaking dries cookies out. Try baking your next batch 1 to 2 minutes less.
■ Use an oven thermometer to check oven temperature. If necessary, adjust the setting.
■ You may have overmixed the dough. After adding the remaining flour, mix *just till combined*.

If cookies are irregularly sized or shaped:
■ You may not be dropping *rounded* spoonfuls of cookie dough. Try scooping equal amounts of dough in rounded shapes.

Oatmeal-Raisin 'n' Walnut Cookies

If you have oat bran (see tip at right) on hand, substitute 1½ cups of it for the rolled oats. Then you won't need to turn oats into oat flour.

    2 cups rolled oats
    ¾ cup margarine *or* butter
    1 cup all-purpose flour
    ¾ cup sugar
    ¾ cup packed brown sugar
    2 eggs
    2 teaspoons finely shredded orange
         peel (optional)
    1 teaspoon baking soda
    1 teaspoon vanilla
    ½ teaspoon ground cinnamon
    ¼ teaspoon ground nutmeg
    1½ cups raisins *or* one 8-ounce package
         chopped dates
    1 cup coarsely chopped walnuts

For oat flour, in a blender container place *½ cup* of the rolled oats. Cover and blend till reduced to a powder. Transfer to a small bowl. Repeat with the remaining oats, ½ cup at a time. (You should have about 1½ cups of oat flour.) Set oat flour aside.

In a large mixing bowl beat margarine or butter with an electric mixer on medium to high speed about 30 seconds or till softened.

Add about *half* of the all-purpose flour to the margarine. Add sugar, brown sugar, eggs, orange peel (if desired), baking soda, vanilla, cinnamon, and nutmeg. Beat till thoroughly combined. Stir in oat flour and remaining all-purpose flour. Stir in raisins and walnuts.

Drop dough from a rounded tablespoon 2 inches apart on an ungreased cookie sheet. Bake in a 375° oven for 8 to 10 minutes or till edges are lightly browned. Cool on cookie sheet for 1 minute. Remove cookies and cool on a wire rack. Makes about 42.

Peanut Butter-Oatmeal Rounds

    ¾ cup margarine *or* butter
    ½ cup peanut butter
    1¼ cups all-purpose flour
    1 cup sugar
    ½ cup packed brown sugar
    2 eggs
    1 teaspoon baking powder
    1 teaspoon vanilla
    ½ teaspoon baking soda
    2 cups rolled oats
    1 cup chopped cocktail peanuts *or* semisweet
         chocolate pieces

In a large bowl beat margarine and peanut butter with an electric mixer on medium speed 30 seconds or till combined. Add *half* of the flour. Add sugar, brown sugar, eggs, baking powder, vanilla, and soda; beat till combined. Stir in remaining flour. Stir in oats and peanuts. Drop dough from a rounded teaspoon 2 inches apart on an ungreased cookie sheet. Bake in a 375° oven about 10 minutes or till edges are lightly browned. Cool on a wire rack. Makes about 60.

Selecting Oat Bran

Don't confuse *oat bran* (resembles coarsely ground oat flour) with *oat bran flake cereals* (similar in appearance to wheat or corn flakes). The oat bran called for in our recipes is available in supermarkets and health food stores. Oat bran flake cereals have a different texture and contain other ingredients in addition to the oats (see ingredient lists on labels). Oat bran cereals won't give you the same baking results as oat bran.

Pineapple Nut Cookies

1   8-ounce can crushed pineapple, (juice pack)
½   cup margarine *or* butter
2   cups all-purpose flour
1   cup packed brown sugar
1   egg
1   teaspoon baking powder
1   teaspoon vanilla
¼   teaspoon baking soda
½   cup chopped pecans
    Pineapple-Cream Cheese Frosting

Grease a cookie sheet; set aside. Drain pineapple, reserving juice for frosting. Set pineapple and juice aside. In a large mixing bowl beat the margarine or butter with an electric mixer on medium to high speed about 30 seconds or till softened.

Add about *half* of the flour to the margarine. Then add brown sugar, egg, baking powder, vanilla, and baking soda. Beat till thoroughly combined. Beat or stir in the remaining flour. Then stir in the drained pineapple and pecans.

Drop dough from a rounded teaspoon 2 inches apart on the prepared cookie sheet. Bake in a 375° oven for 8 to 10 minutes or till edges are lightly browned. Remove cookies from cookie sheet and cool on a wire rack. Frost cookies with Pineapple-Cream Cheese Frosting. Store in refrigerator. Makes about 42.

Pineapple-Cream Cheese Frosting: In a small bowl beat 2 tablespoons *soft-style cream cheese,* 1 tablespoon *margarine or butter,* and 1 tablespoon of *reserved juice* till well combined. Gradually beat in 1½ cups sifted *powdered sugar.* If necessary, beat in an additional *1 to 2 teaspoons* of the reserved juice to make a frosting of spreading consistency. Makes about ¾ cup.

White Chocolate-Hazelnut Cookies

½   cup margarine *or* butter
1¼ cups all-purpose flour
⅔   cup sugar
1   egg
½   teaspoon baking powder
1   6-ounce package white baking bar with cocoa butter, coarsely chopped (about 1 cup)
½   cup coarsely chopped hazelnuts (filberts), pecans, *or* macadamia nuts

In a large mixing bowl beat margarine or butter with an electric mixer on medium to high speed about 30 seconds or till softened. Add about *half* of the flour to the margarine. Add sugar, egg, and baking powder. Beat till thoroughly combined, scraping sides of bowl occasionally. Beat or stir in the remaining flour. Then stir in baking bar and nuts.

Drop dough from a rounded tablespoon 2 inches apart on an ungreased cookie sheet. Bake in a 375° oven about 8 minutes or till edges are lightly browned. Cool on a wire rack. Makes about 30.

Storing Cookies

To preserve the just-baked freshness of cookies, choose tightly covered containers or plastic bags. Either choice will prevent humidity from softening crisp cookies and air from drying out soft cookies. Be sure to store crisp and soft cookies separately. Most cookies can be stored successfully for up to three days at room temperature.

To freeze cookies, tightly package cookies in freezer bags or airtight containers for up to 12 months. Before serving, thaw for 15 minutes.

SHAPED COOKIES

Fun shapes and decorative touches abound in the cookie recipes that follow. Create an array of designs by shaping the dough with your hands or by using a cookie press or cookie molds. Whatever's your fancy—shaping balls for Peanut Butter Crisscross Cookies or molding shell-shaped Madeleines—you'll find it all here in Shaped Cookies.

□ What's the easiest way to get the exact yield from a cookie recipe? Simply pat the dough into a square. Cut the dough into the number of pieces that matches the recipe yield. Then shape and bake them. For instance, for 48 cookies, cut the dough into six equal strips one way and eight equal strips the other way. Then shape the pieces into 48 balls and bake.

□ Some cookie recipes require special tools, such as cookie presses or cookie molds. Because the consistency of the dough was developed with a particular tool in mind, be sure to use the specific tool called for in the recipe.

□ Cookie molds vary, so to ensure good results follow the directions that come with your particular cookie mold.

□ Shaped cookies are done baking when the edges are lightly browned.

Brandy Snaps

Fill them with delicious brandy-flavored whipped cream or serve them plain with your favorite ice cream.

½ **cup packed brown sugar**
⅓ **cup margarine *or* butter, melted**
¼ **cup light molasses *or* dark corn syrup**
1 **tablespoon brandy**
¾ **cup all-purpose flour**
½ **teaspoon ground ginger**
½ **teaspoon ground nutmeg**
   Brandy-Cream Filling (optional)
   Grated semisweet chocolate (optional)

Line a cookie sheet with foil. Grease foil and set cookie sheet aside. In a medium bowl stir together brown sugar, margarine, molasses, and brandy. Stir in flour, ginger, and nutmeg till thoroughly combined.

Drop batter from a *level* teaspoon 3 inches apart on the prepared cookie sheet. (Bake only 4 or 5 cookies at a time.) Bake in a 350° oven for 5 to 6 minutes or till the cookies are bubbly and a deep golden brown.

Cool on sheet about 2 minutes or till set. Quickly remove cookies, one at a time, and roll around a metal cone or the greased handle of a wooden spoon. Cool. (If cookies harden before shaping, reheat about 1 minute or till softened.)

If filling is desired, prepare it just before serving. Then spoon the filling into a decorating bag fitted with a large star tip (about ½ inch in diameter). Pipe filling into each cookie. If desired, sprinkle the cookies with grated chocolate. Makes about 54.

Brandy-Cream Filling: In a small bowl combine 2 cups *whipping cream,* ¼ cup sifted *powdered sugar,* and 2 tablespoons *brandy.* Beat with an electric mixer on medium to high speed till stiff peaks form. Makes about 4 cups.

Orange Crisps
(see recipe, page 144)

Brandy Snaps

Orange Crisps

Don't forget—bake only three cookies at a time so you can shape them while they're warm. (Pictured on page 143.)

> 2 **egg whites**
> ¼ **cup margarine *or* butter**
> 2 **teaspoons finely shredded orange peel**
> ½ **cup sugar**
> ½ **cup all-purpose flour**
> ½ **cup semisweet chocolate pieces (optional)**
> 1 **tablespoon shortening (optional)**

In a medium bowl bring egg whites to room temperature. Set aside. Generously grease a cookie sheet. (Repeat greasing cookie sheet for each batch.) Set aside. In a small saucepan heat margarine over low heat *just till melted.* Stir in peel and set aside to cool.

Beat egg whites with an electric mixer on medium to high speed till soft peaks form (tips curl). Gradually add sugar, beating till stiff peaks form (tips stand straight). Fold in about *half* of the flour. Then gently stir in margarine mixture. Fold in the remaining flour till thoroughly combined.

Drop batter from a *level tablespoon* at least 3 inches apart on prepared cookie sheet. Spread batter into 3-inch circles. (Bake only 3 cookies at a time.) Bake in a 375° oven for 5 to 6 minutes or till done.

Immediately remove cookies from cookie sheet, one at a time. Place cookie upside down on a table or countertop and quickly roll it around the greased handle of a wooden spoon or dowel. Slide the cookie off and cool on a wire rack. Repeat with remaining warm cookies. (If cookies harden before you can shape them, reheat about 1 minute.)

If desired, in a small heavy saucepan heat chocolate and shortening over low heat *just till melted,* stirring occasionally. Remove from heat. Dip one end of each cookie into chocolate mixture. Let excess drip off. Transfer to a waxed-paper-lined cookie sheet. Let stand till chocolate is set. Makes about 30.

Orange Roof Tiles: Prepare batter for Orange Crisps as directed at left, *except* fold in ¼ cup finely chopped *almonds* with the remaining flour. Spread batter on cookie sheets and bake as directed. Remove cookies and immediately wrap them around a rolling pin to give them a curved shape. Instead of dipping in chocolate, lightly sift *powdered sugar* over cookies. Makes about 30.

Chocolate Crinkles

> 3 **beaten eggs**
> 1½ **cups sugar**
> 4 **squares (4 ounces) unsweetened chocolate, melted**
> ½ **cup cooking oil**
> 2 **teaspoons baking powder**
> 2 **teaspoons vanilla**
> 2 **cups all-purpose flour**
> **Powdered sugar**

In a large mixing bowl stir together beaten eggs, sugar, melted chocolate, cooking oil, baking powder, and vanilla. Gradually stir in the flour till thoroughly combined. Cover and chill for 1 to 2 hours or till the dough is easy to handle.

Shape dough into 1-inch balls. Roll balls in powdered sugar to coat. Place 2 inches apart on an ungreased cookie sheet. Bake in a 375° oven for 8 to 10 minutes or till edges are set and tops are crackled.

Remove the cookies from the cookie sheet. Cool on a wire rack. If desired, sift additional powdered sugar over cookies. Makes about 48.

Gingersnaps

Transform gingersnaps into perfect pumpkin faces at Halloween by decorating cookies with colorful icings. (Basic Gingersnaps are pictured on pages 126–127.)

2¼ **cups all-purpose flour**
1 **cup packed brown sugar**
¾ **cup shortening *or* cooking oil**
¼ **cup molasses**
1 **egg**
1 **teaspoon baking soda**
1 **teaspoon ground ginger**
1 **teaspoon ground cinnamon**
½ **teaspoon ground cloves**
¼ **cup sugar**

In a large bowl place about *half* of the flour. Add the brown sugar, shortening or oil, molasses, egg, baking soda, ginger, cinnamon, and cloves. Beat with an electric mixer on medium to high speed till thoroughly combined, scraping sides of bowl occasionally. Then beat or stir in the remaining flour.

Shape the dough into 1-inch balls. Roll the balls in sugar to coat. Place 2 inches apart on an ungreased cookie sheet. Bake in a 375° oven for 8 to 10 minutes or till edges are set and tops are crackled. Cool on cookie sheet for 1 minute. Remove cookies from the cookie sheet. Cool on a wire rack. Makes about 48.

Snickerdoodles

½ **cup margarine *or* butter**
1½ **cups all-purpose flour**
1 **cup sugar**
1 **egg**
½ **teaspoon vanilla**
¼ **teaspoon baking soda**
¼ **teaspoon cream of tartar**
2 **tablespoons sugar**
1 **teaspoon ground cinnamon**

In a large mixing bowl beat margarine or butter with an electric mixer on medium to high speed about 30 seconds or till softened.

Add about *half* of the flour to the margarine. Then add the 1 cup sugar, egg, vanilla, baking soda, and cream of tartar. Beat till thoroughly combined, scraping sides of bowl occasionally. Then beat or stir in the remaining flour. Cover and chill for 1 hour.

In a shallow dish combine the 2 tablespoons sugar and cinnamon. Shape dough into 1-inch balls. Roll balls in the sugar-cinnamon mixture to coat. Place 2 inches apart on an ungreased cookie sheet. Bake in a 375° oven about 10 minutes or till done. Cool on cookie sheet for 1 minute. Remove cookies from cookie sheet; cool on a wire rack. Makes about 36.

Using Margarine in Cookies

The firmness of cookie dough can vary depending on the type of margarine you use. If you choose margarine that's made from 100 percent corn oil, your dough will be softer than dough made from other margarines. So, you may need to adjust the chilling instructions given in the recipe.

How you adjust the chilling will depend on the type of cookie dough with which you're working. For shaped or sliced cookie dough made with 100 percent corn oil margarine, chill the dough in the freezer instead of the refrigerator. If you're using 100 percent corn oil margarine in cutout cookie dough, refrigerate the dough at least 5 hours before rolling it out.

Hazelnut Mocha Morsels

A crunchy nut garnishes each tender cookie.

- ½ teaspoon instant coffee crystals
- 1 tablespoon milk
- 1 teaspoon vanilla
- 1 cup margarine *or* butter
- 1¾ cups all-purpose flour
- ⅔ cup sugar
- ¼ cup unsweetened cocoa powder
- 2 egg yolks
- 42 to 44 hazelnuts (filberts) *or* pecan *or* walnut halves (about ½ cup)
- Hazelnut Icing

In a custard cup dissolve coffee crystals in milk. Add the vanilla; set aside. In a large mixing bowl beat margarine or butter with an electric mixer on medium to high speed about 30 seconds or till softened.

Add about *half* of the flour to the margarine. Then add sugar, cocoa powder, egg yolks, and coffee mixture. Beat till thoroughly combined, scraping bowl occasionally. Then beat or stir in the remaining flour. If necessary, cover and chill dough till easy to handle.

Shape dough into 1-inch balls. Place 2 inches apart on an ungreased cookie sheet. Press a hazelnut or a pecan or walnut half in the center of each ball.

Bake in a 375° oven for 8 to 10 minutes or till the edges are firm. Cool on cookie sheet for 1 minute. Remove cookies from cookie sheet and cool on a wire rack. Drizzle icing over cookies. Makes about 42.

Hazelnut Icing: In a small mixing bowl combine ½ cup sifted *powdered sugar,* ¼ teaspoon *vanilla,* and 2 to 3 teaspoons *hazelnut liqueur or milk* to make an icing of drizzling consistency. Makes about ¼ cup.

Rum Prints

Rich rum-flavored buttercream filling enhances these delectable spiced cookies.

- ⅔ cup margarine *or* butter
- 1¾ cups all-purpose flour
- ⅓ cup sugar
- 1 egg
- 1 teaspoon vanilla
- ¼ teaspoon ground nutmeg
- Rum Buttercream Filling
- Grated chocolate *or* ground nuts (optional)

In a large mixing bowl beat the margarine or butter with an electric mixer on medium to high speed about 30 seconds or till softened.

Add about *half* of the flour to the margarine. Then add the sugar, egg, vanilla, and nutmeg. Beat till thoroughly combined, scraping the sides of the bowl occasionally. Then beat or stir in the remaining flour.

Shape dough into 1-inch balls. Place 2 inches apart on an ungreased cookie sheet. Using your thumb, press an indentation into each cookie. Bake in a 375° oven about 8 minutes or till done. Remove cookies from the cookie sheet and cool on a wire rack.

Prepare the Rum Buttercream Filling. Spoon the filling into a decorating bag fitted with a medium star tip (about ¼ inch in diameter). Pipe about ½ *teaspoon* filling into the center of *each* cookie. If desired, sprinkle filling with grated chocolate or ground nuts. Makes about 36.

Rum Buttercream Filling: In a small bowl beat 1 cup *powdered sugar* and ¼ cup *margarine or butter* till smooth. Stir in 1 tablespoon *rum, or* 1 tablespoon *milk plus* ¼ teaspoon *rum extract,* till smooth. Makes about ½ cup.

Jam Thumbprints
(see recipe, page 148)

Hazelnut Mocha Morsels

Peanut Butter Crisscross Cookies

Create a chocolate kiss version of these cookies. Shape the dough into balls, but do not flatten. After baking, press a milk chocolate kiss into each hot cookie.

- ½ **cup peanut butter**
- ¼ **cup shortening**
- ¼ **cup margarine *or* butter**
- 1⅓ **cups all-purpose flour**
- ½ **cup sugar**
- ½ **cup packed brown sugar**
- 1 **egg**
- 1 **teaspoon vanilla**
- ½ **teaspoon baking powder**
- ½ **teaspoon baking soda**
  Sugar

In a large mixing bowl beat the peanut butter, shortening, and margarine or butter with an electric mixer on medium to high speed about 30 seconds or till mixture is combined.

Add about *half* of the flour to the peanut butter mixture. Then add the ½ cup sugar, brown sugar, egg, vanilla, baking powder, and baking soda. Beat till thoroughly combined, scraping sides of bowl occasionally. Then beat or stir in the remaining flour. If necessary, cover and chill dough till easy to handle.

Shape the dough into 1-inch balls. Place 2 inches apart on an ungreased cookie sheet. Using the tines of a fork dipped in the additional sugar, flatten balls to about ¼-inch thickness by pressing fork in two directions to form crisscross marks.

Bake in a 375° oven for 9 to 11 minutes or till done. Remove the cookies from the cookie sheet. Cool on a wire rack. Makes about 48.

Jam Thumbprints

Feature your favorite jams or preserves in these traditional cookies. (Pictured on page 147.)

- ⅔ **cup margarine *or* butter**
- 1½ **cups all-purpose flour**
- ½ **cup sugar**
- 2 **egg yolks**
- 1 **teaspoon vanilla**
- 2 **slightly beaten egg whites**
- 1 **cup finely chopped walnuts**
- ⅓ **to ½ cup cherry, apricot, *or*
  strawberry jam *or* preserves**

Generously grease a cookie sheet. Set aside. In a large mixing bowl beat margarine or butter with an electric mixer on medium to high speed about 30 seconds or till softened.

Add about *half* of the flour to the margarine. Add sugar, egg yolks, and vanilla. Beat till thoroughly combined, scraping sides of bowl occasionally. Beat or stir in the remaining flour. Cover and chill about 1 hour.

Shape the dough into 1-inch balls. Roll balls in egg whites, then in walnuts. Place 1 inch apart on the prepared cookie sheet. Using your thumb, press an indentation into each cookie. Bake in a 375° oven for 10 to 12 minutes or till done. Remove cookies from cookie sheet and cool on a wire rack. To serve, fill centers with jam or preserves. Makes about 42.

Home Is Where The Hearth Is

Did you know that in the past, home baking served a dual purpose? Food was baked not only for the table, but also to keep the house warm during cold spells.

Chocolate-Covered Cherry Cookies

Cherries soaked in cherry brandy impart a distinct flavor to these cookies. Or if you prefer, use maraschino cherry juice instead of the brandy.

- 1 **10-ounce jar small maraschino cherries (about 48), drained**
- 2 **tablespoons cherry brandy *or* maraschino cherry juice**
- ½ **cup margarine *or* butter**
- 1½ **cups all-purpose flour**
- 1 **cup sugar**
- ½ **cup unsweetened cocoa powder**
- 1 **egg**
- ¼ **teaspoon baking soda**
- ¼ **teaspoon baking powder**
  Chocolate-Cherry Frosting

In a small bowl lightly toss cherries with cherry brandy or maraschino cherry juice. Let stand for 30 minutes, stirring once or twice. Then drain well, reserving liquid for cookie dough and frosting.

In a large mixing bowl beat margarine or butter with an electric mixer on medium to high speed about 30 seconds or till softened.

Add about *half* of the flour to the margarine. Then add sugar, cocoa powder, egg, baking soda, baking powder, and *1 teaspoon* of the reserved liquid. Beat till thoroughly combined, scraping sides of bowl occasionally. Beat or stir in the remaining flour.

Shape *1 scant teaspoon* of the dough around each cherry. Place each ball in a miniature paper or foil bake cup (1 inch in diameter). Place cups 1 inch apart on an ungreased cookie sheet. (*Or,* omit the bake cups and place the dough balls 1 inch apart on an ungreased cookie sheet.)

Bake in a 350° oven for 10 to 12 minutes or till tops look dry. Transfer cookies from cookie sheet to a wire rack. Frost each *warm* cookie with ½ teaspoon frosting. Then cool completely. Makes 48.

Chocolate-Cherry Frosting: In a small heavy saucepan stir together ½ cup *semisweet chocolate pieces* and ⅓ cup *sweetened condensed milk.* Cook over low heat *just till* chocolate is melted, stirring occasionally. Stir in 1 to 2 tablespoons of the *reserved liquid* to make frosting of spreading consistency. Makes about ½ cup.

Pfeffernuss

- ¾ **cup light molasses**
- ½ **cup sugar**
- ½ **cup margarine *or* butter**
- 2 **eggs**
- 4 **cups all-purpose flour**
- 1½ **teaspoons ground cinnamon**
- 1¼ **teaspoons baking soda**
- ½ **teaspoon ground cloves**
- ½ **teaspoon ground nutmeg**
  Powdered sugar

In a large saucepan combine molasses, sugar, and margarine or butter. Heat and stir *just till melted.* Cool mixture.

Add eggs. Using a wooden spoon, beat *just till* combined. Add about *half* of the flour. Then add the cinnamon, baking soda, cloves, and nutmeg. Beat till thoroughly combined. Beat in remaining flour. Cover and chill for several hours or till easy to handle.

Shape the dough into 1-inch balls. Place 1 inch apart on an ungreased cookie sheet. Bake in a 375° oven about 7 minutes or till done. Remove cookies from the cookie sheet and cool on a wire rack. Sift powdered sugar over cookies. Makes about 84.

Sugar 'n' Spice Molded Cookies

Become a cookie artist—highlight molded cookies with food colors that have been diluted with some water.

- ½ **cup butter**
- ¼ **cup shortening**
- 3 **cups all-purpose flour**
- 1 **cup packed brown sugar**
- ¼ **cup milk**
- 1 **egg yolk**
- 1½ **teaspoons finely shredded lemon peel (optional)**
- 1¼ **teaspoons ground cinnamon *or* 1 teaspoon ground cardamom**
- ¾ **teaspoon ground ginger**
- ½ **teaspoon ground nutmeg**
- ½ **teaspoon vanilla**
- ¼ **teaspoon baking powder**
- ⅛ **teaspoon salt**
- ⅛ **teaspoon ground cloves**

Generously grease a cookie sheet. Set cookie sheet aside. In a large mixing bowl beat butter and shortening with an electric mixer on medium to high speed about 30 seconds or till softened.

Add *half* of the flour to butter mixture. Add brown sugar, *half* of the milk, egg yolk, lemon peel (if desired), cinnamon, ginger, nutmeg, vanilla, baking powder, salt, and cloves. Beat till thoroughly combined, scraping bowl. Beat or stir in remaining flour and remaining milk. (If necessary, knead in last portion of flour by hand.) Shape into large or small cookies and bake as directed below or at right. Cool on cookie sheet for 1 minute. Remove and cool on a rack. Makes 10 to 16 large or 48 to 60 small cookies.

For large cookies: *Lightly* oil and flour a ceramic cookie mold. (If using a wooden mold, *only oil* the mold.) Press dough firmly into mold. Level the dough. Loosen molded cookie dough with a toothpick and carefully unmold onto prepared cookie sheet. Repeat flouring the ceramic mold, but *do not oil* again. Repeat with remaining dough, placing cookies 2 inches apart on prepared cookie sheet. Bake in a 375° oven for 12 to 14 minutes or till done.

For small cookies: Shape the dough into 1- to 1¼-inch balls. Place 2 inches apart on the prepared cookie sheet. Using a *floured* cookie stamp or the *floured* bottom of a glass, flatten balls to ⅛- to ¼-inch thickness. If desired, trim the uneven edges from cookies with a round cookie cutter. Bake in a 375° oven for 8 to 10 minutes or till done.

Honey Stamped Cookies

- ½ **cup margarine *or* butter**
- 1¼ **cups all-purpose flour**
- ⅓ **cup sugar**
- 1 **egg yolk**
- 1 **tablespoon honey**
- ½ **teaspoon vanilla**
  Sugar (optional)

In a large bowl beat margarine with an electric mixer on medium to high speed about 30 seconds or till softened. Add about *half* of the flour. Add the ⅓ cup sugar, egg yolk, honey, and vanilla. Beat till thoroughly combined. Beat or stir in the remaining flour.

Shape dough into 1- to 1½-inch balls. Place 2 inches apart on an ungreased cookie sheet. Using a *floured* cookie stamp or the *floured* bottom of a glass, flatten balls to ¼-inch thickness. If desired, trim uneven edges from cookies with a round cookie cutter. If desired, lightly sprinkle cookies with additional sugar.

Bake in a 375° oven about 6 minutes or till done. Cool on cookie sheet for 1 minute. Then remove cookies from cookie sheet and cool on a wire rack. Makes 24 to 36.

Buttery Spritz Cookies

¾ cup margarine *or* butter
1¾ cups all-purpose flour
½ cup sugar
1 egg yolk
½ teaspoon vanilla
¼ teaspoon baking powder
¼ teaspoon coconut flavoring, *or* 2 drops oil of
    cinnamon (optional)
    Desired small decorative candies,
      finely chopped dried fruits *or* nuts, *or*
      colored sugars (optional)

In a large bowl beat margarine with an electric mixer on medium to high speed about 30 seconds or till softened. Add about *half* of the flour. Add sugar, egg yolk, vanilla, and baking powder. If desired, add coconut flavoring. Beat till thoroughly combined. Beat or stir in remaining flour. *Do not chill dough.*

Pack dough into a cookie press. Force dough through press onto an ungreased cookie sheet. If desired, decorate with candies, fruits, nuts, or colored sugars. Bake in a 375° oven for 8 to 10 minutes or till edges are firm but not browned. Remove cookies from cookie sheet; cool on a rack. Makes about 42.

Buttery Chocolate-Mint Spritz Cookies: Prepare Buttery Spritz Cookies as above, *except* reduce flour to *1½ cups.* Stir in 3 tablespoons *unsweetened cocoa powder* with sugar and substitute ¼ teaspoon *mint extract* for coconut flavoring.

Buttery Nut Spritz Cookies with Chocolate Drizzle: Prepare Buttery Spritz Cookies as above, *except* reduce flour to *1½ cups,* omit coconut flavoring, and stir ½ cup ground *hazelnuts (filberts)* or *almonds* into dough.
    For chocolate drizzle, melt ¼ cup *semisweet chocolate pieces* and 1 teaspoon *shortening* over low heat. Drizzle over cookies.

Sandbakkelse

Sandbakkelse, or Norwegian "sand tarts," are rich and delicate molded cookies with a mild almond flavor.

½ cup butter
½ cup sugar
1 egg yolk
¼ teaspoon almond extract
1⅓ cups all-purpose flour
    Sugar (optional)

If necessary, season 2½-inch sandbakkelse molds.* In a large mixing bowl beat the butter with an electric mixer on medium to high speed about 30 seconds or till softened.

Add ½ cup sugar to butter and beat till well combined. Then add egg yolk and almond extract. Beat till thoroughly combined. Beat or stir in the flour.

Place about *2 teaspoons* of dough in the center of *each* seasoned sandbakkelse mold. Press dough in an even, very thin layer along the bottom and up the sides of the mold. Place molds on a cookie sheet.

Or, shape the dough into 1-inch balls. Place 2 inches apart on an ungreased cookie sheet. Using a cookie stamp or bottom of a glass dipped in the additional sugar, flatten balls to ¼-inch thickness.

Bake in a 375° oven about 8 minutes or till done. For molded cookies, *cool in the molds.* To remove, invert molds and tap lightly. If necessary, loosen cookies from molds with a toothpick. For flattened cookies, remove from the cookie sheet. Cool cookies on a wire rack. Makes 30 to 36.

*To season 2½-inch sandbakkelse molds, grease inside of molds with shortening. Heat in a 300° oven for 30 minutes. Cool. Wipe out excess shortening. (After use, rinse with water and wipe out with paper towels. No further seasoning is needed.)

Madeleines

Lemon-Filled Ladyfinger Sandwiches

4 egg whites
½ cup sugar
4 egg yolks
½ teaspoon finely shredded lemon peel
2 teaspoons lemon juice
1 teaspoon vanilla
¾ cup sifted cake flour
4 teaspoons powdered sugar
Lemon Curd Filling

Line a cookie sheet with parchment or plain brown paper. Set aside. In a large mixing bowl beat egg whites and dash *salt* with an electric mixer till soft peaks form (tips curl). Gradually add ¼ *cup* of the sugar, beating till stiff peaks form (tips stand straight).

In a small bowl beat egg yolks on medium speed for 1 minute. Gradually add remaining sugar, beating till thick and lemon-colored. Beat in lemon peel, lemon juice, and vanilla. Fold egg yolk mixture into egg whites. Fold in cake flour. Spoon batter into a decorating bag fitted with a large round tip (about ½ inch in diameter). Pipe 3½x¾-inch strips of batter 1 inch apart on the prepared cookie sheet. (*Or,* spoon batter into ungreased ladyfinger molds till batter is even with top of pan.) Sift powdered sugar over cookies.

Bake in a 350° oven for 8 to 10 minutes or till lightly browned. Transfer cookies on paper or in ladyfinger molds to a wire rack. Cool cookies for 15 minutes. Remove ladyfingers from the paper or molds, then completely cool on the wire rack. If desired, store unfilled ladyfingers in the freezer till the day of serving.

Just before serving, spread about *2 teaspoons* of the Lemon Curd Filling on the flat side of *half* of the ladyfingers. Top with the remaining ladyfingers, forming sandwiches. Makes about 18.

Lemon Curd Filling: In a saucepan combine ⅓ cup *sugar* and 2 teaspoons *cornstarch.* Stir in 2 teaspoons finely shredded *lemon peel,* ¼ cup *lemon juice,* and ¼ cup *margarine or butter.* Cook and stir till thickened and bubbly. Stir *half* of the mixture into 2 beaten *eggs.* Return mixture to pan. Cook and stir for 2 minutes. Cover with waxed paper; cool. Makes about 1 cup.

Madeleines

2 eggs
½ teaspoon vanilla
½ teaspoon finely shredded lemon peel
1 cup sifted powdered sugar
⅔ cup all-purpose flour
¼ teaspoon baking powder
½ cup margarine *or* butter, melted and cooled
Powdered sugar

Grease and flour twenty-four 3-inch madeleine molds; set aside. In a medium bowl beat eggs, vanilla, and lemon peel with an electric mixer on high speed for 5 minutes. Gradually beat in 1 cup powdered sugar. Beat for 5 to 7 minutes or till thick and satiny.

Sift together flour and baking powder. Sift *one-fourth* of flour mixture over egg mixture; gently fold in. Fold in remaining flour by fourths. Fold in margarine. Spoon into the prepared molds, filling ¾ full. Bake in a 375° oven for 10 to 12 minutes or till edges are golden and tops spring back. Cool in molds on a rack for 1 minute. Loosen cookies with a knife. Invert cookies onto rack and cool. Sift additional powdered sugar over tops. Store in freezer. Makes 24.

SLICED COOKIES

Keep sliced cookie dough on hand for the next time you have a craving for homemade cookies. Just slice the roll of cookie dough and pop the cookies into the oven. You'll have warm, yummy cookies in no time. Try Peanut Butter-Fudge Swirls, Praline 'n' Brown Sugar Rounds, or any of the other tempting sliced cookie recipes. They're all convenient and delicious.

☐ For a change of pace, coat a roll of cookie dough in finely chopped nuts, colored sugar, or flaked coconut. Just roll the dough in the coating, pressing to make it stick. Then chill.

☐ To speed dough chilling, freeze the dough for about one-third of the refrigerator time. However, *do not freeze* dough made entirely with butter. It will become too firm to slice (see tip, page 145).

☐ If a recipe makes more than one roll of cookie dough, take only one roll from the refrigerator at a time to slice. Keep the other roll chilled.

☐ To keep all of your cookies nice and round, rotate the roll frequently while you're slicing. This will help you avoid flattening one side.

☐ Sliced cookies have a crisp but tender texture. Bake them till the edges are firm and the bottoms of the cookies are lightly browned.

☐ To keep your baked cookies from sticking to one another, do not stack or store them until they're thoroughly cooled.

Chocolate-Coconut Slices

Fudgy and chewy around the edges, these cookies have moist, soft coconut centers. (Pictured on page 159.)

1	3-ounce package cream cheese, softened
⅓	cup sugar
1	teaspoon vanilla
1	cup coconut
½	cup finely chopped nuts
⅓	cup margarine *or* butter
1½	cups all-purpose flour
1	cup sugar
¼	cup unsweetened cocoa powder
1	egg
3	tablespoons milk
½	teaspoon baking soda

For filling, in a large bowl beat cream cheese, the ⅓ cup sugar, and vanilla with an electric mixer on medium to high speed about 30 seconds or till smooth. Stir in coconut and nuts. Cover and chill.

For dough, in a medium bowl beat margarine or butter on medium to high speed about 30 seconds or till softened. Add about *half* of the flour. Then add the 1 cup sugar, cocoa powder, egg, milk, and baking soda. Beat till thoroughly combined. Beat or stir in remaining flour. Cover and chill for 30 minutes.

To shape, place dough between 2 sheets of waxed paper. Using a rolling pin, roll dough into a 14x6-inch rectangle. Remove top sheet of waxed paper. Remove filling from refrigerator and shape into a 14-inch-long roll. Place filling on top of dough. Roll dough around filling, removing bottom sheet of waxed paper as you roll. Moisten and pinch edges together. Cut roll in half. Wrap each half in waxed paper or plastic wrap, then chill for 4 to 48 hours.

Grease a cookie sheet. Cut dough into ¼-inch-thick slices. Place 2 inches apart on prepared cookie sheet. Bake in a 375° oven for 7 to 9 minutes or till edges are firm. Cool on cookie sheet for 1 minute. Remove cookies and cool on a wire rack. Makes about 52.

Apricot-Hazelnut Spirals

Tender dough wraps around a sweet and tart apricot-hazelnut filling. (Pictured on pages 126–127.)

½ cup margarine *or* butter
¼ cup shortening
2 cups all-purpose flour
¾ cup sugar
2 tablespoons milk
½ teaspoon vanilla
¼ teaspoon baking powder
1 12-ounce can apricot cake and pastry filling
½ cup whole hazelnuts (filberts) *or* almonds, ground

In a large bowl beat margarine or butter and shortening with an electric mixer on medium to high speed about 30 seconds or till softened. Add about *half* of the flour. Then add the sugar, milk, vanilla, and baking powder. Beat till thoroughly combined. Then beat or stir in the remaining flour.

To shape, divide the dough in half. Place *each* half of the dough between 2 sheets of waxed paper. Using a rolling pin, roll *each* half into a 12x6-inch rectangle. Remove top sheets of waxed paper. In a small mixing bowl stir together apricot filling and ground hazelnuts or almonds. Spread *half* of the apricot-nut mixture over *each* rectangle. From a long side, roll up *each* rectangle jelly-roll style, removing bottom sheet of waxed paper as you roll. Moisten and pinch edges to seal each roll. Wrap each roll in waxed paper or plastic wrap, then chill for 4 to 48 hours.

Grease a cookie sheet. Set aside. Cut chilled dough into ¼-inch-thick slices. Place 2 inches apart on the prepared cookie sheet. Bake in a 375° oven for 10 to 12 minutes or till done. Cool on cookie sheet for 1 minute. Remove cookies from the cookie sheet and cool on a wire rack. Makes about 84.

Whole Wheat Slices

Tasty sliced cookies spiced with nutmeg and lightly coated with wheat germ.

½ cup margarine *or* butter
½ cup shortening
1½ cups all-purpose flour
1 cup packed brown sugar
1 egg
2 tablespoons milk
1 teaspoon vanilla
½ teaspoon baking soda
½ teaspoon ground nutmeg
¼ teaspoon salt
1 cup whole wheat flour
¼ cup toasted wheat germ

In a large mixing bowl beat margarine or butter and shortening with an electric mixer on medium to high speed about 30 seconds or till softened. Add about *half* of the all-purpose flour. Then add the brown sugar, egg, milk, vanilla, baking soda, nutmeg, and salt. Beat till thoroughly combined, scraping sides of bowl occasionally. Then beat or stir in the remaining all-purpose flour and the whole wheat flour.

Shape the dough into *two* 7-inch rolls. Roll them in wheat germ to coat. Wrap the rolls in waxed paper or plastic wrap. Chill for 4 to 48 hours.

Cut the dough into ¼-inch-thick slices. Place 2 inches apart on an ungreased cookie sheet. Bake in a 375° oven for 8 to 10 minutes or till done. Remove cookies and cool on a wire rack. Makes about 48.

Selecting Fats

When choosing a product other than butter for baking, select stick products labeled margarine. Avoid diet products and spreads.

Date Pinwheel Cookies

Date Filling
½ **cup margarine *or* butter**
½ **cup shortening**
3 **cups all-purpose flour**
½ **cup sugar**
½ **cup packed brown sugar**
1 **egg**
3 **tablespoons milk**
1 **teaspoon vanilla**
½ **teaspoon baking soda**
¼ **teaspoon salt**

Prepare Date Filling as directed at right. Set aside. In a large mixing bowl beat margarine or butter and shortening with an electric mixer on medium to high speed about 30 seconds or till softened. Add about *half* of the flour. Then add the sugar, brown sugar, egg, milk, vanilla, baking soda, and salt. Beat till thoroughly combined, scraping the sides of the bowl occasionally. Then beat or stir in the remaining flour. Cover and chill about 1 hour or till easy to handle.

To shape, divide the dough in half. Place *each* half of the dough between 2 sheets of waxed paper. Using a rolling pin, roll *each* half into a 12x10-inch rectangle. Remove the top sheets of waxed paper.

Spread Date Filling over *each* half of the dough. From a long side, roll up each half jelly-roll style, removing bottom sheet of paper as you roll. Moisten and pinch edges to seal each roll. Wrap each in waxed paper or plastic wrap. Chill for 4 to 48 hours.

Grease a cookie sheet; set aside. Cut the dough into ¼-inch-thick slices. Place 2 inches apart on the prepared cookie sheet. Bake in a 375° oven for 10 to 12 minutes or till done. Remove cookies from cookie sheet and cool on a wire rack. Makes about 84.

Date Filling: In a small saucepan snip one 8-ounce package (1⅓ cups) pitted whole *dates*. Stir in ½ cup *water* and ⅓ cup *sugar*. Bring to boiling, then reduce heat. Cook and stir about 2 minutes or till thickened. Then stir in 2 tablespoons *lemon juice* and ½ teaspoon *vanilla*. Set filling aside to cool. Makes about 2 cups.

Maple Crisps

Finely chop the nuts to make the dough easy to slice.

⅓ **cup margarine *or* butter**
⅓ **cup shortening**
2¼ **cups all-purpose flour**
½ **cup packed brown sugar**
¼ **cup maple-flavored syrup**
1 **egg**
½ **teaspoon baking soda**
1 **cup finely chopped walnuts *or* pecans**

In a large mixing bowl beat margarine or butter and shortening with an electric mixer on medium to high speed about 30 seconds or till softened.

Add about *half* of the flour to the margarine mixture. Then add brown sugar, syrup, egg, baking soda, and ¼ teaspoon *salt*. Beat till thoroughly combined, scraping the sides of the bowl occasionally. Then beat or stir in the remaining flour. Stir in chopped nuts. Shape dough into *two* 7-inch rolls. Wrap in waxed paper or plastic wrap, then chill for 4 to 48 hours.

Cut dough into ¼-inch-thick slices. Place 1 inch apart on an ungreased cookie sheet. Bake in a 375° oven for 7 to 9 minutes or till done. Remove the cookies from the cookie sheet and cool on a wire rack. Makes about 48.

Peanut Butter-Fudge Swirls

Swirls are both pretty and delicious. (Pictured on page 159.)

- ½ **cup margarine *or* butter**
- ½ **cup peanut butter**
- ¼ **cup shortening**
- 3 **cups all-purpose flour**
- 1¼ **cups sugar**
- 1 **egg**
- ⅓ **cup milk**
- 1 **teaspoon vanilla**
- ½ **teaspoon baking soda**
- ¼ **teaspoon salt**
- 1 **square (1 ounce) unsweetened chocolate, melted and cooled**

In a large mixing bowl beat margarine, peanut butter, and shortening with an electric mixer on medium to high speed about 30 seconds or till combined. Add about *half* of the flour. Add sugar, egg, milk, vanilla, soda, and salt. Beat till thoroughly combined. Beat or stir in remaining flour. Divide dough in half. Set one portion aside. To the remaining portion, knead or stir in melted chocolate till thoroughly combined.

To shape dough, place *each* half of dough between 2 sheets of waxed paper. Using a rolling pin, roll *each* half into a 12x11-inch rectangle. Remove top sheets of waxed paper. Carefully invert peanut butter dough on top of chocolate-peanut butter dough. Remove waxed paper from top. If necessary, pat the 2 layers together to form the 12x11-inch rectangle. If desired, trim dough around edges. From a long side, roll up jelly-roll style, removing bottom sheet of waxed paper as you roll. Cut the roll in half. Wrap in waxed paper or plastic wrap, then chill for 4 to 48 hours.

Cut chilled dough into ¼-inch-thick slices. Place 2 inches apart on an ungreased cookie sheet. Bake in a 375° oven for 10 to 12 minutes or till done. Remove cookies and cool on a wire rack. Makes about 48.

Santa's Whiskers

- ¾ **cup margarine *or* butter**
- 2 **cups all-purpose flour**
- ¾ **cup sugar**
- 1 **tablespoon milk**
- 1 **teaspoon vanilla**
- ¾ **cup finely chopped candied red *or* green cherries**
- ⅓ **cup finely chopped pecans**
- ¾ **cup coconut**

In a large bowl beat margarine with an electric mixer on medium to high speed about 30 seconds or till softened. Add about *half* of the flour. Then add the sugar, milk, and vanilla. Beat till thoroughly combined, scraping sides of bowl occasionally. Beat or stir in remaining flour. Stir in cherries and pecans.

Shape the dough into *two* 8-inch rolls. Roll *each* dough roll in coconut to coat. Wrap in waxed paper or plastic wrap, then chill 4 to 48 hours.

Cut the dough into ¼-inch-thick slices. Place 1 inch apart on an ungreased cookie sheet. Bake in a 375° oven for 10 to 12 minutes or till done. Remove cookies from the cookie sheet and cool on a wire rack. Makes about 56.

▶ *To shape the dough for Peanut Butter-Fudge Swirls, invert the peanut butter dough on top of the chocolate-peanut butter dough. If desired, trim dough around edges. Then, from a long side, roll up the dough, jelly-roll style. As you roll, remove the bottom piece of waxed paper.*

Orange-Molasses Spiced Cookies

Citrus frosting complements these mildly spiced cookies.

  ½ **cup margarine *or* butter**
  ½ **cup shortening**
2½ **cups all-purpose flour**
  ½ **cup sugar**
  ½ **cup packed brown sugar**
  1 **egg**
  2 **tablespoons dark molasses**
  1 **teaspoon ground ginger**
  ½ **teaspoon baking powder**
  ¼ **teaspoon baking soda**
  ¼ **teaspoon ground cinnamon**
  ¼ **teaspoon ground nutmeg**
  2 **tablespoons finely shredded orange peel**
    Orange-Cream Cheese Frosting

In a large bowl beat margarine and shortening with an electric mixer on medium to high speed about 30 seconds or till softened. Add about *half* of the flour. Add sugar, brown sugar, egg, molasses, ginger, baking powder, baking soda, cinnamon, and nutmeg. Beat till thoroughly combined. Stir in peel and remaining flour. Shape dough into *two* 10-inch rolls. Wrap in waxed paper or plastic wrap. Chill for 4 to 48 hours.

Cut dough into ¼-inch-thick slices. Place 2 inches apart on an ungreased cookie sheet. Bake in a 375° oven for 7 to 9 minutes or till done. Remove from cookie sheet and cool on a wire rack. Frost with Orange-Cream Cheese Frosting. Makes about 72.

Orange-Cream Cheese Frosting: In a bowl beat two 3-ounce packages softened *cream cheese,* ¼ cup softened *margarine or butter,* 1 teaspoon *vanilla,* and ½ teaspoon finely shredded *orange peel* till combined. Gradually beat in 4 cups sifted *powdered sugar* till smooth. Makes 2½ cups.

Praline 'n' Brown Sugar Rounds

  ½ **cup margarine *or* butter**
  ½ **cup shortening**
  3 **cups all-purpose flour**
  1 **cup packed brown sugar**
  1 **egg**
  2 **tablespoons milk**
  1 **teaspoon vanilla**
  ½ **teaspoon baking powder**
  ¼ **teaspoon baking soda**
  ¼ **teaspoon salt**
  1 **cup finely chopped pecans**
    Brown Sugar Frosting

In a large bowl beat margarine and shortening with an electric mixer on medium to high speed about 30 seconds or till softened. Add about *half* of the flour. Add brown sugar, egg, milk, vanilla, baking powder, soda, and salt. Beat till thoroughly combined. Stir in remaining flour. Stir in *½ cup* of the pecans. Shape dough into *two* 10-inch rolls. Wrap in waxed paper or plastic wrap, then chill 4 to 48 hours.

Cut dough into ¼-inch-thick slices. Place 2 inches apart on an ungreased cookie sheet. Bake in a 375° oven for 8 to 10 minutes or till edges are firm. Cool cookies on a wire rack. Evenly top with remaining pecans. Drizzle with *warm* frosting. Makes about 72.

Brown Sugar Frosting: In a small saucepan combine 1 cup packed *brown sugar,* ¼ cup *margarine or butter,* and ¼ cup *light cream.* Heat and stir over medium heat till mixture comes to a full boil. Boil 1 minute, stirring constantly. Remove from heat. Add 1⅓ cups sifted *powdered sugar.* Beat with a wire whisk or fork till smooth. (Frosting will thicken as it cools. If necessary, add a few drops of *water* to make of drizzling consistency.) Makes about 1¼ cups.

Praline 'n' Brown Sugar Rounds

Chocolate-Coconut Slices (see recipe, page 154)

Peanut Butter-Fudge Swirls (see recipe, page 157)

CUTOUT COOKIES

Baking cutout cookies can conjure up pleasant memories of holidays and other occasions. Remember choosing your favorite cutout forms . . . moons, stars, hearts, or ginger people? Bring back those wonderful memories by selecting one of our many classic cutout cookie recipes presented here.

☐ To ease handling, work with *half* of the dough at a time. Keep the other half refrigerated until you're ready to roll it out.

☐ To keep your cutout cookie dough from sticking to the countertop, lightly sprinkle the surface with flour. If available, a pastry stocking and cloth also will help prevent sticking.

☐ Keep cookie dough from sticking to the cookie cutter by dipping the cutter in flour between uses.

☐ To get the greatest number of cookies from the rolled-out dough, leave little (if any) space between the cutouts.

☐ You probably will have some dough scraps left after you have cut out your cookie shapes. Just combine the scraps, handling them as little as possible to keep cookies tender, and reroll the dough on a very lightly floured surface.

☐ Cutout cookies are done when the bottoms are very lightly browned and the edges are firm.

☐ Be sure to completely cool the cookies before storing them so that they don't warp.

Swedish Butter Cookies

Lemony butter cookies, dipped in semisweet chocolate.

- ½ **cup butter**
- 1 **cup all-purpose flour**
- ¼ **cup sugar**
- 1½ **teaspoons finely shredded lemon peel**
- ¼ **teaspoon vanilla**
- 4 **squares (4 ounces) semisweet chocolate**
- 2 **tablespoons shortening**

In a medium mixing bowl beat butter with an electric mixer on medium to high speed about 30 seconds or till softened.

Add about *half* of the flour to the butter. Then add the sugar, lemon peel, and vanilla. Beat on medium to high speed about 2 minutes or till thoroughly combined, scraping sides of bowl occasionally. Beat or stir in the remaining flour. Divide dough in half. Cover and chill about 1 hour or till easy to handle.

On a lightly floured surface, roll *each* half of dough to ⅛-inch thickness.* Using 2-inch cookie cutters, cut dough into desired shapes. Place 1 inch apart on an ungreased cookie sheet.

Bake in a 375° oven for 5 to 7 minutes or till done. Cool on cookie sheet 1 minute. Remove cookies from cookie sheet and cool on a wire rack.

In a small heavy saucepan heat semisweet chocolate and shortening over low heat, stirring occasionally. Dip half of *each* cookie in the chocolate mixture. Place on waxed paper about 30 minutes or till the chocolate is set. If necessary, chill the cookies till the chocolate is set. Makes about 80.

*For thicker cookies, roll *each* half of dough to ¼-inch thickness and bake the cookies in the 375° oven for 7 to 9 minutes. Use *3 squares (3 ounces)* semisweet chocolate and *4 teaspoons* shortening for the chocolate mixture. Makes about 36.

Sugar Cookie Cutouts

Perk up cookies with decorative candies, colored sugars, or chopped nuts sprinkled on before baking or after icing.

- ⅓ **cup margarine *or* butter**
- ⅓ **cup shortening**
- 2 **cups all-purpose flour**
- ¾ **cup sugar**
- 1 **egg**
- 1 **tablespoon milk**
- 1 **teaspoon baking powder**
- 1 **teaspoon vanilla**
- 1 **recipe Powdered Sugar Icing (see page 230) (optional)**

In a large bowl beat margarine or butter and shortening with an electric mixer on medium to high speed about 30 seconds or till softened. Add about *half* of the flour. Add sugar, egg, milk, baking powder, vanilla, and dash of *salt*. Beat till combined. Beat or stir in remaining flour. Divide dough in half. Cover and chill about 3 hours or till easy to handle.

On a lightly floured surface, roll *each* half of the dough to ⅛-inch thickness. Using 2½-inch cookie cutters, cut dough into desired shapes. Place 1 inch apart on an ungreased cookie sheet.

Bake in a 375° oven for 7 to 8 minutes or till done. Cool on cookie sheet for 1 minute. Remove cookies from sheet and cool on a wire rack. If desired, frost cookies with Powdered Sugar Icing. Makes about 42.

Candy-Window Sugar Cookie Cutouts: Prepare Sugar Cookie Cutouts as above, *except* before baking, place cookies on a *foil-lined* cookie sheet. Cut out a small shape in the center of each cookie. Finely crush 3 ounces *hard candy* (about ½ cup). Spoon some candy into each cookie center. Bake and cool cookies on foil.

Filled Sugar Cookie Cutouts: Prepare Sugar Cookie Cutouts as at left. Before serving, spread *1 tablespoon* tinted *Butter Frosting* (see recipe, page 224) on *half* of the cookies. Top with the remaining cookies. Makes about 21.

Pineapple Pecan Poppits

Named "poppits" because these cookies pop up during baking.

- 1½ **cups all-purpose flour**
- 1 **cup margarine *or* butter, softened**
- ½ **cup dairy sour cream**
- 3 **tablespoons sugar**
- ½ **cup pineapple spreadable fruit**
- ¼ **cup finely chopped pecans**
- ½ **of a recipe Powdered Sugar Icing (see page 230)**

In a large mixing bowl stir together flour, margarine or butter, and sour cream till thoroughly combined. Divide dough in half. Cover; chill for 3 hours.

On a lightly floured surface, roll out *each* half of dough to ⅛-inch thickness. Using a 1½-inch round cookie cutter, cut dough. Using a ¾-inch round cookie cutter, cut out centers from *half* of the rounds. Lightly brush *water* over one side of cookies *with* holes. Place cookies, brushed side down, on top of cookies *without* holes. Place 1 inch apart on an ungreased cookie sheet.

Brush the tops of the cookies with a mixture of the sugar and 1 tablespoon *water*. Spoon ¼ *teaspoon* pineapple fruit into the center of *each* cookie. Sprinkle with pecans. Bake in a 350° oven for 15 to 20 minutes or till done. Remove cookies; cool on a wire rack. Drizzle with icing. Makes about 72.

Chocolate-Almond Parson's Hats

These cookies resemble the tricornered hats of old with their triangular shape and domed filling in the center.

1⅓ cups margarine *or* butter
3½ cups all-purpose flour
1½ cups sugar
⅔ cup unsweetened cocoa powder
2 eggs
1 teaspoon baking powder
½ teaspoon salt
Almond Filling

In a large mixing bowl beat margarine or butter with an electric mixer on medium to high speed about 30 seconds or till softened. Add about *half* of the flour. Then add the sugar, cocoa powder, eggs, baking powder, and salt. Beat till thoroughly combined, scraping sides of bowl occasionally. Beat or stir in the remaining flour. Divide dough in half. Cover and chill 1 to 2 hours or till easy to handle.

On a lightly floured surface, roll *each* half of dough to ¼-inch thickness. Using a 2½-inch cookie cutter, cut dough into rounds. Spoon *1 teaspoon* of Almond Filling onto the center of *each* round.

To form each tricornered hat, lift up three edges of dough round. Fold the edges toward the filling, *but not over* the filling. Then pinch the three outer points together. Place cookies 2 inches apart on an un-greased cookie sheet. Bake in a 350° oven for 10 to 12 minutes or till edges are firm. Remove the cookies from the cookie sheet and cool them on a wire rack. Makes about 48.

Almond Filling: In a small mixing bowl beat one 8-ounce can *almond paste,* ¼ cup *sugar,* 1 *egg,* and 1 tablespoon *all-purpose flour* until smooth. Makes about 1 cup.

Cinnamon-Almond Stars

2 cups blanched almonds
2 tablespoons all-purpose flour
1½ teaspoons ground cinnamon
3 egg whites
2 cups sifted powdered sugar
1 teaspoon finely shredded lemon peel
Sifted powdered sugar

In a blender container blend almonds in fourths till all are ground. Stir in flour and cinnamon; set aside. In a large bowl beat egg whites with an electric mixer on medium speed till soft peaks form (tips curl). Gradually add the 2 cups powdered sugar and lemon peel, beating till stiff peaks form (tips stand straight). Set ¾ *cup* egg white mixture aside. Fold almond mixture into remaining egg white mixture. Cover and let stand 15 minutes or till mixture stiffens.

Generously grease a cookie sheet. On a surface lightly sprinkled with additional powdered sugar, roll almond mixture to ¼-inch thickness. Using a 1½-inch star-shaped cookie cutter, cut dough into stars. Place 1 inch apart on the prepared cookie sheet. Spread ½ *teaspoon* of the reserved egg white mixture on *each* star. Bake in a 375° oven for 6 to 8 minutes or till done. Remove and cool on a rack. Makes about 60.

◀ *To shape Chocolate-Almond Parson's Hats, lift up one-third of the edge of the dough round. Fold it toward the filling. Raise the other two edges. Bring the three edges around the filling but not over it. (The filling still should be visible.) Then pinch the three outer points of the "hat" together.*

Apple Half-Moons

To keep these moist apple-filled cookies for more than one day, store them in the freezer.

⅓ **cup dairy sour cream**
1 **beaten egg yolk**
1 **teaspoon vanilla**
1½ **cups all-purpose flour**
¼ **cup sugar**
¾ **cup margarine *or* butter**
1 **tablespoon margarine *or* butter**
2 **medium cooking apples, peeled and chopped**
¼ **cup raisins *or* light raisins**
1 **tablespoon brown sugar**
1 **teaspoon apple pie spice**
½ **of a recipe Powdered Sugar Icing**
   (see page 230)

In a small bowl stir together sour cream, egg yolk, and vanilla; set aside. In a large bowl stir together flour and sugar. Cut in the ¾ cup margarine till mixture resembles coarse crumbs. Then stir in egg yolk mixture till well combined. Divide dough in half. Cover and chill about 3 hours or till easy to handle.

Meanwhile, in a small saucepan melt the 1 tablespoon margarine or butter. Add apples, raisins, brown sugar, and apple pie spice. Cook over medium heat about 4 minutes or till apples are *just tender,* stirring occasionally. If necessary, drain off any excess liquid. Cool the apple mixture.

On a lightly floured surface, roll *each* half of dough to ⅛-inch thickness. Using a 2½-inch round cookie cutter, cut dough into rounds. Place ½ inch apart on an ungreased cookie sheet. Spoon a *scant teaspoon* of apple mixture onto the center of *each* round. Fold the rounds in half over the filling. Using the tines of a fork, press edges together to seal.

Bake in a 350° oven for 10 to 12 minutes or till lightly browned. Remove cookies from cookie sheet and cool on a wire rack. Drizzle cookies with icing. Store cookies in the freezer. Makes about 48.

Sour Cream Linzer Cookies

½ **cup margarine *or* butter**
2 **cups all-purpose flour**
1 **cup sugar**
⅓ **cup dairy sour cream**
1 **egg**
1 **teaspoon vanilla**
½ **teaspoon baking powder**
¼ **teaspoon baking soda**
⅔ **cup ground almonds**
2 **tablespoons powdered sugar**
½ **cup red raspberry jelly**

In a large mixing bowl beat margarine or butter with an electric mixer on medium to high speed about 30 seconds or till softened.

Add about *half* of the flour to the margarine. Then add the sugar, sour cream, egg, vanilla, baking powder, and baking soda. Beat till thoroughly combined, scraping sides of bowl occasionally. Then beat or stir in the remaining flour. Stir in almonds. Divide dough in half. Cover and chill the dough about 3 hours or till easy to handle.

On a well-floured pastry cloth or sheet of waxed paper, roll *each* half of dough to ⅛-inch thickness. Using a 2-inch round cookie cutter, cut dough into rounds. Then using a ¾-inch star- or heart-shaped cutter, cut out the desired shape from the centers of *half* of the rounds. Place 1 inch apart on an ungreased cookie sheet. Bake in a 375° oven for 6 to 8 minutes or till done. Remove cookies from cookie sheet and cool on a wire rack.

To assemble, sift powdered sugar over the tops of the cookies *with* holes in centers. Set aside. In a small bowl stir jelly till smooth. Spoon ½ *teaspoon* of jelly onto the center of *each* of the cookies *without* holes. Top each jellied cookie with a cookie with a hole, powdered sugar side up. Store cookies in the freezer. Makes about 40.

Lemon Cream Wafers

Delicate cookie wafers sandwiched with fresh lemon filling.

1 cup all-purpose flour
1 tablespoon sugar
½ cup margarine *or* butter
1 tablespoon lemon juice
1 to 2 tablespoons water
 Sugar
 Sunshine Filling

In a medium mixing bowl stir together flour and 1 tablespoon sugar. Cut margarine or butter into flour mixture till the mixture resembles coarse crumbs. Combine lemon juice and *1 tablespoon* of the water. Sprinkle *half* of the lemon juice mixture over part of the flour mixture, then gently toss with a fork. Push moistened portion to the side of bowl. Repeat with remaining juice mixture. (If necessary, sprinkle with the remaining 1 tablespoon of water to moisten all of the flour mixture.) Form the dough into a ball.

On a lightly floured surface, roll dough to *slightly less* than ⅛-inch thickness. Using a 1½-inch scalloped or plain round cookie cutter, cut dough into rounds. Place 1 inch apart on an ungreased cookie sheet. Lightly sprinkle with additional sugar. Using the tines of a fork, prick 4 parallel rows of holes in each round. Bake in a 375° oven for 8 to 10 minutes or till done. Remove cookies from the cookie sheet and cool on a wire rack. Using half of the cookies, spread about ½ *teaspoon* of Sunshine Filling on *each* cookie. Top with the remaining cookies. Makes about 36.

Sunshine Filling: In a bowl beat 1 cup sifted *powdered sugar*, 1 tablespoon softened *margarine or butter*, ½ teaspoon finely shredded *lemon peel*, 2 to 3 drops *yellow food coloring* (if desired), and 2 to 3 teaspoons *milk* to make a filling of spreading consistency. Makes ⅓ cup.

Cherry Shortbread Sweet Hearts

Surprise your sweetheart on Valentine's Day with a gift of these chocolate-iced heart-shaped cookies.

½ cup maraschino cherries, well drained
  and chopped
1¼ cups all-purpose flour
3 tablespoons sugar
½ cup butter
¼ cup finely chopped almonds
¼ cup semisweet chocolate pieces
½ teaspoon shortening

Using paper towels, pat cherries dry. Set aside. In a medium bowl stir together flour and sugar. Cut in butter till mixture resembles coarse crumbs. Stir in cherries. Knead till well combined and nearly smooth.

On a lightly floured surface, roll dough to ½-inch thickness. Using a 1½-inch heart-shaped cookie cutter, cut dough into heart shapes. Place 1 inch apart on an ungreased cookie sheet. Bake in a 325° oven for 20 to 25 minutes or till done. Remove the cookies from the cookie sheet and cool on a wire rack.

Evenly spread almonds on waxed paper; set aside. In a small heavy saucepan heat chocolate and shortening over low heat just till melted, stirring occasionally. Using a pastry brush, brush bottoms of cookies with chocolate mixture. Press cookies with chocolate sides down into almonds. Place cookies with chocolate-almond sides up on a wire rack. Let stand till the chocolate is set. Makes about 18.

Festive Cranberry Pinwheels

1 cup cranberries
¼ cup orange marmalade
1 tablespoon honey
⅔ cup margarine *or* butter
2 cups all-purpose flour
½ cup sugar
1 egg
1 tablespoon milk
1 teaspoon baking powder
1 teaspoon vanilla
½ teaspoon finely shredded orange peel
½ of a recipe Powdered Sugar Icing
    (see page 230)
¼ cup finely chopped walnuts

For filling, in a covered saucepan cook cranberries, marmalade, and honey over low heat till mixture boils and berries pop. Uncover, then cook about 8 minutes more or till mixture is the consistency of a thick jam. Set filling aside to cool.

In a bowl beat margarine with an electric mixer on medium to high speed about 30 seconds or till softened. Add about *half* of the flour. Add sugar, egg, milk, baking powder, and vanilla. Beat till well combined. Stir in the remaining flour and peel. Divide in half. Cover; chill about 3 hours or till easy to handle.

On a lightly floured surface, roll *each* half into a 10-inch square. Using a fluted pastry wheel, cut *each* half into sixteen 2½-inch squares. Place squares 2 inches apart on an ungreased cookie sheet. Cut 1-inch slits from each corner to the center of *each* square. Spoon ¾ *teaspoon* of the filling on the center of *each* square. Fold every other point to the center to form a pinwheel. Pinch points of dough together to seal.

Bake in a 375° oven for 8 to 10 minutes or till done. Remove cookies from cookie sheet and cool on a wire rack. Drizzle cookies with Powdered Sugar Icing. Sprinkle nuts in the center of cookies. Makes 32.

Butter Tea Cakes

½ cup butter *or* margarine
2¼ cups all-purpose flour
½ cup sugar
¼ cup buttermilk *or* sour milk
1 egg
1 teaspoon baking powder
1 teaspoon vanilla
½ teaspoon baking soda
½ cup dried currants
½ teaspoon finely shredded orange peel
    Powdered sugar

In a bowl beat butter with an electric mixer on medium speed about 30 seconds or till softened. Add *half* of the flour. Add sugar, buttermilk, egg, baking powder, vanilla, and soda. Beat till well combined. Stir in remaining flour, currants, and peel. Divide in half. Cover; chill about 2 hours or till easy to handle.

On a lightly floured surface, roll *each* half of dough to ¼-inch thickness. Using a 3x1½-inch diamond-shaped cutter, cut dough into diamonds. Place 2 inches apart on an ungreased cookie sheet. Bake in a 375° oven for 8 to 10 minutes or till done. Remove cookies from the cookie sheet and cool on a wire rack. Sift powdered sugar over tops of *warm* cookies. Cool cookies completely. Makes about 36.

◄ To assemble Festive Cranberry Pinwheels, cut a 1-inch slit from each corner to the center of each square. Spoon filling on the center. Fold every other point to the center, forming a pinwheel. Pinch points together in the center to seal. (If necessary to seal, lightly moisten points with water.)

Ginger Kids

Whole Wheat
Spiced Wreaths

Ginger Kids

Check the photo at left for some decorating ideas.

  ½ **cup margarine *or* butter**
2½ **cups all-purpose flour**
  ½ **cup sugar**
  ½ **cup molasses**
  1 **egg**
  1 **teaspoon baking soda**
  1 **teaspoon ground ginger**
  ½ **teaspoon ground cinnamon**
  ½ **teaspoon ground cloves**
  4 **ounces (⅔ cup) chopped vanilla-flavored confectioners' coating**
  1 **tablespoon shortening**
  ⅔ **cup semisweet chocolate pieces**
  1 **tablespoon shortening**
  1 **recipe Powdered Sugar Icing (see page 230)**

In a large bowl beat margarine with an electric mixer on medium to high speed about 30 seconds or till softened. Add about *half* of the flour. Then add sugar, molasses, egg, baking soda, ginger, cinnamon, and cloves. Beat till thoroughly combined. Beat or stir in the remaining flour. Divide dough in half. Cover and chill about 3 hours or till easy to handle.

Grease a cookie sheet, then set aside. On a lightly floured surface, roll *each* half of dough to ⅛-inch thickness. Using 3- to 4-inch people-shaped cookie cutters, cut dough into shapes. Place 1 inch apart on the prepared cookie sheet. Bake in a 375° oven for 5 to 6 minutes or till edges are firm. Cool on cookie sheet for 1 minute. Transfer cookies to a wire rack.

In a small heavy saucepan heat and stir vanilla coating and 1 tablespoon shortening over low heat till melted. In another saucepan heat and stir chocolate pieces and 1 tablespoon shortening over low heat till melted. Dip hands, feet, and tops of heads of cookies in either vanilla or chocolate mixture. Place on wire rack till set. If desired, dip cookies again in contrasting mixture; place on wire rack till set. Decorate with Powdered Sugar Icing. Makes about 36.

Whole Wheat Spiced Wreaths

Brighten wreaths by tinting the powdered sugar icing with a few drops of food coloring.

  1 **cup margarine *or* butter**
  3 **cups whole wheat flour**
1¼ **cups packed brown sugar**
  2 **eggs**
  2 **teaspoons baking powder**
  ½ **teaspoon ground cinnamon**
  ¼ **teaspoon ground allspice**
  ⅛ **to ¼ teaspoon ground cloves**
  ⅛ **teaspoon salt**
  2 **recipes Powdered Sugar Icing (see page 230)**

In a large bowl beat margarine with an electric mixer on medium to high speed about 30 seconds or till softened. Add about *1 cup* of the flour. Then add brown sugar, eggs, baking powder, cinnamon, allspice, cloves, and salt. Beat till thoroughly combined. Beat or stir in remaining flour. Divide dough in half.

On a lightly floured surface, roll *each* half to ⅛-inch thickness. Using a 3-inch round cookie cutter, cut dough into rounds. Then using a 1-inch round cookie cutter, cut out the centers of the rounds to form wreaths. Place wreaths 1 inch apart on an ungreased cookie sheet. Bake in a 375° oven for 6 to 8 minutes or till edges are firm. Remove cookies from cookie sheet and cool on a wire rack. Decorate cookies with Powdered Sugar Icing. Makes about 36.

Tree-Trimming Treats

Gingerbread cookies and cookie wreaths make fun, edible, Christmas tree decorations. Just poke a hole in the cookie dough with a drinking straw and bake. After cooling, hang the cookies from the tree with ribbons.

SPECIAL PACKAGING IDEAS

Personalize your cookie and cracker gifts with creative packaging ideas like the ones featured here. Whether you want an old-fashioned, festive, or romantic feel, you can create the mood by selecting different containers and wrappings.

A VARIETY OF CONTAINERS: Choose from old-fashioned tins, baskets, decorative canisters, fancy cookie molds, and colorful gift bags.

If the container you select doesn't have a tight-fitting lid, be sure to keep the cookies fresh by wrapping them in plastic wrap or sealing them in a plastic bag before placing them in the container.

Add extra color to your gift by lining the container with colored tissue paper or napkins. Or, place the cookies in colored paper bake cups in the container. If you like, wrap the entire cookie-filled container in colored cellophane.

COVERED JAR LIDS: You can create a country look by covering the lid of a wide-mouth canning jar with fabric. Using pinking shears, cut a piece of fabric slightly larger than the lid. Place a few cotton balls on the lid for padding, then cover it with the fabric. Secure the fabric to the lid by screwing on the outer metal ring. If you like, glue ribbon around the metal ring.

SPECIAL COOKIE GIFTS: Add a festive flair to your cookie gifts. At Christmas, fill a holiday tin or Christmas stocking with gingerbread people, cookie wreaths, or other seasonal cutout cookie shapes.

At Easter, fill a basket with colored plastic wrap and add a variety of duck-, bird-, bunny-, or egg-shaped cutout cookies.

For birthdays, cut cookie dough the same size as a greeting card or bookmark. After baking and cooling the cookie, place the card or bookmark on top. Wrap with plastic wrap.

For an individualized gift, try attaching a small hobby-related item to your cookie gifts—tie on a fancy key ring, drawing pencils, fun jewelry, colored markers, decorative recipe cards, or a paperback book.

CRACKERS

Accompany hearty soups, create tempting hors d'oeuvres, and complement fresh salads with your own crispy home-baked crackers. Choose from among many different flavors, textures, shapes, and sizes. Imagine how impressed your family and friends will be when sampling your tasty assortment of signature crackers.

☐ If your cracker dough shrinks back when you are rolling it out, cover it and let it rest for a few minutes. Once it has "relaxed," your cracker dough will roll out more easily.

☐ For fancy edges and decorative shapes, use a fluted pastry wheel or various-shaped cookie cutters to cut the dough.

☐ To keep your crackers free of large air bubbles, use the tines of a fork to prick the dough well. Place the prick marks close together. The closer the prick marks, the flatter the crackers.

☐ For evenly baked crackers, leave about a ¼-inch space between the cracker dough shapes on the baking sheets.

☐ Crackers are done when they are lightly browned and firm to the touch.

☐ If crackers lose some of their crispness during storage, just arrange them on a baking sheet and heat them in a 250° oven for 5 to 6 minutes or till warm. Once cooled, store them in a tightly covered container at room temperature.

Buttery Rich Crackers

For a change, stir 2 tablespoons of finely chopped, cooked bacon into the flour mixture and omit the salt.

  1 **beaten egg**
 ⅓ **cup milk**
1½ **cups all-purpose flour**
  1 **tablespoon sugar**
  1 **teaspoon baking powder**
 ½ **teaspoon salt**
 ⅓ **cup butter**
    Coarse salt, toasted sesame seed,
      ***or* poppy seed**

In a small mixing bowl stir together beaten egg and milk. Set milk mixture aside. In a large mixing bowl stir together flour, sugar, baking powder, and the ½ teaspoon salt. Using a pastry blender, cut in the butter till the mixture resembles coarse crumbs. Make a well in the center of the flour mixture. Add the milk mixture all at once. Using a fork, stir till the mixture can be gathered into a ball.

Turn dough out onto a lightly floured surface. Knead dough by gently folding and pressing dough for 10 to 12 strokes or till dough is nearly smooth. Roll dough into a 9-inch square. Brush off excess flour. Fold dough into thirds to form a 9x3-inch rectangle. Repeat rolling into a 9-inch square and folding in thirds 3 more times. Divide dough in half.

Roll *each* half of the dough into a 12-inch square. Using a pastry wheel or sharp knife, cut dough into 1½-inch squares, triangles, or diamond shapes. *Or,* using a 1½-inch round cookie or biscuit cutter, cut dough into rounds. Place on an ungreased baking sheet. Using the tines of a fork, prick crackers well. Lightly brush crackers with *water.* Sprinkle with coarse salt, sesame seed, or poppy seed.

Bake in a 300° oven for 20 to 25 minutes or till done. Remove the crackers from the baking sheet and cool on a wire rack. Makes about 96.

Honey Graham Crackers

Bring out a variety of animal-shaped cookie cutters and let youngsters have a ball creating animal graham crackers.

- ⅓ **cup milk**
- ¼ **cup honey**
- 1½ **cups graham flour**
- 1 **cup all-purpose flour**
- ¼ **cup packed brown sugar**
- 1 **teaspoon baking powder**
- ½ **teaspoon baking soda**
- ⅓ **cup margarine *or* butter**
- ¼ **cup shortening**

In a small bowl stir together milk and honey. Set milk mixture aside. In a large bowl stir together graham flour, all-purpose flour, brown sugar, baking powder, baking soda, and ¼ teaspoon *salt*. Using a pastry blender, cut in margarine and shortening till mixture resembles coarse crumbs. Make a well in center of flour mixture. Add milk mixture all at once. Using a fork, stir till mixture can be gathered into a ball.

Turn dough out onto a lightly floured surface. Knead dough by gently folding and pressing dough for 12 to 15 strokes or till dough is nearly smooth. Divide dough in half.

Sprinkle surface with additional graham flour. Roll *each* half of dough to ⅛-inch thickness. Using a pastry wheel or sharp knife, cut dough into 2-inch squares. Place on an ungreased baking sheet. Using the tines of a fork, prick crackers well. Bake in a 350° oven for 12 to 15 minutes or till done. Remove crackers from sheet and cool on a wire rack. Makes about 72.

Cinnamon Graham Crackers: Prepare Honey Graham Crackers as directed above, *except* stir ¼ teaspoon ground *cinnamon* into the flour mixture. After pricking the crackers, sprinkle crackers with a mixture of 3 tablespoons *sugar* and ½ teaspoon ground *cinnamon*.

Chocolate Graham Crackers: Prepare Honey Graham Crackers as directed at left, *except* reduce graham flour to 1¼ *cups*. Stir ⅓ cup *unsweetened cocoa powder* into the flour mixture and increase the brown sugar to ⅓ *cup*.

Norwegian Flatbread

Take your pick. Choose either rye or whole wheat flour. (Pictured on page 174.)

- 2 **cups all-purpose flour**
- ½ **cup rye *or* whole wheat flour**
- 1 **tablespoon brown sugar**
- ½ **teaspoon baking soda**
- ¼ **teaspoon salt**
- ¼ **cup margarine *or* butter**
- 1 **cup buttermilk *or* sour milk**

In a medium bowl stir together all-purpose flour, rye or whole wheat flour, brown sugar, soda, and salt. Using a pastry blender, cut in margarine or butter till mixture resembles coarse crumbs. Make a well in center of flour mixture. Add buttermilk all at once. Using a fork, stir till mixture can be gathered into a ball.

Lightly grease baking sheets; set aside. Turn dough out onto a lightly floured surface. Knead dough by gently folding and pressing dough for 8 to 10 strokes or till dough is nearly smooth. Divide dough into 10 portions. Roll *each* portion into an 8-inch circle. Place 2 or 3 dough circles on prepared baking sheets. Using the tines of a fork, prick circles well. Bake in a 350° oven for 10 to 12 minutes or till done. Remove from baking sheets and cool on a wire rack. Makes 10.

Scandinavian Oatmeal Crackers

A rich cracker with a slightly sweet, nutty flavor.

2 cups rolled oats
1 cup all-purpose flour
¼ cup packed brown sugar
1 teaspoon baking powder
⅓ cup margarine *or* butter
½ cup *cold* water

For oat flour, in a blender container or food processor bowl place *½ cup* of the oats. Cover and blend or process till reduced to a powder. Transfer to a large bowl. Repeat with the remaining oats, ½ cup at a time. (You should make about 1½ cups of oat flour.)

Add all-purpose flour, brown sugar, and baking powder to the oat flour. Stir till thoroughly combined. Using a pastry blender, cut in the margarine or butter till the mixture resembles coarse crumbs.

Make a well in the center of the flour mixture. Add cold water all at once. Using a fork, stir till the mixture can be gathered into a ball. Divide dough in half.

Turn the dough out onto a lightly floured surface. Roll *each* half of dough to ⅛-inch thickness. Using a 2-inch round cookie cutter, cut dough into rounds. Place on an ungreased baking sheet. Using the tines of a fork, prick crackers well.

Bake in a 350° oven for 18 to 20 minutes or till done. Remove crackers from the baking sheet and cool on a wire rack. Makes about 48.

Apple 'n' Nut Crackers

Apples and nuts make these home-baked crackers deliciously different from their store-bought counterparts.

¾ cup all-purpose flour
½ cup whole wheat flour
½ cup chopped walnuts *or* pecans, toasted and ground
1 tablespoon brown sugar
½ teaspoon baking powder
⅛ teaspoon salt
⅛ teaspoon ground cinnamon *or* apple pie spice
¼ cup margarine *or* butter
½ cup applesauce

In a medium mixing bowl stir together all-purpose flour, whole wheat flour, ground nuts, brown sugar, baking powder, salt, and cinnamon or apple pie spice. Using a pastry blender, cut in margarine or butter till the mixture resembles coarse crumbs.

Make a well in the center of the flour mixture. Add applesauce all at once. Using a fork, stir till the mixture can be gathered into a ball. Divide dough in half.

Lightly grease a baking sheet. Set baking sheet aside. On a lightly floured surface, roll *each* half of dough into a 12x7½-inch rectangle. Using a pastry wheel or sharp knife, cut the dough into 1½-inch squares, triangles, or diamond shapes. *Or,* using a 1½-inch round cookie or biscuit cutter, cut dough into rounds. Place on the prepared baking sheet. Using the tines of a fork, prick crackers well.

Bake in a 350° oven for 15 to 17 minutes or till done. Remove crackers from the baking sheet and cool on a wire rack. Makes 80.

Homemade Plain Crackers

Simple crackers that don't compete with the taste of flavorful spreads and cheeses.

- ½   **package (1 teaspoon) active dry yeast**
- ⅓   **cup warm water (105° to 115°)**
- 2   **tablespoons cooking oil**
- ¼   **teaspoon sugar**
- ¼   **teaspoon salt**
- 1½   **cups all-purpose flour**
- ¼   **teaspoon baking soda**
- 1   **slightly beaten egg white**
  Coarse *or* seasoned salt, grated Parmesan cheese, toasted wheat germ, *or* toasted sesame seed

In a small bowl dissolve yeast in the warm water. Stir in oil, sugar, and the ¼ teaspoon salt; set aside. In a medium bowl stir together flour and soda. Stir water mixture into flour mixture. When the dough becomes too stiff to stir, turn it out onto a lightly floured surface and knead until thoroughly combined. Then knead for 1 to 2 minutes more to make a moderately stiff dough that is smooth and elastic. Place in a sealed plastic bag and chill for 1 hour.

On a lightly floured surface, roll the dough into a 12x10-inch rectangle. Brush off excess flour. Fold dough crosswise into thirds to form a 10x4-inch rectangle. Repeat rolling into a 12x10-inch rectangle and folding in thirds 2 more times. Cover dough and let rest for 10 minutes. Meanwhile, grease a baking sheet. Set baking sheet aside.

Cut dough crosswise in half. Roll *each* portion into a 14x10-inch rectangle. Using a pastry wheel or sharp knife, cut dough into 2-inch squares, triangles, or diamond shapes. *Or,* using a 2-inch round cookie cutter, cut dough into rounds. Place on the prepared baking sheet. Using the tines of a fork, prick crackers well.

In a small mixing bowl stir together egg white and 1 tablespoon *water.* Lightly brush crackers with egg white mixture. Sprinkle with coarse or seasoned salt, Parmesan cheese, toasted wheat germ, or toasted sesame seed. Bake in a 350° oven for 10 to 12 minutes or till done. Remove crackers from the baking sheet and cool on a wire rack. Makes about 60.

Homemade Whole Wheat Crackers: Prepare Homemade Plain Crackers as directed at left, *except* reduce all-purpose flour to *1 cup.* Stir ¼ cup *whole wheat flour* into the flour mixture. Bake in the 350° oven for 12 to 14 minutes or till done.

Rice Crackers

White rice flour lends a slightly sweet flavor and very crisp texture to these chip-thin crackers. (Pictured on page 174.)

- 1   **cup sweet white rice flour**
- ¼   **teaspoon salt**
  Dash to ⅛ teaspoon ground red pepper
- 1¼   **cups water**
- 2   **tablespoons margarine *or* butter**

Line a baking sheet with foil. Grease foil; set aside. In a medium bowl stir together rice flour, salt, and red pepper. Make a well in center of flour mixture; set aside. In a small saucepan heat and stir water and margarine or butter *just till warm* and margarine is melted. Add water mixture to flour mixture. Using a fork, stir till thoroughly combined. (If batter thickens upon standing, stir in 1 to 2 teaspoons *water.*)

Drop batter from a *level teaspoon* 1 inch apart on the prepared baking sheet. Bake in a 350° oven for 17 to 20 minutes or till lightly browned (centers of crackers will become crisp upon cooling). Cool crackers for 1 minute on baking sheet. Then remove from sheet and cool on a wire rack. Makes about 72.

Cheddar Cheese Cracker
(see recipe, page 176)

Norwegian Flatbread
(see recipe, page 171)

Country Flatbread

Rice Crackers
(see recipe, page 173)

Country Flatbread

This flatbread is especially flavorful thanks to the addition of cheese, ham, and onion.

- 2¾ **to 3 cups all-purpose flour**
- 1 **package active dry yeast**
- 1 **cup warm water**
- 2 **tablespoons shortening**
- 1 **egg**
- ½ **cup grated Parmesan cheese**
- ½ **cup finely chopped fully cooked ham *or* prosciutto**
- 2 **large onions, very thinly sliced and separated into rings, *or* chopped**
- 2 **tablespoons margarine *or* butter**
  Cornmeal

In a large mixing bowl combine *1 cup* of the flour and the yeast; set aside. In a small saucepan heat and stir water and shortening *just till warm* (120° to 130°) and shortening almost melts.

Add the water mixture to the flour mixture, then add egg. Beat with an electric mixer on low to medium speed for 30 seconds, scraping the sides of the bowl constantly. Beat on high speed for 3 minutes. Using a wooden spoon, stir in the Parmesan cheese and ham or prosciutto. Then stir in as much of the remaining flour as you can.

Turn the dough out onto a lightly floured surface. Knead in enough of the remaining flour to make a moderately stiff dough that is smooth and elastic (6 to 8 minutes total). Shape the dough into a ball. Place dough in a lightly greased bowl, turning once to grease surface of dough. Cover and let rise in a warm place till double (about 1 hour).

Punch dough down. Turn out onto a lightly floured surface. Divide the dough into 12 portions and shape into balls. Cover and let rest for 10 minutes. Meanwhile, in a skillet cook onion in margarine till very tender but not brown. Set onion mixture aside.

Grease 2 large baking sheets. Sprinkle with cornmeal and set aside. Place 6 of the dough balls in the refrigerator until ready to use. On a lightly floured surface, roll the remaining 6 balls into 6-inch rounds. Place 3 of the dough rounds on each prepared baking sheet. Using the tines of a fork, prick each round well. Evenly top the *six* rounds with *half* of the onion mixture. *Do not allow to rise.*

Bake in a 350° oven for 20 to 25 minutes or till lightly browned and crisp. Remove flatbread from baking sheets and cool on a wire rack. Repeat rolling, pricking, topping, and baking the remaining 6 portions of dough. Makes 12.

Cracker Heritage

Crackers are said to have been developed by a sea captain named Josiah Bent. It was shortly after 1800 that Josiah started a baking business in Massachusetts. There he produced his crackers, which were named for the sound they made upon breaking apart. He made them as a more palatable alternative to what, at that time, was a popular seafarers' staple called hardtack. In this case, the cracker he made was a flatbread, a thinner, lighter version of hardtack. The cracker was a very basic formula of flour and water that was mixed and kneaded to form a dough, then rolled thin and baked.

Homemade Oyster Crackers

These crunchy, seasoned mini-crackers stay crisp in soups and salads.

    2 cups all-purpose flour
    ½ package (1 teaspoon) active dry yeast
    ½ teaspoon salt
    ½ teaspoon dried dillweed, oregano, *or*
           basil, crushed (optional)
    ¼ teaspoon baking soda
    ¼ teaspoon cream of tartar
    ½ cup water
    2 tablespoons shortening

In a large mixing bowl stir together flour; yeast; salt; dillweed, oregano, or basil (if desired); baking soda; and cream of tartar. Set flour mixture aside.

In a small saucepan heat and stir water and shortening *just till warm* (120° to 130°) and shortening almost melts. Stir the water mixture into the flour mixture. When the dough becomes too stiff to stir, turn it out onto a lightly floured surface and knead until thoroughly combined. Then knead for 1 to 2 minutes more to make a moderately stiff dough that is smooth and elastic. Divide dough in half. Cover the dough and let it rest for 10 minutes.

On a lightly floured surface, roll *each* half of the dough to ¼-inch thickness. Using the tines of a fork, prick the dough very well. Using a ¾-inch hors d'oeuvre cutter, a pastry wheel, or a sharp knife, cut the dough into desired shapes. Place the dough shapes on an ungreased baking sheet.

Bake in a 300° oven for 40 to 50 minutes or till done. Remove crackers from the baking sheet and cool on a wire rack. Makes about 10 dozen.

Cheddar Cheese Crackers

Some for now or some for later—just store the roll in the freezer, then thaw for 30 minutes before slicing and baking. (Pictured on page 174.)

    1 5-ounce jar sharp cheddar cheese spread *or*
           cheese spread with bacon
    ¼ cup butter
    1 cup all-purpose flour
    1 tablespoon toasted wheat germ *or*
           sesame seed (optional)

In a medium bowl beat cheese spread and butter with an electric mixer on medium to high speed about 30 seconds or till softened and combined.

Add about *half* of the flour to the cheese mixture. Beat till thoroughly combined, scraping sides of bowl occasionally. Beat or stir in the remaining flour.

Turn the dough out onto a lightly floured surface. Knead the dough by gently folding and pressing it for 10 to 12 strokes or till the dough is smooth. Shape the dough into one 7-inch roll. If desired, press the dough roll in wheat germ or sesame seed to coat. Wrap the dough in waxed paper or plastic wrap; chill in the refrigerator for 3 hours or overnight.

Remove dough roll from the refrigerator. If necessary, reshape roll to round out any flattened surfaces. Using a sharp knife, cut the dough into ⅛-inch-thick slices. Place dough slices on an ungreased baking sheet. Bake in a 400° oven for 9 to 11 minutes or till golden. Remove crackers from the baking sheet and cool on a wire rack. Makes about 48.

Dilly Cheddar Cheese Crackers: Prepare Cheddar Cheese Crackers as directed above, *except* add ¾ teaspoon dried *dillweed* to the cheese and butter before beating.

Nutrition Analysis

Per Serving

Recipes	Servings	Calories	Protein (g)	Carbohydrates (g)	Total Fat (g)	Saturated Fat (g)	Cholesterol (mg)	Sodium (mg)
Apple Half-Moons, 163	48	60	1	7	4	1	5	38
Apple 'n' Nut Crackers, 172	80	19	0	2	1	0	0	12
Apple Squares, 130	16	128	2	21	4	1	14	66
Apricot-Hazelnut Spirals, 155	84	44	0	6	2	0	0	15
Apricot Tea Cookies, 137	30	118	1	17	6	1	7	72
Brandy Snaps, 142	54	28	1	4	1	0	0	14
Buttermilk Brownies, 132	36	164	2	24	7	1	12	107
Butter Tea Cakes, 165	36	71	1	10	3	2	13	45
Buttery Chocolate-Mint Spritz Cookies, 151	42	57	1	6	3	1	5	40
Buttery Nut Spritz Cookies with Chocolate Drizzle, 151	42	71	1	7	5	1	5	40
Buttery Rich Crackers, 170	96	14	0	2	1	0	4	43
Buttery Spritz Cookies, 151	42	59	1	6	3	1	5	40
Candy-Window Sugar Cookie Cutouts, 161	42	72	1	10	3	1	5	29
Carrot-Walnut Bars, 133	24	223	2	26	13	3	22	75
Cheddar Cheese Crackers, 176	48	47	2	3	3	2	8	113
Cherry Shortbread Sweet Hearts, 164	18	114	1	12	7	4	14	44
Chocolate-Almond Parson's Hats, 162	48	127	2	15	7	1	13	93
Chocolate Chip Cookies, 138	60	112	1	13	7	2	7	30
Chocolate-Coconut Slices, 154	52	66	1	9	3	1	6	29
Chocolate-Covered Cherry Cookies, 149	48	71	1	11	3	1	5	33
Chocolate Crinkles, 144	48	82	1	11	4	1	13	16
Chocolate Graham Crackers, 171	84	31	0	4	1	0	0	24
Chocolate-Nut Cheesecake Bars, 128	24	139	3	9	11	5	39	65
Chocolate Revel Bars, 131	64	135	2	19	6	2	9	64
Cinnamon-Almond Stars, 162	60	42	1	5	2	0	0	3
Cinnamon Graham Crackers, 171	84	32	0	5	1	0	0	24
Cocoa-Berry Bars, 129	24	97	1	16	4	1	9	52
Coconut-Lemon Bars, 133	16	148	2	22	6	2	27	79
Country Flatbread, 175	12	188	7	26	6	2	24	169
Cranberry-Date Crumb Bars, 132	24	112	1	18	4	1	0	52
Cranberry-Pecan Bars, 134	24	77	1	10	4	1	9	42
Date Pinwheel Cookies, 156	84	58	1	9	2	1	3	26
Dilly Cheddar Cheese Crackers, 176	48	47	2	3	3	2	8	113
Festive Cranberry Pinwheels, 165	32	106	1	15	5	1	7	57
Filled Sugar Cookie Cutouts, 161	21	157	2	22	7	2	10	66
Florentines, 137	24	122	2	12	8	2	0	44
Fruit Crumb Bars, 132	24	100	1	15	4	1	0	53
Fudge Brownies, 130	24	173	2	23	9	2	18	73
Ginger Kids, 167	36	128	1	18	6	2	6	59
Gingersnaps, 145	48	76	1	11	3	1	4	21
Hazelnut Mocha Morsels, 146	42	89	1	9	6	1	10	52
Holiday Cottage Cookies, 139	48	82	1	10	5	1	5	40
Homemade Oyster Crackers, 176	120	10	0	2	0	0	0	11
Homemade Plain Crackers, 173	60	16	0	2	0	0	0	58
Homemade Whole Wheat Crackers, 173	60	14	0	2	0	0	0	58

Per Serving

Recipes	Servings	Calories	Protein (g)	Carbohydrates (g)	Total Fat (g)	Saturated Fat (g)	Cholesterol (mg)	Sodium (mg)
Honey Graham Crackers, 170	84	30	0	4	1	0	0	24
Honey Stamped Cookies, 150	24	73	1	8	4	1	9	45
Jam Thumbprints, 148	42	80	1	8	5	1	10	38
Lemon Bars, 133	16	127	2	20	4	1	27	74
Lemon Cream Wafers, 164	36	52	0	6	3	1	0	34
Lemon-Filled Ladyfinger Sandwiches, 153	18	102	2	14	4	1	71	57
Madeleines, 153	24	73	1	8	4	1	18	53
Maple Crisps, 156	48	72	1	8	4	1	4	38
Norwegian Flatbread, 171	10	166	4	26	5	1	1	175
Oatmeal-Raisin 'n' Walnut Cookies, 140	42	121	2	17	6	1	10	64
Orange Crisps, 144	30	35	0	5	2	0	0	21
Orange-Date Bars, 134	24	86	1	12	4	1	9	42
Orange-Molasses Spiced Cookies, 158	72	89	1	12	4	1	6	37
Orange Roof Tiles, 144	30	42	1	5	2	0	0	21
Peanut Butter and Chocolate Chip Bars, 131	36	162	4	23	7	2	12	55
Peanut Butter Crisscross Cookies, 148	48	66	1	8	4	1	4	36
Peanut Butter Cup-Chocolate Cookies, 138	30	194	3	22	11	2	15	88
Peanut Butter-Fudge Swirls, 157	48	96	2	12	5	1	5	55
Peanut Butter-Oatmeal Rounds, 140	60	89	2	10	5	1	7	61
Peanutty Chocolate Cookies, 138	30	210	4	22	13	2	14	77
Pfeffernuss, 149	84	46	1	8	1	0	5	27
Pineapple Nut Cookies, 141	42	94	1	14	4	1	6	47
Pineapple Pecan Poppits, 161	72	48	0	5	3	1	1	31
Praline 'n' Brown Sugar Rounds, 158	72	97	1	12	5	1	3	39
Pumpkin Bars, 129	48	126	1	16	7	1	20	63
Rice Crackers, 173	72	10	0	2	0	0	0	11
Rum Prints, 145	36	85	1	9	5	1	6	57
Sandbakkelse, 151	30	62	1	8	3	2	15	26
Santa's Whiskers, 157	56	65	1	8	3	1	0	29
Scandinavian Oatmeal Crackers, 172	48	38	1	5	1	0	0	21
Snickerdoodles, 145	36	68	1	10	3	1	6	39
Sour Cream Linzer Cookies, 163	40	92	1	13	4	1	6	39
Spiced Apple Drops, 136	60	95	1	15	4	1	4	61
Spicy Prune Bars, 134	24	83	1	12	4	1	9	42
Sugar Cookie Cutouts, 161	42	65	1	8	3	1	5	29
Sugar 'n' Spice Molded Cookies (large), 150	10	356	5	51	15	7	47	126
Sugar 'n' Spice Molded Cookies (small), 150	48	74	1	11	3	2	10	26
Swedish Butter Cookies (thick), 160	36	63	1	6	4	2	7	22
Swedish Butter Cookies (thin), 160	80	28	0	3	2	1	3	10
Viennese Raspberry Squares, 134	36	76	1	9	4	1	12	25
White Chocolate-Hazelnut Cookies, 141	30	164	2	17	10	4	7	56
Whole Wheat Spiced Wreaths, 167	36	134	2	20	6	1	12	91
Whole Wheat Slices, 155	56	68	1	8	4	1	4	384

We've analyzed the nutritional content of each recipe using the first choice if ingredient substitutions are given, and using the first serving size if a serving range is given. We've omitted optional ingredients from the analysis.

Almond-Raspberry Torte
(see recipe, page 210)

Checkerboard Cake
(see recipe, page 181)

Petits Fours
(see tip, page 229)

Pineapple Upside-Down Cake
(see recipe, page 180)

Pumpkin Cheesecake Roll
(see recipe, page 202)

FAVORITE CAKES AND FROSTINGS

Craving something sweet, rich, and satisfying? Welcome to the wonderful world of delicious cakes and frostings.

The recipes presented here are a dreamy blend of flavors and textures. We've included a variety of both new and old favorites to please every taste.

In the creamed cakes section, you'll find our recipes for tender cakes. Next, explore our recipes for light angel, sponge, and chiffon cakes. And then discover our recipes for layer upon layer of filled tortes, rich cakes made with little or no flour, and moist pudding cakes.

Finally, check out our recipes for frostings, glazes, and icings. By mixing and matching these frostings with the many cakes in this chapter, you'll discover an endless amount of fabulous combinations.

CREAMED CAKES

Creamed cakes have satisfied sweet tooths for centuries. Many of these classic creamed cake recipes appear here. Some recipes use the traditional method of mixing the ingredients in several different steps, while other recipes use an easy one-bowl technique devised for today's busy cook. Creamed cakes come in a myriad of textures and flavors, like the fine-textured Champagne Celebration Cake, the sumptuous brandy-soaked Dried-Fruit Fruitcake, and the buttery Pound Cake, to name a few.

☐ Our recipes include ranges of beating speeds to help you get the best mixing results when combining ingredients. The lower speed in the range is recommended for freestanding electric mixers. The higher speed is for portable electric mixers.

☐ Creamed cakes are properly baked when a wooden toothpick inserted near the center of the cake comes out clean.

☐ To freeze a creamed cake, place the frosted or unfrosted cake on a baking sheet and freeze until firm. Once firm, place the cake in a freezer bag or an airtight container. Then seal, label, and freeze. An unfrosted cake freezes well for up to six months. Frosted cakes freeze well for up to four months and fruitcakes freeze well for up to 12 months. To thaw the cake, unwrap it and let it stand at room temperature for several hours.

Pineapple Upside-Down Cake

Originally baked in a cast-iron skillet, this cake now is baked in a cake pan. (Pictured on pages 178–179.)

      2 **tablespoons margarine** *or* **butter**
     ⅓ **cup packed brown sugar**
      5 *or* **6 pineapple slices, drained and halved**
      4 **maraschino cherries, halved**
    1⅓ **cups all-purpose flour**
     ⅔ **cup sugar**
      2 **teaspoons baking powder**
     ⅔ **cup milk**
     ¼ **cup margarine** *or* **butter, softened**
      1 **egg**
      1 **teaspoon vanilla**

Melt 2 tablespoons margarine in a 9x1½-inch round baking pan. Stir in brown sugar and 1 tablespoon *water*. Arrange pineapple and cherries in the pan. Set pan aside.

In a medium mixing bowl stir together flour, sugar, and baking powder. Add milk, ¼ cup margarine or butter, egg, and vanilla. Beat with an electric mixer on low to medium speed about 30 seconds or till combined. Then beat on medium to high speed for 1 minute. Pour batter into pan over pineapple slices. Bake in a 350° oven for 30 to 35 minutes or till the cake tests done. Cool the cake in the pan on a wire rack for 5 minutes. Loosen sides and invert the cake onto a plate. Serve warm. Makes 8 servings.

Apricot Upside-Down Cake: Prepare Pineapple Upside-Down Cake as directed above, *except* substitute one 8¾-ounce can *apricot halves,* drained and halved, *or peach slices,* drained, and 2 tablespoons toasted *coconut* for the pineapple and cherries.

Checkerboard Cake

No special pan is needed. (Pictured on pages 178–179.)

2½ cups all-purpose flour
2 teaspoons baking powder
½ teaspoon baking soda
¾ cup shortening
2 cups sugar
1 tablespoon vanilla
5 egg whites, at room temperature
1⅓ cups buttermilk *or* sour milk
⅓ cup unsweetened cocoa powder
1 tablespoon milk
Chocolate Frosting

Grease and flour three 8x1½-inch round baking pans. In a bowl combine flour, baking powder, soda, and ½ teaspoon *salt*. In a very large bowl beat shortening with an electric mixer on medium speed for 30 seconds. Add *1⅔ cups* of sugar and vanilla; beat till combined. Alternately add flour mixture and buttermilk, beating after each addition *just till combined.*

Thoroughly wash beaters. Beat egg whites on medium till soft peaks form (tips curl). Gradually add remaining sugar, beating on medium to high till stiff peaks form (tips stand straight). Gently fold *half* of egg white mixture into beaten mixture. Fold in the remaining egg white mixture. Spoon *half* of batter (about 3¼ cups) into a bowl. Sift cocoa powder over remaining batter. Stir in the 1 tablespoon milk.

Set ¾ *cup* of white batter aside. Spoon *1¼ cups* of remaining white batter around the outer edge of *each* of 2 of the prepared pans. Spoon ¾ *cup* of chocolate batter in a ring right next to the inner edge of white batter in *each* of the pans. Spoon *half* of remaining white batter into center of *each* pan. In the third pan, using *1¼ cups* of chocolate batter, make outer ring. Using the reserved ¾ *cup* white batter, make inner ring. Fill center with remaining chocolate batter.

Bake in a 350° oven about 25 minutes or till cakes test done. Cool in pans for 10 minutes. Remove and cool. Place a cake layer with a white outer ring on serving plate. Frost top with ½ *cup* frosting. Place cake layer with chocolate outer ring on top. Frost top with ½ *cup* frosting. Top with remaining layer. Frost sides and top with remaining frosting. Serves 16.

Chocolate Frosting: Beat together ¼ cup *margarine* and 2 cups sifted *powdered sugar*. Beat in 3 squares (3 ounces) *unsweetened chocolate,* melted and cooled; ½ cup *milk;* and 1 teaspoon *vanilla*. Beat in 2½ to 3 cups sifted *powdered sugar* to reach desired consistency. Makes 4 cups.

◀ *Properly beating the shortening and sugar together helps ensure that your checkerboard cake will have an even texture and will rise properly. To do this, beat the shortening, sugar, and vanilla until they are well combined. The shortening mixture will have a light texture.*

◀ *The third layer is the reverse of the other two layers. First, spoon 1¼ cups chocolate batter around the outer edge of the pan. Next spoon ¾ cup of reserved white batter in a ring right next to the inner edge of the chocolate batter. Fill the center with the remaining chocolate batter.*

Buttermilk White Cake

Fruit preserves make a simple but luscious filling for this layered cake.

2½ **cups all-purpose flour**
  2 **cups sugar**
  1 **teaspoon baking powder**
  ½ **teaspoon baking soda**
  ⅛ **teaspoon salt**
1⅓ **cups buttermilk *or* sour milk**
  ½ **cup shortening, margarine, *or* butter, softened**
  1 **teaspoon vanilla**
  4 **egg whites**
  ½ **cup apricot *or* peach preserves**
  1 **recipe Fluffy White Frosting (see page 228)**

Grease and lightly flour two 9x1½-inch round baking pans. Set pans aside. In a large bowl stir together flour, sugar, baking powder, baking soda, and salt. Then add buttermilk, shortening, and vanilla. Beat with an electric mixer on low speed about 30 seconds or till combined. Beat on medium to high speed for 2 minutes, scraping sides of the bowl occasionally. Add unbeaten egg whites; beat 2 minutes more.

Pour the batter into the prepared pans. Bake in a 350° oven for 30 to 35 minutes or till cakes test done. Cool cakes in pans on wire racks for 10 minutes. Then remove cakes from pans and completely cool them on wire racks. Spread preserves between the layers. Frost sides and top with Fluffy White Frosting. Store in the refrigerator. Makes 12 servings.

Secrets to Successful Creamed Cakes

You can create many mouthwatering cakes using the recipes in this section. If your cakes are less than perfect, use this list of helpful pointers from our Test Kitchen.

If your cake has a coarse texture:
■ This can happen if the fat and sugar are not *well* combined. Next time, try beating longer.
■ Your oven may be too cool. Use an oven thermometer to check the oven temperature. If necessary, adjust the setting.
■ Accurately measure ingredients. It is especially critical for the success of cake recipes. (Review Measuring Tips, page 297).

If your cake is heavy and compact:
■ Stir flour and baking powder before scooping and leveling these ingredients (see page 297). This way you'll get more accurate measurements and lighter, more tender cakes.

If your cake is dry:
■ Overbeating egg whites can make cakes dry. When beating egg whites, first beat them to the soft-peak stage where the tips curl. Then beat them to the stiff-peak stage where the peaks stand straight but are not dry. (See photos, page 195.)
■ Be sure not to overbake the cake. As a general rule, check the cake at the lower end of the baking time range. If the cake doesn't test done, return it to the oven for the full baking time.

If your cake has tunnels:
■ Do not overmix the batter. Remember, mix *just until* the ingredients are combined.
■ Your oven temperature may be too high. Use an oven thermometer to check the oven temperature. If necessary, adjust the setting.
■ Tunnels may occur if too much flour is added. Remember to stir flour before measuring. Then spoon it into a dry measuring cup and level it off.

Lady Baltimore Cake

2 cups all-purpose flour
1 tablespoon baking powder
¼ teaspoon salt
5 egg whites
¾ cup margarine *or* butter
1½ cups sugar
1 teaspoon vanilla
¼ teaspoon almond extract
1 cup milk
1 recipe Seven-Minute Frosting (see page 228)
   Lady Baltimore Filling

Grease and lightly flour two 9x1½-inch round baking pans. In a small mixing bowl stir together flour, baking powder, and salt. In a large mixing bowl bring egg whites to room temperature. Set pans, flour mixture, and egg whites aside.

In a very large bowl beat margarine with an electric mixer on medium to high speed about 30 seconds or till softened. Add sugar, vanilla, and almond extract; beat till combined. Alternately add flour mixture and milk, beating on low to medium speed after each addition *just till combined.* Wash beaters. Beat egg whites till stiff peaks form (tips stand straight); fold into batter. Spread batter in the prepared pans.

Bake in a 350° oven for 30 to 35 minutes or till cakes test done. Cool cakes in pans on wire racks for 10 minutes. Remove cakes and cool them completely on wire racks. Meanwhile, prepare the Seven-Minute Frosting. Prepare Lady Baltimore Filling. Spread one cake layer with the filling. Then top with the second cake layer. Frost with the remaining Seven-Minute Frosting. Store in refrigerator. Makes 12 servings.

> **Lady Baltimore Filling:** Combine *one-fourth* of the *Seven-Minute Frosting* (about 1¼ cups) with 1 cup chopped, pitted *dates or figs,* ½ cup *raisins,* and ½ cup chopped *pecans.* Makes 2 cups.

Choose-a-Pan Cakes

Two-layer cakes suit some occasions, and carry-in-the-pan cakes are handy for picnics and potlucks. For the cake batters on pages 181–189, choose the size pan that best fits your needs.

Fill the baking pans no more than half full. Use any remaining batter to make some cupcakes. Baking times given are approximate and may vary from cake to cake.

Pan Size	Estimated Baking Time in a 350° Oven
Two 8x1½-inch round baking pans	35 to 40 minutes
Two 9x1½-inch round baking pans	30 to 35 minutes
Two 8x8x2-inch baking pans	25 to 35 minutes
Two 9x9x2-inch baking pans	25 to 35 minutes
One 13x9x2-inch baking pan	30 to 35 minutes
One 15x10x1-inch baking pan	25 to 30 minutes
Cupcakes (half full of batter)	18 to 23 minutes

Champagne
Celebration Cake

Champagne Celebration Cake

4 cups all-purpose flour
3 cups sugar
5 teaspoons baking powder
½ teaspoon baking soda
1⅔ cups milk
1 cup shortening
½ cup champagne *or* cream sherry
1 tablespoon vanilla
10 to 12 drops red food coloring (optional)
8 egg whites
9 tablespoons champagne *or* cream sherry
Edible carnations *or* chamomiles (optional)
(see tip, page 123)
Champagne Buttercream Frosting

Grease and lightly flour one 9x1½-inch round baking pan *and* one 13x9x2-inch baking pan; set aside. In a very large bowl stir together flour, sugar, baking powder, soda, and ¼ teaspoon *salt*. Add milk, shortening, ½ cup champagne, vanilla, and, if desired, red food coloring. Beat on low to medium speed about 30 seconds or *just till combined,* scraping bowl constantly. Beat on medium speed 2 minutes. Add unbeaten egg whites; beat 2 minutes. (Batter may appear slightly curdled.) Spread *2¾ cups* of batter in 9x1½-inch round pan, and remaining batter in 13x9x2-inch pan. Bake in a 350° oven 30 to 35 minutes for round cake and 40 to 45 minutes for rectangular cake or till cakes test done. Cool cakes in pans on racks 10 minutes. Remove and cool completely.

Using cardboard circle patterns of 4 inches and 6 inches in diameter, cut out one 4-inch and one 6-inch cake layer from the 13x9x2-inch cake. If desired, drizzle *3 tablespoons* of champagne over the top of *each* round cake layer. Place the 9-inch cake layer on a serving plate; frost sides and top. Lining up the backs of the layers, place the 6-inch cake on top of the 9-inch cake; frost sides and top. Repeat with remaining 4-inch cake. If desired, tint any remaining frosting; decorate with tinted frosting and flowers. Serves 24.

Champagne Buttercream Frosting: In a bowl beat ¾ cup *shortening* and ¾ cup *butter or margarine* till combined. Beat in 1 tablespoon *champagne or cream sherry*. Beat in 4½ cups sifted *powdered sugar* and a few drops *red food coloring*. If necessary, beat in additional *champagne or cream sherry* to make a frosting of spreading consistency. Makes 3¾ cups.

Pineapple Carrot Cake

If you favor raisins and nuts, replace the crushed pineapple and coconut with ½ cup raisins and ½ cup chopped walnuts. Add them after beating the batter.

2 cups all-purpose flour
2 cups sugar
1 teaspoon baking powder
1 teaspoon baking soda
1 teaspoon ground cinnamon
3 cups finely shredded carrot
1 8¼-ounce can crushed pineapple
1 cup cooking oil
½ cup coconut
4 eggs
1 recipe Cream Cheese Frosting (see page 226)

Grease and lightly flour two 9x1½-inch round baking pans; set aside. In a bowl stir together flour, sugar, baking powder, soda, and cinnamon. Add carrot, *undrained* pineapple, oil, coconut, and eggs. Beat with an electric mixer on low to medium speed about 30 seconds or till combined. Spread in prepared pans. Bake in a 350° oven about 35 minutes or till cakes test done. Cool in pans on racks for 10 minutes. Remove from pans; cool on racks. Frost with Cream Cheese Frosting. Store in the refrigerator. Serves 12.

SPECIAL CAKE-DECORATING IDEAS

Whether it's a birthday, wedding, shower, or some other reason to celebrate, tailor your cake to the occasion. Here are easy decorating hints to help you do just that.

PERFECTLY COMBED SIDES

Frost a round layered cake with desired flavor of Butter Frosting (see recipe, page 224) so the frosting is smooth.

To comb, start with the sides. Hold the decorating comb against the side of the cake and gently pull it around the entire cake, guiding it in a straight pattern. (A lazy Susan makes this an easy task.) If desired, pipe a border around the top edge and the base of the combed cake.

OLD-FASHIONED LADY'S HAT AND PETITS FOURS

For a Lady's Hat, bake Buttermilk White Cake (see recipe, page 182). Assemble layers with preserves. Spoon Petits Fours Icing over cake (see recipe and tip, page 229). Transfer cake to a round cake board with a ruffle. Decorate top with purchased icing flowers. Wrap a ribbon around the cake, taping ends. With another ribbon, tie a bow. Tape the bow to the ribbon on the cake.

For the Petits Fours, see the tip on page 229.

HOT-AIR BALLOON CAKES

Bake cupcakes in 2½-inch paper bake cups (see tip, page 183). Frost cupcakes with desired Butter Frosting (see recipe, page 224). If desired, sprinkle cupcake with colored sugars or edible glitter.

For each Hot-Air Balloon Cake, blow up a small round balloon to 5 inches in diameter (not completely full). Knot the balloon and tape it to the end of a straw, *or* attach it to a cello cup on a plastic stick purchased from a balloon shop.

Next, tie ribbons around the straw at the balloon's base; curl the ribbon ends. Insert the end of the straw into the center of a cupcake. (If necessary, trim the length of your straw.) Cut three long pieces of ribbon in lengths that will reach from the top of the balloon down under the base of the cupcake, and back up and over the top of the balloon about 1½ times.

Arrange the three pieces of ribbon on a countertop so that they resemble the spokes of a wheel, crossing in the center. Tape the ribbons together in the center. Set a cupcake on the tape. Bring the ends of the ribbons up and over the top of the balloon. Tie the ribbons together above the balloon. Curl the ribbon ends.

BLOCKBUSTER CAKE

Bake desired cake (see recipes, pages 182–189) in a 13x9x2-inch baking pan (see tip, page 183). Frost cake with Butter Frosting (see recipe, page 224). To decorate, spell out a special wish or name with colorful, lettered building blocks. Decorate with small, colorful candies.

Buttermilk Chocolate Cake

This cake is delicious with the Chocolate Buttermilk Frosting or a butter frosting. (Pictured on the cover.)

  2 cups all-purpose flour
1¾ cups sugar
  1 teaspoon baking powder
  1 teaspoon baking soda
  ¼ teaspoon salt
1⅓ cups buttermilk *or* sour milk
  ½ cup shortening
  1 teaspoon vanilla
  2 eggs
  3 squares (3 ounces) unsweetened chocolate, melted and cooled
    Chocolate Buttermilk Frosting

Grease and lightly flour two 9x1½-inch round baking pans; set aside. In a large bowl combine flour, sugar, baking powder, baking soda, and salt. Add buttermilk, shortening, and vanilla. Beat with an electric mixer on low to medium speed about 30 seconds or till combined. Then beat on medium to high speed for 2 minutes, scraping bowl occasionally. Add eggs and melted chocolate; beat for 2 minutes more.

Pour batter into prepared pans. Bake in a 350° oven for 30 to 35 minutes or till cakes test done. Cool in pans on racks for 10 minutes. Remove cakes from pans; cool completely. Frost with frosting. Serves 12.

Chocolate Buttermilk Frosting: In a medium bowl beat ⅓ cup *margarine or butter* till fluffy. Slowly beat in 2 cups sifted *powdered sugar.* Slowly beat in 2 squares (2 ounces) *unsweetened chocolate,* melted and cooled, ¼ cup *buttermilk or milk,* and 1½ teaspoons *vanilla.* Slowly beat in 2 to 2½ cups sifted *powdered sugar* to make frosting of spreading consistency. Makes about 2¼ cups.

Old-Fashioned Yellow Cake

For a simply delicious variation from the powdered sugar topping, whip 1 cup of whipping cream with 1 tablespoon brandy. Serve this brandy-flavored cream atop your cake.

  3 cups all-purpose flour
  2 cups sugar
  1 tablespoon baking powder
1½ cups milk
  ½ cup margarine *or* butter, softened
1½ teaspoons vanilla
  2 eggs
  1 cup apricot *or* strawberry spreadable fruit *or* preserves
    Powdered sugar

Grease and lightly flour two 9x1½-inch round baking pans. Set pans aside. In a large mixing bowl stir together flour, sugar, and baking powder. Add milk, margarine or butter, and vanilla. Beat with an electric mixer on low to medium speed about 30 seconds or till combined. Then beat on medium to high speed for 2 minutes, scraping sides of the bowl occasionally. Add eggs and beat for 2 minutes more.

Pour batter into the prepared pans. Bake in a 375° oven for 25 to 30 minutes or till cakes test done. Cool cakes in pans on wire racks for 10 minutes. Then remove cakes from pans and cool them completely on the wire racks before filling.

If using preserves, cut up any large pieces of fruit. Place one cake layer on a serving plate. Spread it with spreadable fruit or preserves. Top with second layer. Place a lace doily, cutout paper pattern, or cardboard pattern on top of the cake. Sift powdered sugar over the top. Remove pattern. Makes 12 servings.

Hickory Nut Cake

2¾ cups all-purpose flour
1 cup ground hickory nuts *or* pecans
2½ teaspoons baking powder
¼ teaspoon salt
½ cup margarine *or* butter
1¾ cups sugar
1½ teaspoons vanilla
2 eggs
1¼ cups light cream *or* milk
½ of a recipe Cream Cheese Frosting (see page 226)
½ cup finely chopped hickory nuts *or* pecans

Grease and lightly flour two 8x1½-inch round baking pans. In a large mixing bowl stir together flour, the 1 cup ground nuts, baking powder, and salt. Set pans and flour mixture aside.

In another large mixing bowl beat margarine or butter with an electric mixer on medium to high speed about 30 seconds or till softened. Add sugar and vanilla; beat till combined. Add eggs, one at a time, beating on medium speed till combined. Alternately add flour mixture and light cream or milk, beating on low to medium speed after each addition *just till combined.*

Spread batter into the prepared pans. Bake in a 375° oven for 35 to 40 minutes or till cakes test done. Cool cakes in pans on wire racks for 10 minutes. Remove cakes from pans and completely cool on the racks.

To assemble, place one cake layer on a serving plate. Spread with *half* of the frosting, then sprinkle with *half* of the finely chopped nuts. Top with second layer. Spread top with remaining frosting and sprinkle with remaining chopped nuts. Store in the refrigerator. Makes 12 servings.

High-Altitude Cake Baking

Cakes expand more during baking at high altitudes than at sea level. So baking temperatures, times, and ingredients must be adjusted. At high altitudes, raise the oven temperature by about 25° and decrease baking time slightly. For cakes with a large amount of fat or chocolate, reduce the shortening by 1 to 2 tablespoons and add an egg to keep cakes from falling.

Use these suggestions and the chart at right to adjust the cake recipes.

Ingredients	3,000 ft.	5,000 ft.	7,000 ft.
Liquid: Add for *each* cup	1 to 2 tablespoons	2 to 4 tablespoons	3 to 4 tablespoons
Baking Powder: Decrease for *each* teaspoon	⅛ teaspoon	⅛ to ¼ teaspoon	¼ teaspoon
Sugar: Decrease for *each* cup	0 to 1 tablespoon	0 to 2 tablespoons	1 to 3 tablespoons

Three-Layer Coconut and Spice Cake

A classic spice cake, now with a touch of coconut.

2½ cups all-purpose flour
1½ teaspoons baking powder
1½ teaspoons ground cinnamon
¾ teaspoon baking soda
¼ teaspoon ground nutmeg
⅛ teaspoon ground cloves *or* allspice
⅛ teaspoon ground ginger
½ cup margarine *or* butter
1 cup sugar
½ cup packed brown sugar
1 teaspoon vanilla
4 eggs
1¼ cups light cream *or* milk
¼ cup molasses
½ cup flaked coconut
⅔ cup orange marmalade *or* apricot preserves
    Creamy Orange Frosting
⅓ cup flaked coconut, toasted

Grease and lightly flour three 8x1½-inch round baking pans; set aside. In a medium bowl stir together flour, baking powder, cinnamon, baking soda, ¼ teaspoon *salt,* nutmeg, cloves, and ginger; set aside.

In a large bowl beat margarine or butter with an electric mixer on medium to high speed about 30 seconds or till softened. Add sugar, brown sugar, and vanilla; beat till combined. Add eggs, one at a time, beating on medium speed till combined. In a bowl stir together cream or milk and molasses. Alternately add flour mixture and cream mixture to margarine mixture, beating on low to medium speed after each addition *just till combined.* Stir in ½ cup coconut.

Pour batter into prepared pans. Bake in a 350° oven for 20 to 25 minutes or till cakes test done. Cool in pans on racks for 10 minutes. Remove cakes from pans; cool completely. Spread marmalade between layers. Frost with Creamy Orange Frosting. Sprinkle with toasted coconut. Store in refrigerator. Serves 12.

Creamy Orange Frosting: In a bowl beat one 3-ounce package *cream cheese,* ⅓ cup *margarine or butter,* and 1 teaspoon finely shredded *orange peel* till combined. Beat in 2½ cups sifted *powdered sugar* till smooth. Makes 1½ cups.

Lemon-Iced Ginger Cake

3 cups all-purpose flour
2 teaspoons baking powder
1½ teaspoons ground ginger
½ teaspoon baking soda
½ teaspoon ground nutmeg
¾ cup margarine *or* butter
1¾ cups packed brown sugar
4 eggs
1½ cups buttermilk *or* sour milk
½ cup sifted powdered sugar
2 tablespoons lemon juice

Grease and lightly flour a 10-inch fluted tube pan. In a medium bowl stir together flour, baking powder, ginger, baking soda, and nutmeg; set aside. In a large bowl beat margarine or butter with an electric mixer on medium speed for 30 seconds. Add brown sugar; beat till combined. Add eggs, one at a time, beating on medium speed till combined. Alternately add flour mixture and buttermilk or sour milk, beating on low speed after each addition *just till combined.*

Pour batter into the prepared pan. Bake in a 350° oven for 50 to 55 minutes or till cake tests done. Cool on a rack for 10 minutes. Remove from pan and cool completely. Meanwhile, stir together powdered sugar and lemon juice; drizzle over cake. Makes 16 servings.

Dried-Fruit Fruitcake
(see recipe, page 192)

Dried-Fruit Fruitcake

Our version features dried fruit instead of the traditional candied fruit. (Pictured on page 191.)

1½ **cups all-purpose flour**
½ **teaspoon baking powder**
¼ **teaspoon baking soda**
½ **cup margarine *or* butter**
¾ **cup packed brown sugar**
2 **eggs**
1 **teaspoon finely shredded orange peel**
½ **cup orange juice *or* apple juice**
2 **tablespoons light corn syrup**
1 **teaspoon vanilla**
¾ **cup snipped dried apricots**
½ **cup pitted whole dates, snipped**
½ **cup dried red cherries***
½ **cup chopped pecans *or* walnuts**
  Brandy, *or* orange *or* apple juice

Grease and lightly flour an 8-inch fluted tube mold or a 6½-cup ring mold. *Or,* grease an 8x4x2-inch loaf pan. Line loaf pan with parchment paper; grease paper. In a medium bowl combine flour, baking powder, and baking soda; set aside. In a large bowl beat margarine or butter with an electric mixer on medium to high speed about 30 seconds or till softened. Add brown sugar; beat till combined. Add eggs, one at a time, beating on medium speed till combined. (Batter may appear curdled.) In a small bowl combine peel, the ½ cup orange juice, corn syrup, and vanilla. Alternately add flour mixture and orange juice mixture to margarine mixture, beating on low speed after each addition *just till combined.*

Combine apricots, dates, cherries, and pecans. Fold into batter. Spread in prepared pan. Bake in a 300° oven about 1 hour in tube or ring mold, *or* about 1½ hours in loaf pan or till cake tests done. (If necessary, cover loosely with foil for the last 15 to 30 minutes to prevent overbrowning.) Cool cake in tube or ring mold on rack for 10 minutes. Remove from pan; cool completely. *Or,* completely cool cake in loaf pan on rack; remove from pan. Wrap cake in brandy- or fruit juice-moistened cheesecloth. Place on a piece of foil; wrap well. Store on a plate in refrigerator for 2 to 8 weeks to mellow flavors. Remoisten cheesecloth with brandy or juice once a week or as needed. Serves 16.

*If desired, substitute ¼ cup snipped *dried apricots* plus ¼ cup whole pitted *dates,* snipped, for the ½ cup dried red cherries.

◀ *To remoisten fruit-cake, partially un-wrap it. With foil and cheesecloth around the base of the cake, spoon a small amount of brandy or fruit juice over cake. Rewrap cake, cover-ing it with the moist cheesecloth and foil. Refrigerate for a week before remoistening again, or rewrap un-til ready to serve.*

The Rise of Cakes

Today's cakes have come a long way from their roots, which can be traced back thousands of years to the Middle East. The first known cakes were flat baked mixtures of coarsely ground grain and water. Over the years, honey and sugar became standard ingredients. Then sweet spices such as cinnamon, cloves, and nutmeg were used as seasonings. Eventually, fruits and nuts were added to the cakes. Later, when cakes were brought to Europe, they evolved to the status of sweetened breads, leavened with yeast. But it was not until about the 1600s that cakes took on the rich, delicate qualities that we now enjoy.

Pound Cake

In this time-honored recipe, butter provides the traditional rich flavor and smooth, dense texture.

    1 cup butter
    4 eggs
    2 cups all-purpose flour
    1 teaspoon baking powder
    ¼ teaspoon ground nutmeg (optional)
    1 cup sugar
    1 teaspoon vanilla
    1 recipe Powdered Sugar Icing (see page 230)

Bring butter and eggs to room temperature. Grease and lightly flour a 9x5x3-inch loaf pan. In a medium bowl stir together flour, baking powder, and, if desired, nutmeg. Set eggs, pan, and flour mixture aside.

In a large bowl beat butter with an electric mixer on medium to high speed about 30 seconds or till softened. Gradually add sugar, *2 tablespoons* at a time, beating on medium to high speed about 6 minutes total or till very light and fluffy. Add the vanilla. Then add the eggs, one at a time, beating on low to medium speed for 1 minute after each addition; scrape sides of bowl often. Gradually add the flour mixture, beating on low speed *just till combined.*

Spread batter in the prepared pan. Bake in a 325° oven for 55 to 65 minutes or till cake tests done. Cool cake in pan on a rack for 10 minutes. Then remove cake from pan and cool completely on rack. Drizzle Powdered Sugar Icing over cake. Makes 12 servings.

Chocolate Marble Pound Cake: Prepare Pound Cake as directed above, *except* transfer about *1½ cups* of the batter to a small bowl. Stir in ¼ cup *chocolate-flavored syrup* till combined. Spoon *half* of the plain batter into the prepared pan. Top with the chocolate batter. Then top with the remaining plain batter. Using a knife, *gently* swirl the batter to get a marbled effect.

Sour Cream Pound Cake

    ½ cup butter
    3 eggs
    ½ cup dairy sour cream
    1½ cups all-purpose flour
    ¼ teaspoon baking powder
    ⅛ teaspoon baking soda
    1 cup sugar
    ½ teaspoon vanilla
       Powdered sugar

Bring butter, eggs, and sour cream to room temperature. Grease and lightly flour an 8x4x2-inch or 9x5x3-inch loaf pan. In a bowl stir together flour, baking powder, and soda; set aside. In a large bowl beat butter with an electric mixer on medium to high speed about 30 seconds or till softened. Gradually add sugar, *2 tablespoons* at a time, beating on medium to high speed about 6 minutes total or till very light and fluffy. Add vanilla. Add eggs, one at a time, beating on low to medium speed for 1 minute after each; scrape bowl often. Alternately add flour mixture and sour cream, beating on low speed *just till combined.*

Spread batter in the prepared pan. Bake in a 325° oven for 1 to 1¼ hours or till cake tests done. Cool cake in pan on a wire rack for 10 minutes. Remove cake from pan and cool completely. Sift powdered sugar over the top. Makes 10 to 12 servings.

Lemon-Poppy Seed Pound Cake: Prepare the Sour Cream Pound Cake as directed above, *except* add 1 teaspoon finely shredded *lemon peel* and 2 tablespoons *lemon juice* with vanilla. Substitute *lemon yogurt* for the sour cream. Fold 2 tablespoons *poppy seed* into batter.

Blueberry Sour Cream Pound Cake: Prepare the Sour Cream Pound Cake as directed above, *except* gently fold ½ cup fresh *or* frozen *blueberries* into the batter.

ANGEL, SPONGE, AND CHIFFON CAKES

Angel, sponge, and chiffon cakes are delicate and tender baked works of art. In the following pages, you'll find a variety of cakes ranging from a basic angel cake to a delectable Chocolate Chiffon Loaf with a refreshing mint topping.

□ You'll notice that many recipes in this section give you the choice of using cake flour or all-purpose flour. These recipes have been perfected using either type of flour. Cake flour will give you a slightly more tender cake than all-purpose flour.

□ Since eggs separate more easily when they are cold, separate an egg right after removing it from the refrigerator. Then let it come to room temperature along with the other ingredients.

□ Just one speck of egg yolk in egg whites ruins their beating quality. So separate eggs one at a time into a small bowl. Transfer the single egg white to a large glass or metal bowl in which the egg whites will be beaten. If any yolk does get mixed in with that one egg white, refrigerate that egg white for another use instead of ruining all of the egg whites.

□ The first step in properly beating egg whites is picking the right bowl. Select a glass or metal bowl that is wide and large enough to keep the beaters from becoming buried in the high fluffy egg whites.

□ To freeze an angel, sponge, or chiffon cake, place the unfrosted cake in a freezer bag or an airtight plastic container. Seal, label, and freeze for up to 3 months. Thaw at room temperature about 3 hours.

Angel Cake

Angel cakes are appropriately named—they're light and high-rising.

- 1½ **cups egg whites (10 to 12 large)**
- 1½ **cups sifted powdered sugar**
- 1 **cup sifted cake flour *or* sifted all-purpose flour**
- 1½ **teaspoons cream of tartar**
- 1 **teaspoon vanilla**
- 1 **cup sugar**

In a very large mixing bowl bring egg whites to room temperature. Meanwhile, sift the powdered sugar and flour together 3 times; set aside.

Add cream of tartar and vanilla to egg whites. Beat with an electric mixer on medium to high speed till soft peaks form (tips curl). Gradually add sugar, about *2 tablespoons* at a time, beating on medium to high speed till stiff peaks form (tips stand straight).

Sift about *one-fourth* of the flour mixture over the egg white mixture, then gently fold in. Repeat sifting and folding in the remaining flour mixture, using one-fourth of the flour mixture each time.

Gently pour the batter evenly into an *ungreased* 10-inch tube pan. Gently cut through the cake batter with a knife or narrow metal spatula. Bake on the lowest rack in a 350° oven for 40 to 45 minutes or till the top springs back when lightly touched. *Immediately* invert the cake in the pan and cool completely. Using a narrow metal spatula, loosen the sides of the cake from the pan. Then remove the cake from the pan. Serves 12.

Chocolate Angel Cake: Prepare Angel Cake as directed above, *except* sift ¼ cup *unsweetened cocoa powder* with the flour and powdered sugar.

Peppermint Angel Cake

Here's a "peppermint twist" to the classic angel cake.

1½ cups egg whites (10 to 12 large)
1½ cups sifted powdered sugar
1   cup sifted cake flour *or* sifted all-purpose
    flour
4   striped round peppermint candies, finely
    crushed (2 tablespoons)
1½ teaspoons cream of tartar
1   teaspoon vanilla
1   cup sugar

In a very large mixing bowl bring egg whites to room temperature. Meanwhile, sift powdered sugar and flour together 3 times. In a small mixing bowl stir together *1 tablespoon* of the flour mixture and the crushed candies. Set the flour mixture and the candy mixture aside.

Add cream of tartar and vanilla to the egg whites. Beat with an electric mixer on medium to high speed till soft peaks form (tips curl). Gradually add sugar, about *2 tablespoons* at a time, beating on medium to high speed till stiff peaks form (tips stand straight).

Sift about *one-fourth* of the plain flour mixture over the egg white mixture, then gently fold in. Repeat sifting and folding in the remaining flour mixture, using one-fourth of the flour mixture each time. Gently fold in the candy mixture.

Gently pour the batter evenly into an *ungreased* 10-inch tube pan. Gently cut through the cake batter with a knife or narrow metal spatula. Bake on the lowest rack in a 350° oven for 40 to 45 minutes or till the top springs back when lightly touched. *Immediately* invert the cake in the pan and cool completely. Using a narrow metal spatula, loosen the sides of the cake from the pan. Then remove the cake from the pan. Makes 12 servings.

▶ *To properly beat egg whites for angel cakes, first beat the egg whites, cream of tartar, and vanilla with an electric mixer set on medium to high speed, until they reach the soft-peak stage. At the soft-peak stage, the peak curls when the beaters are lifted from the egg white mixture.*

▶ *After the soft-peak stage, gradually add the sugar to the egg white mixture, 2 tablespoons at a time, while beating on medium to high speed. Beat the egg white-sugar mixture until stiff peaks form. At the stiff-peak stage, the peak stands straight up when the beaters are lifted out of the mixture.*

▶ *To fold the candy mixture into the stiffly beaten egg white-sugar mixture, cut down through the mixture with a rubber spatula. Scrape across bottom of bowl and bring the spatula up and over the mixture, close to the surface. Repeat this circular down-up-and-over motion while turning bowl.*

Luscious Lemon Angel Cake

Inviting on the outside—irresistible on the inside.

1½ **cups egg whites (10 to 12 large)**
1½ **cups sifted powdered sugar**
 1 **cup sifted cake flour *or* sifted all-purpose flour**
1½ **teaspoons cream of tartar**
 1 **teaspoon vanilla**
 1 **cup sugar**
 1 **teaspoon finely shredded lemon peel**
    Lemon Cake Filling
    Powdered sugar
    Lemon slices, quartered (optional)

In a very large mixing bowl bring egg whites to room temperature. Meanwhile, sift powdered sugar and flour together 3 times. Set flour mixture aside. Add cream of tartar and vanilla to egg whites. Beat with an electric mixer on medium to high speed till soft peaks form (tips curl). Gradually add the sugar, *2 tablespoons* at a time, beating on medium to high speed till stiff peaks form (tips stand straight).

Sift about *one-fourth* of the flour mixture over the egg white mixture, then gently fold in. Repeat sifting and folding in the remaining flour mixture, using one-fourth of it each time. Gently fold in lemon peel.

Gently pour batter evenly into an *ungreased* 10-inch tube pan. Gently cut through cake batter with a knife or metal spatula. Bake on lowest rack in a 350° oven for 40 to 45 minutes or till top springs back when lightly touched. *Immediately* invert cake in pan; cool completely. Using a narrow metal spatula, loosen sides of cake from pan. Remove cake from pan.

Using a serrated or very sharp knife, cut off the top 1 inch of the cake; set aside. With the knife held parallel to the side of the cake, cut around the hole in the center of the cake, leaving a 1-inch thickness of cake around hole. Then cut around inside the outer edge of the cake, leaving the outer cake wall 1 inch thick. Using a spoon, remove center of cake, leaving a

1-inch-thick base (see photo, page 198). Place the hollowed-out cake on a serving plate. Spoon filling into the hollowed-out section. Replace the top of the cake. Cover and chill for 4 to 24 hours. Before serving, sift powdered sugar over the cake. If desired, garnish with lemon slices. Makes 12 servings.

Lemon Cake Filling: In a saucepan stir together ¾ cup *sugar,* 1 envelope *unflavored gelatin,* and a dash *salt*. Gradually stir in ¾ cup *cold water*. Stir in 1 teaspoon finely shredded *lemon peel* and 3 tablespoons *lemon juice*. Heat and stir *just till gelatin dissolves*. If desired, stir in a few drops *yellow food coloring*. Cool lemon-gelatin mixture in a bath of ice water, stirring constantly for 5 to 8 minutes or till mixture is the consistency of corn syrup. Remove lemon-gelatin mixture from ice water; set aside. In a medium bowl beat 1 cup *whipping cream* till soft peaks form. Fold *one-fourth* of the whipped cream into the lemon-gelatin mixture. Then fold the lemon-gelatin mixture back into the remaining whipped cream. Chill about 5 minutes or till the mixture mounds when spooned. Makes 3 cups.

High-Altitude Cake Baking

Angel, sponge, and chiffon cakes can over-expand easily at high altitudes because so much air is beaten into the eggs. To adapt these recipes to high-altitude baking, see the tip on page 189 for suggestions on adjusting oven temperature, baking times, and amount of sugar. Also as suggestions, beat egg whites till soft peaks form, not till they're stiff, and increase flour by 1 or 2 tablespoons.

Luscious Lemon Angel Cake

Strawberry Angel Cake

1½ **cups egg whites (10 to 12 large)**
1½ **cups sifted powdered sugar**
 1 **cup sifted cake flour *or* sifted**
     all-purpose flour
1½ **teaspoons cream of tartar**
 1 **teaspoon vanilla**
 1 **cup sugar**
    Strawberry Filling
1½ **cups whipping cream**
 3 **tablespoons sugar**
    Strawberry halves (optional)

In a very large mixing bowl bring egg whites to room temperature. Meanwhile, sift powdered sugar and flour together 3 times. Set flour mixture aside.

Add cream of tartar and vanilla to the egg whites. Beat with an electric mixer on medium speed till soft peaks form (tips curl). Gradually add the 1 cup sugar, about *2 tablespoons* at a time, beating on medium to high speed till stiff peaks form (tips stand straight). Sift about *one-fourth* of the flour mixture over the egg white mixture, then gently fold in. Repeat sifting and folding in the remaining flour mixture, using one-fourth of the flour mixture each time.

Gently pour batter evenly into an *ungreased* 10-inch tube pan. Gently cut through cake batter with a knife or narrow metal spatula. Bake on the lowest rack in a 350° oven for 40 to 45 minutes or till top springs back when lightly touched. *Immediately* invert cake in pan and cool completely. Using a narrow metal spatula, loosen cake from pan; remove cake.

Using a very sharp knife, cut off the top 1 inch of the cake. Set top of cake aside. With the knife held parallel to the side of the cake, cut around the hole in the center of the cake, leaving a 1-inch thickness of cake around hole. Then cut around inside the outer edge of the cake, leaving the outer cake wall 1 inch thick. Using a spoon, remove center of the cake, leaving a 1-inch-thick base. Place hollowed-out cake on a

serving plate. Spoon filling into hollowed-out section. Replace top of cake. Cover and chill for 4 to 24 hours.

Up to 1 hour before serving, in a medium bowl beat the whipping cream and 3 tablespoons sugar till soft peaks form. Frost cake with the cream. If desired, garnish with strawberries. Makes 12 servings.

Strawberry Filling: In a small bowl mash 2 cups whole *strawberries*. Stir in ¼ cup *sugar*. Set mixture aside. In a glass measuring cup or custard cup combine ¼ cup *cold water* and 1 envelope *unflavored gelatin*. Let stand 5 minutes to soften. Place the cup containing the gelatin mixture in 1 inch of water in a small saucepan. Heat and stir *just till gelatin dissolves*. Stir gelatin mixture into strawberry mixture. Cool the strawberry-gelatin mixture in a bath of ice water, stirring constantly about 5 minutes or till mixture is the consistency of corn syrup. Remove from ice water; set aside. In a medium bowl beat ¾ cup *whipping cream* till soft peaks form. Fold *one-fourth* of the whipped cream into the strawberry-gelatin mixture. Then fold the strawberry-gelatin mixture back into the remaining whipped cream. Chill about 5 minutes or till slightly thickened. Makes about 3 cups.

◀ *To hollow out the cake, cut off the top 1 inch. Then cut around the hole, leaving a 1-inch thickness of cake around the hole. Next, cut around inside the outer edge, leaving the outer cake wall 1 inch thick. Using a spoon, remove the center of the cake, leaving a 1-inch base.*

Pecan Angel Cake

A light, nutty cake served with a custard sauce.

1½   cups egg whites (10 to 12 large)
1½   cups sifted powdered sugar
  1   cup sifted cake flour *or* all-purpose flour
  ¼   cup very finely chopped pecans, toasted
1½   teaspoons cream of tartar
  1   teaspoon vanilla
  ¾   cup sugar
  ¼   cup packed brown sugar
       Stirred Custard

In a very large bowl bring egg whites to room temperature. Sift powdered sugar and flour together 3 times. In a small bowl combine *½ cup* of flour mixture and pecans. Add cream of tartar and vanilla to egg whites. Beat with an electric mixer on medium to high speed till soft peaks form (tips curl). In a bowl combine sugar and brown sugar; add to egg white mixture, *2 tablespoons* at a time, beating on medium to high speed till stiff peaks form (tips stand straight).

Sift *one-fourth* of plain flour mixture over the egg white mixture; gently fold in. Repeat with remaining plain flour mixture by fourths. Fold in flour-nut mixture. Pour into an *ungreased* 10-inch tube pan. Using a knife, cut through batter. Bake on lowest rack in a 350° oven for 40 to 45 minutes or till the top springs back when touched. *Immediately* invert cake in pan and cool completely. Loosen cake from pan and remove. Serve Stirred Custard with cake. Serves 12.

Stirred Custard: In a heavy medium saucepan stir together 2 beaten *eggs,* 1 cup *milk,* and 2 tablespoons *sugar.* Heat and stir over medium heat *just till mixture coats a metal spoon.* Stir in ½ teaspoon *vanilla.* Place in a bath of ice water for 1 to 2 minutes, stirring constantly. Pour into a bowl. Cover surface with plastic wrap and chill.
   Just before serving, stir in ½ cup toasted broken *pecans.* Makes about 1⅓ cups.

Hot Milk Sponge Cake

The broiled coconut topping makes a great-tasting, easy frosting.

  1   cup all-purpose flour
  1   teaspoon baking powder
       Dash salt
  2   eggs
  1   cup sugar
  ½   cup milk
  5   tablespoons margarine *or* butter
  ½   cup packed brown sugar
  2   tablespoons milk
  1   cup coconut

Grease the bottom of a 9x9x2-inch metal baking pan. In a small bowl combine flour, baking powder, and salt. Set flour mixture aside.

In a large mixing bowl beat eggs with an electric mixer on high speed about 4 minutes or till thick and lemon-colored. Gradually add the 1 cup sugar, beating on medium speed about 5 minutes or till sugar is *almost* dissolved. Add flour mixture. Beat on low to medium speed *just till combined.*

In a small saucepan heat the ½ cup milk and *2 tablespoons* of the margarine just till margarine melts. Stir warm milk mixture into the beaten egg mixture.

Pour batter into the prepared baking pan. Bake in a 350° oven about 25 minutes or till the top springs back when touched. Slightly cool the cake in the pan on a wire rack.

Meanwhile, for a coconut topping, in a bowl stir together the remaining *3 tablespoons* of margarine or butter and brown sugar till combined. Stir in 2 tablespoons milk, then stir in coconut. Spread on top of the *warm* cake. Broil 3 to 4 inches from heat about 2 minutes or till golden. Serve warm. Serves 9.

Lively Lime Sponge Cake

This moist cake, flavored with lime or orange, is delicious.

1¼ cups all-purpose flour
⅓ cup sugar
6 egg yolks
2 teaspoons finely shredded lime peel
       (set aside)
¼ cup lime juice
¼ cup water
⅔ cup sugar
6 egg whites
¾ teaspoon cream of tartar
½ cup sugar
1 cup whipping cream (optional)
2 tablespoons sugar (optional)
       Lime slices (optional)

In a small bowl stir together flour and the ⅓ cup sugar. Set flour mixture aside.

In a medium bowl beat egg yolks with an electric mixer on high speed about 6 minutes or till thick and lemon-colored. Add lime juice and water. Beat on low speed about 30 seconds or till combined. Gradually add the ⅔ cup sugar, beating on medium speed about 5 minutes or till sugar is *almost* dissolved.

Gradually add *one-fourth* of the flour mixture to the egg yolk mixture, beating on low to medium speed *just till moistened.* Repeat beating in the remaining flour mixture by fourths. Stir in lime peel.

Thoroughly wash beaters. In a large mixing bowl beat egg whites and cream of tartar on medium to high speed till soft peaks form (tips curl). Gradually add the ½ cup sugar, about *2 tablespoons* at a time, beating on medium to high speed till stiff peaks form (tips stand straight).

Fold about *1 cup* of the egg white mixture into the the egg yolk mixture. Then fold egg yolk mixture into

remaining egg white mixture. Gently pour batter into an *ungreased* 10-inch tube pan. Bake in a 325° oven about 60 minutes or till top springs back when lightly touched. *Immediately* invert cake in pan; completely cool. Using a narrow metal spatula, loosen sides of cake from pan. Then remove cake from pan.

If desired, for a whipped cream topping, in a medium mixing bowl beat whipping cream and 2 tablespoons sugar till stiff peaks form. Pipe on top of cake. If desired, garnish with lime slices. Makes 12 servings.

Orange Sponge Cake: Prepare Lively Lime Sponge Cake as directed at left, *except* substitute 1 tablespoon finely shredded *orange peel* for lime peel and ½ cup *orange juice* for the lime juice and water. If desired, for an orange topping, in a medium bowl beat one 8-ounce package *cream cheese,* softened, ⅓ cup *sugar,* and ⅓ cup *orange juice* till smooth. Then, beat in one 8-ounce container *dairy sour cream.* Stir in 1 teaspoon finely shredded *orange peel.* Serve orange topping with Orange Sponge Cake.

◄ *To properly beat egg yolks for a sponge cake, place the yolks in a medium mixing bowl. Then beat with an electric mixer on high speed about 6 minutes or till thick and lemon-colored. When sufficiently beaten, the yolks will flow from the beaters in a thick stream when the beaters are lifted from the bowl.*

Cassata Rum Cake

6 **slightly beaten eggs**
1 **cup sugar**
1 **cup all-purpose flour**
¼ **cup margarine** *or* **butter, melted and cooled**
2 **tablespoons light rum**
1 **tablespoon amaretto**
1½ **cups whipping cream**
3 **tablespoons sugar**
½ **teaspoon vanilla**
½ **cup ricotta cheese**
2 **tablespoons sugar**
⅛ **teaspoon ground cinnamon**
 Dash ground nutmeg
½ **cup finely chopped almonds, toasted**
1 **square (1 ounce) semisweet chocolate, grated**

Grease and flour two 8-inch round baking pans. In a large bowl combine eggs and 1 cup sugar. Beat with an electric mixer on high speed about 6 minutes or till thick and more than doubled in volume. Fold in flour by thirds. Fold in melted margarine or butter. Spread into prepared pans. Bake in a 350° oven fir 30 to 35 minutes or till tops spring back when lightly touched. Cool in pans for 10 minutes. Remove cakes from pans; cool on wire racks.

In a bowl combine rum and amaretto; brush on bottoms of cake layers. Set aside. In a bowl combine whipping cream, 3 tablespoons sugar, and vanilla. Beat till soft peaks form. Set whipped cream aside.

In a bowl combine ricotta cheese, 2 tablespoons sugar, cinnamon, and nutmeg. Fold in ¾ *cup* of the whipped cream. Transfer one cake layer, bottom side up, to a serving plate. Spread cheese mixture on the top of the cake on plate. Sprinkle with *1 tablespoon* of the almonds and *half* of the grated chocolate. Top with remaining cake layer, bottom side down. Frost sides and top with remaining whipped cream. Sprinkle with remaining grated chocolate. Then press remaining almonds onto the sides of the cake. Chill for up to 4 hours. Makes 12 servings.

Secrets to Successful Angel and Sponge Cakes

Angel and sponge cakes rise high and have light textures. If you have any problems with these cakes, here are some tips on how to improve your results next time.

If angel or sponge cakes have poor volume:
■ Try not to underbeat *or* overbeat the egg whites. The egg whites should be stiff (see photo, page 195) but not dry.
■ Remember to fold in the flour mixture just until batter is smooth (see photo, page 195). Overmixing decreases cake volume.

If your angel or sponge cake falls:
■ Be sure to beat egg whites until they're stiff (see photo, page 195) but not dry.
■ Cool these cakes upside down. If your tube pan doesn't have legs for this purpose, invert it on a funnel or long-necked bottle.

If your angel or sponge cake is tough:
■ The amounts of sugar and flour are particularly critical to the tenderness of these cakes. Be sure to measure accurately (see page 297).
■ Fold in ingredients *just until combined.* Avoid overmixing (see photo, page 195).

If your sponge cake appears layered:
■ To avoid an eggy bottom layer, beat the egg yolks until they're thick and lemon-colored (see photo, page 200).
■ Too little sugar or liquid causes a layered appearance. So, use appropriate dry and liquid measuring cups (see page 297).

Pumpkin-Cheesecake Roll

For an attractive presentation, garnish with orange-peel curls and pecan halves. (Pictured on pages 178–179.)

　1　**8-ounce container soft-style cream cheese**
　⅓　**cup sugar**
　4　**eggs**
　1　**tablespoon milk**
　¾　**cup all-purpose flour**
　1　**teaspoon baking powder**
　1　**teaspoon ground cinnamon**
　1　**cup sugar**
　⅔　**cup canned pumpkin**
　　　Powdered sugar
　　　Cream Cheese Icing

Grease a 15x10x1-inch jelly-roll pan. Line with waxed paper; grease paper. Set pan aside. Set *2 tablespoons* of the cream cheese aside. In a bowl beat the remaining cream cheese and ⅓ cup sugar with an electric mixer on low speed till smooth. Beat in *one* egg and milk; spread in the prepared pan.

In a bowl combine flour, baking powder, cinnamon, and ¼ teaspoon *salt;* set aside. In a medium bowl beat remaining 3 eggs on high speed for 5 minutes. Gradually add 1 cup sugar, beating about 3 minutes or till sugar is *almost* dissolved. Stir in pumpkin. Fold in flour mixture. Carefully spread batter over cheese mixture. Bake in a 375° oven about 15 minutes or till top springs back. *Immediately* loosen cake from pan; invert cake onto a towel sprinkled with powdered sugar. Peel off paper. Roll up cake *without* towel from a short side. Cool on a rack. Frost with icing. Store in refrigerator. Makes 10 servings.

> **Cream Cheese Icing:** In a bowl combine the reserved 2 tablespoons cream cheese, 2 teaspoons *milk,* and ¼ teaspoon *vanilla.* Slowly beat in 1 cup sifted *powdered sugar* till smooth. If necessary, beat in ½ to 1 teaspoon *milk* to make icing of drizzling consistency. Makes about ½ cup.

Jelly Roll

Fill and roll this traditional jelly-roll cake with your favorite preserves.

　½　**cup all-purpose flour**
　1　**teaspoon baking powder**
　4　**egg yolks**
　½　**teaspoon vanilla**
　⅓　**cup sugar**
　4　**egg whites**
　½　**cup sugar**
　　　Powdered sugar
　½　**cup desired fruit preserves**
　1　**to 2 tablespoons desired fruit brandy**

Grease and flour a 15x10x1-inch jelly-roll pan; set aside. In a bowl combine flour and baking powder; set aside. In a large bowl beat egg yolks and vanilla with an electric mixer on high speed about 5 minutes or till thick and lemon-colored. Gradually add ⅓ cup sugar, beating on medium speed about 5 minutes or till sugar is *almost* dissolved.

Thoroughly wash beaters. In a very large mixing bowl beat egg whites on medium to high speed till soft peaks form (tips curl). Gradually add ½ cup sugar, about *2 tablespoons* at a time, beating on medium to high speed till stiff peaks form (tips stand straight).

Fold *1 cup* of the egg white mixture into egg yolk mixture. Then fold egg yolk mixture into remaining egg white mixture. Gently fold in flour mixture; spread in prepared pan. Bake in a 375° oven for 12 to 15 minutes or till cake springs back when touched. *Immediately* loosen cake from pan. Invert cake onto a towel sprinkled with powdered sugar. Roll up warm cake and towel, jelly-roll style, starting from one of the short sides. Cool completely on a wire rack.

Meanwhile, in a small bowl combine preserves and brandy. Gently unroll cake. Spread preserve mixture on cake to within ½ inch of the edges. Roll up cake *without* towel, jelly-roll style, starting from one of the short sides. Sift powdered sugar over cake. Serves 12.

Yule Log

Shape marzipan tinted with green food coloring into leaves for an easy garnish. (Pictured on page 205.)

- 1 **cup all-purpose flour**
- ¼ **teaspoon salt**
- 5 **egg yolks**
- 2 **tablespoons dry** *or* **cream sherry**
- 1 **cup sugar**
- 5 **egg whites**
- ¼ **teaspoon cream of tartar**
  Powdered sugar
  Coffee Cream Filling
  Rich Chocolate Frosting

Grease and lightly flour a 15x10x1-inch jelly-roll pan; set aside. In a small bowl stir together flour and salt. In a large bowl beat egg yolks and sherry with an electric mixer on high speed about 5 minutes or till thick and lemon-colored. Gradually add *½ cup* of the sugar, beating till sugar is *almost* dissolved.

Wash beaters. In a very large bowl beat egg whites and cream of tartar on medium to high speed till soft peaks form (tips curl). Gradually add remaining sugar, *2 tablespoons* at a time, beating on medium to high speed till stiff peaks form (tips stand straight). Fold *1 cup* of the egg white mixture into egg yolk mixture. Fold egg yolk mixture into remaining egg white mixture. Fold in flour mixture; spread in the prepared pan. Bake in a 375° oven for 12 to 15 minutes or till top springs back. *Immediately* loosen cake from pan. Invert cake onto a towel sprinkled with powdered sugar. Roll up warm cake and towel, jelly-roll style, starting from a short side. Cool on a rack.

Gently unroll cake. Spread filling on cake to within 1 inch of the edges. Roll up cake without towel, jelly-roll style, starting from one of the short sides. Cut a 2-inch slice from one end of cake. Place the slice at the side of the "log" to form a "branch." Frost with Rich Chocolate Frosting. Using the tines of a fork, score the cake lengthwise to resemble tree bark. Serves 10.

Coffee Cream Filling: In a mixing bowl beat 1 cup *whipping cream,* ¼ cup sifted *powdered sugar,* and 1½ teaspoons *instant coffee crystals* till soft peaks form. Makes about 2 cups.

Rich Chocolate Frosting: In a saucepan heat and stir 2 squares (2 ounces) *unsweetened chocolate,* and 2 tablespoons *margarine or butter* till chocolate melts. Remove from heat; stir in 2 cups sifted *powdered sugar,* ½ teaspoon *vanilla,* and 2 to 3 tablespoons *milk* to make a frosting of spreading consistency. Makes 1¼ cups.

▶ *To roll the cake, it is necessary for it to still be warm. Start at a short side; roll up the cake and the powdered-sugar-coated towel together. The towel prevents the cake from sticking together as it cools. The powdered sugar helps keep the towel from sticking to the cake.*

Layered Cherry-Almond Chiffon Cake

2¼ cups sifted cake flour *or* 2 cups sifted
    all-purpose flour
1½ cups sugar
 1 tablespoon baking powder
 ½ cup cooking oil
 7 egg yolks
 ¼ cup cherry brandy
 ¼ teaspoon almond extract
 7 egg whites
 ½ teaspoon cream of tartar
    Double Almond Frosting
    Cherry Filling
    Almond Frosting
    Sliced almonds

In a large bowl stir together flour, sugar, baking powder, and ¼ teaspoon *salt;* make a well in center. Add oil, egg yolks, brandy, almond extract, and ½ cup *cold water.* Beat with an electric mixer on low to medium speed till combined. Beat on high speed about 5 minutes or till satin smooth; set aside.

Thoroughly wash beaters. In a very large bowl beat egg whites and cream of tartar on medium to high speed till stiff peaks form (tips stand straight). Pour beaten egg yolk mixture in a thin stream over egg whites; fold in. Gently pour batter into an *ungreased* 10-inch tube pan. Bake in a 325° oven for 65 to 70 minutes or till top springs back when touched. *Immediately* invert cake in the pan and cool completely. Loosen the cake from the pan and then remove it.

To assemble, cut cake horizontally into *three* even layers. Place bottom layer on a serving plate. Pipe *half* of the Double Almond Frosting on the cake layer in a ring around hole in center and in a ring inside outer edge. Spoon *half* of Cherry Filling between rings. Place second layer on top; repeat piping and filling. Top with third layer. Frost top of cake with Almond Frosting. Sprinkle top with almonds. Serves 16.

Cherry Filling: In a saucepan combine ⅓ cup *sugar,* 2 tablespoons *cornstarch,* and one 16-ounce can *undrained* pitted *tart red cherries.* Cook and stir till thick and bubbly. Reduce heat; cook and stir 2 minutes. Remove from heat. Stir in 1 tablespoon *cherry brandy.* Transfer to a bowl. Cover surface with plastic wrap; cool to room temperature without stirring. Chill about 2 hours or till well chilled. Makes about 2 cups.

Almond Frosting: In a bowl beat ⅓ cup *margarine or butter* with an electric mixer till softened. Beat in 2 cups sifted *powdered sugar* till smooth. Slowly beat in ¼ cup *milk* and 6 drops of *almond extract.* Slowly beat in 2½ cups additional sifted *powdered sugar.* Makes 2¼ cups.

Double Almond Frosting: Transfer 1¼ cups of the *Almond Frosting* to another bowl. Beat in ⅓ cup *almond paste.* Set this frosting aside. If necessary, beat additional *milk* into remaining Almond Frosting to make the frosting of spreading consistency. Makes about 1⅔ cups.

Historic Roots of the Yule Log Cake

Over the centuries, cakes have been prepared to mark celebrations and holidays. Traditionally, different cakes were designed to symbolize different occasions. For instance, in France, at Christmas a sponge cake was rolled with a filling and made to resemble a Yule log. The Yule log was a large log put on the hearth on Christmas Eve as the foundation of the fire.

Yule Log
(see recipe, page 203)

Tropical Chiffon Cake

Pineapple and orange complement each other in this cake.

1 8-ounce can pineapple slices (juice pack)
2¼ cups sifted cake flour *or* 2 cups sifted
    all-purpose flour
1½ cups sugar
1 tablespoon baking powder
½ cup cooking oil
7 egg yolks
2 teaspoons finely shredded
    orange peel (set aside)
½ cup orange juice
7 egg whites
½ teaspoon cream of tartar
1 3½-ounce can (1⅓ cups) flaked coconut
    Rich Orange Frosting

Drain pineapple, reserving *¼ cup* of juice; set aside. In a large mixing bowl combine flour, sugar, baking powder, and ½ teaspoon *salt*. Make a well in the center of the flour mixture. Then add oil, egg yolks, orange juice, and reserved pineapple juice. Beat with an electric mixer on low to medium speed till combined. Then beat on high speed about 5 minutes or till smooth. Fold in orange peel. Set beaten mixture aside.

Thoroughly wash beaters. In a very large bowl beat egg whites and cream of tartar on medium to high speed till stiff peaks form (tips stand straight). Pour beaten mixture in a thin stream over egg white mixture; gently fold in. Fold in *1 cup* of the coconut. Pour batter into an *ungreased* 10-inch tube pan. Bake in a 325° oven for 55 to 60 minutes or till top springs back when lightly touched. *Immediately* invert cake in pan; cool completely. Place remaining coconut in an 8x8x2-inch baking pan. Bake in the 325° oven for 5 to 10 minutes or till toasted, stirring once; set aside. Remove cake from pan. Frost sides and top with frosting. Quarter pineapple slices and arrange on top of the cake. Sprinkle with toasted coconut. Serves 12.

Rich Orange Frosting: In a bowl beat one 3-ounce package *cream cheese*, ¼ cup *margarine or butter*, and 1 teaspoon *vanilla* till fluffy. Slowly beat in 3 cups sifted *powdered sugar* and 1 to 2 tablespoons *orange juice* to make a frosting of spreading consistency. Makes 1¾ cups.

Secrets to Successful Chiffon Cakes

Chiffon cakes are prepared similarly to angel and sponge cakes. Many of the steps and results are the same. If your chiffon cake is anything less than perfect, consult our helpful tips below and on page 201.

If your chiffon cake has an eggy bottom layer:
■ Underbeating *or* overbeating egg whites may give you an eggy layer. Beat egg whites till stiff peaks form when the beaters are lifted from the beaten egg whites. They should be stiff (see photo, page 195) but not dry.

If your chiffon cake has eggy streaks:
■ Be sure to *first* add the cooking oil to the flour mixture, then add the yolks. If egg yolks are placed directly in the flour mixture, they will bind with the flour and form streaks.

Chocolate Chiffon Loaf With Mint Topping

If your loaf cake rises above the pan, you can cool it upside down without crushing the cake. Invert the cake in the pan with its edges resting on two other pans of equal height.

- 2 squares (2 ounces) unsweetened chocolate
- 2 tablespoons sugar
- 1 cup *plus* 2 tablespoons sifted cake flour *or* 1 cup sifted all-purpose flour
- ¾ cup sugar
- 1½ teaspoons baking powder
- ¼ teaspoon salt
- ⅓ cup cooking oil
- 4 egg yolks
- ½ teaspoon vanilla
- 4 egg whites
- ½ teaspoon cream of tartar
  Mint Topping
- 5 layered chocolate-mint candies

In a saucepan combine ⅓ cup *water,* chocolate, and 2 tablespoons sugar. Heat and stir over low heat till chocolate melts; set aside to cool. In a large bowl combine flour, ¾ cup sugar, baking powder, and salt; make a well in center. Add oil, egg yolks, vanilla, and ⅓ cup *cold water.* Beat with an electric mixer on low to medium speed till combined. Beat on high speed about 3 minutes or till smooth. Beat in chocolate mixture on low speed; set aside.

Thoroughly wash beaters. In a very large bowl beat egg whites and cream of tartar on medium to high speed till stiff peaks form (tips stand straight). Pour beaten mixture in a thin stream over egg white mixture and gently fold in.

Pour batter into an *ungreased* 9x5x3-inch loaf pan. Bake in a 325° oven for 50 to 55 minutes or till top springs back. *Immediately* invert cake in pan; cool completely. Loosen cake from pan. Remove cake from pan. Frost sides and top of cake with Mint Topping. Shave chocolate-mint candies over cake. Serves 8.

Mint Topping: In a medium bowl beat 1 cup *whipping cream,* 2 tablespoons *powdered sugar,* and 2 tablespoons *crème de menthe* till stiff peaks form. Makes about 2¼ cups.

Chiffon Cake

- 2¼ cups sifted cake flour *or* 2 cups sifted all-purpose flour
- 1½ cups sugar
- 1 tablespoon baking powder
- ½ cup cooking oil
- 7 egg yolks
- 1 teaspoon vanilla
- 2 teaspoons finely shredded orange peel
- 1 teaspoon finely shredded lemon peel
- 7 egg whites
- ½ teaspoon cream of tartar

In a large bowl combine flour, sugar, baking powder, and ¼ teaspoon *salt;* make a well in center. Add oil, egg yolks, vanilla, and ¾ cup *cold water.* Beat with an electric mixer on low speed till combined. Beat on high speed about 5 minutes or till satin smooth. Fold in orange and lemon peels; set aside.

Thoroughly wash beaters. In a very large mixing bowl beat egg whites and cream of tartar on medium to high speed till stiff peaks form (tips stand straight). Then pour beaten mixture in a thin stream over egg white mixture and gently fold in. Gently pour batter into an *ungreased* 10-inch tube pan. Bake in a 325° oven for 65 to 70 minutes or till top springs back when lightly touched. *Immediately* invert cake in pan and cool completely. Using a narrow metal spatula, loosen the sides of the cake from the pan. Then remove cake from pan. Makes 12 servings.

Boston Cream Pie

A great trio—cake, pudding filling, and chocolate glaze.

   1 cup *plus* 2 tablespoons sifted cake flour
      or 1 cup sifted all-purpose flour
   ⅔ cup sugar
   1½ teaspoons baking powder
   ¼ teaspoon salt
   ½ cup milk
   ¼ cup cooking oil
   2 egg yolks
   1 teaspoon vanilla
   2 egg whites
   ¼ teaspoon cream of tartar
      Vanilla Pudding Filling
      Chocolate Glaze

In a medium mixing bowl combine flour, sugar, baking powder, and salt. Make a well in the center of the flour mixture. Add milk, oil, egg yolks, and vanilla. Beat with an electric mixer on low to medium speed till combined. Then beat on high speed for 3 minutes. Set beaten mixture aside.

Thoroughly wash beaters. In a large mixing bowl beat egg whites and cream of tartar on medium to high speed till stiff peaks form (tips stand straight). Pour the beaten mixture over the egg white mixture and gently fold in.

Gently pour batter into an *ungreased* 9-inch springform pan. Bake in a 350° oven for 25 to 30 minutes or till top springs back when lightly touched. *Immediately* invert the cake in the pan on a wire rack. Cool completely. Remove the cake from the pan.

To assemble, cut cake horizontally in half. Place bottom layer on a serving plate or board. Spread filling on top. Top with second layer. Pour glaze over cake and down sides. Store in refrigerator. Serves 8.

Vanilla Pudding Filling: In a saucepan combine ½ cup *sugar,* 2 tablespoons *flour,* 1 tablespoon *cornstarch,* and ⅛ teaspoon *salt.* Stir in 1¼ cups *milk.* Cook and stir till thickened. Reduce heat; cook and stir 2 minutes more. Set aside. In a bowl slightly beat 2 *eggs.* Stir *1 cup* of hot mixture into eggs; return to saucepan. Cook and stir 2 minutes more. (*Do not boil.*) Remove from heat. Stir in 1 tablespoon *margarine or butter* and 1½ teaspoons *vanilla* till combined. Cover surface with plastic wrap; cool. Makes 1¾ cups.

Chocolate Glaze: In a saucepan melt 1 square (1 ounce) *unsweetened chocolate* and 1 tablespoon *margarine or butter* over low heat. Remove from heat. Stir in ¾ cup sifted *powdered sugar* and ½ teaspoon *vanilla* till crumbly. Stir in 2 teaspoons *very hot water.* Stir in 3 to 4 teaspoons additional *hot water,* 1 teaspoon at a time, to a make a glaze of pouring consistency. Makes ½ cup.

Newest Cake: Chiffon

Chiffon cake is said to have been the invention of one Harry Baker. At the time he developed the cake, Baker was a 64-year-old insurance salesman in the Los Angeles area.

The story goes that he became renown in that part of the country for his new cake, which was both light and rich. He kept the recipe a closely guarded secret, making his cake for the public only on very special occasions. Finally he decided to divulge his secret recipe to a radio food show personality, traveling to Minneapolis to do so. In 1948, the cake was introduced to the U.S. by a flour milling company as the first new cake in 100 years.

Boston Cream Pie

SPECIALTY CAKES

Specialty cakes are rightfully named because of their excellence. On the following pages, you'll find legendary thinly layered tortes, flourless cakes that use nuts or bread crumbs in place of flour, and cakes that have a unique spongy top and a puddinglike bottom. Whichever type you choose to make, these fabulous cakes surely will impress all who taste them.

☐ Some specialty cakes use nuts, bread crumbs, or cracker crumbs in place of the flour. For these recipes, it is important to use *very fine* and *dry* ground nuts or crumbs. Grinding nuts to the right stage can be tricky because nuts will form a paste if ground too much. To prevent this, grind the nuts in small batches with a food grinder, blender, or food processor. (If using a blender or food processor, quickly start and stop it for better control over the fineness of the ground nuts.)

☐ For many recipes, you will need to beat the egg yolks until they are thick and lemon-colored (see photo, page 200). Follow the beating time given in the recipe to achieve this stage.

☐ To test the doneness of a cake made with ground nuts or crumbs, touch the top lightly. If the cake springs back slightly, the cake is done. Cakes made with ground nuts or crumbs will not have a domed top like most other cakes. Instead, they will have a flat or slightly depressed top.

☐ Since pudding cakes have a moist bottom layer, a toothpick will not come out clean when inserted near the center. Pudding cakes are done if the top springs back slightly when lightly touched.

Almond-Raspberry Torte

Feature this scrumptious torte at your next dinner party. (Pictured on pages 178–179.)

1½ **cups all-purpose flour**
2¼ **teaspoons baking powder**
 ¾ **cup margarine *or* butter**
 1 **cup sugar**
1½ **teaspoons vanilla**
 3 **eggs**
 ¾ **cup milk**
 1 **8-ounce can almond paste**
 ⅓ **cup margarine *or* butter, softened**
 2 **tablespoons milk**
 ¾ **cup seedless red raspberry preserves, stirred**
 1 **cup whipping cream**
 ⅔ **cup sliced almonds, toasted**

For cake, grease and lightly flour two 9x1½-inch round baking pans; set aside. Combine flour, baking powder, and ¼ teaspoon *salt;* set aside. In a large bowl beat ¾ cup margarine with an electric mixer on medium to high speed for 30 seconds. Add sugar and vanilla; beat well. Add eggs, one at time, beating till combined. Alternately add flour mixture and ¾ cup milk, beating after each *just till combined* (may look curdled). Pour into pans. Bake in a 375° oven 20 to 25 minutes or till wooden toothpick comes out clean. Cool on racks 10 minutes. Remove; completely cool.

For almond filling, in a small mixing bowl beat almond paste, ⅓ cup margarine or butter, and 2 tablespoons milk with an electric mixer till smooth.

To assemble, cut *each* cake horizontally in half. Place first layer on serving plate. Spread with *one-third* of the almond filling, then with *2 rounded tablespoons* of preserves. Repeat layering twice more. Finally, top with remaining cake layer. Cover tightly; chill 6 to 24 hours. Reserve remaining preserves.

Beat cream just to stiff peaks; spread over cake. Gently press nuts around sides. Just before serving, drizzle remaining preserves on top. Makes 12 servings.

Fresh Pineapple Torte

To choose a pineapple at its peak of ripeness and flavor, look for one that's plump, slightly soft to the touch, fresh looking, and heavy for its size.

 1 **small fresh pineapple*, peeled, cored, and cut into ½-inch chunks (about 2 cups)**
 ¼ **cup sugar**
 1 **tablespoon cornstarch**
 1 **cup all-purpose flour**
 ½ **teaspoon baking powder**
 ¼ **teaspoon baking soda**
 ⅛ **teaspoon salt**
 2 **eggs**
 ½ **teaspoon vanilla**
 1 **cup sugar**
 2 **tablespoons margarine *or* butter**
 1 **cup whipping cream**
 2 **tablespoons sugar**
 ¼ **cup shredded coconut, toasted**

Divide pineapple chunks into thirds; set *two* of the portions aside.

In a blender container or food processor bowl place remaining portion of the pineapple. Cover; blend or process till pureed. If necessary, add enough *water* to measure ⅔ *cup* pureed pineapple. Set puree aside.

For filling, in a small saucepan combine *one* of the reserved portions of pineapple and ⅓ cup *water*. Bring to boiling. Stir together the ¼ cup sugar and cornstarch; add to hot pineapple mixture all at once. Cook, stirring constantly, till very thick and bubbly. Cook and stir for 1 minute more. Remove from heat. Cover and cool to room temperature.

For cake, grease and lightly flour two 8x1½-inch round baking pans. In a small mixing bowl stir together flour, baking powder, baking soda, and salt. Set pans and flour mixture aside. In a large mixing bowl beat eggs and vanilla with an electric mixer on high speed for 4 minutes. Gradually add the 1 cup sugar,

beating on medium speed for 4 to 5 minutes or till sugar is *almost* dissolved. Gradually add flour mixture, beating on low speed *just till combined.*

In a small saucepan heat pineapple puree and margarine or butter till margarine melts; add to beaten mixture and beat at low speed *just till combined.* Pour batter into the prepared pans. Bake in a 350° oven 20 to 25 minutes or till a wooden toothpick inserted near centers of cakes comes out clean. Cool cakes in pans on wire racks for 10 minutes. Remove cakes from pans; completely cool on wire racks.

In a medium mixing bowl beat whipping cream and the 2 tablespoons sugar just till stiff peaks form. Place first cake layer on a large serving plate; spread with pineapple filling. Top with second cake layer. Frost sides and top with whipped cream. Arrange the remaining reserved portion of pineapple on top. Sprinkle coconut on top. Makes 12 servings.

*You can substitute 2 cups well-drained *canned pineapple chunks* (juice pack) for the fresh pineapple.

Serving Cakes with Whipped Cream

Cakes filled or frosted with whipped cream can get soggy quite quickly. In storage, whipped cream breaks down and becomes watery. So, to serve cream-filled cakes at their best, whip the cream and assemble the cake no more than 2 hours before serving. *Or,* use our stabilized whipped cream (see tip, page 226) and assemble the cake up to 24 hours before serving. Be sure to store the cream-filled cake in the refrigerator until you are ready to serve it.

Sacher Torte

The apricot preserves filling adds just the right touch of tartness to the rich chocolate cake and glaze.

  4 **egg whites**
  6 **tablespoons margarine *or* butter**
  3 **squares (3 ounces) semisweet chocolate, cut up**
  4 **slightly beaten egg yolks**
  1 **teaspoon vanilla**
  ⅓ **cup sugar**
  ½ **cup all-purpose flour**
  ⅓ **cup apricot preserves**
     Sacher Torte Chocolate Glaze
     Chocolate leaves (see page 301) (optional)

In a large mixing bowl bring egg whites to room temperature. Meanwhile, grease and flour a 9x1½-inch round baking pan. In a medium saucepan melt the margarine or butter and semisweet chocolate over low heat, stirring occasionally; cool. Stir in egg yolks and vanilla. Set pan and chocolate mixture aside.

Beat egg whites with an electric mixer on medium to high speed till soft peaks form (tips curl). Gradually add sugar, about *2 tablespoons* at a time, beating on high speed about 4 minutes or till stiff peaks form (tips stand straight). Gently fold about *1 cup* of the egg white mixture into the egg yolk mixture. Then fold egg yolk mixture into remaining egg white mixture. Sift flour over egg mixture; gently fold in. *Do not overfold.* Spread batter into prepared pan. Bake in a 350° oven about 35 minutes or till a wooden toothpick inserted near center comes out clean. Cool in the pan on a wire rack for 10 minutes. Remove cake from pan; completely cool cake on the wire rack.

To assemble, cut cake horizontally into *two* even layers. Press apricot preserves through a sieve. Place first cake layer on wire rack covered with waxed paper. Spread preserves on top. Top with second cake layer. Spoon Sacher Torte Chocolate Glaze over cake. Carefully transfer cake to a serving plate. If desired, garnish with chocolate leaves. Makes 12 servings.

Sacher Torte Chocolate Glaze: In a saucepan heat 2 squares (2 ounces) *semisweet chocolate,* cut up, and 2 tablespoons *margarine or butter* over low heat just till melted, stirring occasionally. Remove from heat. Stir in ¾ cup sifted *powdered sugar* and 4 teaspoons *hot water* till smooth. If necessary, stir in additional *hot water* to make of drizzling consistency. Makes ½ cup.

The Sacher Torte Story

HISTORY OF BAKING

This famous cake was at the heart of a controversy in Austria for six years. It seems some Austrians took their baking so seriously that an argument over what constituted a true Sacher Torte erupted and had to be decided in court. In the early 1800s, the Congress of Vienna ruled on the matter. It decided that the true Sacher Torte was made of two chocolate cake layers separated by apricot jam with a chocolate glaze over the top and sides of the cake. Justice was served!

Orange Torte
(see recipe, page 214)

Orange Torte

1¼ **cups all-purpose flour**
¼ **cup sugar**
   Dash salt
6 **egg yolks**
1 **tablespoon finely shredded orange peel**
   (set aside)
½ **cup orange juice**
⅔ **cup sugar**
6 **egg whites**
1 **teaspoon cream of tartar**
½ **cup sugar**
   Creamy Butter Filling
3 **oranges, peeled and thinly sliced**
½ **cup apricot jam *or* preserves, sieved**
1 **cup sliced almonds**

In a small mixing bowl stir together flour, ¼ cup sugar, and salt. Set flour mixture aside. In a medium bowl beat egg yolks with an electric mixer on high speed 6 minutes or till thick and lemon-colored.

Add orange juice to beaten egg yolks. Beat on low speed till combined. Gradually add ⅔ cup sugar, beating till sugar is *almost* dissolved. Gradually add about *one-fourth* of the flour mixture, beating on low speed *just till moistened.* Repeat beating in the remaining flour mixture by fourths. Stir in shredded orange peel.

Thoroughly wash beaters. In a large mixing bowl beat egg whites and cream of tartar on medium to high speed till soft peaks form (tips curl). Gradually add the ½ cup sugar, about *2 tablespoons* at a time, beating on medium to high speed till stiff peaks form (tips stand straight).

Fold about *1 cup* of the egg white mixture into the egg yolk mixture. Then fold yolk mixture into remaining egg white mixture. Spoon batter into an *ungreased* 10-inch springform pan. Bake in a 325° oven for 1 to 1¼ hours or till done. *Immediately* invert cake and pan. Cool completely. Using a narrow metal spatula, loosen sides of cake from pan. Remove cake.

To assemble, cut cake horizontally into *three* even layers. Place first layer on a large serving plate. Spread *half* of the Creamy Butter Filling on top of the cake layer. Top with second layer, then spread on remaining filling. Finally, top with remaining layer. Cover and chill for 3 to 4 hours. Just before serving, arrange orange slices on top of the cake. In a small saucepan heat jam just till melted; cool slightly. Brush jam over orange slices and around sides of cake. Then press almonds on sides of cake. Makes 12 to 16 servings.

Creamy Butter Filling: In a medium saucepan stir together ⅓ cup *sugar* and 2 tablespoons *cornstarch*. Stir in 1¼ cups *milk*. Cook and stir over medium heat till thickened and bubbly. Reduce heat, then cook and stir 2 minutes more. Gradually stir about *half* of the mixture into 1 slightly beaten *egg yolk;* return to remaining hot mixture. Bring to a gentle boil. Cook and stir for 2 minutes. Remove from heat. Cover surface with plastic wrap. Cool to room temperature without stirring. In a medium mixing bowl beat ¾ cup softened *butter or margarine* and ¾ cup sifted *powdered sugar* with electric mixer on medium speed till light and fluffy. Gradually beat in cornstarch mixture till smooth. Makes 2¾ cups.

◀ *To split the cake horizontally, first use toothpicks to mark the midpoint on the cake's side. Then, carefully slice the cake using a long serrated knife.*

Easy Raspberry Torte

Both the mixing and the assembly have been streamlined.

- ¾ **cup chopped *or* broken walnuts**
- ½ **cup sugar**
- 1 **tablespoon all-purpose flour**
- 2 **teaspoons baking powder**
- 3 **eggs**
- ½ **cup seedless raspberry preserves**
- 1 **cup whipping cream**
- 2 **tablespoons sugar**

Generously grease and lightly flour an 11x7x1½-inch baking pan. Set pan aside.

In a blender container or food processor bowl combine walnuts, the ½ cup sugar, the flour, and baking powder. Cover and blend or process till nuts are ground. Add eggs. Blend or process till *nearly* smooth.

Spread walnut mixture evenly in the prepared pan. Bake in a 350° oven about 20 minutes or till the cake tests done. Cool the cake in the pan on a wire rack for 10 minutes. Loosen edges. Then remove cake from the pan and completely cool it on the wire rack.

Spread raspberry preserves on top of the cake. In a medium mixing bowl beat whipping cream and 2 tablespoons sugar just till stiff peaks form. Spread about *½ cup* of the whipped cream on top of the preserves.

To assemble, cut the cake vertically into thirds. On a serving plate, stack the 3 frosted cake pieces. If desired, reserve *½ cup* of the whipped cream for piping. Frost the sides of the cake with the remaining whipped cream. If desired, spoon the reserved whipped cream into a decorating bag fitted with a medium star tip (about ¼-inch opening). Pipe stars around top and bottom edges of cake. Serves 8.

White Chocolate-Filled Coffee Torte

Choose either coffee liqueur or crème de cacao to flavor the whipped cream filling and topping.

- 4 **eggs**
- ¾ **cup sugar**
- 2½ **teaspoons instant coffee crystals**
- 1 **cup hazelnuts (filberts) *or* chopped pecans**
- 2 **tablespoons all-purpose flour**
- 2½ **teaspoons baking powder**
- 1½ **cups whipping cream**
- 2 **tablespoons coffee liqueur or creme de cacao**
- 1 **teaspoon vanilla**
- 2 **ounces white baking bar with cocoa butter, chopped (about ½ cup)**
  White baking bar with cocoa butter (optional)
  Hazelnuts (filberts) *or* pecan halves (optional)

Generously grease and lightly flour two 8x1½-inch round baking pans. Set pans aside.

In a blender container or food processor bowl combine eggs, sugar, and coffee crystals. Cover and blend or process till smooth. Add 1 cup nuts, flour, and baking powder. Cover and blend or process till *nearly* smooth. Spread mixture evenly in prepared pans. Bake in a 350° oven 20 to 25 minutes or till done. Cool cakes in pans on wire racks for 10 minutes. Remove cakes and completely cool them on the racks.

In a medium mixing bowl beat whipping cream, liqueur, and vanilla just till stiff peaks form. Transfer *1 cup* of the whipped cream mixture to a small bowl; fold in the 2 ounces chopped white baking bar.

To assemble, place first cake layer on a serving plate. Spread with the whipped cream-baking bar mixture. Top with remaining cake layer. Frost sides and top with remaining plain whipped-cream mixture. If desired, garnish with curls made from the additional white baking bar (see page 301) and hazelnuts or pecan halves. Makes 10 servings.

Meringue-Topped Torte

Two-treats-in-one: Spread a meringue on top of the cake batter, then bake as one luscious dessert.

> 3 **egg whites**
> 1 **cup all-purpose flour**
> 1 **teaspoon baking powder**
> ¼ **teaspoon salt**
> ½ **cup margarine** *or* **butter**
> ½ **cup sugar**
> 3 **egg yolks**
> 1 **teaspoon vanilla**
> ¼ **cup milk**
> ¼ **teaspoon cream of tartar**
> ¾ **cup sugar**
> 3 **tablespoons sliced almonds**
> 1 **cup whipping cream**
> 1 **tablespoon amaretto** *or* **powdered sugar**
> 1 **to 1½ cups sliced fresh strawberries** *or* **sliced pitted peaches,** *or* **whole raspberries**

Grease two 9x1½-inch round baking pans. Line the bottoms of the pans with waxed paper. Grease waxed paper, then set pans aside. In a large mixing bowl bring egg whites to room temperature. In a small mixing bowl stir together flour, baking powder, and salt. Set the egg whites and the flour mixture aside.

In a medium mixing bowl beat margarine or butter with an electric mixer on medium to high speed about 30 seconds or till softened. Add the ½ cup sugar, the egg yolks, and vanilla. Beat till fluffy. Alternately add the flour mixture and the milk, beating on low to medium speed after each addition *just till combined.* Spread batter into the prepared pans.

For meringue, add cream of tartar to egg whites in bowl. Beat with an electric mixer on medium speed till soft peaks form (tips curl). Gradually add the ¾ cup sugar, *1 tablespoon* at a time, beating on high speed about 4 minutes or till stiff peaks form (tips stand straight) and sugar is *almost* dissolved. Carefully spread egg white mixture evenly over the cake batter in pans. Sprinkle almonds on top. Bake in a 350°

oven about 30 minutes or till meringue is golden. Cool in pans on wire racks for 10 minutes. Loosen edges and gently invert cakes onto wire racks. Remove pans, then place a second wire rack on cake bottoms and invert again so meringue sides are up. Completely cool on wire racks, meringue sides up.

In a mixing bowl beat whipping cream and amaretto or powdered sugar till soft peaks form. Place one cake layer on a serving plate, meringue side up. Spread about *two-thirds* of the whipped cream on top of the meringue. Arrange fruit in a single layer on the whipped cream. Top with remaining cake layer, meringue side up. Dollop remaining whipped cream on top of meringue. Makes 10 to 12 servings.

Tips for Assembling Tortes

Since tortes are made up of several layers of cake and filling, their assembly is as much a part of the preparation as mixing and baking. Here are some hints for successfully assembling tortes.

■ Chilling the cake makes it easier to split it horizontally into layers (see photo, page 214).

■ Use a *long serrated* knife when splitting the cake into layers. This type of knife will make a clean cut and minimize crumbs.

■ If the cake has a slightly domed top, horizontally slice a thin layer off the top to make it flat. This will result in level cake layers, making it easier to assemble a torte.

Triple Nut Torte

⅔ cup *each* chopped walnuts *and* pecans
½ cup blanched almonds
6 egg yolks
½ cup sugar
¼ cup fine dry bread crumbs
1 tablespoon finely shredded orange peel
2 tablespoons orange juice
6 egg whites
   Orange-Date Filling
¾ cup whipping cream

Generously grease and lightly flour three 8x1½-inch round baking pans. Grind walnuts, pecans, and almonds separately. Set pans and nuts aside.

In a medium mixing bowl beat egg yolks and sugar with an electric mixer on high speed for 6 minutes. Stir in crumbs, peel, and juice. Thoroughly wash beaters. In a large bowl beat egg whites on medium speed till stiff peaks form (tips stand straight). Fold about *1 cup* egg whites into egg yolk mixture. Fold yolk mixture into remaining egg whites. Equally divide mixture into 3 bowls. Fold one type of nut into each. Spread each mixture into a prepared pan. Bake in a 350° oven about 20 minutes or till done. Cool on racks 10 minutes; remove from pans. Cool completely.

To assemble, place pecan cake on a plate. Spread with *half* of filling. Top with almond cake and remaining filling. Top with walnut layer. Whip cream till soft peaks form; spread on top. Serves 12.

Orange-Date Filling: In a saucepan combine one 8-ounce package pitted whole *dates,* snipped; 2 teaspoons finely shredded *orange peel;* 1 cup *orange juice;* ½ cup *water;* and ¼ cup *each* chopped *almonds, walnuts,* and *pecans.* Bring to boiling. Cook and stir over medium heat about 5 minutes or till thickened. Cool. Makes 1⅔ cups.

Greek Walnut Cake

A blend of lemon and cinnamon subtly flavors this moist, delectable cake.

1 cup chopped *or* broken walnuts
½ cup crushed zwieback
4 egg yolks
½ cup sugar
¾ teaspoon baking powder
½ teaspoon finely shredded lemon peel
½ teaspoon ground cinnamon
4 egg whites
   Lemon Syrup
12 lemon peel twists

Grease an 8x8x2-inch baking pan. Grind walnuts. In a small mixing bowl stir together ground walnuts and zwieback. Set pan and nut mixture aside.

In a medium mixing bowl beat egg yolks and sugar with an electric mixer on high speed for 5 minutes. Stir in baking powder, lemon peel, and cinnamon. Thoroughly wash beaters. In a large mixing bowl beat egg whites on medium to high speed till stiff peaks form (tips stand straight). Fold about *1 cup* of the egg whites into the egg yolk mixture. Fold yolk mixture into remaining egg white mixture. Sprinkle about *one-third* nut mixture at a time over batter; gently fold in. Spread batter into the prepared pan. Bake in a 350° oven for 25 to 30 minutes or till the cake tests done. Completely cool cake in the pan on a wire rack.

Cut cake into 12 pieces. Pour *hot* Lemon Syrup over cake. Completely cool cake with Lemon Syrup. Garnish with a lemon peel twists. Makes 12 servings.

Lemon Syrup: In a small saucepan combine ⅓ cup *sugar,* ⅓ cup *water,* ½ teaspoon finely shredded *lemon peel,* and 2 teaspoons *lemon juice.* Bring to boiling; reduce heat. Simmer, uncovered, for 10 minutes. Remove from heat. Stir in ¼ teaspoon *vanilla.* Makes about ⅓ cup.

**Cherry-Topped
Almond Cake**

**Chocolate
Mousse Cake**
(see recipe, page 222)

**Apricot-Glazed
Chocolate Nut Cake**

Cherry-Topped Almond Cake

A splash of orange liqueur is a delightful accent to the cherries in the sauce.

1¼ **cups whole blanched almonds, toasted**
¼ **cup fine dry bread crumbs**
3 **egg yolks**
¼ **cup sugar**
3 **egg whites**
½ **teaspoon cream of tartar**
3 **tablespoons sugar**
   Cherry Sauce

Generously grease and lightly flour the bottom of a 9x1½-inch round baking pan. Grind almonds. In a small mixing bowl stir together ground almonds and bread crumbs. Set pan and almond mixture aside.

In a medium bowl beat egg yolks and the ¼ cup sugar with an electric mixer on high speed for 5 minutes. Thoroughly wash beaters. In a large bowl beat egg whites and cream of tartar on medium to high speed till soft peaks form (tips curl). Gradually add the 3 tablespoons sugar, beating till stiff peaks form (tips stand straight). Fold about *1 cup* egg white mixture into yolk mixture. Then fold yolk mixture into remaining egg white mixture. Sprinkle about *one-third* nut mixture at a time over batter; gently fold in. Spread batter evenly into the prepared pan. Bake in a 350° oven for 20 to 25 minutes or till cake tests done.

Cool cake in the pan on a wire rack for 10 minutes. Remove cake from the pan and completely cool on the rack. Serve with Cherry Sauce. Makes 8 servings.

Cherry Sauce: In a saucepan combine ⅓ cup *sugar* and 1 tablespoon *cornstarch*. Stir in ¼ cup *water* and, if desired, 2 tablespoons *orange liqueur*. Stir in 2 cups fresh *or* thawed frozen unsweetened pitted *tart red cherries*. Cook and stir till thickened and bubbly. Cook and stir for 2 minutes more. Cool. Makes 1½ cups.

Apricot-Glazed Chocolate Nut Cake

As easy as 1-2-3—just whip up the batter in your blender or food processor, bake, and glaze.

1½ **cups broken walnuts *or* pecans**
¾ **cup sugar**
¼ **cup unsweetened cocoa powder**
¼ **cup semisweet chocolate pieces**
1 **teaspoon baking powder**
¼ **teaspoon baking soda**
5 **eggs**
1 **teaspoon vanilla**
3 **apricots, pitted and sliced, *or* one 8-ounce can unpeeled apricot halves, drained and sliced**
   Apricot Glaze
   Walnut *or* pecan halves (optional)

Grease and flour a 9-inch springform pan. In a blender container or food processor bowl combine the 1½ cups broken nuts, sugar, cocoa powder, chocolate pieces, baking powder, and baking soda. Cover and blend or process till nuts are ground. Add eggs and vanilla. Blend or process till *nearly* smooth.

Spread nut mixture in the prepared pan. Bake in a 350° oven for 35 minutes or till the cake tests done. Cool in springform pan on a wire rack for 10 minutes. Remove sides of springform pan. Cool completely. Place the cake on a serving platter. Arrange apricot slices on top of the cake. Top with Apricot Glaze. If desired, garnish with walnut or pecan halves. Chill for 2 hours before serving. Makes 8 to 10 servings.

Apricot Glaze: In a small saucepan combine ⅔ cup *apricot preserves* and 2 teaspoons *cornstarch*. (Cut up any large pieces of fruit.) Stir in 2 tablespoons *brandy or orange juice*. Cook, stirring constantly, till bubbly. Cook and stir for 2 minutes more. Cover surface with plastic wrap. Cool without stirring. Makes about ⅔ cup.

Pumpkin Praline Cake

　2　**cups chopped *or* broken pecans, toasted**
⅔　**cup finely crushed vanilla wafers**
　1　**teaspoon pumpkin pie spice**
　1　**teaspoon baking powder**
½　**teaspoon finely shredded orange peel**
　6　**egg yolks**
½　**cup sugar**
⅔　**cup canned pumpkin**
　1　**teaspoon vanilla**
　6　**egg whites**
½　**cup sugar**
　　Powdered sugar
　　Vanilla-Rum Filling
　　Whipped Cream Topping
　　Ground pecans

Grease a 15x10x1-inch baking pan. Line the bottom of the pan with waxed paper, then set the pan aside. Grind the 2 cups toasted pecans. Transfer ground pecans to a bowl. Stir in crushed vanilla wafers, pumpkin pie spice, baking powder, and orange peel. Set pecan mixture aside.

In a large mixing bowl beat egg yolks and ½ cup sugar with an electric mixer on high speed for 6 minutes. Stir in canned pumpkin and vanilla. Then fold in the pecan mixture.

Thoroughly wash beaters. In a very large mixing bowl beat egg whites on medium to high speed till soft peaks form (tips curl). Gradually add the ½ cup sugar, *2 tablespoons* at a time, beating on medium to high speed till stiff peaks form (tips stand straight).

Fold about *1 cup* egg white mixture into pumpkin mixture. Then fold pumpkin mixture into remaining egg white mixture. Spread into the prepared pan. Bake in a 350° oven for 20 to 25 minutes or till the cake tests done. *Immediately* loosen the cake from the pan. Invert the cake onto a towel sprinkled with powdered sugar. Peel off paper. *Do not roll up cake.* Completely cool cake on the towel on a wire rack.

To assemble, cut cake vertically into three 10x5-inch pieces. Place first piece on a serving plate; spread with *half* of the Vanilla-Rum Filling. Top with second piece and remaining filling. Top with remaining piece. Frost sides and top with Whipped Cream Topping. Garnish with ground pecans. Chill at least 1 hour before serving. Makes 10 to 12 servings.

Vanilla-Rum Filling: Cook one 4-serving-size package *regular vanilla pudding mix* according to package directions, *except* reduce milk to *1⅓ cups* and add ¼ cup canned *pumpkin.* Remove from heat. Stir in 3 tablespoons *rum.* Cover surface with plastic wrap and cool. Makes 1½ cups.

Whipped Cream Topping: In a bowl beat 1 cup *whipping cream* and 2 tablespoons *brown sugar* just till stiff peaks form. Makes 2 cups.

Secrets to Successful Flourless Cakes

Cakes made with little or no flour typically are flat on top and may even have a slight depression. However, if your cake has fallen or has a sunken center, try these tips next time:

■ Bake the cake slightly longer.
■ Check your oven temperature with an oven thermometer to make sure that it's not too cool. If necessary, adjust the setting.
■ Grind the nuts in small batches (and if you are using a blender or food processor, be sure not to blend or process the nuts too much). Grinding the nuts in small batches will keep them *very fine* and *dry.* If the nuts are coarse or oily, they will make the cake fall.

Hazelnut-Chocolate Cake

A chocolate lover's delight—there's chocolate in the cake, filling, and glaze.

    2 cups hazelnuts (filberts) *or* almonds
    ¾ cup margarine *or* butter
    ⅔ cup sugar
    9 egg yolks
    5 squares (5 ounces) semisweet chocolate,
        melted and cooled
    ⅓ cup fine dry bread crumbs
    2 tablespoons milk
    9 egg whites
      Chocolate-Liqueur Filling
      Semisweet Chocolate Glaze
      Whole blanched hazelnuts (filberts)
        or almonds (optional)

Generously grease and lightly flour four 8x1½-inch round baking pans. Grind the 2 cups nuts. Set pans and nuts aside.

In a large mixing bowl beat margarine or butter with an electric mixer on medium to high speed about 30 seconds or till softened. Add sugar and beat on medium speed till fluffy. Then add egg yolks, 3 at a time, beating on medium speed till smooth. Beat in melted chocolate. Stir in the ground nuts, bread crumbs, and milk.

Thoroughly wash beaters. In a very large mixing bowl beat egg whites on medium to high speed till stiff peaks form (tips stand straight). Fold about *1 cup* of the egg whites into the chocolate mixture. Then fold chocolate mixture into remaining egg whites. Spread batter into prepared pans. Bake in a 350° oven for 18 to 20 minutes or till cakes test done. Cool cakes in pans on wire racks for 10 minutes. Remove the cakes from the pans; completely cool on wire racks.

To assemble, place first cake layer on a large serving plate. Spread *one-third* of the Chocolate-Liqueur Filling on top of the cake layer. Top with second cake layer, then spread on another third of filling. Top with third cake layer, then spread on remaining filling. Finally, top with remaining cake layer. Pour Semisweet Chocolate Glaze over cake. If desired, garnish with whole nuts. Store in refrigerator. Makes 16 servings.

Chocolate-Liqueur Filling: In a small saucepan combine 4 beaten *egg yolks* and ¼ cup *milk*. Gradually stir in 1 cup sifted *powdered sugar* and 1 tablespoon *all-purpose flour*. Cook, stirring constantly, over medium heat till mixture is very thick. Remove from heat. Stir in 2 tablespoons *crème de almond, amaretto, or cherry, almond, or hazelnut liqueur* and 1 teaspoon *vanilla*. Cover surface with waxed paper; cool.

In a medium mixing bowl beat ½ cup *margarine or butter* with electric mixer about 30 seconds or till softened. Beat in 2 squares (2 ounces) melted and cooled *semisweet chocolate*. Then gradually beat cooled egg yolk mixture into chocolate mixture. Makes 1⅔ cups.

Semisweet Chocolate Glaze: In a saucepan heat 1 square (1 ounce) *semisweet chocolate* and 1 tablespoon *margarine or butter* over low heat just till melted, stirring occasionally. Remove from heat. Stir in 1 cup sifted *powdered sugar* and 1 teaspoon *vanilla* until crumbly. Stir in 1 to 2 tablespoons *hot water* to make a glaze of pouring consistency. Quickly pour glaze over cake. Makes ¾ cup.

Chocolate Mousse Cake

*This rich cake has the texture of a firm cheesecake.
(Pictured on page 218.)*

1¾ cups hazelnuts (filberts), finely chopped
   3 tablespoons margarine *or* butter, melted
   2 8-ounce packages semisweet chocolate,
        cut up
   1 cup whipping cream
   6 eggs
   1 teaspoon vanilla
⅓ cup all-purpose flour
¼ cup sugar
½ cup whipping cream
      Whole hazelnuts (filberts)

In a bowl stir together 1¾ cup hazelnuts and margarine. Press onto bottom and 1½ inches up the sides
of an ungreased 9-inch springform pan; set aside.

In a heavy saucepan heat chocolate and 1 cup
whipping cream over low heat just till melted, stirring
constantly. Then cool to room temperature.

In a large mixing bowl beat eggs and vanilla with
an electric mixer on low speed till well combined.
Add flour and sugar. Then beat on high speed about
10 minutes or till slightly thick. Fold about *one-fourth*
of the egg mixture into chocolate mixture. Then fold
chocolate mixture into remaining egg mixture.

Spread batter into the prepared pan. Bake in a 325°
oven for 40 to 45 minutes or till slightly puffed
around the outer edge (center will be slightly soft).
Cool the cake in the pan on a wire rack for 20 minutes. Remove sides of the pan. Cool for 3 to 4 hours
more. Store, covered, in the refrigerator.

To serve, let stand at room temperature for 30 minutes. Meanwhile, in a small mixing bowl beat ½ cup
whipping cream just till stiff peaks form. Spoon cream
into a decorating bag fitted with a medium star tip
(about ¼-inch opening). Pipe cream on top of cake.
Garnish with whole hazelnuts. Serves 16 to 20.

Walnut Fudge Pudding Cake

*You can't miss with this cake that tastes like brownies
with hot fudge sauce.*

   1 cup all-purpose flour
½ cup sugar
   2 tablespoons unsweetened cocoa powder
   2 teaspoons baking powder
¼ teaspoon salt
½ cup light cream *or* milk
   2 tablespoons margarine *or* butter, melted
   1 teaspoon vanilla
   1 cup chopped walnuts
¾ cup sugar
¼ cup unsweetened cocoa powder
1½ cups *boiling* water
      Whipped cream

In a large mixing bowl stir together flour, the ½
cup sugar, the 2 tablespoons cocoa powder, baking
powder, and salt. Add cream or milk, melted margarine or butter, and vanilla. Stir just till smooth. Stir in
nuts. Spread in an ungreased 8x8x2-inch baking pan.

In a medium mixing bowl stir together the ¾ cup
sugar and the ¼ cup cocoa powder. Stir in boiling
water. Pour evenly over batter in pan. Bake in a 350°
oven about 30 minutes or till the cake tests done.
Serve warm with whipped cream. Makes 8 servings.

Rum-Date Pudding Cake

1½ cups all-purpose flour
½ cup packed brown sugar
1 teaspoon baking soda
½ teaspoon baking powder
¼ teaspoon salt
⅛ teaspoon ground nutmeg
1 8-ounce package pitted whole dates, snipped
¼ cup margarine *or* butter, cut up
1 cup *boiling* water
¼ cup dark rum
1 teaspoon vanilla
½ cup chopped walnuts
1½ cups *boiling* water
1 cup packed brown sugar
  Whipped cream *or* rum-raisin ice cream

In a large mixing bowl stir together flour, the ½ cup brown sugar, the baking soda, baking powder, salt, and nutmeg. Set flour mixture aside.

In a medium mixing bowl place dates and margarine or butter. Add the 1 cup boiling water. Stir till the margarine or butter melts. Stir in rum and vanilla. Stir the date mixture and walnuts into the flour mixture just till smooth. Spread in an ungreased 9x9x2-inch baking pan.

In a medium mixing bowl stir together the 1½ cups boiling water and the 1 cup brown sugar. Pour evenly over batter in pan. Bake in a 350° oven about 55 minutes or till done. Serve warm with whipped cream or rum-raisin ice cream. Makes 9 servings.

Lemon Pudding Cake

½ cup sugar
3 tablespoons all-purpose flour
1 teaspoon finely shredded lemon peel
¼ cup lemon juice
2 tablespoons margarine *or* butter, melted
2 slightly beaten egg yolks
1 cup milk
2 egg whites
  Whipped cream (optional)

In a large mixing bowl stir together sugar and flour. Then stir in lemon peel, lemon juice, and melted margarine or butter. Stir together egg yolks and milk; add to the flour mixture. Stir just till combined.

In a bowl beat egg whites with an electric mixer on medium to high speed till stiff peaks form (tips stand straight). Gently fold egg whites into lemon batter. Spoon into an ungreased 1-quart casserole.

Place casserole in a 13x9x2-inch baking pan; set on the oven rack. Pour *boiling or hottest tap water* into the 13x9x2 inch pan to a depth of 1 inch. Bake in a 350° oven 40 to 45 minutes or till done. Serve warm with whipped cream, if desired. Makes 4 servings.

A Pudding Cake by Any Other Name

Over the years, pudding cakes have had different names such as sponge pudding, cake-top pudding, sponge custard, and upside-down pudding. But no matter what the name, this informal dessert is basically pudding topped by a cake layer that forms during baking. They've remained popular because they're tasty and easy to make.

FROSTINGS

Swirl a coat of fluffy frosting on a great cake or cookie and it becomes a spectacular dessert.

☐ Allow about 4 hours for the cake to completely cool before frosting it. After frosting the cake, let it stand for at least 1 hour before slicing it.

☐ Using a flexible spatula, spread the frosting with light back and forth strokes. Avoid lifting up the spatula so you don't pull the crust away from the cake.

☐ If the frosting becomes too thick to spread easily, stir in a few more drops of the liquid.

☐ To frost 24 cupcakes, you'll need about 2 cups of frosting.

☐ Cutting cakes with a fluffy frosting, such as Seven-Minute Frosting, is easier if between cuts, you dip the knife in hot water, then shake it to remove excess water. Don't, however, dry the knife completely.

☐ To improvise a cake cover, turn a very large bowl upside down over the cake.

☐ Store cakes in the refrigerator if the frosting or filling contains whipped cream, cream cheese, yogurt, or eggs.

To freeze frosted creamed cakes, see the freezing information on page 180. Freezing frosted angel, sponge, and chiffon cakes is not recommended.

Choose a creamy frosting for best results. Frostings made with egg whites and boiled frostings do not freeze well. To thaw, unwrap the cake and let it stand at room temperature for several hours.

Butter Frosting

⅓ cup butter *or* margarine
4½ cups sifted powdered sugar
¼ cup milk
1½ teaspoons vanilla
Milk (optional)
Food coloring (optional)

In a large mixing bowl beat butter or margarine with an electric mixer on medium to high speed till light and fluffy. Gradually add *2 cups* of the powdered sugar, beating well on low to medium speed. Slowly beat in the ¼ cup milk and vanilla.

Gradually beat in the remaining powdered sugar. If necessary, beat in additional milk to make a frosting of spreading consistency. If desired, tint the frosting with food coloring. Frosts the sides and tops of two 8- or 9-inch cake layers or the top of one 13x9-inch cake. Makes about 2 cups.

Chocolate Butter Frosting: Prepare Butter Frosting as directed above, *except* beat ½ cup *unsweetened cocoa powder* into butter or margarine.

Mocha Butter Frosting: Prepare Butter Frosting as directed above, *except* beat ½ cup *unsweetened cocoa powder* into butter or margarine. Add 1 tablespoon instant *coffee crystals* to the ¼ cup milk. Let stand 3 minutes, then stir to dissolve.

Lemon *or* Orange Butter Frosting: Prepare Butter Frosting as directed above, *except* substitute fresh *lemon juice or orange juice* for the ¼ cup milk. Add ½ teaspoon finely shredded *lemon peel or* 1 teaspoon finely shredded *orange peel* to the juice.

Creamy Peanut-Butter Frosting: Prepare Butter Frosting as directed above, *except* substitute creamy *peanut butter* for butter or margarine.

▶ Before frosting the cake, brush off the crumbs with a pastry brush or your fingers. Then, transfer the first layer to the serving plate, placing the top side down.

▶ Place the second cake layer, top side up, on top of the frosted layer. Spread a thin coating of frosting on the sides of the cake to seal in any crumbs so they won't show in the final coating.

▶ To keep the plate clean, tuck strips of waxed paper under the edge of the cake before frosting it. Then spread about ½ cup of the frosting or a filling on top of the cake layer. Spread creamy frosting to the edge of the layer, but spread fluffy frosting only to within ¼ inch of the edge.

▶ Add a thicker coating of frosting to the sides of the cake. Then go around the cake again, swirling and building up the top edge about ¼ inch above the cake. Finally, spread the remaining frosting on top of the cake, blending the frosting at the edges.

Creamy White Frosting

It's just the right consistency for piping decorations.

> 1 cup shortening
> 1½ teaspoons vanilla
> ½ teaspoon lemon extract, orange extract, *or* almond extract
> 4½ cups sifted powdered sugar
> 3 to 4 tablespoons milk

In a large mixing bowl beat shortening, vanilla, and lemon, orange, or almond extract with an electric mixer on medium to high speed for 30 seconds.

Gradually add *2 cups* of the powdered sugar, beating well. Slowly beat in *2 tablespoons* of the milk.

Gradually beat in the remaining powdered sugar and enough of the remaining milk to make frosting of spreading consistency. Frosts the sides and tops of two 8- or 9-inch cake layers. Makes about 3 cups.

Cream Cheese Frosting

> 2 3-ounce packages cream cheese
> ½ cup margarine *or* butter, softened
> 2 teaspoons vanilla
> 4½ to 4¾ cups sifted powdered sugar

In a large mixing bowl beat cream cheese, margarine or butter, and vanilla with an electric mixer on medium to high speed till light and fluffy.

Gradually add *2 cups* of the powdered sugar, beating well. Gradually beat in enough of the remaining powdered sugar to make the frosting of spreading consistency. Store the frosted cake, covered, in the refrigerator. Frosts the sides and tops of two 8- or 9-inch cake layers. Makes about 3 cups.

Chocolate Cream Cheese Frosting: Prepare Cream Cheese Frosting as directed above, *except* beat ¼ cup *unsweetened cocoa powder* into the cream cheese mixture. Reduce powdered sugar to *4¼ to 4½ cups.*

Stabilize Whipped Cream for Frosting and Garnishing

Whipped cream makes a light, simple frosting or garnish for cakes, pies, and other desserts. Stabilizing the whipped cream with a little unflavored gelatin gives the whipped cream more body so it will hold its shape for two days and even can be piped. Here's the way to prepare it:

In a 1-cup glass measuring cup, combine 1 tablespoon *cold water* and ½ teaspoon *unflavored gelatin.* Stir well and let stand for 2 minutes. Then place the measuring cup in a pan of boiling water. Cook and stir about 1 minute or till the gelatin is *completely* dissolved.

Place 1 cup *whipping cream* and, if desired, 2 tablespoons *sugar* in a small mixing bowl. Beating the whipped cream mixture with an electric mixer on high speed, gradually drizzle the dissolved gelatin over it. Continue beating till stiff peaks form. Use the cream mixture to frost a cake or pipe it onto desserts. Store, covered, in the refrigerator for up to 48 hours. Makes about 2 cups.

Chocolate-Sour-Cream Frosting

1 6-ounce package (1 cup) semisweet chocolate pieces
¼ cup margarine *or* butter
½ cup dairy sour cream
2½ cups sifted powdered sugar

In a heavy medium saucepan heat chocolate pieces and margarine or butter over low heat just till melted, stirring occasionally. Cool about 5 minutes. Stir in sour cream.

Gradually add powdered sugar, beating till frosting is smooth and of spreading consistency. Store frosted cake, covered, in the refrigerator. Frosts the sides and tops of two 8- or 9-inch cake layers or the top of one 13x9-inch cake. Makes about 2 cups.

Chocolate Glaze

4 squares (4 ounces) semisweet chocolate, cut up
3 tablespoons margarine *or* butter
1½ cups sifted powdered sugar
3 tablespoons *hot* water

In a small heavy saucepan heat chocolate and margarine or butter over low heat just till melted, stirring occasionally. Remove from heat. Stir in powdered sugar and the 3 tablespoons hot water. If necessary, stir in additional *hot water,* 1 teaspoon at a time, till the glaze is smooth and of drizzling consistency.

Spoon Chocolate Glaze over the top of a cake, allowing the excess to drip down the sides. Glazes the tops of two 8- or 9-inch cake layers or the top of one 10-inch tube cake. Makes about 1¼ cups.

No-Cook Fudge Frosting

A snap to make.

4¾ cups sifted powdered sugar
½ cup unsweetened cocoa powder
½ cup margarine *or* butter, softened
⅓ cup *boiling* water
1 teaspoon vanilla

In a large mixing bowl combine powdered sugar, cocoa powder, margarine or butter, boiling water, and vanilla. Beat with an electric mixer on low to medium speed till combined. Then beat on medium speed for 1 minute more.

Cool for 20 to 30 minutes or till the frosting is of spreading consistency. Frosts the sides and tops of two 8- or 9-inch cake layers or the top of one 13x9-inch cake. Makes about 2 cups.

Penuche Frosting

Reminiscent of brown-sugar fudge, this frosting is great on any yellow cake.

½ cup margarine *or* butter
1 cup packed brown sugar
¼ cup milk
3½ cups sifted powdered sugar

In a heavy medium saucepan melt margarine or butter. Stir in brown sugar. Cook and stir till bubbly. Remove from the heat. Add milk. Using a wooden spoon, vigorously beat till smooth. Add powdered sugar, then beat till of spreading consistency.

Immediately spread frosting on cake. Frosts the tops of two 8- or 9-inch cake layers or the top of one 13x9-inch cake. Makes about 2 cups.

Fluffy White Frosting

1 cup sugar
⅓ cup water
¼ teaspoon cream of tartar
2 egg whites
1 teaspoon vanilla

In a small saucepan combine sugar, water, and cream of tartar. Bring mixture to boiling over medium-high heat, stirring constantly till sugar dissolves.

In a medium mixing bowl combine egg whites and vanilla. While beating the egg white mixture with an electric mixer on high speed, very slowly add the sugar mixture. Then beat about 7 minutes or till stiff peaks form (tips stand straight). Frosts the sides and tops of two 8- or 9-inch cake layers or one 10-inch tube cake. Makes about 4 cups.

▲ *The finished Fluffy White Frosting will be smooth and fluffy yet hold stiff peaks. At the stiff peak stage, the peaks will stand straight without curling over.*

Seven-Minute Frosting

Beating this frosting about 7 minutes makes it as fluffy and glossy as divinity.

1½ cups sugar
⅓ cup *cold* water
2 egg whites
¼ teaspoon cream of tartar *or* 2 teaspoons light corn syrup
1 teaspoon vanilla

In the top of a double boiler combine sugar, water, egg whites, and cream of tartar or corn syrup. Beat with an electric mixer on low speed for 30 seconds.

Place the upper pan over gently boiling water (upper pan should be near but not touching water). Cook, beating constantly with the electric mixer on high speed, about 7 minutes or till stiff peaks form (tips stand straight). Remove from heat. Add vanilla.

Beat frosting for 2 to 3 minutes more or till the frosting is of spreading consistency. Frosts the sides and tops of two 8- or 9-inch cake layers or one 10-inch tube cake. Makes about 5 cups.

Peppermint Seven-Minute Frosting: Prepare Seven-Minute Frosting as directed above, *except* substitute a few drops of *peppermint extract* for the vanilla. Frost the cake and garnish with crushed striped, round *peppermint candies*.

Petits Fours Icing

3 cups sugar
1½ cups *hot* water
¼ teaspoon cream of tartar
1 teaspoon clear vanilla flavoring *or* vanilla
　Sifted powdered sugar
　Food coloring (optional)

In a medium saucepan combine sugar, hot water, and cream of tartar. Bring the mixture to boiling over medium-high heat, stirring constantly for 5 to 9 minutes or till the sugar dissolves.

Reduce heat to medium-low. Clip a candy thermometer to the side of the saucepan. Cook till thermometer registers 226°, stirring only when necessary to prevent sticking. Remove the saucepan from the heat. Cool at room temperature, *without stirring,* to 110° (allow about 1 hour).

Add vanilla flavoring or vanilla. Stir in enough powdered sugar (about 4 cups) to make the icing of drizzling consistency. If necessary, beat the icing with a rotary beater or wire whisk to remove any lumps. If desired, stir in a few drops of food coloring. Frosts 36 to 40 petits fours. Makes about 3½ cups.

Note: If the icing becomes too thick to drizzle, beat in a few drops of *hot water.*

Frosting Petits Fours

Dainty individual cakes are beautiful for bridal showers, baby showers, luncheons, birthdays, and weddings. (Pictured on pages 178–179 and 186–187.)

To make these little treats, prepare Buttermilk White Cake as directed on page 182, *except* bake batter in a greased and floured 13x9x2-inch baking pan for 40 to 45 minutes or till a wooden toothpick inserted near the center comes out clean. *Or,* prepare Hot Milk Sponge Cake as directed on page 199, *except* bake batter in two greased and floured 8x1½-inch round baking pans about 18 minutes or till top springs back when lightly touched. Cool cake on a wire rack for 10 minutes. Remove from the pan and cool completely.

Trim the sides of the cake to make the edge smooth and straight. Cut the cake into 1½-inch squares, diamonds, or circles. Brush off crumbs. Place cake pieces on wire racks with waxed paper underneath the racks.

Insert a 2- or 3-prong long-handled fork into the side of one cake piece. Holding the cake over the saucepan of Petits Fours Icing, spoon on enough icing to cover the sides and top. Place the frosted cake piece on the wire rack, making sure the other cake pieces do not touch it. Repeat with the remaining cake pieces. Let cake pieces dry for 15 minutes.

Repeat with a second layer of icing, *except* set cake pieces *on top* of the prongs of the fork (do not spear them). If desired, repeat with a third layer of icing. If necessary, reuse the icing that has dripped onto the waxed paper, straining to remove crumbs.

Decorate the petits fours with candied violets or edible flowers (see tip, page 123), or drizzle with melted chocolate.

Powdered Sugar Icing

Flavor this easy icing with fruit juice or liqueur to match the flavor of the cake, cookies, or nut bread.

> 1 **cup sifted powdered sugar**
> ¼ **teaspoon vanilla**
> **Milk *or* orange juice**

In a small mixing bowl, combine powdered sugar and vanilla. Stir in *1 tablespoon* milk or orange juice. Stir in additional milk or orange juice, *1 teaspoon* at a time, till icing is smooth and of drizzling consistency.

Drizzle icing over cake, bread, or cookies. Let the cake stand for 2 hours before slicing. Frosts one 10-inch tube cake. Makes about ½ cup.

Chocolate Powdered Sugar Icing: Prepare Powdered Sugar Icing as directed above, *except* add 2 tablespoons *unsweetened cocoa powder* to the powdered sugar.

Liqueur Powdered Sugar Icing: Prepare Powdered Sugar Icing as directed above, *except* substitute 1 tablespoon desired *liqueur* for the first 1 tablespoon milk or orange juice.

Coconut-Pecan Frosting

A rich, crunchy topping for a chocolate or yellow cake.

> 1 **egg**
> 1 **5-ounce can (⅔ cup) evaporated milk**
> ⅔ **cup sugar**
> ¼ **cup margarine *or* butter**
> 1⅓ **cups flaked coconut**
> ½ **cup chopped pecans**

In a heavy medium saucepan slightly beat the egg with a fork. Stir in the evaporated milk and sugar. Add margarine or butter. Cook and stir over medium heat about 12 minutes or till thickened and bubbly.

Stir in coconut and pecans. Cool thoroughly. Spread on cake. Frosts tops of two 8- or 9-inch cake layers or the top of one 13x9-inch cake. Makes about 1¾ cups.

Margarine Wins The Prize

Napoléon III inspired the development of margarine by offering a prize to anyone who could produce a substitute for butter. In 1869, French chemist Hippolyte Mège-Mouriès won the prize for oleomargarine or "oil of pearls."

When oleomargarine was introduced in America, dairy farmers were upset by this new product, which hurt the sale of butter. Their protests resulted in laws and taxes on oleomargarine. Until the 1950s, it was against the law in some states to sell oleomargarine that was yellow like butter. Instead, white oleomargarine was sold with a packet of yellow coloring, which the buyer mixed with the margarine to get the traditional color.

Nutrition Analysis

Recipes	Servings	Calories	Protein (g)	Carbohydrates (g)	Total Fat (g)	Saturated Fat (g)	Cholesterol (mg)	Sodium (mg)
Almond-Raspberry Torte, 210	12	534	8	54	33	9	82	328
Angel Cake, 194	12	155	3	36	0	0	0	68
Apricot-Glazed Chocolate Nut Cake, 219	8	388	8	50	20	4	133	108
Apricot Upside-Down Cake, 180	8	292	4	17	10	2	29	197
Blueberry Sour Cream Pound Cake, 193	10	280	4	37	13	8	94	121
Boston Cream Pie, 208	8	378	7	56	15	4	111	252
Butter Frosting, 224	12	192	0	37	5	3	14	46
Buttermilk Chocolate Cake, 188	12	523	6	83	21	7	37	243
Buttermilk White Cake, 182	12	418	5	81	9	2	1	141
Cassata Rum Cake, 201	12	365	7	35	22	10	150	102
Champagne Celebration Cake, 185	24	446	4	61	22	8	17	175
Checkerboard Cake, 181	16	448	5	75	16	5	2	206
Cherry-Topped Almond Cake, 219	8	260	7	31	13	2	80	60
Chiffon Cake, 207	12	288	5	40	12	2	124	160
Chocolate Angel Cake, 194	12	160	4	37	0	0	0	68
Chocolate Butter Frosting, 224	12	201	1	39	6	4	14	47
Chocolate Chiffon Loaf with Mint Topping, 207	8	424	6	41	27	11	147	180
Chocolate Cream Cheese Frosting, 226	12	259	1	36	13	5	16	132
Chocolate Glaze, 227	12	121	0	18	6	3	0	35
Chocolate Marble Pound Cake, 193	12	348	5	45	17	10	113	181
Chocolate Mousse Cake, 222	16	380	6	24	32	13	110	62
Chocolate Powdered Sugar Icing, 230	12	35	0	9	0	0	0	1
Chocolate-Sour-Cream Frosting, 227	12	326	2	43	19	10	4	56
Coconut-Pecan Frosting, 230	12	196	3	19	13	5	10	84
Cream Cheese Frosting, 226	12	262	1	38	13	5	16	132
Creamy Peanut-Butter Frosting, 224	12	189	2	39	4	1	0	32
Creamy White Frosting, 226	12	299	0	37	17	4	0	3
Dried-Fruit Fruitcake, 192	16	228	3	25	9	2	27	104
Easy Raspberry Torte, 215	8	322	5	34	20	8	121	111
Fluffy White Frosting, 228	12	67	1	17	0	0	0	13
Fresh Pineapple Torte, 211	12	242	3	35	11	6	63	93
Greek Walnut Cake, 217	12	176	5	23	8	1	71	901
Hazelnut-Chocolate Cake, 221	16	454	7	35	33	8	174	230
Hickory Nut Cake, 189	12	557	7	74	27	7	53	282
Hot Milk Sponge Cake, 199	9	302	4	49	11	4	49	151
Jelly Roll, 202	12	139	3	28	2	1	71	45
Lady Baltimore Cake, 183	12	483	6	84	15	3	2	297

Recipes	Servings	Calories	Protein (g)	Carbohydrates (g)	Total Fat (g)	Saturated Fat (g)	Cholesterol (mg)	Sodium (mg)
Layered Cherry-Almond Chiffon Cake, 204	16	421	5	69	14	3	94	169
Lemon Butter Frosting, 224	12	191	0	38	5	3	14	44
Lemon-Iced Gingercake, 190	16	294	5	46	10	2	54	213
Lemon-Poppy Seed Pound Cake, 193	10	273	5	38	12	6	89	121
Lemon Pudding Cake, 223	4	240	6	34	10	3	112	127
Liqueur Powdered Sugar Icing, 230	12	37	0	9	0	0	0	0
Lively Lime Sponge Cake, 200	12	183	5	36	3	1	106	42
Luscious Lemon Angel Cake, 196	12	210	4	50	0	0	0	80
Meringue-Topped Torte, 216	10	353	4	38	21	8	97	225
Mocha Butter Frosting, 224	12	201	1	39	6	4	14	47
No-Cook Fudge Frosting, 227	12	230	1	41	8	2	0	91
Old-Fashioned Yellow Cake, 188	12	405	5	75	9	2	38	189
Orange Butter Frosting, 224	12	192	0	38	5	3	14	44
Orange Sponge Cake, 200	12	186	5	36	3	1	106	43
Orange Torte, 214	12	448	8	64	19	9	158	170
Pecan Angel Cake, 199	12	236	6	41	6	1	37	91
Penuche Frosting, 227	12	251	0	47	8	2	0	101
Peppermint Angel Cake, 195	12	160	3	37	0	0	0	68
Peppermint Seven-Minute Frosting, 228	12	99	1	25	0	0	0	13
Petits Fours Icing, 229	12	321	0	83	0	0	0	6
Pineapple Carrot Cake, 185	12	694	6	95	34	8	87	257
Pineapple Upside-Down Cake, 180	8	297	4	49	10	2	29	196
Pound Cake, 193	12	334	4	41	17	10	113	176
Powdered Sugar Icing, 230	12	33	0	8	0	0	0	1
Pumpkin-Cheesecake Roll, 202	10	302	5	49	10	6	110	178
Pumpkin Praline Cake, 220	10	490	8	45	32	9	167	170
Rum-Date Pudding Cake, 223	9	432	4	72	14	5	18	249
Sacher Torte, 212	12	234	3	28	14	5	71	111
Seven-Minute Frosting, 228	12	99	1	25	0	0	0	13
Sour Cream Pound Cake, 193	10	276	4	36	13	8	94	121
Strawberry Angel Cake, 198	12	347	5	46	17	10	61	86
Three-Layer Coconut and Spice Cake, 190	12	555	6	86	22	8	88	295
Triple Nut Torte, 217	12	362	8	32	25	6	127	52
Tropical Chiffon Cake, 206	12	496	6	72	21	7	132	272
Walnut Fudge Pudding Cake, 222	8	382	5	49	20	6	26	188
White Chocolate-Filled Coffee Torte, 215	10	335	5	24	24	11	134	117
Yule Log, 203	10	385	6	55	17	9	139	126

We've analyzed the nutritional content of each recipe using the first choice if ingredient substitutions are given, and using the first serving size if a serving range is given. We've omitted optional ingredients from the analysis.

Strawberry Strudel Torte
(see recipe, page 283)

Coconut Cream Pie
(see recipe, page 256)

Chocolate-Apricot Éclairs
(see recipe, page 264)

Apple Dumplings
(see recipe, page 253)

COUNTRY PIES AND PASTRIES

Take a little flour, some water, a bit of shortening, and maybe some eggs, and you can work miracles. With these simple ingredients and some special techniques, you can make an old-fashioned fruit pie, easy cream puffs, sophisticated puff pastry, or flaky strudel or phyllo.

Complete directions and how-to pictures for each type of pastry will speed you on your way to becoming a great pastry baker.

PIES AND DUMPLINGS

Any way you shape it, a plain pastry with a sweet filling makes a delicious combination. Shape pastry into a shell and it's a pie. Wrap pastry around fruit and call it a dumpling. Make the filling shallow for a tart, or layer pastry and filling and you've got a torte.

☐ Use either a lattice or a double-crust top as the recipe specifies. It does not work to substitute one for the other because some fillings require the extra venting of the lattice. Also, some fillings won't cook properly if not covered with a top crust.

☐ Make several cuts in the top of a double-crust pie before baking. This allows the steam to escape so the top crust does not get soggy on the underside. It also prevents excessive bubbling.

☐ For an attractive glazed crust, brush the top crust with milk and then sprinkle it with sugar before baking.

☐ To cover the edge of the unbaked pie with foil, tear off a 12-inch square of foil. Fold the foil in quarters and cut a quarter circle off the folded corner (about 3 inches from the tip). Unfold the piece of foil and place it on the pie, slightly molding the foil over the edge.

☐ Place a pizza pan or baking sheet under a double-crust fruit pie when you put it in the oven to catch any filling that bubbles over.

☐ To get the best flavor, and so the slices won't fall apart when serving, let a pie cool for 3 to 4 hours before you cut and serve it.

Pastry for Single-Crust Pie

1¼ cups all-purpose flour
⅓ cup shortening *or* lard
3 to 4 tablespoons *cold* water

In a medium mixing bowl stir together flour and ¼ teaspoon *salt*. Using a pastry blender, cut in shortening or lard till pieces are the size of small peas. Sprinkle *1 tablespoon* of the water over part of mixture, then gently toss with a fork. Push moistened dough to side of the bowl. Repeat, using 1 tablespoon of water at a time, till all is moistened. Form dough into a ball.

On a lightly floured surface, use your hands to slightly flatten dough. Roll dough from center to edges, forming a 12-inch circle. Wrap pastry around the rolling pin. Unroll onto a 9-inch pie plate. Ease pastry into pie plate, being careful not to stretch it.

Trim pastry to ½ inch beyond edge of plate. Fold under extra pastry. Crimp edge (see pages 250–251). *Do not prick pastry.* Bake as directed in recipes.

Baked Pastry Shell: Prepare Pastry for Single-Crust Pie as above, *except* prick bottom and sides of pastry generously with the tines of a fork. Prick pastry where bottom and sides meet all around the pie shell. Bake in a 450° oven for 10 to 12 minutes or till golden. Cool on a wire rack.

Whole Wheat Pastry: Prepare Pastry for Single-Crust Pie as above, *except* substitute ½ cup *whole wheat flour* for ½ cup of all-purpose flour.

Cinnamon Pastry: Prepare Pastry for Single-Crust Pie as directed above, *except* stir 1 teaspoon ground *cinnamon* into the flour mixture.

Pecan Pastry: Prepare Pastry for Single-Crust Pie as directed above, *except* stir ¼ cup finely chopped *pecans* into the flour mixture.

Pastry for Double-Crust Pie

2 cups all-purpose flour
⅔ cup shortening *or* lard
6 to 7 tablespoons *cold* water

In a large bowl stir together flour and ½ teaspoon *salt.* Using a pastry blender, cut in shortening or lard till pieces are the size of small peas. Sprinkle *1 tablespoon* of the water over part of mixture, then gently toss with a fork. Push to side of the bowl. Repeat, using 1 tablespoon of water at a time, till all is moistened. Divide dough in half. Form *each* half into a ball.

On a lightly floured surface, use your hands to slightly flatten *one* ball of dough. Roll dough from center to edges, forming a 12-inch circle. Wrap the pastry around the rolling pin. Unroll onto a 9-inch pie plate. Ease pastry into the pie plate, being careful not to stretch it.

For top crust, repeat rolling remaining dough. Cut slits in crust. Transfer filling to pastry-lined pie plate; trim bottom pastry even with rim of plate. Place top crust on filling. Trim top crust ½ inch beyond edge of plate. Fold top crust under bottom pastry. Seal; crimp edge (see page 251). Bake as directed in recipes.

Pastry for Lattice-Top Pie: Prepare Pastry for Double-Crust Pie as above, *except* after rolling top crust, cut into ½-inch-wide strips. Transfer desired filling to pastry-lined pie plate. Trim bottom pastry to ½ inch beyond edge of plate. Weave strips on top of filling to make a lattice. Press ends of strips into rim of bottom crust. Fold bottom pastry over strips; seal and crimp edge (see page 251). Bake as directed in recipes.

Whole Wheat Pastry for Double-Crust Pie: Prepare Pastry for Double-Crust Pie as directed above, *except* substitute ¾ cup *whole wheat flour* for ¾ cup of the all-purpose flour.

Old-Fashioned Raisin Pie

Tangy lemon and orange accent the sweet raisin filling.

⅔ cup packed brown sugar
2 tablespoons cornstarch
2 cups raisins
1 teaspoon finely shredded orange peel
½ cup orange juice
2 tablespoons lemon juice
½ cup chopped walnuts
1 recipe Pastry for Double-Crust Pie (at left)

In a heavy medium saucepan stir together sugar and cornstarch. Stir in raisins, orange peel, orange juice, lemon juice, and 1⅓ cups *cold water.* Cook and stir over medium heat till thickened and bubbly. Remove from heat. Stir in nuts. Set mixture aside.

Prepare and roll out Pastry for Double-Crust Pie as directed. Line a 9-inch pie plate with *half* of the pastry. Transfer raisin mixture to the pastry-lined pie plate. Trim pastry to edge of pie plate. Cut slits in top crust. Place top crust on filling. Seal and crimp edge.

To prevent overbrowning, cover the edge of the pie with foil. Bake in a 375° oven for 25 minutes. Remove foil. Bake for 20 to 25 minutes more or till top is golden. Cool on a wire rack. Makes 8 servings.

▶ *Use a pastry blender to cut the shortening or lard into the flour mixture until the pieces are about the size of small peas, as shown. If you do not have a pastry blender, try using two knives in a crisscross motion to cut in shortening.*

Apple Pie

For a new twist on an old favorite, add raisins to the filling. (Pictured on the cover.)

  6 **cups thinly sliced, peeled, cooking apples**
       (about 2¼ pounds)
  1 **tablespoon lemon juice (optional)**
  ¾ **cup sugar**
  2 **tablespoons all-purpose flour**
  ½ **teaspoon ground cinnamon**
  ⅛ **teaspoon ground nutmeg**
  ½ **cup raisins (optional)**
  1 **recipe Pastry for Double-Crust Pie**
       (see page 235)

If the apples lack tartness, sprinkle with lemon juice. In a large mixing bowl stir together the ¾ cup sugar, flour, cinnamon, and nutmeg. Add apple slices and, if desired, raisins. Toss till apples and raisins are coated. Set apple mixture aside.

Prepare and roll out Pastry for Double-Crust Pie as directed. Line a 9-inch pie plate with *half* of the pastry. Transfer apple mixture to the pastry-lined pie plate. Trim pastry to the edge of the pie plate. Cut slits in the top crust. Place the top crust on the filling. Seal and crimp the edge.

To prevent overbrowning, cover the edge of the pie with foil. Bake in a 375° oven for 25 minutes. Remove foil. Bake for 20 to 25 minutes more or till the top is golden. Cool on a wire rack. Makes 8 servings.

Crumb-Topped Apple Pie

  6 **cups thinly sliced, peeled, cooking apples**
  1 **tablespoon lemon juice (optional)**
  ½ **to ⅔ cup sugar**
  2 **tablespoons all-purpose flour**
  ½ **teaspoon ground cinnamon**
  1 **recipe Pastry for Single-Crust Pie**
       (see page 234)
     Crumb Topping

If the apples lack tartness, sprinkle with lemon juice. In a large bowl stir together sugar, flour, and cinnamon. Add apples, then toss till coated. Set apple mixture aside. Prepare and roll out pastry as directed. Line a 9-inch pie plate with pastry. Trim and crimp the edge of the pastry. Transfer apple mixture to pie plate. Sprinkle topping over pie. To prevent overbrowning, cover edge of pie with foil. Bake in a 375° oven 25 minutes. Remove foil. Bake 20 to 25 minutes more or till top is golden. Cool on wire rack. Serves 8.

Crumb Topping: In a medium mixing bowl stir together ½ cup *all-purpose flour*, ½ cup *sugar*, ½ teaspoon ground *cinnamon*, and ¼ teaspoon ground *nutmeg*. Cut in ¼ cup *margarine or butter* till crumbly. Makes about 1¼ cups.

All-American Pie

Which pie is the number-one American favorite? You guessed it—apple pie. Apple pies date back to fourteenth-century England when apple filling was substituted in traditional meat pies. The Pilgrims brought apples to America and served apple pie for breakfast. In colonial America, apple pie was served with, not after, the main course at lunch or dinner.

Upside-Down Apple Pie

Flip the pie upside down and you've got a crunchy, brown-sugar-topped pie.

½ **cup chopped walnuts**
½ **cup packed brown sugar**
¼ **cup margarine *or* butter, melted**
½ **to ¾ cup sugar**
1 **tablespoon all-purpose flour**
½ **teaspoon ground cinnamon**
⅛ **teaspoon ground allspice**
6 **cups thinly sliced, peeled, cooking apples**
   (about 2¼ pounds)
1 **recipe Pastry for Double-Crust Pie**
   (see page 235)

In a 9-inch pie plate stir together walnuts, brown sugar, and melted margarine or butter. Spread walnut mixture evenly over bottom of the pie plate. Set pie plate aside.

In a large mixing bowl stir together sugar, flour, cinnamon, and allspice. Add apples, then gently toss till coated. Set apple mixture aside.

Prepare and roll out Pastry for Double-Crust Pie as directed. Ease *half* of the pastry into the prepared pie plate over the walnut mixture, being careful not to stretch the pastry.

Transfer apple mixture to the pastry-lined pie plate. Trim the bottom pastry to the edge of pie plate. *Do not cut slits* in top crust. Place top crust on filling. Seal and crimp edge.

To prevent overbrowning, cover edge of pie with foil. Bake in a 375° oven for 25 minutes. Remove foil. Bake for 20 to 25 minutes more or till top is golden. *Immediately* place a serving plate upside down on top of the pie plate, then turn the pie plate and serving plate over together. Remove the pie plate. Cool pie for at least 45 minutes. Serve warm. Serves 8.

Secrets to Successful Pastries

Tender, flaky pastries are a perfect partner to any pie filling. If your pastry has one of the following problems, look below for a solution.

If your pastry is crumbly and hard to roll:
■ Add more water, *1 teaspoon* at a time.
■ Toss the flour mixture and water together a little more or *just till evenly moistened.*

If your pastry is tough:
■ Use a pastry blender to cut in the shortening or lard till well mixed and all of the mixture resembles small peas.
■ Use less water to moisten the flour mixture.
■ Toss the flour mixture and water together only till all of the flour mixture is moistened.
■ Use less flour when rolling out the pastry.

If your crust shrinks excessively:
■ Roll the pastry to an even thickness.
■ Mix in water only till evenly moistened.
■ Don't stretch pastry when transferring it.

If the bottom crust is soggy:
■ Use a dull metal or glass pie plate, not a shiny metal pan.
■ Patch any cracks in the pastry with a scrap of the pastry before adding the filling.
■ Be sure the oven temperature is accurate. If the temperature is too low, the bottom crust will not bake properly.

If a single-crust pastry blisters excessively:
■ Lightly press pastry into pan so that there are no air pockets under crust.
■ Prick the pastry more with the fork.

Choose-a-Berry Pie

¾ **to 1 cup sugar**
¼ **cup all-purpose flour**
½ **teaspoon finely shredded lemon peel**
4 **cups fresh *or* frozen unsweetened**
   blackberries, blueberries, *or* gooseberries*
1 **recipe Pastry for Double-Crust Pie**
   (see page 235)

In a large mixing bowl stir together sugar, flour, and lemon peel. Add fresh or frozen berries, then gently toss till berries are coated. If using frozen berries, let them stand for 15 to 30 minutes or till berries are *partially* thawed but still icy.

Prepare and roll out Pastry for Double-Crust Pie as directed. Line a 9-inch pie plate with *half* of the pastry. Stir berry mixture, then transfer berry mixture to the pastry-lined pie plate. Trim the bottom pastry to the edge of the pie plate. Cut slits in the top crust. Place top crust on filling. Seal and crimp the edge. To prevent overbrowning, cover the edge of the pie with foil. Bake in a 375° oven for 25 minutes for fresh berries (50 minutes for frozen berries). Remove foil. Bake for 20 to 25 minutes more for fresh berries (20 to 30 minutes for frozen berries) or till top is golden. Cool pie on a wire rack. Makes 8 servings.

*If using gooseberries, use the *1 cup* sugar.

Tri-Berry Pie

1 **cup fresh *or* frozen unsweetened whole**
   strawberries
½ **to ¾ cup sugar**
3 **tablespoons cornstarch**
2 **cups fresh *or* frozen red raspberries**
1½ **cups fresh *or* frozen blueberries**
1 **recipe Pastry for Lattice-Top Pie**
   (see page 235)

Partially thaw strawberries, if frozen. *Do not drain.* Cut strawberries in half. In a large mixing bowl stir together sugar and cornstarch. Add strawberries and their juice, fresh or frozen raspberries, and fresh or frozen blueberries. Then gently toss till berries are coated. If using frozen fruit, let it stand for 15 to 30 minutes or till fruit is *partially* thawed but still icy.

Prepare and roll out Pastry for Lattice-Top Pie as directed. Line a 9-inch pie plate with *half* of the pastry. Stir berry mixture; transfer mixture to the pastry-lined pie plate. Trim the pastry to ½ inch beyond the edge of the plate. Top with lattice crust. Seal and crimp the edge. To prevent overbrowning, cover the edge of the pie with foil. Bake in a 375° oven for 25 minutes for fresh fruit (50 minutes for frozen fruit). Remove foil. Bake for 20 to 25 minutes more for fresh fruit (20 to 30 minutes for frozen fruit) or till the top is golden. Cool on a wire rack. Makes 8 servings.

Freezing Pastry for Pies

Get a step ahead on your next pie by making some extra pastry to freeze. Roll the pastry into rounds and stack them with two sheets of waxed paper between layers. *Or,* fit the pastry into pie plates or tart pans. Place the pastry into freezer bags, then seal, label, and freeze. Plan to use the frozen pastry within 6 to 8 weeks.

To use the frozen pastry, thaw the flat rounds, covered, at room temperature while making the filling. Frozen pastry shells may be baked without thawing. When using frozen pastry shells, you may need to add an extra 5 to 10 minutes to the baking time.

Tri-Berry Pie

Raspberry Pie

This pie is simple to make and simply delicious to eat.

½ to ¾ cup sugar
3 tablespoons all-purpose flour
5 cups fresh *or* frozen red raspberries
1 recipe Pastry for Double-Crust Pie
   (see page 235)

In a bowl combine sugar and flour. Add fresh or frozen raspberries. Gently toss till berries are coated. If using frozen raspberries, let stand for 15 to 30 minutes or till berries are *partially* thawed but still icy.

Prepare and roll out the pastry as directed. Line a 9-inch pie plate with *half* of the pastry. Stir berry mixture, then transfer mixture to the pastry-lined pie plate. Trim pastry to edge of pie plate. Cut slits in top crust. Place top crust on filling. Seal and crimp edge. To prevent overbrowning, cover edge of pie with foil. Bake in a 375° oven 25 minutes for fresh berries (50 minutes for frozen). Remove foil. Bake 20 to 25 minutes more for fresh berries (20 to 30 minutes for frozen) or till top is golden. Cool on a rack. Serves 8.

Choosing Pie Plates

For pies that are evenly browned underneath as well as on top, select standard glass or *dull* metal pie plates. Use shiny metal pie pans for crumb-crust pies. Pastry crust may turn out soggy if baked in a shiny pan.

Ceramic or pottery pie plates may not be a standard size. (A standard-size plate holds about 3¾ cups liquid.) Therefore, you may need to adjust the amount of filling and the baking time.

Disposable foil pie pans usually are smaller than a standard pie plate. A foil *deep-dish* pie pan will be closer to the standard size.

Strawberry-Rhubarb Pie

3 cups fresh *or* frozen unsweetened whole
   strawberries
1¼ cups sugar
3 tablespoons quick-cooking tapioca
2 cups fresh *or* frozen unsweetened sliced
   rhubarb
½ teaspoon finely shredded lemon peel
1 teaspoon lemon juice
1 recipe Pastry for Double-Crust Pie
   (see page 235)

Partially thaw strawberries, if frozen. *Do not drain.* Slice strawberries. In a large mixing bowl stir together the 1¼ cups sugar and the tapioca. Add the strawberries and their juice, fresh or frozen rhubarb, lemon peel, and lemon juice, then gently toss till fruit is coated. Let fruit mixture stand about 15 minutes (about 60 minutes for frozen fruit) or till syrup forms, stirring mixture occasionally.

Prepare and roll out Pastry for Double-Crust Pie as directed. Line a 9-inch pie plate with *half* of the pastry. Stir fruit mixture, then transfer fruit mixture to the pastry-lined pie plate. Trim the bottom pastry to the edge of pie plate. Cut slits in the top crust. Place top crust on filling. Seal and crimp edge of pastry.

To prevent overbrowning, cover the edge of the pie with foil. Bake in a 375° oven for 25 minutes for fresh fruit (50 minutes for frozen fruit). Remove foil. Bake for 20 to 25 minutes more for fresh fruit (20 to 30 minutes for frozen fruit) or till the top is golden. Cool on a wire rack. Makes 8 servings.

Rhubarb Pie

1 cup sugar
¼ cup all-purpose flour
4 cups fresh *or* frozen unsweetened sliced
    rhubarb
1 recipe Pastry for Double-Crust Pie
    (see page 235)

In a bowl stir together sugar and flour. Add fresh or frozen rhubarb, then gently toss till rhubarb is coated. If using fresh rhubarb, let mixture stand for 15 minutes. If using frozen rhubarb, let stand for 15 to 30 minutes or till *partially* thawed but still icy.

Prepare and roll out Pastry for Double-Crust Pie as directed. Line a 9-inch pie plate with *half* of the pastry. Stir rhubarb mixture, then transfer to pastry-lined pie plate. Trim pastry to edge of pie plate. Cut slits in top crust; place crust on filling. Seal and crimp edge.

To prevent overbrowning, cover edge of pie with foil. Bake in a 375° oven 25 minutes for fresh rhubarb (50 minutes for frozen). Remove foil. Bake 20 to 25 minutes more for fresh rhubarb (20 to 30 minutes for frozen) or till top is golden. Cool on a rack. Serves 8.

Cranberry Lore

At the first Thanksgiving feast, the Indians are believed to have brought gifts of cranberries as a symbol of peace. The Pilgrims named them "crane berries" because the cranberry blossoms looked like the heads of cranes.

Wild cranberries became very popular with the colonists. To control the picking of cranberries, some settlements passed laws imposing a penalty for picking more than a quart before September 20.

Gingerberry Lattice Pie

Cranberries spiced with ginger make a terrific holiday pie. (Pictured on the cover.)

1 15¼-ounce can crushed pineapple
    (juice pack)
3 cups cranberries
1⅓ cups sugar
¼ cup cornstarch
1 to 2 tablespoons finely chopped crystallized
    ginger *or* ½ teaspoon ground ginger
1 recipe Pastry for Lattice-Top Pie
    (see page 235)
    Orange Cream

Drain pineapple, reserving juice. Add water to the pineapple juice to make *1 cup*. In a medium saucepan combine cranberries and pineapple juice mixture. Bring to boiling. Reduce heat and simmer, uncovered, about 5 minutes or till cranberries pop. In a small bowl stir together sugar and cornstarch. Add sugar mixture to cranberries. Cook and stir till bubbly. Remove from heat. Stir in pineapple and ginger.

Prepare and roll out Pastry for Lattice-Top Pie as directed. Line a 9-inch pie plate with *half* of the pastry. Transfer cranberry mixture to the pastry-lined pie plate. Trim bottom pastry to ½ inch beyond edge of pie plate. Top with lattice crust. Seal and crimp edge.

To prevent overbrowning, cover edge of pie with foil. Bake in a 375° oven for 25 minutes. Remove foil. Bake for 20 to 25 minutes more or till golden. Cool on a wire rack. Serve with Orange Cream. Serves 8.

Orange Cream: In a medium mixing bowl beat 1 cup *whipping cream* and 2 tablespoons *sugar* till soft peaks form. Fold in 1 teaspoon finely shredded *orange peel*. Serve immediately with pie. Makes 2 cups.

Cranberry-Cherry Pie

Celebrate the holidays—Valentine's Day or the Fourth of July—with this festive red pie.

  2 **16-ounce cans pitted tart red cherries (water pack)**
  1 **cup cranberries**
1½ **cups sugar**
  ¼ **cup cornstarch**
  ¼ **teaspoon ground nutmeg**
      Dash ground cloves
  1 **recipe Pastry for Double-Crust Pie (see page 235)**

Drain cherries, reserving ⅓ *cup* liquid. In a medium saucepan combine the reserved cherry liquid and cranberries. Bring mixture to boiling. Reduce heat and simmer, uncovered, about 3 minutes or till the cranberries pop.

In a small mixing bowl stir together ¾ *cup* of the sugar, the cornstarch, nutmeg, and cloves. Add sugar mixture to hot cranberries. Cook and stir constantly till mixture is thickened and bubbly. Remove from heat. Stir in remaining ¾ cup sugar and cherries.

Prepare and roll out Pastry for Double-Crust Pie as directed. Line a 9-inch pie plate with *half* of the pastry. Transfer cranberry-cherry mixture to the pastry-lined pie plate. Trim the bottom pastry to the edge of the pie plate. Cut slits in the top crust. Place the top crust on the filling. Seal and crimp the edge.

To prevent overbrowning, cover the edge of the pie with foil. Bake in a 375° oven for 25 minutes. Remove foil. Bake for 20 to 25 minutes more or till top is golden. Cool on a wire rack. Makes 8 servings.

Cherry Lattice Pie

  2 **16-ounce cans pitted tart red cherries (water pack)**
  1 **cup sugar**
  ¼ **cup cornstarch**
  1 **tablespoon margarine *or* butter**
  3 **or 4 drops almond extract**
10 **drops red food coloring (optional)**
  1 **recipe Pastry for Lattice-Top Pie (see page 235)**

Drain cherries, reserving *1 cup* liquid. In a large saucepan combine ¾ *cup* of the sugar and the cornstarch. Stir in the reserved cherry liquid. Cook and stir over medium heat till thickened and bubbly. Cook and stir for 2 minutes more. Remove from heat. Stir in the remaining sugar, margarine or butter, and almond extract. Stir in cherries and, if desired, food coloring. Cool the mixture slightly.

Prepare and roll out Pastry for Lattice-Top Pie as directed. Line a 9-inch pie plate with *half* of the pastry. Transfer cherry mixture to the pastry-lined pie plate. Trim pastry to ½ inch beyond the edge of the pie plate. Top with lattice crust. Seal and crimp the edge.

To prevent overbrowning, cover the edge of the pie with foil. Bake in a 375° oven for 25 minutes. Remove foil. Bake for 25 to 30 minutes more or till top is golden. Cool on a wire rack. Makes 8 servings.

Cherry Pie

Choose a traditional cherry pie or a fancy one that has a touch of cherry brandy.

1¼ to 1½ cups sugar
2 tablespoons quick-cooking tapioca
5 cups fresh *or* frozen unsweetened pitted tart red cherries
¼ teaspoon almond extract
1 recipe Pastry for Double-Crust Pie (see page 235)

In a large mixing bowl stir together the sugar and quick-cooking tapioca. Add fresh or frozen cherries and almond extract, then gently toss till cherries are coated. Let the mixture stand about 15 minutes for fresh cherries (about 60 minutes for frozen cherries) or till syrup forms, stirring occasionally.

Prepare and roll out Pastry for Double-Crust Pie as directed. Line a 9-inch pie plate with *half* of the pastry. Stir cherry mixture, then transfer cherry mixture to the pastry-lined pie plate. Trim the bottom pastry to edge of pie plate. Cut slits in the top crust. Place top crust on filling. Seal and crimp edge of pastry.

To prevent overbrowning, cover edge of pie with foil. Bake in a 375° oven for 25 minutes for fresh cherries (50 minutes for frozen cherries). Remove foil. Bake for 25 to 35 minutes more for fresh cherries (20 to 30 minutes for frozen cherries) or till top is golden. Cool pie on a wire rack. Makes 8 servings.

Cherry-Brandy Pie: Prepare Cherry Pie as directed above, *except* omit almond extract. Stir 1 teaspoon finely shredded *lemon peel* and 2 tablespoons *cherry brandy* into the cherry mixture. Continue as directed above. Completely cool the pie before serving.

Pear-Date Pie

¾ cup pitted whole dates, snipped
¾ cup unsweetened pineapple *or* orange juice
1 tablespoon cornstarch
⅛ teaspoon ground ginger
⅛ teaspoon ground nutmeg
½ cup rolled oats
½ cup packed brown sugar
¼ cup all-purpose flour
¼ cup margarine *or* butter
1 recipe plain Pastry *or* Whole Wheat Pastry for a Single-Crust Pie (see page 234)
6 cups sliced, peeled pears (6 *or* 7 medium pears)
2 tablespoons all-purpose flour

In a small saucepan stir together dates, pineapple or orange juice, cornstarch, ginger, and nutmeg. Cook and stir till thickened and bubbly. Cool slightly.

For topping, in a medium mixing bowl stir together rolled oats, brown sugar, and the ¼ cup flour. Using a pastry blender, cut in margarine or butter till mixture resembles coarse crumbs. Set topping aside.

Prepare and roll out Pastry for Single-Crust Pie as directed. Line a 9-inch pie plate with the pastry. Trim and crimp the edge of the pastry. Spread the date mixture over bottom of the pastry shell.

In a medium mixing bowl toss pears with the 2 tablespoons flour. Arrange pears on top of date mixture. Sprinkle the topping mixture on top of the pears.

To prevent overbrowning, cover the edge of the pie with foil. Bake in a 375° oven for 25 minutes. Remove foil. Bake for 20 to 25 minutes more or till pears are tender. Cool on a wire rack. Serves 8.

Mince-Peach Pie

Mince-Pear Pie

Convenience products aren't new to the kitchen. Canned mincemeat has been saving cooks time since the 1870s.

- 1 **27- *or* 28-ounce jar (2⅔ cups) mincemeat**
- 2 **cups sliced, peeled pears**
- 3 **tablespoons orange juice**
- 1 **recipe Pastry for Double-Crust Pie (see page 235)**
  Vanilla ice cream (optional)

In a large mixing bowl stir together mincemeat, sliced pears, and orange juice. Set mixture aside.

Prepare and roll out Pastry for Double-Crust Pie as directed. Line a 9-inch pie plate with *half* of the pastry. Transfer pear mixture to the pastry-lined pie plate. Trim pastry to the edge of the pie plate. Cut slits in the top crust (if desired, use a miniature cookie cutter). Place top crust on filling. Seal and crimp edge.

To prevent overbrowning, cover the edge of the pie with foil. Bake in a 375° oven for 25 minutes. Remove foil. Bake for 20 to 25 minutes more or till the top is golden. Cool on a wire rack. If desired, serve warm with vanilla ice cream. Makes 8 servings.

Mince-Peach Pie: Prepare Mince-Pear Pie as directed above, *except* substitute one 29-ounce can *peach slices,* drained and cut up, for the sliced pears. Omit the orange juice.

Mince-Orange Pie: Prepare Mince-Pear Pie as directed above, *except* substitute 3 *oranges,* peeled, sectioned, and halved, for the pears.

Mince-Apple Pie: Prepare Mince-Pear Pie as directed above, *except* substitute 3 cups thinly sliced, peeled cooking *apples* (about 1 pound) for the sliced pears. Stir ¼ cup packed *brown sugar* into the mincemeat mixture.

Fig-Nut Tarts

- ½ **cup margarine *or* butter, melted**
- 1 **3-ounce package cream cheese, softened**
- 1 **cup all-purpose flour**
- ½ **cup packed brown sugar**
- 4 **teaspoons cornstarch**
- 1½ **cups dried golden figs, stems removed and finely chopped**
- ½ **teaspoon finely shredded orange peel**
- 1 **cup orange juice**
- ⅓ **cup chopped walnuts *or* pecans**

For pastry, in a medium bowl stir together melted margarine or butter and cream cheese. Stir in flour. Press dough into 16 ungreased 3-inch round sandbakkelse molds or 2½-inch muffin pans, pressing an even layer onto the bottom and up the sides of each mold (for muffin pans, press dough halfway up the sides).

In a small saucepan stir together brown sugar and cornstarch. Stir in figs, orange peel, and orange juice. Cook and stir over medium heat till thickened and bubbly. Remove from heat, then stir in nuts.

Spoon fig mixture into pastry-lined molds. Bake in a 350° oven for 20 to 30 minutes or till the crust is golden. Cool tarts in molds on a wire rack. Then remove the tarts from the molds. Makes 16 servings.

Christmas Pie

Mincemeat pie has been a traditional Christmas pie since the thirteenth century. These early pies were baked in a rectangular crust that symbolized the manger. The spices were symbolic of the wise men's gifts. For good luck, it was a custom to eat a mincemeat pie each day for the 12 days between Christmas and the Twelfth Night.

Peach Pie

½ to ¾ **cup sugar**
3 **tablespoons all-purpose flour**
½ **teaspoon ground cinnamon**
  Dash ground nutmeg
6 **cups thinly sliced, peeled peaches** *or* **frozen
    unsweetened peach slices**
1 **recipe plain Pastry for Double-Crust Pie** *or*
    **Whole Wheat Pastry for Double-Crust Pie
    (see page 235)**
1 **teaspoon sugar**
  Dash ground cinnamon
  Milk

In a large mixing bowl stir together the ½ to ¾ cup sugar, the flour, the ½ teaspoon cinnamon, and nutmeg. Add fresh or frozen peaches. Gently toss till the peaches are coated. If using frozen peaches, let stand for 15 to 30 minutes or till the peaches are *partially* thawed but still icy.

Prepare and roll out plain Pastry or Whole Wheat Pastry for Double-Crust Pie as directed. Line a 9-inch pie plate with *half* of the pastry. Stir peach mixture, then transfer to the pastry-lined pie plate. Trim the bottom pastry to the edge of the pie plate.

Cut slits in the top crust. Place top crust on filling. Seal and crimp edge. In a small bowl stir together 1 teaspoon sugar and dash cinnamon. Brush top crust with milk and sprinkle with sugar-cinnamon mixture.

To prevent overbrowning, cover edge of pie with foil. Bake in a 375° oven for 25 minutes for fresh peaches (50 minutes for frozen peaches). Remove foil. Bake for 20 to 25 minutes more for fresh peaches (20 to 30 minutes for frozen peaches) or till top is golden. Cool pie on a wire rack. Makes 8 servings.

Country-Style Peach Tart

For a folksy look, this pie is baked on a pizza pan with the edge of the pastry folded over the filling instead of crimped.

½ **cup sugar**
1 **tablespoon all-purpose flour**
½ **teaspoon ground cinnamon**
¼ **teaspoon ground nutmeg**
4 **cups thinly sliced, peeled peaches** *or* **frozen
    unsweetened peach slices**
1 **teaspoon lemon juice**
1 **recipe Pastry for Single-Crust Pie
    (see page 234)**
⅓ **cup finely crushed vanilla wafers**
2 **tablespoons chopped almonds**
1 **tablespoon margarine** *or* **butter, melted**

In a large mixing bowl stir together the sugar, flour, cinnamon, and nutmeg. Add peaches and lemon juice, then gently toss till peaches are coated. If using frozen peaches, let stand for 15 to 30 minutes or till the peaches are *partially* thawed but still icy.

Prepare Pastry for Single-Crust Pie as directed, *except* roll dough into a *13-inch* circle. Transfer dough to an ungreased 12-inch pizza pan or a 15x10x1-inch baking pan. Stir peach mixture, then mound it in the center of pastry, leaving about a 3-inch border. Fold the border up over the peach mixture.

In a small mixing bowl stir together crushed vanilla wafers, chopped almonds, and margarine or butter. Sprinkle crumb mixture on the peaches.

To prevent overbrowning, cover the edge of the tart with foil. Bake in a 375° oven for 20 minutes for fresh peaches (40 minutes for frozen peaches). Remove foil. Bake for 20 to 25 minutes more or till the crust is golden. Cool the tart in the pan on a wire rack. Serve warm or cool. Makes 8 servings.

Sour Cream Peach Pie

2 slightly beaten eggs
1 8-ounce container dairy sour cream
1 cup sugar
3 tablespoons all-purpose flour
½ teaspoon ground cinnamon
⅛ teaspoon ground nutmeg
3 cups thinly sliced, peeled peaches *or* frozen
    unsweetened peach slices
1 recipe Pastry for Single-Crust Pie
    (see page 234)
⅓ cup all-purpose flour
⅓ cup packed brown sugar
2 tablespoons margarine *or* butter

In a large mixing bowl stir together eggs and sour cream. Stir in sugar, the 3 tablespoons flour, cinnamon, nutmeg, and ¼ teaspoon *salt*. Add fresh or frozen peaches, then gently toss till peaches are coated. If using frozen peaches, let stand about 45 minutes or till peaches are *partially* thawed but still icy.

Prepare and roll out Pastry for Single-Crust Pie as directed. Line a 9-inch pie plate with pastry. Trim and crimp edge of pastry. Transfer peach mixture to pastry-lined pie plate. To prevent overbrowning, cover edge of pie with foil. Bake in a 375° oven 15 minutes.

Meanwhile, in a small mixing bowl stir together the ⅓ cup flour and brown sugar. Cut in the margarine or butter till crumbly. Remove foil from pie. Sprinkle brown sugar mixture on top of pie. Bake for 25 to 30 minutes more for fresh peaches (about 40 minutes more for frozen) or till pie appears *nearly* set in the center when gently shaken. Cool the pie on a wire rack. Store in the refrigerator. Makes 8 servings.

Sour Cream Apple Pie: Prepare Sour Cream Peach Pie as directed above, *except* substitute 3 cups thinly sliced, peeled, cooking *apples* (about 1 pound) for the peaches.

Storing Pies and Dumplings

Whether you're storing a few leftover pieces or making pies ahead, proper storage is important to preserve the fresh flavor and texture of pies and dumplings.

Fruit pies and dumplings may stand at room temperature for up to 24 hours, but cover and refrigerate them for longer storage. Custard and cream pies should be served as soon as they are cool. Leftovers should be covered and refrigerated. (To cover a meringue-topped pie, place toothpicks halfway between the center and the edge of the pie to hold the wrap away from the meringue.) Plan to use the pies within 1 or 2 days.

To freeze unbaked fruit pies, treat any light-colored fruit with an ascorbic-acid color keeper. Assemble the pie as directed in a metal or freezer-to-oven pie plate. Place it in a freezer bag, then seal, label, and freeze. Frozen pies should be used within 2 to 4 months.

To bake a frozen pie, unwrap it and cover it with foil. Bake in a 450° oven for 15 minutes. Reduce oven temperature to 375° and bake for 15 minutes. Uncover and continue baking about 30 minutes more or till golden.

To freeze baked fruit pies, bake and cool the pie. Place it in a freezer bag, then seal, label, and freeze. Use frozen baked pies within 6 to 8 months. To use the pie, thaw it, covered, at room temperature. If desired, reheat it.

Do not freeze cream, custard, or pecan pies.

SPECIAL PIE-TOP IDEAS

I t can be simple to turn out a picture-perfect pie. Even if you're all thumbs, you'll find it easy to make creative pie tops using these ideas.

HERRINGBONE LATTICE TOP: Prepare a lattice-top pie according to the recipe, using a fluted pastry wheel to cut the ½-inch-wide strips, if desired. For this lattice top, begin by weaving four strips of pastry on top of the filling to form a small square in the center of the pie. Working toward the edge of the pie, continue weaving strips parallel to the first four strips, forming progressively larger squares. Trim and crimp the edge.

DOTTED PASTRY TOP: Prepare a double-crust pie according to the recipe, *except* do not cut slits in the top crust. Instead, use a wooden skewer or toothpick to prick a design in the pastry, enlarging each hole so the steam can escape. Press the edge with the tines of a fork to seal.

QUICK LATTICE TOP: Prepare a lattice-top pie according to the recipe, *except do not* cut the top crust into strips. For this top, use a miniature cookie or canapé cutter to make a cut-out in the center of the pastry. Repeat the cutouts in a *regular* pattern, an equal distance apart, working from the center to the edge of the pastry. Be careful not to make the cutouts too close together or the pastry may rip when transferred to the pie. (A rolling pin makes it easy to transfer the cutout pastry.) Trim and crimp the edge.

APPLIQUÉ PASTRY TOP: Prepare a double-crust pie according to the recipe, *except* do not cut slits in the top crust. Place the top crust on the filling. Trim and crimp edge. Use a cookie cutter to cut shapes from dough scraps. Brush the back sides of the shapes with water, and arrange on the top crust. Cut slits in the top crust as part of the design, or cut along the edge of the shapes.

SPECIAL PIE-EDGE IDEAS

The edge of the pastry sets off the pie like a picture frame sets off a painting. Try a few of these quick crimping tricks and your pie will be unforgettable.

CUTOUT EDGE: Line the pie plate with pastry and trim pastry to the edge of the pie plate. Roll out pastry scraps very thin. Use a knife or canapé cutter to cut the pastry into desired shapes. Brush the edge of the pastry shell with water. Arrange the cutouts on the edge of the pastry shell and lightly press to secure. Pour the filling into the pastry shell.

Bake as directed in the recipe. If desired, after removing the pie from the oven, arrange semisweet chocolate pieces around the cutouts on the edge of the hot pastry.

TWISTED EDGE: Line the pie plate with pastry and trim pastry to edge of the pie plate. Brush the edge of the pastry shell with water. Loosely twist two ½-inch-wide strips of pastry dough around the edge of the pastry shell. As a strip runs out, seal another strip to it by pressing the ends together. Secure the twist by lightly pressing the bottom strip against the edge of the pastry shell.

ROPE-SHAPED EDGE: Trim and fold under the edge of the pastry for a single-crust, double-crust, or lattice-top pie. Then crimp around the edge of the pie by pinching it. When pinching, push forward on a slant with a bent finger and pull back with the thumb.

FLOWER-PETAL EDGE: Trim and turn under the edge of the pastry for a single- or double-crust pie. Make a large scallop by placing the thumb flat against the inside pastry edge and pressing the dough around the thumb with the thumb and index finger of the other hand (as shown in insert). Then lightly press the tines of a fork in the center of each scallop.

Nectarine Dumplings

1 recipe Pastry for Single-Crust Pie
  (see page 234)
4 medium nectarines *or* peaches, peeled,
  halved, and pitted
3 tablespoons finely chopped pecans
3 tablespoons brown sugar
1 egg white
  Sugar
  Light cream

Lightly grease a 13x9x2-inch baking dish. Set the baking dish aside. Prepare Pastry for Single-Crust Pie as directed, *except* roll the pastry into a 14-inch square. Cut the pastry into four 7-inch squares.

Place *one* nectarine or peach half, cut side up, on the center of *each* pastry square. Combine pecans and brown sugar, then spoon mixture into centers of fruit. Place remaining fruit halves on top of filled fruit.

Moisten edges of pastry with *water.* Fold corners to the center on top of the fruit, pinching edges together to seal. Place in the prepared baking dish. In a small bowl beat together egg white and 1 tablespoon *water.* Brush dumplings with egg white mixture. Sprinkle with sugar. Bake in a 400° oven about 35 minutes or till golden. Serve warm with light cream. Serves 4.

Fruit Dumplings

The Shakers, members of a religious sect, were noted for their simple style. They also were among the cooks who are thought to have influenced American cuisine. Shakers were well known for their fruit dumplings. To make these dumplings, they chose a rich pastry to complement the fresh fruit, and then they topped the dumplings with maple syrup.

Plum Dumplings

Elegant dumplings feature plums stuffed with a cream cheese filling.

¼ cup sugar
¼ teaspoon ground nutmeg
½ of a 3-ounce package cream cheese, softened
1½ cups all-purpose flour
¼ teaspoon salt
½ cup margarine *or* butter
4 to 5 tablespoons *cold* water
6 plums, halved and pitted
  Light cream *or* milk

Lightly grease a 13x9x2-inch baking dish. Set baking dish aside. In a small mixing bowl stir together sugar and nutmeg. In another small mixing bowl stir together *3 tablespoons* of the sugar mixture and the cream cheese. Set cream cheese mixture aside.

For pastry, in a medium bowl stir together flour and salt. Using a pastry blender, cut in margarine or butter till pieces are the size of small peas. Sprinkle *1 tablespoon* of the water over part of the mixture; gently toss with a fork. Push to the side of the bowl. Repeat till all is moistened. Form dough into a ball.

On a lightly floured surface, flatten dough with your hands. Roll dough from center to edges, forming an 18x12-inch rectangle. Cut into six 6-inch squares.

Spread about *2 teaspoons* of the cream cheese mixture over the cut sides of *six* plum halves. Place remaining plum halves on top of the the filled plums. Place *one* stuffed plum in the center of *each* pastry square. Moisten edges of pastry with *water.* Fold corners of the pastry square to the center on top of the plum, pinching the edges together to seal.

Place plum dumplings in the prepared baking dish. Brush dumplings with light cream or milk, then sprinkle with the remaining sugar mixture. Bake in a 375° oven about 40 minutes or till pastry is golden. Serve warm with light cream or milk. Makes 6 servings.

Apple Dumplings

Maple syrup in both the dumpling and the whipped cream topping complements the fresh apple flavor. (Pictured on pages 232–233.)

⅓ **cup snipped dried figs *or* pitted whole dates**
2 **tablespoons chopped walnuts**
2 **tablespoons maple *or* maple-flavored syrup**
1 **tablespoon margarine *or* butter, melted**
2 **cups all-purpose flour**
½ **teaspoon salt**
⅓ **cup margarine *or* butter**
⅓ **cup shortening**
6 **to 7 tablespoons cold water**
4 **medium cooking apples**
　　(about 6 ounces each)
2 **tablespoons maple *or* maple-flavored syrup**
½ **cup whipping cream**
3 **tablespoons maple *or* maple-flavored syrup**

Lightly grease a 15x10x1-inch baking pan. Set pan aside. In a small mixing bowl stir together figs or dates, walnuts, the 2 tablespoons maple syrup, and 1 tablespoon melted margarine or butter. Set aside.

For pastry, in a medium mixing bowl stir together the flour and salt. Using a pastry blender, cut in the ⅓ cup margarine or butter and shortening till pieces are the size of small peas. Sprinkle *1 tablespoon* of the water over part of the flour mixture, then gently toss with a fork. Push moistened dough to the side of the bowl. Repeat till all is moistened. Divide into 4 equal portions. Form each into a ball. Cover; set aside.

Core and peel apples. Press *one-fourth* of the fig or date mixture into the core of *each* apple. Set aside.

On a lightly floured surface, roll *each* portion of dough into a circle about ⅛ inch thick. Trim each portion to an 8-inch circle. Place an apple in the center of each circle. Moisten the edge of the pastry with *water*. Bring dough up around apple to resemble a bundle, pressing the edges together at the top to seal.

Using a knife or small cookie cutter, cut leaf shapes from pastry scraps. Moisten bottom sides of pastry leaves with *water* and place leaves on top of the wrapped apples, gently pressing to seal. If desired, cut small circles and place them on the tops of the apples.

Place wrapped apples in the prepared baking pan. Bake in a 375° oven for 35 minutes, then brush with the 2 tablespoons of the maple syrup. Bake for 5 to 10 minutes more or till pastry is golden. Transfer dumplings to dessert dishes. In a small mixing bowl beat whipping cream and the 3 tablespoons maple syrup till soft peaks form. Serve dumplings warm with the maple whipped cream. Makes 4 servings.

▶ *Place a filled apple in the center of a pastry circle. Bring the pastry up around the apple, making small tucks. Press the pastry together at the top of the apple to seal the tucks.*

▶ *Cut small leaf shapes from the pastry scraps. Then use a knife to mark them with a leaf vein pattern. Moisten the back side of each leaf with water and place it on the top of the apple. Press gently to attach the leaf. Repeat, overlapping the leaves slightly.*

Custard Pie

1 recipe Pastry for Single-Crust Pie
   (see page 234)
4 eggs
½ cup sugar
1 teaspoon vanilla
⅛ teaspoon salt
2½ cups milk
   Ground nutmeg

Prepare and roll out Pastry for Single-Crust Pie as directed. Line a 9-inch pie plate with pastry. Trim and crimp edge of pastry. Line the bottom of pastry shell with a double thickness of foil. Bake in a 450° oven for 5 minutes. Remove foil. Bake for 5 minutes more.

Meanwhile, for filling, in a large mixing bowl use a rotary beater or wire whisk to lightly beat eggs *just till mixed.* Stir in sugar, vanilla, and salt. Gradually stir in milk. Mix well.

With the partially baked pastry shell on the oven rack, pour the filling into the pastry shell. Sprinkle with nutmeg.

To prevent overbrowning, cover the edge of the pie with foil. Reduce oven temperature to 350° and bake for 25 minutes. Remove foil. Bake for 15 to 20 minutes more or till a knife inserted near the center comes out clean. Completely cool on a wire rack. Store, covered, in the refrigerator. Makes 8 servings.

Coconut Custard Pie: Prepare Custard Pie as directed above, *except* stir in ½ cup toasted *coconut* with the milk. Mix well.

Chocolate-Pecan Pie

It's as rich as a candy bar.

3 eggs
1 cup light corn syrup
½ cup sugar
⅓ cup margarine *or* butter, melted
1 cup pecan halves
1 recipe Pastry for Single-Crust Pie
   (see page 234)
½ cup semisweet chocolate pieces
2 tablespoons semisweet chocolate pieces
   (optional)

For filling, in a large bowl use a rotary beater or wire whisk to lightly beat eggs *just till mixed.* Stir in corn syrup, sugar, and melted margarine or butter. Mix well. Stir in pecans. Set filling aside.

Prepare and roll out Pastry for Single-Crust Pie as directed. Line a 9-inch pie plate with pastry. Trim the pastry to the edge of the pie plate.

Roll out the pastry scraps very thin. Use a knife or a very small cookie or canapé cutter to cut shapes from pastry. Brush the edge of the shell with water. Arrange the cutouts on the edge of the shell and lightly press to secure (see page 250). Sprinkle the ½ cup chocolate pieces over the bottom of the pastry shell.

With the pastry shell on the oven rack, pour the filling into the pastry shell.

To prevent overbrowning, cover the edge of pie with foil. Bake in a 350° oven for 25 minutes. Remove foil. Bake for 20 to 25 minutes more or till a knife inserted near the center of the pie comes out clean. If desired, arrange the 2 tablespoons chocolate pieces around the cutouts on the edge of pastry (see page 250). Completely cool on a wire rack. Store, covered, in the refrigerator. Makes 8 servings.

Pecan Pie

A fantastic blend of sweet filling and crunchy nuts.

    3 eggs
    1 cup corn syrup
    ⅔ cup sugar
    ⅓ cup margarine *or* butter, melted
    1 teaspoon vanilla
    1¼ cups pecan halves
    1 recipe Pastry for Single-Crust Pie
        (see page 234)

For filling, in a large bowl use a rotary beater or wire whisk to lightly beat eggs *just till mixed.* Stir in corn syrup, sugar, margarine or butter, and vanilla. Mix well. Stir in pecan halves. Set filling aside.

Prepare and roll out Pastry for Single-Crust Pie as directed. Line a 9-inch pie plate with the pastry. Trim and crimp the edge of the pastry.

With the pastry shell on the oven rack, pour the filling into the pastry shell.

To prevent overbrowning, cover the edge of the pie with foil. Bake in a 350° oven for 25 minutes. Remove foil. Bake for 20 to 25 minutes more or till a knife inserted near the center comes out clean. Completely cool the pie on a wire rack. Store, covered, in the refrigerator. Makes 8 servings.

Maple Pecan Pie: Prepare Pecan Pie as directed above, *except* substitute *maple syrup or maple-flavored syrup* for the corn syrup.

Coconut-Oatmeal Pie: Prepare Pecan Pie as above, *except* substitute ¾ cup *coconut* and ½ cup *quick-cooking rolled oats* for pecans.

Peanut Pie: Prepare Pecan Pie as directed above, *except* substitute coarsely chopped *peanuts, macadamia nuts, or cashews* for the pecans.

Pumpkin Pie

    1 16-ounce can (1¾ cups) pumpkin*
    ⅔ cup sugar
    1 teaspoon ground cinnamon
    ½ teaspoon ground ginger
    ½ teaspoon ground nutmeg
    3 eggs
    1 5-ounce can (⅔ cup) evaporated milk
    ½ cup milk
        Pastry for Single-Crust Pie
          (see page 234)
        Whipped cream (optional)

For filling, in a large mixing bowl stir together pumpkin, sugar, cinnamon, ginger, and nutmeg. Add eggs. Use a rotary beater or wire whisk to lightly beat till combined. Gradually stir in evaporated milk and milk. Mix well. Set pumpkin mixture aside.

Prepare and roll out Pastry for Single-Crust Pie as directed. Line a 9-inch pie plate with pastry. Trim and crimp the edge of the pastry. With the pastry shell on the oven rack, pour the pumpkin filling into the pastry shell.

To prevent overbrowning, cover the edge of the pie with foil. Bake in a 375° oven for 25 minutes. Remove foil. Bake about 25 minutes more or till a knife inserted near the center comes out clean. Completely cool the pie on a wire rack. If desired, serve with whipped cream. Store, covered, in the refrigerator. Makes 8 servings.

*To substitute fresh pumpkin for canned pumpkin, cut a medium pumpkin into 5-inch-square pieces. Remove seeds and fibrous strings. Arrange pieces in a single layer, skin side up, in a large shallow baking pan. Cover with foil. Bake in a 375° oven for 1 to 1½ hours or till tender. Scoop pulp from rind. Place part of the pulp at a time in a blender container or food processor bowl. Cover; blend or process till smooth. Place pumpkin in a cheese-cloth-lined strainer and press out excess liquid. Makes 1¾ cups.

Vanilla Cream Pie

It's equally good with whipped cream for the topping or with the traditional meringue. (Coconut Cream Pie with whipped cream is pictured on pages 232–233.)

    1 **recipe Baked Pastry Shell (see page 234)**
    ¾ **cup sugar**
    ¼ **cup cornstarch** *or* **½ cup all-purpose flour**
    3 **cups milk**
    4 **beaten egg yolks**
    1 **tablespoon margarine** *or* **butter**
 1½ **teaspoons vanilla**
    1 **recipe Four-Egg-White Meringue**
       (see page 257)

Prepare and bake pastry shell as directed; set aside. For filling, in a heavy medium saucepan stir together sugar and cornstarch or flour. Gradually stir in milk. Cook and stir over medium heat till the mixture is thickened and bubbly. Reduce heat. Cook and stir for 2 minutes more. Remove from heat.

Gradually stir about *1 cup* of the hot filling into the beaten egg yolks. Return filling and egg yolk mixture to the saucepan. Bring to a gentle boil. Cook and stir for 2 minutes more. Remove from heat. Stir in margarine or butter and vanilla. Set filling aside.

Prepare Four-Egg-White Meringue as directed. Pour *hot* filling into pastry shell. Evenly spread meringue over *hot* filling, sealing to the edge. Bake in a 350° oven for 15 minutes. Completely cool pie on a wire rack. Store in the refrigerator. Makes 8 servings.

Coconut Cream Pie: Prepare Vanilla Cream Pie as directed at left, *except* stir in 1 cup flaked *coconut* with margarine or butter and vanilla. Sprinkle another ⅓ cup flaked *coconut* over meringue before baking.

Banana Cream Pie: Prepare Vanilla Cream Pie as directed at left, *except* before adding filling, arrange 3 medium *bananas,* sliced (about 2¼ cups), over the bottom of the Baked Pastry Shell.

Dark-Chocolate Cream Pie: Prepare Vanilla Cream Pie as directed at left, *except* increase the sugar to *1 cup*. Stir in 3 squares (3 ounces) chopped *unsweetened chocolate* with the milk.

Milk-Chocolate Cream Pie: Prepare Vanilla Cream Pie as at left, *except* stir in 3 squares (3 ounces) chopped *semisweet chocolate* with milk.

Secrets to Successful Meringue for Pies

A golden, tender meringue can be the crowning glory of a cream pie. If your meringue has one of the following problems, here's the solution.

If your meringue is low in volume:
■ Start adding the sugar to the egg whites as soon as soft peaks form (tips bend over slightly).
■ After adding the sugar, beat till stiff peaks form and the sugar is *completely* dissolved (see photos, pages 195 and 95).

If your meringue shrinks:
■ Beat meringue till stiff peaks form and sugar is *completely* dissolved (see photos, pages 195; 95).

If your meringue beads or weeps:
■ Be sure the oven temperature is not too low.

If your meringue leaks:
■ Spread the meringue on the filling while filling is still *hot,* sealing it well to edges of the pastry.

Lemon Meringue Pie

A refreshing ending to any meal.

  1 **recipe Baked Pastry Shell (see page 234)**
1½ **cups sugar**
  3 **tablespoons all-purpose flour**
  3 **tablespoons cornstarch**
  3 **beaten egg yolks**
  2 **tablespoons margarine *or* butter**
  1 **to 2 teaspoons finely shredded lemon peel**
 ⅓ **cup lemon juice**
  1 **recipe Meringue for Pie (at right)**

Prepare and bake pastry shell as directed; set aside. For filling, in a heavy medium saucepan stir together sugar, flour, cornstarch, and dash *salt*. Gradually stir in 1½ cups *water*. Cook and stir over medium heat till thickened and bubbly. Reduce heat. Cook and stir for 2 minutes more. Remove from heat.

Gradually stir about *1 cup* of the hot filling into the beaten egg yolks. Return filling and egg yolk mixture to the saucepan. Bring to a gentle boil. Cook and stir 2 minutes more. Remove from heat. Stir in margarine or butter and lemon peel. Gradually stir in lemon juice till well combined. Set filling aside.

Prepare Meringue for Pie as directed. Pour *hot* filling into baked pastry shell. Spread meringue over hot filling, sealing to edge. Bake in a 350° oven for 15 minutes or till meringue is golden. Completely cool on a rack. Store, covered, in refrigerator. Serves 8.

Cutting Cream Pies

Cutting a pie with a meringue can be difficult when the meringue sticks to the knife. There is an easy way to prevent that problem. Dip the knife in water (don't dry it off) before cutting each slice.

Meringue for Pie

  3 **egg whites**
 ½ **teaspoon vanilla**
 ¼ **teaspoon cream of tartar**
  6 **tablespoons sugar**

In a large mixing bowl bring egg whites to room temperature. Add vanilla and cream of tartar. Beat with an electric mixer on medium to high speed about 1 minute or till soft peaks form (tips curl).

Gradually add sugar, *1 tablespoon* at a time, beating on high speed about 4 minutes more or till stiff, glossy peaks form (tips stand straight) and sugar is *completely* dissolved. Immediately spread meringue over *hot* pie filling, carefully sealing to edge of pastry shell to prevent shrinkage. Bake as directed in recipes.

Four-Egg-White Meringue: Prepare Meringue for Pie as directed above, *except* use *four* egg whites, *1 teaspoon* vanilla, *½ teaspoon* cream of tartar, and *½ cup sugar.* Increase beating time while adding sugar to about 5 minutes.

▶ *Use a spatula to spread the meringue over the hot pie filling. Push the meringue into the tips of the fluted pastry edge so that the pie is completely sealed. Then make swirls and peaks in the meringue for an attractive top.*

Strawberries 'n' Cream Tart

Feature this cool combination of vanilla pudding and fresh berries at a dessert party.

½ **cup sugar**
2 **tablespoons cornstarch**
1¾ **cups milk**
2 **beaten egg yolks**
½ **teaspoon vanilla**
1 **cup all-purpose flour**
2 **tablespoons sugar**
⅓ **cup margarine *or* butter**
1 **beaten egg yolk**
2 **tablespoons *ice* water**
2 **cups strawberries, sliced, *or* raspberries**
⅓ **cup currant jelly**
  Mint sprigs (optional)

For filling, in a heavy medium saucepan stir together the ½ cup sugar and the cornstarch. Gradually stir in milk. Cook and stir over medium heat till thickened and bubbly, then cook for 2 minutes more. Remove from heat. Stir about *1 cup* of the hot mixture into the 2 beaten egg yolks. Return hot mixture and egg yolk mixture to the saucepan. Bring to a gentle boil. Cook and stir for 2 minutes more. Remove from heat. Add vanilla. Cover surface with plastic wrap. Cool to room temperature without stirring. Chill the filling about 4 hours or till cold.

Meanwhile, for pastry, in a medium mixing bowl stir together flour and the 2 tablespoons sugar. Using a pastry blender, cut in margarine or butter till pieces are the size of small peas. Combine the one beaten egg yolk and ice water. Gradually stir egg yolk mixture into flour mixture. Using your fingers, gently knead just till ball forms. Cover and chill for 30 to 60 minutes or till dough is easy to handle.

On a lightly floured surface, roll pastry dough from center to edge, forming a 12-inch circle. Ease pastry into an ungreased 10-inch tart pan with a removable bottom. Press pastry into fluted sides of tart pan and trim edges. Prick pastry. Line pastry shell in tart pan with foil. Bake in a 375° oven for 10 minutes. Remove foil and bake 5 to 10 minutes more or till pastry is lightly browned. Completely cool pastry shell in pan on a wire rack.

Spread the chilled filling in the cooled pastry shell. Arrange sliced strawberries or raspberries on top of the filling.

In a small saucepan heat and stir currant jelly over medium heat till jelly is melted and bubbly. Brush melted jelly over berry-covered tart. Chill for 1 hour or till jelly is set. To serve, remove sides of the tart pan. If desired, garnish with mint sprigs. Serves 8.

Make Mine Vanilla

Do you love vanilla pudding, vanilla cream pie, vanilla everything? That marvelous vanilla flavor hasn't always been so available. Cooks used to cut up vanilla beans, tie the pieces in a sack, and immerse the sack in the food for several hours to get a vanilla flavor.

In 1847, Joseph Burnett, a specialist in household remedies, developed vanilla extract. Vanilla quickly became a basic ingredient to accentuate the sweet flavor of desserts.

If you would like to try the authentic flavor of vanilla beans, here's a simplified method. Purchase a vanilla bean in the spice section of the supermarket. Place the pod in a 1-quart jar of sugar. Let the sugar stand about 2 weeks or until it picks up the vanilla flavor. Use this vanilla-flavored sugar in your next dessert recipe, omitting the vanilla extract. To make another batch, just split the vanilla bean pod and refill the jar with more sugar.

Strawberries 'n' Cream Tart

Sweet Cherry-Nut Tart

- 1 slightly beaten egg yolk
- ¼ cup dairy sour cream
- 2 tablespoons sugar
- ¾ teaspoon vanilla
- 1¼ cups all-purpose flour
- ⅓ cup margarine *or* butter
- 1 cup chopped pecans
- ½ cup sugar
- 1 tablespoon milk
- 1½ pounds dark sweet cherries (about 5 cups) *or* 1½ pounds frozen, unsweetened, pitted, dark sweet cherries (about 6 cups)
- 4 teaspoons cornstarch
  Powdered sugar

For pastry, in a small bowl stir together egg yolk, sour cream, the 2 tablespoons sugar, and ¼ *teaspoon* of the vanilla. In a medium mixing bowl combine flour and ¼ teaspoon *salt*. Using a pastry blender, cut in margarine or butter till pieces are the size of small peas. Make a well in the center of the mixture. Add sour cream mixture. Using a fork, stir till all is moistened. Press dough evenly onto the bottom and 1½ inches up the sides of an ungreased 9-inch springform pan. Bake in a 350° oven for 15 minutes.

Meanwhile, in a small bowl stir together pecans, ¼ *cup* sugar, milk, and the remaining vanilla. Spoon pecan mixture evenly over the partially baked crust. Bake in the 350° oven for 10 to 15 minutes more or till crust is golden. Cool in pan on a wire rack.

Stem and pit fresh cherries. In a large saucepan stir together fresh or frozen cherries, the remaining ¼ cup sugar, and 2 tablespoons *water*. Cook over medium-high heat for 5 to 10 minutes or till heated through, stirring often. In a small bowl stir together cornstarch and 2 tablespoons *water*. Stir into cherry mixture. Cook and stir till thickened and bubbly. Cook and stir 2 minutes more. Spoon cherry mixture into pastry shell. Cool completely. Loosen crust from sides of pan. Remove sides. Sift powdered sugar over tart. Serves 8.

Linzer Torte

A classic Austrian dessert featuring a raspberry filling.

- ⅔ cup margarine *or* butter
- ⅔ cup sugar
- 1 egg
- 2 hard-cooked egg yolks, sieved
- 1 tablespoon kirsch *or* water
- 1 teaspoon finely shredded lemon peel
- ¼ teaspoon ground cinnamon
- ¼ teaspoon ground cloves
- 1½ cups all-purpose flour
- 1¼ cups finely ground hazelnuts (filberts) *or* almonds
- 1 10-ounce jar seedless red raspberry preserves
- ⅓ cup sifted powdered sugar
- 1 teaspoon kirsch (optional)
- 2 to 3 teaspoons milk

In a medium bowl beat margarine or butter with an electric mixer about 30 seconds or till softened. Add sugar, whole egg, hard-cooked egg yolks, 1 tablespoon kirsch or water, lemon peel, cinnamon, and cloves. Beat till well combined. Stir in flour and nuts. Wrap dough in plastic wrap and chill for 1 hour.

On a floured surface, use your hands to slightly flatten *two-thirds* of the dough. (Refrigerate remaining dough till ready to use.) Roll dough into an 11-inch circle. Ease pastry into an ungreased 10-inch springform pan, pressing dough about 1 inch up the sides. Spread preserves over bottom of dough in pan.

Roll the remaining dough into a 10x6-inch rectangle. Cut six 1-inch-wide strips. Carefully weave strips on top of preserves to make a lattice. Press ends of strips into rim of crust. Trim ends of the strips to make an even edge around the pastry shell.

Bake in a 325° oven 35 to 40 minutes or till crust is golden. Cool on a rack. Remove sides of pan. In a bowl, stir together powdered sugar, the 1 teaspoon kirsch (if desired), and enough milk to make a glaze of drizzling consistency. Drizzle on torte. Serves 8.

Sweetheart Torte

Swirls of chocolate add the finishing touch to this handsome heart-shaped torte.

1 recipe Pastry for Double-Crust Pie
    (see page 235) *or* two 9-inch folded
    refrigerated unbaked pie crusts
1 cup whipping cream
¼ cup sifted powdered sugar
1 8-ounce carton strawberry *or* raspberry
    yogurt
1 drop red food coloring (optional)
2 tablespoons semisweet chocolate pieces
1 teaspoon shortening
1 cup sliced strawberries

Prepare and roll out Pastry for Double-Crust Pie as directed. *Or,* unfold refrigerated unbaked pie crusts. Using a 10-inch heart-shaped pattern and a fluted pastry wheel, cut *each* pastry portion into a heart shape.

Wrap *one* heart-shaped pastry piece around the rolling pin, then unroll it onto an ungreased baking sheet. Prick generously with the tines of a fork. Repeat with the remaining pastry. Bake in a 450° oven for 7 to 8 minutes or till golden. Remove the pastries from the baking sheet and cool on a wire rack.

For filling, in a small mixing bowl beat whipping cream and powdered sugar till stiff peaks form. Fold in yogurt and, if desired, red food coloring. Let stand for 5 to 10 minutes or till slightly thickened.

To assemble, place *one* cooled pastry heart on a flat serving plate. Spread *half* of the filling on top of the pastry to within ½ inch of the edge. Top with the second pastry, then spread with remaining filling. Chill the torte for 1 to 2 hours before serving.

To serve, in a small heavy saucepan heat chocolate pieces and shortening over low heat just till melted, stirring occasionally. Arrange strawberries around the edge of the torte. Using a spoon, drizzle or swirl the chocolate mixture over the top of the torte. Serves 8.

Mexican Appetizer Torte

1½ cups all-purpose flour
1½ cups Masa Harina tortilla flour
⅛ teaspoon ground red pepper
¾ cup margarine *or* butter
1 beaten egg
1 8¼-ounce can refried beans
⅓ cup taco sauce
1 large avocado, halved, seeded, and peeled
1 tablespoon lemon juice
⅛ teaspoon garlic powder
1 4-ounce can diced green chili peppers
1 8-ounce container dairy sour cream
½ cup shredded cheddar cheese (2 ounces)
    Taco sauce

For pastry, in a large mixing bowl stir together flour, Masa Harina flour, and red pepper. Using a pastry blender, cut in margarine or butter till pieces are the size of small peas. Combine egg and ⅓ cup *water,* then add to flour mixture. Using a fork, lightly stir till all is moistened. Divide dough into 3 equal portions.

Between 2 pieces of waxed paper, flatten *one* portion of dough; roll into a 10½-inch circle. Remove top sheet of paper. Using a fluted pastry wheel, trim edge, making a 10-inch circle. Invert dough onto an ungreased baking sheet. Remove paper. Generously prick with a fork. Repeat with remaining dough portions. Bake in a 450° oven 9 to 11 minutes or till golden, reversing sheets on oven racks after 5 minutes. Remove pastries from sheets. Cool on wire racks.

In a small bowl stir together refried beans and the ⅓ cup taco sauce. Cut up avocado. In another small bowl mash avocado with lemon juice and garlic powder. Drain chilies and stir them into avocado mixture.

To serve, place *one* cooled pastry on a serving plate. Spread with bean mixture. Top with another pastry, then spread with avocado mixture. Top with the remaining pastry, then spread with sour cream. Sprinkle with cheese. Pass additional taco sauce. Serves 16.

CREAM PUFFS

Almost like magic, little dabs of dough inflate into crisp, airy, hollow puffs. And it takes no special technique to perform this magic— steam in the batter does it for you. Once you've tried making cream puffs, you'll want to have them on hand for everything from appetizers to desserts.

□ The recipes in this book were tested using large eggs. To assure the right balance of ingredients, use large eggs, also. Be sure to add the eggs *one at a time* to the dough for easier stirring and so the cream puffs will fully puff during baking.

□ For evenly shaped puffs, drop the dough into mounds onto the baking sheet and avoid going back to add more dough to the mounds.

□ For éclairs, if you don't have a decorating bag, use two spoons to drop and shape the dough.

□ Use a fork to remove any soft dough inside the cream puff or éclair shells before filling them.

□ Vary the filling and topping for cream puffs to suit the occasion. Prepare the Cream Puff Pastry (see recipe at right) and bake according to the Cream Puffs recipe (see page 263). Then use the cream puff shells as containers for a main-dish salad, ice cream, whipped cream, or pudding. If desired, drizzle the tops of the dessert puffs with ice cream topping or chocolate glaze, or sprinkle them with powdered sugar.

□ To keep the bottoms of cream puffs and éclairs from getting soggy, fill the shells just before serving or fill and chill for up to 2 hours.

Cream Puff Pastry

The French named this pastry "chou" or cabbage because they thought the rough top resembled that garden plant.

> ½ **cup margarine *or* butter**
> 1 **cup all-purpose flour**
> 4 **eggs**

In a medium saucepan combine margarine or butter, 1 cup *water,* and ¼ teaspoon *salt.* Bring mixture to boiling, stirring till margarine or butter melts. Then add flour all at once, stirring vigorously. Cook and stir till the mixture forms a ball that doesn't separate. Remove from heat and cool for 10 minutes.

Add eggs, one at a time, to the margarine mixture, beating with a wooden spoon after each addition about 1 minute or till smooth. Use the pastry dough as directed in the recipes.

Chocolate Cream Puff Pastry: Prepare Cream Puff Pastry as above, *except* in a small bowl stir together the flour, 3 tablespoons *unsweetened cocoa powder,* and 2 tablespoons *sugar.* Add the flour mixture all at once to the boiling mixture, stirring vigorously. Continue as directed above.

◄ *Add the eggs to the dough one at a time. As you begin stirring an egg into the batter, the batter will appear moist and will separate into clumps, as shown. After a minute or two of stirring, the batter will become thick, smooth, and slightly sticky. Now it's time to add another egg.*

Pastry Cream

½ cup sugar
⅓ cup all-purpose flour
¼ teaspoon salt
2 cups light cream
4 slightly beaten egg yolks
1½ teaspoons vanilla

In a heavy medium saucepan stir together sugar, flour, and salt. Slowly stir in light cream. Cook and stir over medium heat till mixture is thickened and bubbly. Cook and stir for 1 minute more.

Gradually stir about *1 cup* of the hot mixture into beaten egg yolks. Return it all to the saucepan. Cook and stir for 2 minutes more. Remove from heat. Stir in vanilla. Cover surface with plastic wrap or waxed paper. Cool. *Do not stir* during cooling. Store, covered, in the refrigerator. Makes about 2½ cups.

Chocolate Pastry Cream: Prepare Pastry Cream as directed above, *except* reduce flour to *¼ cup* and add 2 squares (2 ounces) *semisweet chocolate,* chopped, with the light cream.

Storing Cream Puffs

After cream puff and éclair shells have cooled, place them in a plastic bag so they won't dry out. Then store them in the refrigerator for up to 24 hours.
To freeze, place the unfilled shells in an airtight container, then seal, label, and freeze. Use them within 1 to 2 months. To thaw the shells, let them stand at room temperature for 5 to 10 minutes.

Cream Puffs

1 recipe Pastry Cream *or* Chocolate Pastry
    Cream (at left)
½ cup whipping cream
1 recipe Cream Puff Pastry (see page 262)
    Powdered sugar

Prepare Pastry Cream or Chocolate Pastry Cream as directed. Let it cool. In a small mixing bowl beat whipping cream till soft peaks form. Fold whipped cream into cooled pastry cream, then chill well.

Grease a baking sheet. Set baking sheet aside. Prepare Cream Puff Pastry as directed. Drop dough by heaping tablespoons into 10 mounds, 3 inches apart, on prepared baking sheet. *Or,* spoon dough into a decorating bag fitted with a large star tip (about ⅝-inch opening). Pipe 10 fleurettes or rosettes, 3 inches apart, on the prepared baking sheet.

Bake in a 400° oven about 30 minutes or till golden brown and puffy. Remove puffs from the baking sheet and cool on a wire rack.

To assemble, cut off the top fourth of *each* cream puff. Remove any soft dough from inside.

Spoon about *¼ cup* of the chilled pastry cream mixture into *each* cream puff. *Or,* spoon pastry cream into a decorating bag fitted with a large plain-round tip (about ⅝-inch opening), then pipe the pastry cream into the cream puffs. Replace the tops. If desired, chill them for up to 2 hours. Before serving, lightly sift powdered sugar over the tops of the cream puffs. Makes 10 servings.

Strawberry 'n' Chocolate Cream Puffs

1   **recipe Chocolate Cream Puff Pastry**
    (see page 262)
3   **cups strawberries, sliced, *or* red raspberries**
1½ **cups whipping cream**
2   **tablespoons sugar**
2   **to 3 tablespoons white creme de cacao**
½   **teaspoon vanilla**
    Powdered sugar

Grease a baking sheet. Set baking sheet aside. Prepare Chocolate Cream Puff Pastry as directed. Drop dough by heaping tablespoons into 12 mounds, 3 inches apart, on the prepared baking sheet. Bake in a 400° oven for 25 to 30 minutes or till puffed. Remove puffs from the baking sheet and cool on a wire rack.

To assemble, cut off the top fourth of *each* puff. Remove any soft dough from inside. Arrange *half* of the berries inside the puffs. In a medium mixing bowl combine whipping cream, sugar, crème de cacao, and vanilla. Beat just till stiff peaks form. Spoon about ¼ *cup* of the whipped cream mixture into *each* puff. Top with remaining berries, then replace the tops of the puffs. Before serving, sift powdered sugar over the tops. Makes 12 servings.

Sophisticated Choux

Cream puffs, or choux à la crème pâtissière, were introduced in America at the time San Francisco was evolving from a frontier town into a cosmopolitan city. Citizen François Pioche determined then that the city's cuisine should reflect its new elegance and sophistication, and he arranged for several French chefs to come to San Francisco. These chefs were experts in making everything from delicate sauces to delectable cream puffs.

Chocolate-Apricot Éclairs

Glazing with apricot preserves sets off the rich chocolate filling. (Pictured on pages 232–233.)

1   **recipe Chocolate Pastry Cream (see page 263)**
½   **cup whipping cream**
1   **recipe Cream Puff Pastry (see page 262)**
½   **cup apricot preserves**

Prepare Chocolate Pastry Cream as directed, then let it cool. In a small mixing bowl beat whipping cream till soft peaks form. Fold whipped cream into cooled pastry cream, then chill well.

Grease a baking sheet. Set baking sheet aside. Prepare Cream Puff Pastry as directed. Spoon cream puff dough into a decorating bag fitted with a large plain round tip (½-inch to 1-inch opening). Slowly pipe strips of dough 3 inches apart on the prepared baking sheet, making 12 éclairs, each about 4½ inches long, 1 inch wide, and ¾ inch high.

Bake in a 400° oven for 30 to 40 minutes or till golden brown and puffy. Remove éclairs from the baking sheet and cool on a wire rack.

In a small heavy saucepan heat and stir apricot preserves till melted. Remove from heat, set aside.

To assemble, horizontally cut off tops of éclairs. Remove any soft dough from inside. Spoon about ¼ *cup* of the chilled pastry cream mixture into *each* éclair. *Or,* spoon filling into a decorating bag fitted with a large star tip (about ⅝-inch opening), then pipe filling into the éclairs. Replace the éclair tops. Using a pastry brush, generously brush melted apricot preserves over tops. Chill for up to 2 hours. Serves 12.

Vanilla Cream Éclairs

Imagine a rich vanilla filling, crisp shells, and a chocolate glaze, and you'll be dreaming of these éclairs.

> 1   **recipe Pastry Cream (see page 263)**
> ½   **cup whipping cream**
> 1   **recipe Cream Puff Pastry (see page 262)**
> 2   **squares (2 ounces) semisweet chocolate,**
>   **finely chopped**
> 1   **tablespoon margarine *or* butter**
> 1   **teaspoon light corn syrup**
> ½   **cup sifted powdered sugar**
> ½   **teaspoon vanilla**
>   **Whipping cream**

Prepare Pastry Cream as directed, then let it cool. In a small mixing bowl beat the ½ cup whipping cream till soft peaks form. Fold whipped cream into the cooled pastry cream, then chill well.

Grease a baking sheet. Set baking sheet aside. Prepare Cream Puff Pastry as directed. Spoon cream puff dough into a decorating bag fitted with a large plain round tip (½- to 1-inch opening). Slowly pipe strips of dough 3 inches apart on the prepared baking sheet, making 12 éclairs, each about 4½ inches long, 1 inch wide, and ¾ inch high. Bake in a 400° oven for 30 to 40 minutes or till golden brown and puffy. Remove from the baking sheet and cool on a wire rack.

For chocolate glaze, in a small heavy saucepan combine the semisweet chocolate, margarine or butter, and corn syrup. Cook and stir over low heat till the chocolate is melted. Stir in powdered sugar and vanilla. If necessary, stir in enough of the additional whipping cream to make a glaze of drizzling consistency. Keep glaze warm while assembling the éclairs.

To assemble, horizontally cut off the tops of the éclairs. Remove any soft dough from inside. Spoon about *¼ cup* of the chilled pastry cream mixture into *each* éclair. Replace tops. Spoon or brush the chocolate glaze over the tops of the éclairs. If desired, chill for up to 2 hours. Makes 12 servings.

Secrets to Successful Cream Puffs

Perfect cream puffs are puffy, crisp, and tender. If your cream puffs fall short of your expectations, review these tips before making them again.

If your cream puffs are heavy or don't "puff":
■ Be sure to measure the water carefully. (Review Measuring Tips on page 297.)
■ Add the flour as soon as the margarine or butter is melted and the water boils, so the water does not boil away.
■ Set a minute timer so the pastry dough cools exactly 10 minutes. Then beat in the first egg.

If your cream puffs fall:
■ Be sure your cream puffs are golden brown, firm, and dry before removing them from the oven.

Ham-Onion Bites

2 **cups finely chopped celery**
4 **green onions, finely chopped (¼ cup)**
¼ **cup water**
½ **cup (3 ounces) finely chopped
    fully cooked ham**
⅓ **cup fine dry seasoned bread crumbs**
¼ **teaspoon ground nutmeg**
1 **slightly beaten egg**
1 **recipe Cream Puff Pastry (see page 262)**
⅛ **teaspoon pepper**
⅓ **cup grated Parmesan cheese**

Line baking sheets with foil, then grease foil. Set baking sheets aside.

For filling, in a small saucepan combine celery, onions, and water. Bring the mixture to boiling and reduce heat. Cover and simmer for 6 to 8 minutes or till vegetables are tender. Drain well. Stir in ham, bread crumbs, and nutmeg. Slightly cool filling mixture.

Stir egg into filling mixture. Drop filling from a rounded teaspoon 2 inches apart on the prepared baking sheets, mounding the filling slightly. Set aside.

Prepare Cream Puff Pastry as directed, *except* omit salt. Add the pepper with the flour to the pastry dough. After beating the eggs into the pastry dough, stir in the Parmesan cheese.

Spoon the dough into a decorating bag fitted with a large star tip (about ⅜-inch opening). Pipe the dough around the filling mounds in concentric circles, starting at the base and working toward the top, leaving the tops of the filling uncovered.

Bake in a 400° oven for 18 to 20 minutes or till golden brown. Remove cream puffs from the baking sheets and cool slightly on wire racks. Serve warm. Makes 35 to 40.

Swiss-Dill Puffs

A ring of puff pull-aparts highlights an appetizer buffet.

1 **recipe Cream Puff Pastry (see page 262)**
½ **cup shredded Swiss cheese (2 ounces)**
½ **to 1 teaspoon dried dillweed**

Grease a baking sheet; set aside. Prepare Cream Puff Pastry as directed, *except* reduce margarine to ⅓ *cup.* After beating in eggs, stir in cheese and dillweed.

Drop dough by heaping tablespoons into 10 mounds about ½ inch apart in the shape of a ring on the prepared baking sheet. *Or,* spoon dough into a decorating bag fitted with a large plain round tip (about ⅝-inch opening) and pipe dough into 10 mounds, forming a ring shape. Bake in a 400° oven for 30 to 35 minutes or till golden brown and puffy. Remove from baking sheet; cool slightly on a wire rack. Serve warm. Makes 10 servings.

Cheddar-Onion Puffs: Prepare Swiss-Dill Puffs as directed above, *except* substitute ½ cup shredded *cheddar cheese* for the Swiss cheese and ½ teaspoon *onion powder* for the dillweed.

Make-Ahead Appetizers

Serving cream puff appetizers warm from the oven is easy if you make them ahead and reheat them at the last minute. Bake the Ham-Onion Bites or Swiss-Dill Puffs, then cool them completely. Place the appetizers in an airtight container and chill them for 1 to 2 days or freeze them for up to 1 month.

To serve, transfer the chilled or frozen puffs to an ungreased baking sheet. Heat them in a 350° oven for 5 to 10 minutes or till warm.

Swiss-Dill Puffs

Ham-Onion Bites

PUFF PASTRIES

Layer upon layer of crisp, buttery pastry is the beginning of marvelous desserts, cookies, and appetizers. Whether you make the puff pastry or purchase it, you'll be creating masterpieces.

☐ For the best results, make the entire recipe of Quick-Method or Classic Puff Pastry dough even though most of the recipes using the pastry will call for half of the amount of that dough. You can store the remaining portion to use at another time (see tip, page 274).

☐ Butter is used in the puff pastry recipes in this book. Its flavor and firm texture are preferred for rich-tasting, flaky puff pastries.

☐ For Classic Puff Pastry, the butter mixture is properly chilled and ready to place on the dough when you can slightly bend the rectangle and it does not break. If the butter is too hard, it may poke holes in the dough. If the butter is too soft, it melts into the dough.

☐ If the dough is too elastic to roll, return it to the refrigerator for about 5 minutes so it can relax.

☐ Mark a tally sheet as you complete each rolling and folding step to keep track of how many steps of the recipe you have completed.

☐ Use a very sharp knife, such as a chef's knife or cleaver, to cut *straight down* through the dough. Don't pull the knife or cut the dough at a slant because the edges will puff unevenly during baking.

☐ When lining baking sheets with parchment paper or brown paper, don't let the paper hang over the edges of the baking sheet because it will burn.

Quick-Method Puff Pastry

Tossing the butter with the flour instead of making a butter layer saves steps without sacrificing quality.

  4 **cups all-purpose flour**
  1 **teaspoon salt**
  2 **cups** *cold* **butter (1 pound)**
1¼ **cups** *ice* **water**

In a large mixing bowl stir together flour and salt. Cut the cold butter into ½-inch-thick *slices* (not cubes). Add the butter slices to the flour mixture, then toss till the butter slices are coated with the flour mixture and are separated.

Pour ice water over the flour mixture. Using a spoon, quickly mix (butter will remain in large pieces and flour will not be completely moistened).

Turn dough out onto a lightly floured pastry cloth. Knead the dough 10 times by pressing and pushing dough together to form a rough-looking ball, lifting the pastry cloth if necessary to press dough together. Shape dough into a rectangle (dough still will have some dry-looking areas). Make the corners as square as possible. Slightly flatten dough.

Working on a well-floured pastry cloth, roll the dough into a 15x12-inch rectangle. Fold dough crosswise into thirds to form a 12x5-inch rectangle. Give dough a quarter turn, then fold crosswise into thirds to form a 5x4-inch rectangle and to create 9 layers.

Repeat the rolling, folding, turning, and folding process once more, forming a 5x4-inch rectangle. Wrap the dough with plastic wrap. Chill the dough for 20 minutes in the refrigerator. Repeat the rolling and folding process 2 more times. Before using, chill the dough for 20 minutes more in the refrigerator.

To use the dough in a recipe, with a sharp knife, cut dough *crosswise* in half. Then use as directed in the recipe. Makes 2 portions.

Classic Puff Pastry

Numerous layers of paper-thin pastry and butter make pastry that actually melts in your mouth.

3½ **cups all-purpose flour**
½ **teaspoon salt**
6 **tablespoons *cold* butter**
1 **cup *ice* water**
1½ **cups butter**
¼ **cup all-purpose flour**

For dough, in a large mixing bowl stir together the 3½ cups all-purpose flour and salt. Using a pastry blender, cut in the 6 tablespoons cold butter till pieces are the size of small peas.

Sprinkle *2 tablespoons* of the ice water over part of the flour mixture, then gently toss with a fork. Push moistened dough to side of bowl. Repeat, using 2 tablespoons of water at a time, just till all dough is moistened. Form dough into a ball. Wrap it in plastic wrap and chill for 2 to 24 hours in the refrigerator.

In the same mixing bowl beat the 1½ cups butter and ¼ cup flour with an electric mixer till smooth. Roll butter mixture between 2 large sheets of waxed paper into a 12x8-inch rectangle. Chill for 1 hour in the refrigerator or for 20 minutes in the freezer.

On a lightly floured surface, roll the dough into an 18x15-inch rectangle. Remove the top sheet of waxed paper from the chilled butter rectangle. Invert the butter rectangle onto half of the dough to within about 1 inch of the edges. Remove waxed paper. Fold over the other half of the dough. Using the heel or side of your hand, press edges together to seal. Wrap the dough in plastic wrap and chill for 1 hour in the refrigerator or for 20 minutes in the freezer.

On a lightly floured surface, roll chilled dough into an 18x15-inch rectangle. Brush excess flour from the dough. Fold the dough crosswise into thirds to form a 15x6-inch rectangle. Give the dough a quarter turn, then fold crosswise into thirds to form a 6x5-inch

rectangle and to create 9 layers. Wrap the dough in plastic wrap and chill for 1 hour in the refrigerator or for 20 minutes in the freezer.

Repeat the rolling, folding, turning, folding, and chilling process 2 more times.

To use the dough in a recipe, with a sharp knife, cut the dough *crosswise* in half. Then use as directed in the recipe. Makes 2 portions.

◄ *Seal the edges of the puff pastry around the butter layer by pressing lightly with the side or heel of your hand. It is important to seal the edges so the butter does not leak out during baking. Don't, however, pinch the edges together because then they won't puff well during baking.*

◄ *To roll the dough, always roll from the center to the edges. Roll smoothly and evenly, without pressing hard on the rolling pin. Stop just short of the edges so the ends are not pinched together.*

Palmiers

Named palmiers because their double pinwheel shape makes them look like palm leaves.

1 portion Classic Puff Pastry *or* Quick-Method Puff Pastry (see recipes, pages 269 and 268), *or* one 17¼-ounce package (2 sheets) frozen puff pastry, thawed and unfolded
½ cup sugar

Line baking sheets with parchment or plain brown paper. Set baking sheets aside.

If using Classic or Quick-Method Puff Pastry, cut the portion of dough *crosswise* in half. Cover and return one piece of the dough to the refrigerator. On a lightly floured surface, roll remaining piece of dough or *one* sheet of purchased pastry into a 14x10-inch rectangle. Sprinkle the rectangle with *¼ cup* of the sugar. Lightly press sugar into the dough. Roll the 2 short sides, jelly roll-style, to meet in the center.

Cut the pastry roll crosswise into about ¼-inch-thick slices. If the roll is too soft to slice easily, chill it for a few minutes. Place slices 2 inches apart on the prepared baking sheets.

Bake in a 375° oven for 15 to 20 minutes or till golden and crisp. Remove from baking sheet and cool on a wire rack. Repeat with remaining piece of dough or sheet of purchased pastry and remaining sugar. Makes about 60.

Cinnamon Palmiers: Prepare Palmiers as directed above, *except* stir 1 teaspoon ground *cinnamon* into the sugar.

Patty Shells

Ladle a creamy seafood or chicken sauce into these crisp shells for a main dish. Or, for a dessert, fill them with Pastry Cream (see recipe, page 263) or whipped cream.

1 portion Classic Puff Pastry *or* Quick-Method Puff Pastry (see recipes, pages 269 and 268), *or* one 17¼-ounce package (2 sheets) frozen puff pastry, thawed and unfolded

Line a baking sheet with parchment or plain brown paper. Set baking sheet aside.

If using Classic or Quick-Method Puff Pastry, cut the portion of dough *crosswise* in half. Cover and return one piece to the refrigerator. On a lightly floured surface, roll the remaining piece of dough or *one* sheet of purchased pastry into a 12-inch square.

Using a 3½-inch round or scalloped cookie cutter, cut pastry. *Do not twist* cutter. Dip cutter in flour between cuts. Using a 2½-inch round cutter, make a cut in center of each 3½-inch circle, cutting *to but not completely through* pastry. Place on prepared sheet.

Bake in a 425° oven for 10 to 15 minutes or till golden and crisp. Using the tines of a fork, remove the centers from the shells. Cool shells on a wire rack. Repeat with remaining puff pastry. Makes 18.

◄ *Slice the Palmiers or Cinnamon Palmiers (shown) straight down with a thin, sharp knife. If the roll becomes soft and hard to slice, return it to the refrigerator for a few minutes.*

Strawberry Tart

Pile strawberries into the puff pastry basket and then glaze them with the ruby red sauce.

1 **portion Classic Puff Pastry** *or* **Quick-Method Puff Pastry (see recipes, pages 269 and 268),** *or* **½ of a 17¼-ounce package (1 sheet) frozen puff pastry, thawed and unfolded**
1 **slightly beaten egg white**
3 **cups medium strawberries**
¼ **cup sugar**
1 **tablespoon cornstarch**
3 **drops red food coloring (optional)**
 Whipped cream (optional)

If using Classic or Quick-Method Puff Pastry, cut the portion of dough *crosswise* in half. Cover and return one piece of dough to the refrigerator.

For pastry shell, on a lightly floured surface roll the remaining piece of dough or the sheet of purchased pastry into a 14¼x9¼-inch rectangle. Using a ruler and a very sharp knife, trim edges of pastry to form a 14x9-inch rectangle. Then cut the rectangle into one 14x6-inch rectangle and three 14x1-inch strips. Cut one of the 14x1-inch strips crosswise into two 4½-inch pieces. (There will be a 5-inch piece left over.)

Transfer the 14x6-inch rectangle to an ungreased baking sheet. Using the tines of a fork, generously prick the pastry making definite holes in it so the baking sheet shows through. Brush the edges with egg white. Gently twist all strips several times. Place them within ¼ inch of the edges of the pastry rectangle to form a rim around the edges. Moisten ends with egg white, then lightly press together to seal.

Bake in a 375° oven for 30 to 35 minutes for classic or quick pastry (about 20 minutes for purchased pastry) or till golden. To prevent overbrowning, cover with foil for the last 5 to 10 minutes of baking. Carefully loosen pastry shell from baking sheet and transfer it to a wire rack. Cool the shell completely.

For glaze, in a small saucepan crush *1 cup* of the smaller strawberries. Add ⅔ cup *water*. Bring to boiling. Reduce heat. Simmer, uncovered, for 2 minutes. Sieve strawberry mixture, then discard pulp. In the same saucepan stir together sugar and cornstarch. Stir in the sieved strawberry mixture. Cook and stir over medium heat till thickened and bubbly. Cook and stir for 2 minutes more. If desired, stir in red food coloring. Cool the glaze slightly.

To assemble, transfer pastry shell to a flat serving platter or board. Halve remaining strawberries and arrange them in the shell. Pour glaze over berries, thoroughly covering each berry. Chill for 3 to 4 hours. If desired, garnish with whipped cream. Serves 8.

No Clear Winner In Puff Pastry Debate

Have you ever wondered who dreamed up the idea of folding pastry into hundreds of layers? Historians still debate the issue of who created puff pastry, with two Frenchmen in the middle of the dispute.

Some believe Claude Gellée was the one who perfected the light, airy pastry. Gellée, who was better known as seventeenth-century landscape painter Claude Lorrain, was a pastry cook's apprentice in his early years.

Others feel that Feuillet, a renowned French chef and the chief pastry cook for the house of Condé, should get the credit. The fact that puff pastry often is called pâte feuilletée adds support to the argument that Feuillet did indeed create the puff pastry we enjoy today.

Cream Horns

Also delicious filled with sweetened whipped cream.

1 portion Classic Puff Pastry *or* Quick-Method Puff Pastry (see recipes, pages 269 and 268), *or* one 17¼-ounce package (2 sheets) frozen puff pastry, thawed
1 slightly beaten egg white
1 tablespoon extra-fine granulated sugar *or* sugar
1 recipe Pastry Cream (see page 263)
Chopped nuts

Line a baking sheet with parchment or plain brown paper. Set baking sheet aside.

If using Classic or Quick-Method Puff Pastry, on a lightly floured surface, roll the portion of dough into a 16x12-inch rectangle. Using a sharp knife, cut pastry lengthwise into twelve 16x1-inch strips. *Or,* if using purchased pastry, unfold and roll *each* sheet into a 12x10-inch rectangle. Cut *each* sheet into *twelve* 10x1-inch strips. Press *two* strips of purchased pastry together at the ends to make a long strip, then repeat with remaining strips.

Wrap *each* strip of dough around a well greased cream horn mold or cannoli tube. Place 1 inch apart

◄ *Begin wrapping the strip of pastry around the cream horn mold at the point, then rotate the mold to wind the strip around it. Overlap the strip slightly.*

on prepared sheet. Brush with a mixture of egg white and 1 tablespoon *water.* Then sprinkle with sugar.

Bake in a 425° oven for 15 to 20 minutes or till golden for classic or quick pastry (12 to 15 minutes for purchased pastry). While still warm, slightly twist the molds and remove from pastry horns. Transfer pastry horns to a wire rack and cool completely.

Prepare Pastry Cream. Spoon cooled pastry cream into a decorating bag fitted with a large star tip (about 1-inch opening); pipe cream into each horn. Sprinkle tops with nuts. Chill up to 1 hour. Serves 12.

Cream Turnovers: Roll Classic or Quick-Method Puff Pastry into a 16x12-inch rectangle as directed at left. Using a sharp knife, cut the rectangle *crosswise* in half to make two 12x8-inch rectangles. Cover and return *one* rectangle to the refrigerator. On a lightly floured surface, roll remaining rectangle or *one* sheet of purchased pastry into a 12-inch square. Cut the pastry square into nine 4-inch squares.

Cut three ¼-inch slits near, *but not through,* the edge of one corner of each square to prevent over-puffing. Brush the edges of the squares with 2 tablespoons melted *margarine or butter.* Fold each pastry square diagonally in half with slits on top. Slip a small piece of foil between the layers of each triangle to prevent edges from sticking together. Place on prepared baking sheet.

Brush the triangles with a mixture of egg white and 1 tablespoon *water,* then sprinkle with sugar. Bake in the 425° oven about 20 minutes or till golden and crisp. While still warm, remove foil, then transfer triangles to a wire rack to cool completely. Repeat with remaining 12x8-inch rectangle or sheet of pastry.

Prepare Pastry Cream. Spoon cooled cream into a decorating bag fitted with a large star tip, then pipe around edges of turnovers. Sprinkle with nuts or garnish with fresh *fruit.* Serves 18.

Easy Coconut Diamonds

Make a second batch to freeze for impromptu desserts.

- **1 slightly beaten egg yolk**
- **¼ cup flaked coconut**
- **2 teaspoons brown sugar**
- **½ of a 17¼-ounce package (1 sheet) frozen puff pastry, thawed**
- **1 slightly beaten egg white**
- **1 tablespoon water**

Line a baking sheet with parchment or plain brown paper. Set baking sheet aside. In a small mixing bowl stir together egg yolk, coconut, and brown sugar. Set mixture aside.

On a lightly floured surface, unfold pastry. Using a fluted pastry wheel, cut six ¼-inch-wide strips off one side of the pastry square. Set strips aside. Using a sharp knife or a cookie cutter, cut remaining pastry into 12 diamonds measuring about 3½x2½ inches.

Spoon about *1 teaspoon* of the coconut mixture on top of *six* diamonds. In a small bowl, stir together egg white and water. Brush egg white mixture around edges of pastry diamonds. Top with the remaining pastry diamonds. Gently press edges together to seal. Brush tops of diamonds with the egg white mixture. Decorate by placing reserved pastry strips around the top edge of each diamond, trimming the strips to fit.

If desired, cut additional ¼-inch-wide strips or decorative shapes from pastry scraps. Brush pieces with remaining egg white mixture and continue decorating diamonds by placing pastry pieces on top. Bake the diamonds immediately or seal them in an airtight container and freeze for up to 3 months.

To serve, place fresh or frozen diamonds on prepared baking sheet. Bake in a 400° oven for 18 to 20 minutes or till golden. Serve warm. Makes 6 servings.

Secrets to Successful Puff Pastries

If your puff pastries aren't as flaky and tender as you expect them to be, here's how to solve the problem next time:

If your puff pastries shrink when baked or are tough:
- Be sure to use *ice* water when making the pastry dough.
- Give the dough a quarter turn between rolling and folding as directed so the dough is stretched in all directions.
- Be sure the pastries are fully baked. They will look golden when done.

If your puff pastries don't at least triple in height:
- Cover the dough with plastic wrap during rest periods to retain moisture.
- Wait until you are ready to bake the pastries to place them on the paper-lined baking sheet so the paper doesn't absorb any moisture.
- Use an oven thermometer to check the oven temperature. If necessary, adjust the setting.

If your pastries aren't uniform in shape:
- When rolling the dough, roll just to the edge (see photo, page 269).
- Cut the dough straight down with a sharp knife. Placing pastries on the baking sheet upside down sometimes gives a more even puff.

If your pastries aren't flaky:
- Keep the pastry dough in the refrigerator until you're ready to roll it out. That way the butter won't soften and melt into the dough when rolled.

Dutch Letters

Shape the dough into the traditional "S," into your initials, or into letters to spell a word.

4½ **cups all-purpose flour**
2 **cups *cold* butter (1 pound)**
1 **beaten egg**
1 **cup *ice* water**
1 **egg white**
1 **8-ounce can almond paste**
½ **cup sugar**
½ **cup packed brown sugar**
   Sugar

In a large mixing bowl stir together flour and 1 teaspoon *salt*. Cut cold butter into ½-inch-thick *slices* (not cubes). Add slices to flour mixture, then toss till slices are coated with flour mixture and are separated.

In a small mixing bowl stir together egg and ice water. Add all at once to flour mixture. Using a spoon, quickly mix (butter will remain in large pieces and flour will not be completely moistened).

Turn the dough out onto a lightly floured pastry cloth. Knead the dough 10 times by pressing and pushing dough together to form a rough-looking ball, lifting pastry cloth if necessary to press the dough together. Shape the dough into a rectangle (dough still will have some dry-looking areas). Make the corners as square as possible. Slightly flatten the dough.

Working on a well-floured pastry cloth, roll the dough into a 15x10-inch rectangle. Fold the 2 short sides to meet in center, then fold in half like a book to form 4 layers each measuring about 7½x5 inches.

Repeat rolling and folding process once more. Wrap dough with plastic wrap. Chill dough for 20 minutes in refrigerator. Repeat rolling and folding process 2 more times. Chill dough 20 minutes before using.

For filling, in a bowl stir together egg white, almond paste, ½ cup sugar, and brown sugar. Set aside.

Using a sharp knife, cut dough *crosswise* into 4 equal parts. Wrap *three* portions in plastic wrap and return to the refrigerator. On a well-floured surface, roll *one* portion into a 12½x10-inch rectangle. Cut rectangle into five 10x2½-inch strips.

Shape a *slightly rounded tablespoon* of filling into a 9-inch rope and place it down the center third of *one* strip. Roll up the strip lengthwise. Brush edge and ends with *water;* pinch to seal. Place, seam side down, on an ungreased baking sheet, shaping strip into a letter. Brush with *water* and sprinkle with additional sugar. Repeat with remaining dough strips and filling. Then repeat with remaining dough portions and filling. Bake in a 375° oven for 20 to 25 minutes or till golden. Cool on wire racks. Makes 20.

Easy Dutch Letters: Prepare Dutch Letters as directed at left, *except* substitute two 17¼-ounce packages (4 sheets) frozen *puff pastry,* thawed, for the flour, salt, butter, egg, and ice water. Unfold and roll *one* sheet into a 12½x10-inch rectangle. Cut, fill, and shape as above. Repeat with remaining sheets. Bake in a 375° oven 15 to 20 minutes or till golden. Cool on wire racks.

Storing Puff Pastry

Most of the pastry recipes in this section call for half of a recipe (one portion) of Classic or Quick-Method Puff Pastry (see recipes pages 269 and 268). To store the other portion until needed, wrap the dough in plastic wrap and refrigerate it for up to 3 days.

To freeze, wrap the puff pastry dough in *heavy* foil, seal well, label, and then freeze for up to 3 months. Thaw the dough, covered, in the refrigerator for 24 hours.

Dutch Letters

Napoleons

Collect the compliments when you serve this classic dessert.

1 portion Classic Puff Pastry *or* Quick-Method Puff Pastry (see recipes, pages 269 and 268), *or* one 17¼-ounce package (2 sheets) frozen puff pastry, thawed
Napoleon Filling
2 cups sifted powdered sugar
¼ teaspoon vanilla
2 to 3 tablespoons *boiling* water
2 squares (2 ounces) semisweet chocolate, melted and cooled

Line 2 baking sheets with parchment paper or plain brown paper. Set baking sheets aside.

If using Classic or Quick-Method Puff Pastry, on a lightly floured surface, roll the portion of dough into a 15x9-inch rectangle. Using a sharp knife, cut off ½ inch on all 4 sides to make a 14x8-inch rectangle. *Or,* if using purchased puff pastry, unfold sheets and trim *each* sheet to an 8x7-inch rectangle.

Using a sharp knife, cut puff pastry into sixteen 3½x2-inch rectangles. Transfer pastry rectangles to the prepared baking sheets. Using the tines of a fork, prick pastry rectangles.

Bake in a 425° oven for 18 to 23 minutes or till golden. Carefully remove pastries from baking sheets and cool on a wire rack.

For glaze, in a medium mixing bowl combine powdered sugar and vanilla. Stir in enough boiling water to make a glaze of spreading consistency; set aside.

To assemble, use the tines of a fork to separate *each* pastry rectangle horizontally into *three* layers. Spread about 1½ tablespoons Napoleon Filling on *each* bottom layer, then replace the middle pastry layers.

Spread another *1½ tablespoons* of filling on *each* middle pastry layer, then replace top layers. Spread glaze over the tops of the napoleons. Drizzle chocolate on the tops of the napoleons. If desired, chill for up to 1 hour. Makes 16 servings.

Napoleon Filling: In a heavy medium saucepan stir together 1 cup *sugar,* ¼ cup *all-purpose flour,* ¼ cup *cornstarch,* and ⅛ teaspoon *salt.* Gradually stir in 3 cups *milk.* Cook and stir over medium heat till thickened and bubbly. Reduce heat. Cook and stir for 2 minutes more. Remove from heat. Gradually stir about *1 cup* of the hot mixture into 4 beaten *egg yolks.* Return all to saucepan. Bring to a gentle boil. Cook and stir for 2 minutes more. Remove from heat. Stir in 2 teaspoons *vanilla.* Cover surface with plastic wrap, then cool and chill without stirring. Just before using, gently stir. Makes about 3 cups.

Napoleon Who?

Although it might seem like napoleons must have been named after Napoléon Bonaparte, the French emperor, it's more likely they were not. It's believed napoleons got their name from a large, elaborately decorated cake called a napolitain. This magnificent cake was featured as the centerpiece at grand French buffets. There are similarities between the napolitain and napoleons. Both are rectangles made of many layers with rich filling between the layers. Today's napoleons, however, are smaller.

Ham 'n' Pastry Twists

½ **cup dairy sour cream**
2 **tablespoons mustard-mayonnaise sandwich and salad sauce**
½ **of a 17¼-ounce package (1 sheet) frozen puff pastry, thawed**
1 **slightly beaten egg white**
1 **tablespoon water**
5 **ounces thinly sliced ham or corned beef**

For sauce, stir together sour cream and mustard-mayonnaise sauce. Cover sauce and chill till serving time. Line a baking sheet with parchment paper or plain brown paper. Set baking sheet aside.

Unfold puff pastry sheet. On a lightly floured surface, roll pastry into a 12x9-inch rectangle. Stir together egg white and water. Brush egg mixture on pastry.

Place ham or corned beef on top of the pastry. Using a sharp knife, cut pastry lengthwise in half, forming two 12x4½-inch rectangles. Cut *each* rectangle crosswise into *twenty-four* 4½x½-inch strips. Twist each strip of dough 3 or 4 times, then place them on the prepared baking sheet, pressing ends down.

Bake in a 425° oven for 8 to 10 minutes or till golden. Remove twists from baking sheet and slightly cool on a wire rack. Serve warm with sauce. Makes 48.

Ham 'n' Pastry Pinwheels: Prepare Ham 'n' Pastry Twists as directed above, *except* omit the sour cream, mustard-mayonnaise sauce, egg white, and water. Roll the pastry into a 12x9-inch rectangle and brush the pastry with 2 tablespoons *brown mustard or Dijon-style mustard*. Place ham or corned beef on top of the pastry. Roll up, jelly-roll style, beginning from a long side. Using a sharp knife, cut roll into ½-inch-thick slices. Place on the prepared baking sheet. Bake and cool as above. Makes 24.

Cheesy Twists

Great to serve with a salad or soup.

¼ **cup grated Parmesan or Romano cheese**
¾ **teaspoon dried Italian seasoning**
¼ **teaspoon garlic powder**
1 **portion Classic Puff Pastry or Quick-Method Puff Pastry (see recipes, pages 269 and 268), or one 17¼-ounce package (2 sheets) frozen puff pastry, thawed**
1 **beaten egg**

Line a baking sheet with parchment paper or plain brown paper. Set baking sheet aside.

In a small mixing bowl stir together Parmesan or Romano cheese, Italian seasoning, and garlic powder. Set cheese mixture aside.

If using Classic or Quick-Method Puff Pastry, on a lightly floured surface, roll the portion of dough into a 14x10-inch rectangle. *Or,* if using purchased pastry, unfold the sheets and stack them. Then roll the purchased pastry into a 14x10-inch rectangle. Brush beaten egg over the surface of the pastry. Sprinkle the cheese mixture evenly over the pastry.

Using a sharp knife, cut the pastry lengthwise into two 14x5-inch rectangles. Cut *each* rectangle crosswise into *twenty-eight* 5x½-inch strips. Twist each strip of dough 3 or 4 times, then place them on the prepared baking sheet, pressing ends down.

Bake in a 425° oven about 10 minutes or till golden. Remove twists from the baking sheet and cool on a wire rack. Makes 56.

STRUDELS AND PHYLLO

Ultra-flaky strudels and phyllo pastries are utterly delicious. Whether you make the strudel dough or use purchased phyllo sheets, you'll be serving the ultimate in pastry.

☐ For strudels, prepare the filling first or while the dough is resting. That way the dough won't dry out.

☐ Keep strudel or phyllo dough covered with a damp cloth when not working with it. This will keep the dough from drying out.

☐ A fabric sheet or tablecloth makes a good pastry cloth on which to stretch the strudel dough.

☐ Before stretching the strudel dough, remove any jewelry from your hands that might tear the thin dough. If you still tear large holes during stretching, check to see if a long or rough fingernail may be the cause. Another cause of tearing is lifting the dough too high as you stretch it.

☐ When stretching strudel dough with a partner, work on opposite sides of the dough so you are stretching across from each other. The stretching will take about 5 minutes. If you are working alone, place a heavy rolling pin on one edge and pull from the opposite side. Stretching will take about 15 minutes if you are working alone.

☐ If a large hole appears while you're stretching strudel dough, patch it with dough from the edge. Don't worry about small holes. They will not cause leakage once the strudel is rolled up.

☐ Use two wide metal spatulas to carefully transfer the strudel from the pan to a rack after baking.

Strudel Dough

1½ cups all-purpose flour
¼ cup margarine *or* butter
1 beaten egg yolk
⅓ cup warm water (110° to 115°)
2 tablespoons margarine *or* butter, melted

In a large mixing bowl stir together flour and ¼ teaspoon *salt.* Using a pastry blender, cut in the ¼ cup margarine or butter till pieces are the size of small peas. In a small mixing bowl stir together egg yolk and warm water. Add egg yolk mixture to flour mixture. Stir till combined.

Turn the dough out onto a lightly floured surface. Knead dough for 5 minutes. Cover with plastic wrap, then let dough stand at room temperature for 1 hour.

Cover a large surface (at least 4x3 feet) with a cloth; flour the cloth. On the cloth roll dough into a 15-inch square. Brush with 2 tablespoons melted margarine or butter. Cover dough with plastic wrap. Let dough rest for 30 minutes. Meanwhile, prepare filling.

To stretch dough, use the palms of your hands and work underneath dough. Starting from the middle and working toward edges, gently stretch from one corner to the next. Continue stretching till dough is paper thin, forming a 40x20-inch rectangle. Trim thick or uneven edges with scissors. Fill, roll; bake as directed in recipes. Makes dough for 1 strudel.

Note: To substitute phyllo dough for Strudel Dough, cover a large surface with a cloth; flour cloth. Unfold 10 to 12 sheets frozen *phyllo dough,* thawed. Stack 2 sheets of phyllo on the floured cloth. (*Do not brush margarine or butter between sheets.*) Arrange another stack of 2 sheets on the cloth, overlapping the stacks 2 inches. Add 3 or 4 more stacks, forming a rectangle about 40x20 inches (stagger stacks so all seams are not down the middle). Trim to a 40x20-inch rectangle. Use as directed in strudel recipes, *except* brush with *⅓ cup* melted margarine or butter before filling.

Cranberry Strudel

Serve with small glasses of sherry for a holiday dessert.
(Pictured on page 280.)

- 1 **recipe Strudel Dough**
  (see page 278)
- 2 **cups cranberries**
- ½ **cup dried apples, cut up**
- ½ **cup chopped pecans**
- ¼ **cup currants**
- ¾ **cup sugar**
- ¼ **cup margarine *or* butter, melted**
- 1 **slightly beaten egg white**
- 1 **tablespoon water**
  Powdered sugar

Prepare Strudel Dough as directed. Meanwhile, in a medium saucepan combine cranberries and ¾ cup *water*. Bring to boiling. Reduce heat and simmer, uncovered, about 5 minutes or till cranberries pop. Drain cranberries. In a mixing bowl combine drained cranberries, dried apple, pecans, and currants. Add sugar, then gently toss till mixed; set aside. Lightly grease a 15x10x1-inch baking pan; set aside.

To assemble strudel, stretch dough as directed. Brush stretched dough with melted margarine or butter. Beginning 4 inches from a short side of dough, spoon filling in a 4-inch-wide band across dough.

Using the cloth underneath the dough as a guide, gently lift the 4-inch piece of dough and lay it over the filling. Then slowly and evenly lift cloth and roll up the dough and filling, jelly-roll style, into a tight roll. If necessary, cut off excess dough from ends to within 1 inch of the filling. Fold ends under to seal.

Carefully transfer strudel roll to the prepared baking pan. Slightly curve the roll to form a crescent shape. Stir together egg white and water. Brush top of strudel with egg white mixture. Bake in a 350° oven for 35 to 40 minutes or till golden. Carefully remove strudel from pan and cool on a wire rack. Sift powdered sugar over strudel before serving. Serves 12 to 16.

▶ *To stretch the strudel dough, gently lift and stretch the dough with the palms of your hands. This stretches the dough two ways as you pull your hands apart and, at the same time, pull the dough away from the middle toward yourself. Stretch until the dough is paper-thin.*

▶ *To assemble the strudel, spoon the filling in a 4-inch-wide band 4 inches from one of the short sides of the dough. Then lift the cloth underneath the dough and flip the edge of the dough on top of the filling.*

▶ *Gently pull up on the cloth to roll up the dough and filling, jelly-roll style. Don't allow any slack as you lift the cloth so that the strudel roll will be as tight as possible.*

Cranberry Strudel
(see recipe, page 279)

Apple Strudel Ring

The aroma of cinnamon and apples fills the air while this strudel bakes.

- 1 **recipe Strudel Dough**
     (see page 278)
- ½ **cup packed brown sugar**
- ¾ **teaspoon ground cinnamon**
- ½ **teaspoon finely shredded orange peel**
- 3 **cups thinly sliced, peeled tart apples *or* pears**
- ⅓ **cup raisins**
- ¼ **cup margarine *or* butter, melted**
- 2 **tablespoons margarine *or* butter, melted**
- 2 **tablespoons finely crushed vanilla wafers**
     (optional)
- 1 **cup whipping cream**

Prepare Strudel Dough as directed. Meanwhile, for filling, in a large mixing bowl stir together brown sugar, cinnamon, and orange peel. Add apples or pears and raisins, then gently toss till coated. Set filling aside. Lightly grease a 15x10x1-inch baking pan. Set baking pan aside.

To assemble strudel, stretch dough as directed. Brush stretched dough with the ¼ cup melted margarine or butter. Beginning 4 inches from a short side of dough, spoon the filling in a 4-inch-wide band across dough. Using the cloth underneath dough as a guide, gently lift the 4-inch piece of dough and lay it over the filling. Slowly and evenly lift the cloth and roll up the dough and filling, jelly-roll style, into a tight roll. If necessary, cut excess dough from ends to within 1 inch of filling. Fold ends under to seal.

Carefully transfer strudel roll to the prepared baking pan. Curve ends together to form an 8-inch ring. Brush top of strudel with the 2 tablespoons melted margarine. If desired, sprinkle with vanilla wafer crumbs. Bake in a 350° oven for 35 to 40 minutes or till golden. Carefully remove from pan and cool on a wire rack. Meanwhile, in a medium mixing bowl beat whipping cream till stiff peaks form. Pass whipped cream with strudel. Makes 12 to 16 servings.

Cream Cheese Strudel

- 1 **recipe Strudel Dough**
     (see page 278)
- 1 **8-ounce package cream cheese, softened**
- ¾ **cup sifted powdered sugar**
- 1 **egg yolk**
- ½ **teaspoon finely shredded lemon peel *or*
     orange peel**
- ½ **teaspoon vanilla**
- ¼ **cup margarine *or* butter, melted**
- 1 **slightly beaten egg white**
     Powdered sugar

Prepare Strudel Dough as directed. Meanwhile, for filling, in a medium mixing bowl beat cream cheese and the ¾ cup powdered sugar with an electric mixer till combined. Beat in egg yolk, lemon or orange peel, and vanilla just till combined. Lightly grease a 15x10x1-inch baking pan. Set filling and pan aside.

To assemble strudel, stretch dough as directed. Brush dough with melted margarine. Beginning 4 inches from a short side of dough, spread filling in a 4-inch-wide band across dough. Using the cloth underneath as a guide, lift the 4-inch piece of dough and lay it over the filling. Slowly and evenly lift cloth and roll up dough and filling, jelly-roll style, into a tight roll. If necessary, cut excess dough from ends to within 1 inch of filling. Fold ends under to seal.

Carefully transfer the strudel to the prepared pan. Slightly curve roll into a crescent shape. Brush strudel with a mixture of egg white and 1 tablespoon *water.* Bake in a 350° oven about 35 minutes or till golden. Carefully remove from pan and cool on a rack. Sift powdered sugar over strudel. Serves 12 to 16.

Cream Cheese-Pineapple Strudel: Prepare Cream Cheese Strudel as directed above, *except* stir one 8¼-ounce can *crushed pineapple,* well-drained, into the cream cheese filling.

Cherry-Almond Strudel

1 **recipe Strudel Dough**
   (see page 278)
¾ **cup dried cherries**
1 **tablespoon margarine *or* butter**
¾ **cup soft bread crumbs (1 slice)**
½ **cup chopped slivered almonds**
⅓ **cup sugar**
⅓ **cup cherry jelly**
¼ **cup light raisins**
¼ **cup margarine *or* butter, melted**
1 **slightly beaten egg white**
   Sugar (optional)

Prepare Strudel Dough as directed. Meanwhile, pour enough *boiling water* over dried cherries to cover them, then let stand for 20 minutes. Drain cherries. In a medium saucepan melt the 1 tablespoon margarine or butter. Add bread crumbs and cook over medium heat for 4 to 5 minutes or till golden brown, stirring occasionally. Remove from heat. Stir in drained cherries, almonds, ⅓ cup sugar, jelly, and raisins. Lightly grease a 15x10x1-inch baking pan. Set cherry filling and baking pan aside.

To assemble strudel, stretch dough as directed. Brush stretched dough with the ¼ cup melted margarine. Beginning 4 inches from a short side of the dough, spoon the cherry filling in a 4-inch-wide band across the dough. Using the cloth underneath as a guide, gently lift the 4-inch piece of dough and lay it over the filling. Slowly and evenly lift the cloth and roll up the dough and filling, jelly-roll style, into a tight roll. If necessary, cut excess dough from ends to within 1 inch of filling. Fold ends under to seal.

Carefully transfer strudel roll to the prepared pan. Slightly curve the roll to form a crescent or heart shape. Brush top of strudel with beaten egg white. If desired, sprinkle with sugar. Bake in a 350° oven for 35 to 40 minutes or till golden. Carefully remove strudel from pan; cool on a wire rack. Serves 12 to 16.

Mixed-Fruit Almond Strudel: Prepare Cherry-Almond Strudel as directed at left, *except* substitute 1 cup diced *mixed dried fruit bits* for the cherries. Omit the raisins. Substitute ⅓ cup *apple jelly* for the cherry jelly.

Secrets to Successful Strudels and Phyllo

Flaky strudels and phyllo pastries are satisfying to make and a delight to eat. If you have a problem with your pastries, here's the way to prevent the problem next time:

If your pastries aren't flaky:
■ Brush the strudel dough or between *each* layer of the phyllo dough with melted margarine or butter. It's the margarine or butter that keeps the layers separate and flaky.

If your pastries seem soggy:
■ When covering the strudel or phyllo dough with a damp cloth, be sure the cloth is only *slightly* damp. Otherwise it will get the dough too wet.

Strawberry Strudel Torte

An 8-inch round cake pan makes a handy pattern when cutting the strudel dough into circles. (Pictured on pages 232–233.)

2 **cups medium strawberries, sliced**
¾ **cup fresh *or* frozen unsweetened sliced rhubarb**
½ **cup sugar**
4 **teaspoons cornstarch**
1 **teaspoon lemon juice**
1 **recipe Strudel Dough***
   (see page 278)
¼ **cup margarine *or* butter, melted**
½ **cup whipping cream**
1 **tablespoon sugar**
   Sliced strawberries

For glaze, in a small saucepan combine *1 cup* of the strawberries, the rhubarb, and 2 tablespoons *water.* Bring just to boiling. Reduce heat. Cover and simmer for 5 minutes. Sieve the mixture and discard pulp. Add water to the juice to make *½ cup.*

In the small saucepan, stir together the ½ cup sugar and cornstarch. Stir in reserved ½ cup juice-water mixture and lemon juice. Cook and stir till thickened and bubbly. Cook and stir for 2 minutes more. Remove from heat and cover. Cool mixture, then chill.

Meanwhile, lightly grease a baking sheet; set aside. Prepare and stretch Strudel Dough as directed, *except* stretch it into a 40x30-inch rectangle. Using a sharp knife or pastry wheel, cut nine 8-inch circles from the dough. Brush rounds with melted margarine or butter. Stack *three* rounds on the prepared baking sheet. Generously prick with a fork. Cover remaining dough rounds with a damp cloth. Bake in a 425° oven 4 to 6 minutes or till golden. Remove from baking sheet and cool on a wire rack. Repeat with remaining rounds.

In a small bowl beat whipping cream and the 1 tablespoon sugar just till stiff peaks form. Place *one* stack of strudel rounds on a plate. Spread with *half* of the glaze. Top with another stack of strudel. Spread with *half* of the whipped cream.

Top with the remaining stack of strudel. Spread with some of the glaze. Top with remaining berries. Spoon remaining glaze over berries. Spoon remaining whipped cream in center. Garnish with additional berries. Chill for up to 1 hour. Makes 6 servings.

*To substitute phyllo dough for Strudel Dough, use nine 18x12-inch sheets frozen *phyllo dough,* thawed. Cut *one* phyllo sheet into *two* 8-inch round circles. Stack the 2 rounds on the prepared baking sheet, then brush with some of the melted margarine or butter. Repeat 2 more times to make a stack of 6 phyllo rounds. Generously prick phyllo rounds with a fork. Cover remaining phyllo sheets with a damp cloth. Bake in a 425° oven for 4 to 6 minutes or till golden. Remove phyllo rounds from the baking sheet and cool on a wire rack. Repeat cutting rounds and stacking 2 more times to make 3 stacks of phyllo rounds.

It's All Greek

Pastry making began with the ancient Greeks. Using a few simple tools and basic ingredients, they made honey cakes with many of the same ingredients found in today's baklava (see our recipe, page 284).

Through the centuries, pastry making has expanded. The Romans took the techniques back to Italy after their conquest of Greece. From Italy, the art of pastry making spread to France.

In France, the first trade union of pastry chefs was formed in 1270. The union was divided into branches or specialities such as wafer-makers. Under the strict laws of the union, member chefs were never allowed to cross over to another branch.

Baklava

With little effort, you can make wonderful homemade baklava for entertaining, gifts, and fund-raisers.

> **4 cups (1 pound) walnuts, finely chopped**
> **½ cup sugar**
> **1 teaspoon ground cinnamon**
> **1¼ cups margarine *or* butter, melted**
> **1 16-ounce package frozen phyllo dough, thawed**
> **1½ cups sugar**
> **¼ cup honey**
> **½ teaspoon finely shredded lemon peel**
> **2 tablespoons lemon juice**
> **2 inches stick cinnamon**

For walnut filling, in a large mixing bowl stir together chopped walnuts, the ½ cup sugar, and ground cinnamon. Set filling aside.

Brush the bottom of a 15x10x1-inch baking pan with some of the melted margarine or butter. Unfold phyllo. Layer about *one-fourth* of the phyllo sheets in the pan, brushing each sheet generously with melted margarine or butter and allowing phyllo to extend up the sides of the pan. Sprinkle about *1½ cups* of the filling over the phyllo in the pan. Repeat layering phyllo and filling 2 more times.

Layer remaining phyllo sheets in the pan, brushing each sheet with margarine or butter. Drizzle any remaining margarine or butter over top layer. Trim edges of phyllo to fit pan. Using a sharp knife, cut through all layers to make triangle- or diamond-shaped pieces or squares. Bake in a 325° oven for 45 to 50 minutes or till golden. Slightly cool baklava in its pan on a wire rack.

Meanwhile, in a medium saucepan stir together the 1½ cups sugar, honey, lemon peel, lemon juice, stick cinnamon, and 1 cup *water*. Bring to boiling. Reduce heat and simmer, uncovered, for 20 minutes. Remove cinnamon. Pour honey mixture over warm baklava in the pan. Cool completely. Makes about 60 pieces.

Pecan-Coconut Baklava: Prepare Baklava as directed at left, *except* omit the walnut filling. For the pecan-coconut filling, stir together 3 cups finely chopped *pecans,* 1 cup *coconut,* ⅓ cup packed *brown sugar,* 1 teaspoon ground *cinnamon,* and ¼ teaspoon ground *nutmeg.*

Storing Strudels and Phyllo Pastries

Strudels do not store well and should be eaten the same day they are made.

However, most phyllo pastries can be stored. The filling determines whether or not they need to be refrigerated. (Phyllo pastry recipes with cream cheese or pudding fillings, for instance, need to be stored tightly covered in the refrigerator.)

Phyllo cookies, such as Baklava, Choclava, and Chocolate-Tipped Fans (see recipes at left and on pages 285 and 287), may be stored in an airtight container at room temperature for 2 or 3 days. For longer storage, place the phyllo cookies in an airtight container or freezer bag, then seal, label, and freeze for up to 3 months. Thaw the phyllo cookies, covered, at room temperature.

Choclava

Baklava + 2 chocolates = 1 terrific dessert.

  4 cups (1 pound) walnuts, finely chopped
  1 cup miniature semisweet chocolate pieces
  ¾ cup sugar
1½ teaspoons ground cinnamon
1¼ cups margarine *or* butter, melted
  1 16-ounce package frozen phyllo dough,
      thawed
  ¾ cup orange juice
  ½ cup sugar
  ½ cup honey
  2 squares (2 ounces) semisweet chocolate

For filling, in a large mixing bowl stir together walnuts, chocolate pieces, the ¾ cup sugar, and cinnamon. Set filling aside.

Brush the bottom of a 15x10x1-inch baking pan with some of the melted margarine or butter. Unfold phyllo. Layer about *one-fourth* of the phyllo sheets in the pan, brushing each sheet with margarine or butter and allowing the phyllo to extend up sides of pan. Sprinkle about *2 cups* of the filling over phyllo in the pan. Repeat layering phyllo and filling 2 more times.

Layer remaining phyllo sheets in pan, brushing each sheet with margarine or butter. Drizzle any remaining margarine over top layer. Trim edges of phyllo to fit pan. Using a sharp knife, cut through all layers to make triangle- or diamond-shaped pieces or squares. Bake in a 325° oven for 45 to 50 minutes or till golden. Slightly cool in pan on rack.

Meanwhile, in a medium saucepan stir together orange juice, the ½ cup sugar, honey, and ½ cup *water*. Bring to boiling. Reduce heat and simmer, uncovered, for 20 minutes. Pour over warm choclava in pan. Cool completely.

In a heavy small saucepan heat and stir chocolate squares and 2 tablespoons *water* over low heat till smooth. Drizzle over choclava. Makes about 60 pieces.

Apricot Cups

These petite cheesecake cups are ideal to serve at a buffet. (Pictured on page 286.)

  1 8-ounce package cream cheese, softened
  ⅓ cup sugar
  1 tablespoon lemon juice
  1 egg
  ¼ cup apricot *or* peach preserves
  6 18x12-inch sheets frozen phyllo dough,
      thawed
  ¼ cup margarine *or* butter, melted
  ¼ cup apricot *or* peach preserves

Grease twenty-four 1¾-inch muffin cups. Set muffin cups aside.

For filling, in a medium mixing bowl beat the cream cheese, sugar, and lemon juice with an electric mixer on low to medium speed till creamy. Add the egg and beat just till combined. Stir in the ¼ cup apricot or peach preserves. Set filling aside.

Unfold phyllo dough. Place *one* sheet of phyllo dough on a waxed-paper-lined cutting board, then brush with some of the melted margarine or butter. Top with a second sheet of phyllo, then brush with more margarine or butter. Repeat layering with remaining phyllo sheets and margarine or butter. Using a sharp knife, cut the stack *crosswise* into six 3-inch-wide strips. Then cut the stack *lengthwise* into fourths, forming twenty-four 3-inch squares.

Carefully press phyllo squares into the prepared muffin cups. Spoon *1 tablespoon* of the filling into *each* phyllo cup. Bake in a 375° oven about 20 minutes or till phyllo is golden. Cool in the muffin cups for 5 minutes. Remove phyllo cups from the muffin cups and completely cool on a wire rack.

Spoon about *½ teaspoon* preserves on top of *each* cup. Store, covered, in the refrigerator for up to 2 days. Makes 24.

**Chocolate-Tipped
Fans**

Apricot Cups
(see recipe, page 285)

Blueberry Tarts

Blueberry Tarts

For the garnish, use a vegetable peeler to cut thin strips of orange peel. Then twist the strips into loose knots or curls.

- **8 18x12-inch sheets frozen phyllo dough, thawed**
- **⅓ cup margarine *or* butter, melted**
- **½ cup sugar**
- **1 tablespoon cornstarch**
- **4 cups fresh blueberries *or* one 16-ounce package frozen blueberries**
- **½ teaspoon vanilla**
- **¼ teaspoon finely shredded orange peel**
- **½ cup whipping cream**
- **6 orange peel strips (optional)**

Grease six 6-ounce custard cups. Set cups aside. Unfold phyllo dough. Place *one* sheet of phyllo on a waxed-paper-lined cutting board, then brush with some of the melted margarine or butter. Top with a second sheet of phyllo, then brush with more margarine. Repeat layering with the remaining phyllo and margarine. Using a sharp knife, cut the stack *crosswise* into six 3-inch-wide strips. Then cut *lengthwise* into thirds, forming eighteen 4x3-inch rectangles.

Press *three* rectangles into *each* prepared custard cup with shorter edges overlapping in the bottoms of the cups. Place cups in a 15x10x1-inch baking pan. Bake in a 350° oven for 15 to 18 minutes or till golden. Cool phyllo shells in custard cups on a wire rack.

Meanwhile, in a large saucepan stir together sugar and cornstarch. Add blueberries and ¼ cup *water*. Cook and stir over medium heat till thickened and bubbly. Cook and stir for 2 minutes more. Remove from heat. Stir in vanilla and shredded orange peel. Cool about 15 minutes. Spoon blueberry mixture into baked phyllo shells. Chill tarts for 1 to 4½ hours.

To serve, in a small mixing bowl beat whipping cream till stiff peaks form. Remove tarts from custard cups. Spoon whipped cream on top of the tarts. If desired, garnish with orange peel strips. Serves 6.

Chocolate-Tipped Fans

- **6 18x12-inch sheets frozen phyllo dough, thawed**
- **¼ cup margarine *or* butter, melted**
- **½ cup semisweet chocolate pieces**
- **1 tablespoon shortening**
- **½ teaspoon finely shredded orange peel**
- **¼ teaspoon ground cinnamon**
- **⅛ teaspoon ground nutmeg**
- **¼ cup coconut *or* very finely chopped pistachio nuts, pecans, *or* walnuts**

Unfold phyllo dough. Place *one* sheet of phyllo dough on a waxed-paper-lined cutting board, then brush with some of the melted margarine or butter. Top with a second sheet of phyllo, then brush with more margarine or butter. Top with a third sheet of phyllo dough, then brush with more margarine or butter. (Cover remaining sheets and set aside.)

Using a sharp knife, cut stack *crosswise* into five 3½-inch-wide strips. Then cut *lengthwise* in half, making ten 6x3½-inch rectangles. Starting at a short end, fold each rectangle accordion-style, making ¾-inch folds. Pinch folds together at one end. Spread the folds apart at the other end, forming a fan shape.

Place fans on an ungreased baking sheet. Bake in a 350° oven for 7 to 8 minutes or till golden. Carefully remove fans from baking sheet and cool on a wire rack. Repeat stacking and forming fans with remaining sheets of phyllo and margarine or butter.

In a small saucepan heat chocolate pieces and shortening over low heat just till melted, stirring occasionally. Remove from heat and stir in orange peel, cinnamon, and nutmeg. Dip about ¼ inch of the wide ends of the fans in the melted chocolate, then dip ends in coconut or finely chopped nuts. Place fans on a wire rack till chocolate is set. Makes 20.

Pudding in Chocolate-Nut Cups

½ cup sugar
2 tablespoons cornstarch
2 cups milk
2 beaten egg yolks
6 tablespoons margarine *or* butter
1 teaspoon vanilla
1 teaspoon finely shredded lemon peel
1 cup ground pecans *or* walnuts
½ of a 4-ounce package German sweet
   chocolate, grated
2 tablespoons sugar
6 18x12-inch sheets frozen phyllo dough,
   thawed
   Chopped pecans *or* walnuts

For pudding, in a heavy medium saucepan combine the ½ cup sugar, cornstarch, and ¼ teaspoon *salt*. Stir in milk. Cook and stir till thickened. Cook and stir 2 minutes more. Remove from heat. Gradually stir *1 cup* of the mixture into egg yolks. Return all to saucepan. Cook and stir 2 minutes. Remove from heat. Add *2 tablespoons* margarine or butter, vanilla, and peel, then stir till smooth. Pour into a bowl. Cover surface with plastic wrap. Chill without stirring.

In a bowl combine ground nuts, grated chocolate, and 2 tablespoons sugar. Grease twelve 2½-inch muffin cups. Set nut mixture and muffin cups aside.

Melt remaining margarine or butter. Unfold phyllo. Place *one* sheet of phyllo on a waxed-paper-lined cutting board, then brush with some of the melted margarine. Sprinkle evenly with about *3 tablespoons* of the nut mixture. Repeat layering 4 times. Top with remaining phyllo. Brush with margarine or butter. Using a sharp knife, cut stack *crosswise* into four 4½-inch-wide strips. Then cut *lengthwise* into thirds, forming twelve 4x4½-inch rectangles. Press rectangles into prepared cups. Bake in a 350° oven for 15 to 18 minutes or till golden. Remove phyllo cups from pan and cool on a rack. Spoon pudding into phyllo cups. Sprinkle with nuts. Chill up to 4 hours. Serves 12.

Cheese-Nut Triangles

Serve warm or cool for a snack, brunch, or dessert.

¼ cup mixed dried fruit bits
2 beaten egg yolks
1 cup ricotta cheese
½ cup sifted powdered sugar
½ cup chopped walnuts
12 18x12-inch sheets frozen phyllo dough,
   thawed
½ cup margarine *or* butter, melted

For filling, place fruit bits in a small mixing bowl. Pour enough *boiling water* over dried fruit bits to cover them, then let stand for 10 minutes. Drain fruit bits. In a small mixing bowl stir together the egg yolks, ricotta cheese, and powdered sugar till smooth. Stir in fruit bits and walnuts. Set filling aside.

Unfold phyllo dough. Using a sharp knife, cut sheets *lengthwise* in half into 18x6-inch rectangles. Place *one* of the half sheets on a waxed-paper-lined surface. (Cover the remaining phyllo dough with a damp towel, then set aside.)

Lightly brush the half sheet of phyllo with some of the melted margarine or butter. Fold the sheet *lengthwise* in half, making an 18x3-inch strip. Brush again with more margarine or butter.

Spoon *2 rounded teaspoons* of filling about 1 inch from a short end of *each* strip of phyllo. Fold the end over the filling at a 45-degree angle. Continue folding to form a triangle that encloses the filling. Brush the folded triangle with melted margarine or butter. Place on an ungreased baking sheet.

Repeat with the remaining phyllo, margarine or butter, and filling. Bake in a 375° oven for 15 to 18 minutes or till golden. Cool triangles on a wire rack. Serve warm or cool. Makes 24.

Nutrition Analysis

Recipes	Servings	Calories	Protein (g)	Carbohydrates (g)	Total Fat (g)	Saturated Fat (g)	Cholesterol (mg)	Sodium (mg)
Apple Dumplings, 253	4	861	9	100	49	15	41	497
Apple Pie, 236	8	394	4	56	18	4	0	135
Apple Strudel Ring, 281	12	295	3	29	19	7	45	191
Apricot Cups, 285	24	120	2	17	5	3	19	76
Baklava, 284	60	139	2	15	9	1	0	78
Banana Cream Pie, 256	8	416	9	64	15	4	115	172
Blueberry Tarts, 287	6	372	4	51	18	7	27	251
Cheddar-Onion Puffs, 266	10	152	5	10	10	3	91	185
Cheese-Nut Triangles, 288	24	115	3	11	7	2	21	104
Cheesy Twists, 277	56	46	1	3	3	2	12	43
Cherry-Almond Strudel, 282	12	277	4	35	14	3	18	189
Cherry-Brandy Pie, 243	8	448	4	69	18	4	0	135
Cherry Lattice Pie, 242	8	431	4	62	19	5	0	159
Cherry Pie, 243	8	439	4	68	18	4	0	135
Choclava, 285	60	155	2	16	10	2	0	78
Chocolate-Apricot Éclairs, 264	12	339	6	33	21	9	170	224
Chocolate-Pecan Pie, 254	8	556	6	67	32	7	80	199
Chocolate-Tipped Fans, 287	20	72	1	7	5	2	0	55
Choose-a-Berry Pie, 238	8	389	4	55	18	4	0	134
Cinnamon Palmiers, 270	60	46	0	5	3	2	8	33
Cinnamon Pastry, 234	8	147	2	15	9	2	0	67
Coconut Cream Pie, 256	8	433	9	60	19	8	115	174
Coconut Custard Pie, 254	8	253	5	30	13	4	107	133
Coconut-Oatmeal Pie, 255	8	471	6	69	21	6	80	199
Country-Style Peach Tart, 246	8	276	3	41	12	3	2	98
Cranberry-Cherry Pie, 242	8	472	4	76	18	4	0	143
Cranberry Strudel, 279	12	227	3	34	10	2	18	123
Cream Cheese-Pineapple Strudel, 281	12	224	4	23	13	6	56	174
Cream Cheese Strudel, 281	12	210	4	19	13	6	56	174
Cream Horns, 272	12	329	5	29	22	13	125	233
Cream Puffs, 263	10	341	7	26	23	9	204	266
Cream Turnovers, 272	18	219	3	19	14	8	83	156
Crumb-Topped Apple Pie, 236	8	378	3	60	15	3	0	135
Custard Pie, 254	8	232	5	28	11	3	107	132
Dark-Chocolate Cream Pie, 256	8	455	10	63	20	8	115	172
Dutch Letters, 274	20	362	5	37	22	12	60	271
Easy Coconut Diamonds, 273	6	206	4	18	13	1	36	204
Easy Dutch Letters, 274	20	305	5	34	17	0	0	242
Fig-Nut Tarts, 245	16	183	2	24	9	2	6	88
Four-Egg-White Meringue, 257	8	56	2	13	0	0	0	38
Gingerberry Lattice Pie, 241	8	577	4	78	29	11	41	147
Ham 'n' Pastry Pinwheels, 277	24	54	2	4	3	0	3	143
Ham 'n' Pastry Twists, 277	48	35	1	2	2	0	3	69
Ham-Onion Bites, 266	35	37	2	4	1	0	32	92
Lemon Meringue Pie, 257	8	404	5	68	14	3	80	145
Linzer Torte, 260	8	547	8	67	29	4	80	209
Maple Pecan Pie, 255	8	530	6	61	31	5	80	185

Recipes	Servings	Calories	Protein (g)	Carbohydrates (g)	Total Fat (g)	Saturated Fat (g)	Cholesterol (mg)	Sodium (mg)
Meringue for Pie, 257	8	42	1	10	0	0	0	25
Mexican Appetizer Torte, 261	16	258	6	24	16	5	23	376
Milk-Chocolate Cream Pie, 256	8	431	9	60	18	7	115	173
Mince-Apple Pie, 245	8	518	4	85	19	4	0	397
Mince-Orange Pie, 245	8	492	5	78	19	4	0	394
Mince-Peach Pie, 245	8	534	5	90	19	4	0	400
Mince-Pear Pie, 245	8	493	4	79	19	4	0	394
Mixed-Fruit Almond Strudel, 282	12	272	4	34	14	3	18	197
Napoleons, 276	16	315	4	44	14	8	87	167
Nectarine Dumplings, 252	4	486	8	60	25	7	11	163
Old-Fashioned Raisin Pie, 235	8	506	6	75	22	5	0	147
Palmiers, 270	60	46	0	5	3	2	8	33
Pastry for Double-Crust Pie, 235	8	266	3	24	18	4	0	134
Pastry for Single-Crust Pie, 234	8	146	2	15	9	2	0	67
Patty Shells, 270	18	132	1	10	10	6	26	110
Peach Pie, 246	8	382	5	53	18	4	0	135
Peanut Pie, 255	8	551	11	67	29	6	80	296
Pear-Date Pie, 243	8	424	4	71	15	3	0	142
Pecan-Coconut Baklava, 284	60	132	1	14	8	1	0	78
Pecan Pastry, 234	8	171	2	16	11	2	0	67
Pecan Pie, 255	8	544	6	66	31	5	80	198
Plum Dumplings, 252	6	249	5	42	7	4	19	127
Pudding in Chocolate-Nut Cups, 288	12	258	4	25	17	3	39	179
Pumpkin Pie, 255	8	291	7	39	12	4	87	120
Raspberry Pie, 240	8	362	4	47	18	4	0	134
Rhubarb Pie, 241	8	389	4	54	18	4	0	137
Sour Cream Apple Pie, 247	8	435	5	62	19	7	66	136
Sour Cream Peach Pie, 247	8	438	6	63	19	7	66	137
Strawberries 'n' Cream Tart, 258	8	284	5	43	11	3	85	121
Strawberry 'n' Chocolate Cream Puffs, 264	12	272	3	22	19	11	127	76
Strawberry-Rhubarb Pie, 240	8	422	4	63	18	4	0	137
Strawberry Strudel Torte, 283	6	461	5	50	28	9	63	323
Strawberry Tart,	8	195	2	22	11	7	29	131
Sweet Cherry-Nut Tart, 260	8	389	5	50	21	4	30	96
Sweetheart Torte, 261	8	433	5	36	30	12	42	161
Swiss-Dill Puffs, 266	10	151	5	10	10	3	90	164
Tri-Berry Pie, 238	8	360	4	48	18	4	0	136
Upside-Down Apple Pie, 237	8	517	5	64	28	6	0	209
Vanilla Cream Éclairs, 265	12	338	6	29	23	9	173	235
Vanilla Cream Pie, 256	8	377	8	54	14	4	115	171
Whole Wheat Pastry for Double-Crust Pie, 235	8	260	4	23	18	4	0	134
Whole Wheat Pastry for Single-Crust Pie, 234	8	142	2	14	9	2	0	67

We've analyzed the nutritional content of each recipe using the first choice if ingredient substitutions are given, and using the first serving size if a serving range is given. We've omitted optional ingredients from the analysis.

BAKING BASICS

Whether you're making a double-crust pie, mixing up cookies, or baking a loaf of bread, there are some baking basics that can improve your products.

The keys to baking success are here—everything from facts on ingredients and measuring to features of equipment and bakeware. Turn to these pages of useful information whenever you have a baking question.

Also, look to this section for easy ways to enhance your baked goods—discover successful methods for melting chocolate, garnishing ideas using off-the-shelf ingredients, techniques for piping frosting, and the secret to painting chocolate leaves. Once you've mastered these tips, you'll be able to personalize your baked products in a number of ways.

Baking Ingredients

Do you know . . . the difference between baking powder and baking soda? . . . another name for light cream? . . . what size eggs to use for the recipes in this book? The following notes give you the basics about frequently used ingredients.

FLOUR is one of the most common ingredients used in baking. Some flours are made from soft wheats, others from hard wheats, and still others are a combination of the two. Available in many varieties, each type of flour gives a different flavor or texture to baked products.

All-purpose flour, a blend of soft- and hard-wheat flours, serves as a multipurpose flour in many baked goods. Store it in an airtight container at room temperature.

Cake flour is the flour many bakers choose when making angel and chiffon cakes. Since it's made from a soft wheat, it produces a tender, delicate cake. However, all recipes in this book were perfected using all-purpose flour. If you would like to use cake flour and it's not an option in the recipe, sift it before measuring; use 1 cup *plus* 2 tablespoons cake flour for every 1 cup all-purpose flour.

Self-rising flour is an all-purpose flour that contains baking powder, baking soda, and salt. You may use it as a substitute for all-purpose flour in quick bread recipes. *Be sure,* though, to omit the salt, baking powder, and baking soda from the recipe.

Specialty flours, such as wheat, rye, oat, and graham, generally are combined with all-purpose flour in baked products. Because whole grain flours may become rancid quickly, be sure to store them in the refrigerator or freezer.

SWEETENERS are essential when it comes to baking. They add flavor, tenderness, and a bit of browning to baked goods.

Granulated sugar is used more than any other form of sweetener for baking. It is made from sugar cane or sugar beets. In this cookbook, it's referred to as "sugar."

Brown sugar, a less refined form of cane or beet sugar, has a special flavor and moistness that comes from the molasses that clings to the granules. It is available in "light" and "dark" varieties; the dark brown sugar has a stronger flavor. The recipes in this cookbook were tested using light brown sugar, unless specified.

If you run low on brown sugar, you may substitute granulated sugar, measure for measure, except in items where color and flavor might be important, such as a caramel sauce. To use brown sugar instead of granulated sugar in baked products that use baking powder or baking soda, add ¼ teaspoon more baking soda for each 1 cup brown sugar.

Powdered sugar, often referred to as confectioners' sugar, is crushed granulated sugar with cornstarch added to prevent lumping. We recommend sifting powdered sugar before using. Do not use as a substitute for granulated sugar.

Honey, made by bees from flower nectar, is sweeter than sugar. In baked products it not only adds moisture and sweetness, but also a characteristic flavor. Although available in whipped forms, for the recipes in this cookbook that call for honey, use pure unwhipped honey.

Corn syrup has half the sweetness of sugar and is available in light and dark forms. Dark corn syrup has a stronger flavor than light corn syrup.

FATS AND OILS are added for flavor and tenderness in baked products such as cakes and cookies. In general, fats are solid at room temperature, while oils are liquid. Since fat has the ability to incorporate air and oils do not, the success of a recipe depends on your using the product specified.

Butter and margarine give flavor to baked goods. Butter is made from the natural sweet cream of milk and must contain 80 percent butterfat. Margarine consists of 80 percent vegetable or animal fat and is made to resemble butter. In baking, if you choose margarine instead of butter, be sure to choose a stick product labeled margarine and avoid stick or tub products labeled spreads.

Hydrogenated vegetable shortening, referred to as shortening in this book, is solid at room temperature. It's made by processing oils, such as soy or palm, until they have a creamy, airy texture. Shortening doesn't need to be refrigerated.

Lard is rendered pork fat. It's often used for tender, flaky pie crusts and biscuits. Lard is not recommended for making cakes or other products that require beating.

Cooking oils and flavored oils are not able to hold air when creamed, so they cannot be used interchangeably with solid fats. Vegetable oil, generally made from corn, soybeans, sunflowers, or peanuts, is light in color with a mild flavor. Nut oils, such as walnut oil, have a pronounced nutty flavor and sometimes are darker in color.

LEAVENERS are yeast, baking soda, or baking powder. They cause a product to rise in the oven. In some products no leavening ingredients are needed. For example, in cream puffs and popovers water turns to steam, causing the products to expand. In angel cakes and meringues, the air in the egg-white foam expands and leavens the products.

Yeast is a microscopic plant that causes bread to rise by producing carbon dioxide bubbles that are trapped in the dough. Yeast also adds flavor and aroma. All recipes in this cookbook were tested using active dry yeast. In some yeast bread recipes you may use quick-rising active dry yeast as a substitute for active dry yeast (see tip, page 45).

Baking soda reacts with acid ingredients such as buttermilk, brown sugar, or molasses to release carbon dioxide bubbles. Because baking soda and acid begin to react as soon as liquid is added, a product containing only soda should be baked immediately.

Baking powder, a combination of baking soda and an acid ingredient, starts to produce carbon dioxide bubbles when it's combined with a liquid or dough. However, it doesn't produce its full degree of leavening until it's heated.

EGGS are used to thicken mixtures, bind ingredients, or form a structure in baked goods. All recipes in this cookbook were perfected using "large" eggs.

MILK AND MILK PRODUCTS used in baking provide moisture, flavor, and color. You may use whole, low-fat, and skim milk interchangeably in baking since they vary only in fat content and in the richness of flavor they lend foods.

Buttermilk is made commercially by adding bacteria to skim milk. Sour milk can be substituted for buttermilk. You can make sour milk by combining milk with vinegar or lemon juice (see substitution chart, page 296).

Whipping cream contains 30 to 49 percent fat. To speed up whipping, use a chilled bowl and chilled beaters when whipping the cream.

Light cream or table cream contains 10 to 30 percent fat. Since light cream will not whip, you can't substitute it for whipping cream. Half-and-half, a mixture of milk and cream, can be substituted for light cream.

Evaporated milk is milk with 60 percent of the water removed and is sold in cans. Do not use this form of milk as a substitute for other milk products.

Sweetened condensed milk has about half the amount of water as regular milk and has sugar added. It, too, is sold in cans.

Nonfat dry milk, a product with both the fat and water removed, is sold as a powder. You may mix it with water according to the package directions to form milk. Some of our recipes call for it as a dry ingredient to add richness.

Nuts and Dried Fruits

Pack some pizzazz into your favorite baked goods with nuts and dried fruits.

NUTS, whether they're whole or chopped, plain or salted, add a special touch to baked products, not to mention an appealing crunch and a mild to rich flavor. Stir a handful or two into a batter or dough, or use a sprinkling as a garnish.

Because nuts are somewhat high in oil, they can become rancid quickly. Store unopened packages in a cool dark place. Store opened packages in an airtight container in the refrigerator for 6 months or in the freezer for 2 years.

DRIED FRUITS are great for adding a sweet flavor and specks of color to baked goods.

Because dried fruits have very little moisture, a batter or dough sometimes isn't moist enough to soften them, and they'll remain chewy. If that's the case, soak them in hot water, fruit juice, or liqueur to soften them before adding them to the batter. In this cookbook, the recipes that require soaking the dried fruits have this step incorporated into the method.

To store dried fruits, place unopened packages in a cool, dry place or in the refrigerator. Store opened packages in an airtight container in the refrigerator or freezer for 6 to 8 months.

Almonds *have a rich but mild flavor that enables them to be used in both sweet and savory baking. They're available with or without the skin (blanched) as whole, sliced, and slivered nuts.*

Cashews *are kidney-shaped nuts with a rich, buttery flavor. Their flavor and crunchy texture make them a favorite not only of snackers, but also of bakers.*

Hickory nuts *resemble walnuts. However, these small nuts have a rich flavor similiar to that of toasted pecans. They are available through mail order catalogs or speciality shops.*

Black walnuts *are rich and oily nuts with a very intense flavor. If you choose to use them in a recipe, the flavor will be distinctively different than that from English walnuts.*

Hazelnuts, *also known as filberts, are small and round. Their mild, sweet flavor makes them a popular choice for nut crusts and easy garnishes.*

Macadamia nuts *have a meat that is smooth and round, creamy beige in color, and very rich in flavor. Their popularity is growing as an ingredient in cookies.*

Peanuts *commonly are available in many varieties for both snacking and baking. Their rich, buttery flavor is intensified by roasting.*

Pine nuts, *also known as pignolias, are seeds from a variety of pine trees. The pale yellow to creamy white kernels are sometimes toasted to enhance their slightly pine flavor.*

Walnuts, *other than the black walnut variety, are called English walnuts. More commonly used in baking than black walnuts, these walnuts have a milder flavor.*

Dried cherries, cranberries, and blueberries *are available through mail order catalogs or specialty shops. The drying has preserved their wonderful sweet to tart natural flavors.*

Prunes, raisins, and currants *differ in both size and flavor. Prunes are larger and available pitted. Raisins and currants, sometimes used interchangeably, differ mostly in size (currants being smaller).*

Pecans *are oily textured nuts with a very delicate flavor. It's quite common to use pecans and walnuts interchangeably in baked goods.*

Pistachio nuts *feature a pale green meat inside a medium brown skin and usually are available in split shells. Sometimes the shells are dyed red. The mild flavor is a superb accent to sweet and savory cooking.*

Dried apples, apricots, pears, and peaches *are available in most grocery stores. You can use these fruits whole or chopped.*

Dates and figs *come in a variety of forms. When a recipe calls for "dates, snipped," cut up whole dates rather than using the purchased sugar-coated chopped dates. Figs are available in light or dark varieties.*

Candied fruit *is available as citron, peels, mixed fruit, cherries, and pineapple. Used to add color and flavor to fruit cakes, quick breads, and cookies, candied fruits are most commonly used during the holiday season.*

Emergency Substitutions

To get the best results in baking, use the ingredients called for in the recipe. But if you're in the middle of making a baked product when you discover you're short on sugar or out of baking soda, check the chart at the right for handy substitutions. Some substitutions may cause a change in flavor or texture of the baked product. So, use these substitutions only as a last resort.

Ingredient	Substitution
1 teaspoon baking powder	½ teaspoon cream of tartar *plus* ¼ teaspoon baking soda
1 cup sugar	1 cup packed brown sugar
1 cup cake flour	1 cup *minus* 2 tablespoons all-purpose flour
1 cup self-rising flour	1 cup all-purpose flour *plus* 1 teaspoon baking powder, ½ teaspoon salt, and ¼ teaspoon baking soda
1 cup whole milk	½ cup evaporated milk *plus* ½ cup water, *or* 1 cup water *plus* ⅓ cup nonfat dry milk powder
1 cup light cream	1 tablespoon melted margarine *or* butter *plus* enough milk to make 1 cup
1 cup buttermilk	1 tablespoon lemon juice *or* vinegar *plus* enough milk to make 1 cup (let stand 5 minutes before using), *or* 1 cup milk *plus* 1¾ teaspoons cream of tartar
1 cup honey	1¼ cups sugar *plus* ¼ cup liquid
1 cup corn syrup	1 cup sugar *plus* ¼ cup liquid
1 teaspoon apple pie spice	½ teaspoon ground cinnamon *plus* ¼ teaspoon ground nutmeg, ⅛ teaspoon ground allspice, and dash ground ginger
1 teaspoon pumpkin pie spice	½ teaspoon ground cinnamon *plus* ¼ teaspoon ground ginger, ¼ teaspoon ground allspice, and ⅛ teaspoon ground nutmeg
1 square (1 ounce) unsweetened chocolate	3 tablespoons unsweetened cocoa powder *plus* 1 tablespoon shortening *or* cooking oil
1 square (1 ounce) semisweet chocolate	1 square (1 ounce) unsweetened chocolate *plus* 1 tablespoon sugar, *or* 3 tablespoons semisweet chocolate pieces
6 squares (6 ounces) semisweet chocolate	6 squares (6 ounces) unsweetened chocolate *plus* ⅓ cup sugar, *or* 1 cup semisweet chocolate pieces
4 squares (4 ounces) German sweet chocolate	¼ cup unsweetened cocoa powder *plus* ⅓ cup sugar and 3 tablespoons shortening

Measuring and Temperature Tips

Both correctly measuring ingredients and using the proper oven temperature are important in achieving accurate recipe results. However, not all ingredients are measured the same way, and not all recipes are baked at the same temperature. Follow these pointers for great baked goods every time.

WHEN MEASURING LIQUIDS, use a standard glass or clear plastic liquid measuring cup. Place the cup on a level surface; bend down so your eye is level with the marking you wish

to read. Fill the cup up to the marking. Don't lift the cup off the counter to your eye; your hand is not as steady as the countertop.

WHEN MEASURING DRY INGREDIENTS, use a dry measuring cup that is the exact capacity you wish to measure. Using a spoon, lightly pile the ingredient into the cup. Then, using a metal spatula, level off the measure. Never pack dry ingredients except brown sugar. You should pack brown sugar into the cup just enough that it holds the shape of the measure when turned out.

Is sifting necessary? Years ago it was essential to sift flour to remove any lumps and to lighten it enough for accurate measuring. But today's all-purpose flour is no longer lumpy and compact. That's why simply stirring it before measuring is sufficient. Stirring works well for most other flours, too.

One notable exception, however, is *cake flour*. Cake flour is very soft and tends to pack down in shipping. We recommend that you do sift it to remove any lumps and to lighten it before measuring.

What's a dash? A dash is a measure of less than ⅛ teaspoon (the smallest amount you can accurately measure using standard measuring spoons). To get a dash, just add a quick shake or a sprinkle of the ingredient. When a dash is used, it's usually for flavor, and the actual amount is up to you.

WHEN MONITORING OVEN TEMPERATURE, use an oven thermometer. Since temperature variances of up to 25° are quite common, it's a good idea to check the internal temperature of your oven before baking. If the temperature's too high or low, adjust the settings accordingly.

Preheating the oven will give you the best results when making baked goods. *All recipe timings in this cookbook are based on a preheated oven.*

If the appearance or texture of a baked product does not seem correct, review the oven manufacturer's instructions for the proper procedure in preheating your oven. Also, after preheating your oven, double-check the oven's internal temperature with an oven thermometer.

Mixing Equipment And Bakeware

You'll get the best results with your baked goods if you use the right mixing equipment and bakeware. Here's what to look for.

ELECTRIC MIXERS help to ease the work in baking. The *portable electric mixer* (hand-held mixer) is great to use for light jobs and short mixing periods. But for heavy-duty jobs and long mixing periods, a *freestanding electric mixer* works best.

BAKEWARE is made in an array of materials—aluminum, tin, stainless steel, black steel, and pottery. The material it's made from, and the finish it has, influences the quality of baked products. Shiny bakeware reflects heat, making the browning process slower. In contrast, dark bakeware and bakeware with a dull finish absorb more heat, thus increasing browning of baked goods.

Use the following bakeware tips as guidelines to get the results you're looking for when baking.

☐ For a piecrust that's nicely browned underneath as well as on top, bake your pie in a dull aluminum or tin pan or glass pie plate.

☐ If you bake your cake in a shiny aluminum, tin, or stainless steel pan, the cake crust will be lighter than one baked in a dull aluminum or tin pan or a glass dish.

☐ Cookies baked on new or shiny cookie sheets, as well as on insulated cookie sheets, do not brown as quickly, tend to spread more, and may be softer set than those baked on dull or dark cookie sheets.

☐ Breads baked in dull aluminum or tin pans or glass dishes will have nicely browned crusts that are somewhat crisp. Black steel pans, however, will give the bread a crisp dark crust. You'll see black steel pans most commonly used for French bread, since this is a bread that you want crisp.

☐ Popovers work well in individual custard cups or special dark-colored popover pans.

Index of Baking Basics

Simply Chocolate

Whether you nestle it in cookie dough, drizzle it over cakes, or sprinkle it over frosting, chocolate reigns as an all-ages, American favorite. You'll find the next three pages chock-full of tidbits on everything from melting chocolate to garnishing with chocolate.

MELTING CHOCOLATE is easy with any of these methods. Choose the method that suits the equipment you have available.

Direct Heat: One of the most common and convenient methods for melting chocolate is using direct heat. Place the chocolate in a heavy saucepan over very low heat, stirring constantly till the chocolate *begins* to melt. Immediately remove the chocolate from the heat and stir till smooth.

Double Boiler: The best way to avoid scorching chocolate when melting it is to use this method. Place water in the bottom pan of a double boiler so that it comes to within ½ inch of the upper pan (water should not touch the upper pan). Put the chocolate in the upper pan and place the upper pan over the water in the lower pan.

Then place the entire double boiler over low heat. Stir constantly till chocolate is melted. (The water in the bottom of the double boiler should not come to boiling while the chocolate is melting.)

Microwave Oven: A handy way to melt chocolate is to use your microwave oven. Heat chocolate in a microwave-safe bowl, custard cup, or measuring cup, uncovered, on 100% power (high) till soft enough to stir smooth. Stir every minute during heating. (You may not be able to tell if chocolate is melted until you stir it.)

For squares, in a 1-cup measuring cup, allow 1 to 2 minutes for 1 square (1 ounce) and 1½ to 2½ minutes for 2 squares (2 ounces).

For chocolate pieces, allow 1 to 2 minutes for ½ cup in a 1-cup measuring cup, 1½ to 2½ minutes for one 6-ounce package (1 cup) in a 2-cup measuring cup, and 2 to 3 minutes for one 12-ounce package (2 cups) in a 4-cup measuring cup.

To assure success in whatever method you choose, follow these guidelines.

☐ The equipment you use for melting chocolate must be completely dry. Any moisture on the utensils or in the container may cause the chocolate to stiffen. If this happens, stir in ½ to 1 teaspoon shortening or oil for every ounce of melted chocolate.

☐ To avoid scorching the chocolate, don't turn up the heat to speed up the melting process. Coarsely chopping the squares before melting will enable you to melt the chocolate as quickly and evenly as possible.

☐ Stir the chocolate while it is melting since semisweet, sweet, and milk chocolate hold their shape while melting.

STORING CHOCOLATE properly will keep it from developing a gray film (called "bloom") and will prevent moisture from forming on it after it's chilled.

Wrap the chocolate in foil, then in plastic wrap, and place it in a cool, dry place. The ideal storage conditions are between 60° and 78°, with less than 50 percent relative humidity. You also can refrigerate chocolate. Just make sure to wrap the chocolate tightly so odors are not absorbed and so moisture doesn't form on its surface when it's removed from the refrigerator. Chocolate becomes hard and brittle when it's chilled, so let it stand, tightly wrapped, at room temperature before using.

Although cocoa powder is less sensitive than chocolate, it's still a good idea to store it in a tightly covered container in a cool, dry place. High temperatures and high humidity tend to cause cocoa powder to lump and lose its rich brown color.

Grated Chocolate

Chocolate Cutouts

Chocolate-Dipped Nuts

Chocolate Leaves

Chocolate Curls

CHOCOLATE AND COCOA PRODUCTS are available in a variety of forms. Because they differ in flavor and consistency when melted, always use the type of chocolate called for in the recipe.

Unsweetened chocolate, sometimes referred to as bitter or baking chocolate, is pure chocolate with no sugar or flavoring added.

German sweet chocolate consists of at least 15 percent pure chocolate with extra cocoa butter and sugar added.

Semisweet chocolate is made of pure chocolate, extra cocoa butter, and sugar. It contains at least 35 percent pure chocolate.

Milk chocolate, made of pure chocolate, extra cocoa butter, sugar, and milk solids, contains at least 10 percent pure chocolate and 12 percent milk solids.

White chocolate is composed of sugar, cocoa butter, dry milk solids, and vanillin or vanilla. Because it lacks pure chocolate, it can't legally be called chocolate in the United States. You will find it labeled white baking bars (or pieces) with cocoa butter.

Confectioners' coating is a chocolate-like product with most of the cocoa butter removed and replaced by vegetable fat. It is available in assorted colors and flavors, and sometimes is referred to as "summer coating."

Unsweetened cocoa powder, primarily used for baking, is pure chocolate with most of the cocoa butter removed. Once the cocoa butter is extracted from the pure chocolate, the remaining chocolate solids are ground into a powder.

CHOCOLATE GARNISHES can make the simplest desserts quite showy. To ensure success, make sure you use clean and dry utensils and the recommended kind of chocolate. Once the garnish is made, handle it as little as possible to keep it from melting. If you don't use the garnish immediately, be sure to refrigerate it.

Chocolate curls are easiest to make using milk chocolate, but can be made with white chocolate, too. To make curls, let a bar of chocolate come to room temperature, then carefully draw a vegetable peeler at an angle across the chocolate. For small curls use the narrow side of the chocolate piece and for large curls use the wide surface.

Shaved chocolate can be made using unsweetened, semisweet, German sweet, or white chocolate. Use a vegetable peeler to make short, quick strokes across the surface of a firm chocolate piece.

Grated chocolate also can be made using unsweetened, semisweet, German sweet, or white chocolate. Start with a cool, firm square of chocolate and rub it across the grating section of a

hand-held grater. Select from among the fine or large grating surfaces to get the size you want.

Chocolate leaves should be made using nontoxic fresh leaves such as mint, lemon, ivy, or strawberry. Use melted chocolate (3 ounces makes six small leaves). With a small paint brush, brush several coats of the melted chocolate on the *underside* of each leaf. Wipe off any chocolate on the topside of the leaf. Then place the leaves, chocolate side up, on a waxed-paper-lined baking sheet or a curved surface such as a rolling pin; chill or freeze till hardened. Before using, peel the leaf away from the chocolate.

Chocolate-dipped nuts are easy to make using semisweet or milk chocolate, or confectioners' coating. For large nuts, dip the nut halfway into melted chocolate; let excess chocolate drip off. For small nuts, use a small paintbrush to stroke on the chocolate. Place nuts on waxed paper to dry.

Chocolate cutouts are made by melting together one 6-ounce package semisweet chocolate pieces or 6 ounces white chocolate *and* 1 tablespoon shortening; cool slightly. Pour chocolate mixture onto a waxed-paper-lined baking sheet, spreading 1/8 to 1/4 inch thick. Chill till almost set. Firmly press hors d'oeuvre or small cookie cutters into the chocolate. Chill. Before serving, lift cutouts from baking sheet.

Easy Extras

Perk up cookies, cup-cakes, cakes, or any dessert you wish with some fun-to-do garnishes. These garnishes may look extravagant, but they're simple enough that with a few ingredients from your kitchen cupboard, you can put them together in a matter of minutes. Get some ideas below, then let your creativity flow.

TOASTED NUTS OR COCONUT can add a little pizzazz to all types of desserts. Prepare your favorite frosted cake or cookie recipe and then add a sprinkling of toasted nuts or coconut

evenly over the top. And you don't need to stop there. Try sprinkling the nuts or coconut in a pattern on the top, around the edge, or on each serving.

To toast nuts or coconut, spread them into a thin layer in a shallow baking pan. Bake in a 350° oven for 5 to 10 minutes or till golden brown, stirring once or twice. While you're at it, toast some extra. Place the excess amount in a freezer bag and store it in the freezer until you need some again.

COLORED FROSTINGS can help to brighten up a batch of sugar cookies, a birthday cake, or your favorite cupcakes. With an array of liquid, paste, and powdered food colorings available, you can tint frosting almost any color of the rainbow. Look for liquid food colorings at the supermarket. They are available in the primary colors. Paste and powdered food colorings can be pur-

chased through mail order catalogs or at stores carrying cake decorating supplies. They are available in assorted colors.

To tint a small batch of frosting or to tint frosting a light shade of color, liquid colorings are best because the amount you add will not thin the frosting. However, a large batch of frosting or a deep shade of color requires more coloring to tint. In these cases it's best to use paste or powdered colorings so the frosting doesn't thin. Because paste and powdered colorings are highly concentrated, start with a small amount and mix thoroughly before adding more.

GUMDROP DECORATIONS add a touch of color to baked products. Gumdrops can be used whole, flattened and cut into a variety of shapes such as stars, or rolled up to form three-dimensional shapes such as roses.

To make gumdrop cutouts, sprinkle sugar on a flat surface and place slightly flattened gumdrops, one at a time, on the surface. Then using a rolling pin, roll out the gumdrop. To cut flattened gumdrops into desired shapes, use a knife or hors d'oeurve or small cookie cutters.

To make roses, roll the gumdrops into ovals. Then cut ovals in half crosswise. Starting at one corner, roll up a half-oval diagonally to form rose center. Press on additional half-ovals, curving the outer edges to resemble petals. Trim the base if necessary.

PURCHASED CANDIES, including everything from chocolate-flavored sprinkles to rainbow-colored edible glitter, give cookies a festive look. Sprinkle them on a batch of unbaked cookies and they'll bake right on.

Or, frost a batch of cookies, cupcakes, or a cake and arrange candies in a simple but stunning pattern on top.

You can purchase decorative candies, colored sugars, and colored marzipan at the supermarket. Check mail order catalogs or stores that carry cake decorating supplies for edible glitter and a unique selection of decorative candies and colored sprinkles.

A DUSTING OF POWDERED SUGAR over the tops of cakes or cookies can give you either a simple or an elegant-looking garnish, depending on the technique you use. To sift powdered sugar over a baked product, spoon the powdered sugar into a sifter or sieve. Sift directly onto the cake or cookies.

For a patterned look, place a paper doily or a small craft stencil on top of the baked product. Lightly sift the powdered sugar over the doily or stencil. Remove the doily or stencil carefully.

For chocolate-flavored powdered sugar, in a small bowl combine 2 tablespoons powdered sugar and 1 to 1½ teaspoons unsweetened cocoa powder. Spoon into a sifter or sieve and sift.

DRESS UP THE SIDES OF A CAKE OR TORTE by lightly patting some nuts or coconut onto the frosting- or glaze-covered sides. Whole, slivered, or sliced nuts and flaked, toasted, or tinted coconut add both flavor and texture. Also, candies of all shapes and colors make suitable sidekicks on many cakes and cupcakes.

For a simple side-decorating idea that requires no additional ingredients, just make impressions in the frosting with cookie cutters or the tines of a fork.

Piping Techniques

Jazz up the frosting on a cake by piping on some "extras" with a decorating bag and tips. By using a variety of tips, you can pipe frosting to look like ruffles, hearts, stars, leaves, or just about anything you'd like. The following is a potpourri of piping basics, ranging from how to hold a decorating bag to several decorations you can make using just three basic tips.

DECORATING BAGS come in different sizes and materials. You can find big ones, small ones, cloth ones, plastic-lined ones, and plastic disposable ones, or you can even make your own paper ones (see tip, page 306).

Each type of bag has advantages. Decorating bags that are made from a synthetic material or of plastic-lined cloth are reusable. All you have to do is wash and dry them each time you change the frosting color. On the other hand, plastic disposable and paper decorating bags require no cleaning. Just throw them away when you're finished. Look in supermarkets, mail order catalogs, or any store carrying cake decorating supplies for the kind of decorating bag you prefer.

Holding the bag properly is essential. If you're holding the bag awkwardly, or applying pressure incorrectly, your arm will tire.

To use, fill the bag half to two-thirds full of frosting. Then, fold the corners over and roll the bag down to the frosting level. With your writing hand, grip the bag near the roll above the frosting level with the full end in your palm. Then apply pressure from the *palm* of your hand, forcing frosting toward the tip. Use your other hand to guide the tip of the bag. With a little practice, you'll learn to control the flow of the frosting by changing the pressure.

DECORATING TIPS are available in many shapes and sizes, from basic shapes to specialty shapes. You don't need specialty tips, however, to make a beautifully decorated masterpiece. With a few basic tips and decorating techniques, you can make borders, flowers, leaves, stars . . . the possibilities are endless. To get maximum use out of the basic tips, try some of the ideas below.

Round tips have a simple round opening used for writing and for making dots, lines, beads, and hearts.

☐ To make *dots,* hold the bag at a 90-degree angle (straight up and down) with the tip *almost* touching the surface. Squeeze out a dot of frosting till it's the size you want. Stop pressure and pull away.

☐ For *lines or writing,* hold the bag at a 45-degree angle. Guiding tip just above surface with your free hand, squeeze with your writing hand. To end each letter or line, touch the tip to the surface, release pressure, and pull away.

☐ To make *beads,* hold the bag at a 45-degree angle. With the tip just above the surface, squeeze out some frosting till you've formed a small mound; ease the pressure and pull the tip down till it touches the surface. Stop pressure and pull the bead to a point.

☐ For *hearts,* pipe two beads next to each other and join the points.

Star tips are used to make stars, drop flowers, shells, and zigzags.

☐ For *stars,* hold the bag at a 90-degree angle with the tip just above the surface. Squeeze out some frosting, stop pressure, then pull away.

☐ To make *drop flowers,* choose a star tip that is the size flower you want (the number of prongs the tip has determines how many petals the flower will have). Hold the bag at a 90-degree angle with the tip barely touching the surface. Squeeze out the frosting as you would for a star. Make a dot in the center with a small round tip.

☐ For *shells,* hold the bag at a 45-degree angle. With the tip just above the surface, squeeze out some frosting till you've formed a

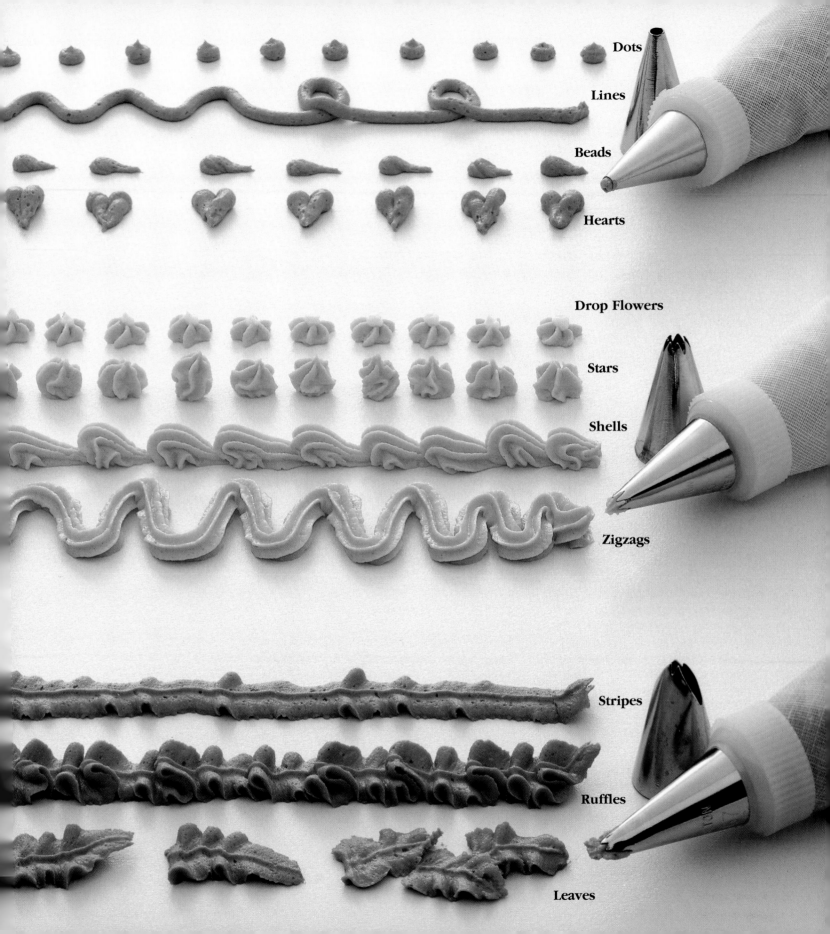

Dots

Lines

Beads

Hearts

Drop Flowers

Stars

Shells

Zigzags

Stripes

Ruffles

Leaves

and pull the tip down till it touches the surface. Stop pressure and pull away. Start the next shell at the stopping point of the previous one (shells will overlap slightly).

□ For *zigzags,* hold the bag at a 45-degree angle. Touch tip to surface; squeeze out frosting as you move tip from side to side. Stop pressure and pull away.

Leaf tips are great for making leaves, stripes, and ruffles.

□ For *leaves,* hold the bag at a 45-degree angle with the tip opening parallel to the cake top. Holding point just above the surface, squeeze out some frosting to make the base of the leaf. Continue squeezing, but ease up on the pressure as you pull away. Stop the pressure and lift off.

□ For *stripes,* hold the bag at a 45-degree angle with the tip opening parallel to the cake top. Touch tip to surface; apply pressure as you pull away. Stop pressure; lift off.

□ For *ruffles,* hold the bag at a 45-degree angle with the tip opening parallel to the cake top. Touch the tip to the surface and move up and down as you squeeze. Stop pressure and pull away.

HINTS FOR PIPING: If you get the jitters when it comes to decorating with frosting . . . relax. With frosting, you always can fix your mistakes. Try these hints.

□ To make sure your lines are straight or your writing is evenly spaced, use a toothpick to lightly sketch out the lines or words prior to piping on the frosting. Then, if you discover a line is crooked, just smooth out your sketched line or lettering and start over again.

□ Try making drop flowers on waxed paper and put them in the freezer to "set." Then transfer them to the baked product.

□ Use the tip of a toothpick to lift off any flower, shell, or other design that doesn't look quite right.

Making Parchment Cones

To make your own cones out of parchment triangles, hold a 12x12x17-inch parchment triangle with the long side at the bottom. Curl the lower right corner (A) over to the top point (B) to form a cone. Hold points (A) and (B) together with your right hand. Wrap corner (C) around the front of the cone to the top point so points A, B, and C meet and there is not an opening at the tip. Fold the points down into the cone. Tape the outside seam to about 1 inch from the tip. With scissors, snip off ½ to ¾ inch from the tip, depending on the size of the decorating tip you'll be using. Drop desired tip into the cone. Half-fill the cone with frosting using a knife or metal spatula. Fold in the top, then roll the top down to the frosting level and begin decorating.

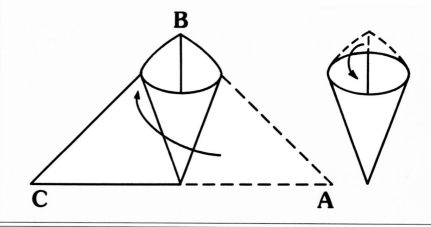

INDEX

If you would like to order any
additional copies of our books,
call 1-800-678-2803 or check
with your local bookstore.